Time, Temporality, and Imperial Transition

ASIAN INTERACTIONS AND COMPARISONS
General Editor Joshua A. Fogel

ASIAN INTERACTIONS AND COMPARISONS

Time, Temporality, and Imperial Transition

East Asia from Ming to Qing

Edited by Lynn A. Struve

ASSOCIATION FOR ASIAN STUDIES

and

UNIVERSITY OF HAWAI'I PRESS

Honolulu

Asian Interactions and Comparisons, published jointly by the University of Hawai'i Press and the Association for Asian Studies, seeks to encourage research across regions and cultures within Asia. The Series focuses on works (monographs, edited volumes, and translations) that concern the interaction between or among Asian societies, cultures, or countries, or that deal with a comparative analysis of such. Series volumes concentrate on any time period and come from any academic discipline.

Library of Congress Cataloging-in-Publication Data
Time, temporality, and imperial transition : East Asia from Ming to Qing / Edited by Lynn A. Struve.
 p.   cm. — (Asian interactions and comparisons)
Includes bibliographical references and index.
ISBN 0-8248-2827-5 (hardcover : alk. paper)
1. East Asia—History. 2. Time perception—East Asia—History.
I. Title: East Asia from Ming to Qing. II. Struve, Lynn A. III. Series.
DS514.T55   2005
950—dc22

                                          2004018504

Designed by University of Hawai'i Press production staff
Printed by The Maple-Vail Book Manufacturing Group

CONTENTS

SERIES EDITOR'S PREFACE

Time is one of those things we take for granted, personally and as scholars. No matter what we do, we assume, time proceeds on its way and, in a saying popular in the West, it may even heal all wounds. We also know that it doesn't. But just what does time "do"? Does it actually, as many middle-aged people believe, run more quickly as we get older? We occasionally speak of wishing that time would stand still for more than an instant or that we might be transported back in time so that we might enjoy some thing or fleeting moment more fully. In these and many other ways, we express a desire to alter the droning manner in which ordinary time seems to pass with the regularity of a metronome.

Do all peoples, however, conceptualize time in ways similar to this? How have people in the past understood temporality? What are the cultural and social components of our constructions of time? These and like questions about time and temporality have not been the subject of concerted scholarly attention in East Asian studies until the appearance of this volume edited by Lynn Struve of Indiana University. Asian Interactions and Comparisons is thus extremely proud to share in the responsibility for its publication and the contribution it is certain to make to this fascinating set of issues.

The six essays that compose this book focus on East and Northeast Asia in the early and mid-seventeenth century. They examine Chinese (in Henan and in Fujian), Korean, Manchu, Mongolian, and Christian (specifically, Dominican Catholic) conceptions of time in their distinctive historical settings. They draw on a wealth of primary and secondary writings in an extraordinary array of languages, offering an utterly original feast of ideas both as a guide to better understanding the era under study and for future scholarship.

Recent work in the West has acquainted (or, more accurately, re-acquainted) us with the rich and complex ethnic dimension of East Asian history over the past few centuries. Building on this new sensibility, the authors in this volume now take a topic we all think we have something of a handle on and demonstrate just how fecund an approach this can be.

Joshua A. Fogel

ACKNOWLEDGMENTS

The chapters in this volume arose from a conference called "The Qing Formation in World and Chinese Time," which was held on the Bloomington campus of Indiana University in June of 1999. That conference was made possible by fiscal and administrative support from the IU East Asian Studies Center—the key figures being Professor George M. Wilson, then director of the center; Dr. Jason Lewis, then associate director; and the continuing administrative coordinator, Benita Brown Banning. Helpful in many ways, too, was the conference rapporteur, Arthur Ling. Support also was provided by the IU Office of International Programs and by certain of the conference participants who voluntarily paid their own transportation expenses.

Financial assistance for the preparation of this volume was provided by the IU Office of Research and the University Graduate School as well as by the East Asian Studies Center. John Hollingsworth continued, despite his retirement from the IU Department of Geography, to meet my needs for professionally executed maps. And indispensable skills in multilingual word processing were brought to this project by Dr. Hiromi Oda and Vanessa Nolan, to both of whom I am deeply grateful for their unfailing patience, good sense, and cooperativeness as well as for their technical abilities. And colleagues in the IU Department of Central Eurasian Studies—especially Professors Elliot Sperling and Christopher Atwood, who participated actively in the conference —were helpful to me, as ever, in editing materials that relate to Tibet and Mongolia. The errors of editorial judgment that may remain, however, are entirely due to my own shortcomings.

My thanks, also, to Patricia Crosby of the University of Hawai'i Press and to members of the editorial board of the Asian Interactions and Comparisons series—particularly the general editor, Professor Joshua Fogel, and the anonymous reviewer—for their support in the acceptance and production of this volume.

And yes, Xiaohuang lives!—still taking seriously her feline "supervisory" responsibilities.

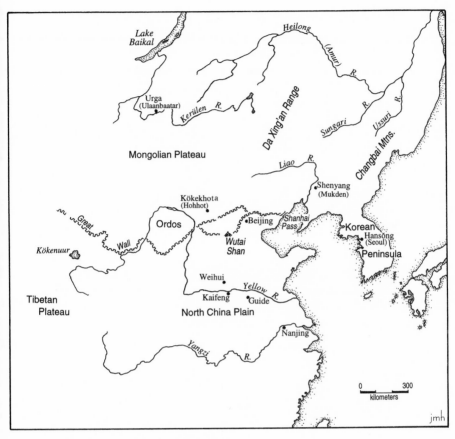

Map 1: Northeastern Asia in Ming and Qing Times

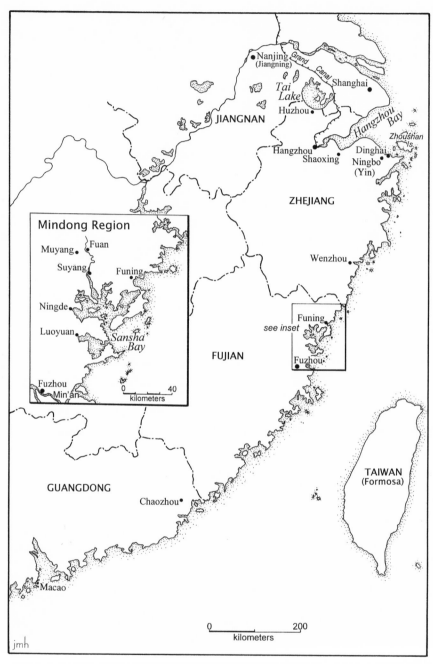

Map 2: Southeastern Coastal China and Mindong

INTRODUCTION

Lynn A. Struve

By one Chinese view of time, the future is behind you, above you,
where you cannot see it. The past is before you, below you, where
you can examine it. Man's position in time is that of a person sitting
beside a river, facing always downstream as he watches the river flow
past.

In America and other Western countries, the commonest view of
abstract time seems to be the opposite of the old Chinese one. In
this, man faces in the other direction, with his back to the past,
which is sinking away behind him, and his face is turned toward the
future, which is floating down upon him.

So wrote Graham Peck in *Two Kinds of Time* (1967: 7, 8), which re-
counts his experiences and observations in Guomindang-held China
during two years of the Japanese occupation, 1940 and 1941, and
which makes palpable for any reader why it was that no Chinese or
Western sense of being-in-time, stereotypical or otherwise, could hold
up under the dislocations and uncertainties of those years. His por-
trayal of people being dragged by events through a maelstrom, one
that buffets conventional orientations and leaves the tatters at new
angles, reminds us of how inextricable human self-understanding is
from constructed matrixes of time.

Now, more than a half century later, we are moving beyond this
sort of binary construction.[1] But scholars of East Asia have been

slow to build on thorough explications of sinitic horology, temporal ordination, and abstract concepts of time that emerged in the 1960s and 1970s.[2] Time in our work remains largely as it was in Peck's—a chronological backdrop to comprehensible narration and beyond that, at most, a conceit to heighten literary interest.[3] Now, more than a half century later, we no longer write in Peck's idiom of "old Chinese" ways that still were loath to change in the mid-twentieth century. Rather, we debate over how best to replace "old" and "traditional" with period terms—late imperial, early modern, advanced premodern—that avoid earlier connotations of stagnation or repetition, ones that highlight or at least do not occlude the vigorous changes that we've come to see especially in the four centuries before the twentieth (Struve 2004b). Yet we have attended little to the resources of time perception that sustained and guided the peoples of the sinitic imperium through the thick and thin of those centuries.

A central premise of this volume is that disrupted *times*, that is, ones of disrupted *time*, reveal those resources most vividly in drawing upon them most exigently. A corollary of this premise is that the well-recorded middle of the seventeenth century in mainland East Asia— when the desultory fall of one great dynasty and rise of another in China were attended by adversities in the climatic, microbic, and economic environments, and when peoples of eastern, central, and western Eurasia came into epochal compacts and conflicts—offers the best possibility for broad examination of temporality-under-duress before the twentieth century.[4] The contributors to this volume hope to show some of the ways—certainly not all—in which the lens of temporality can bring into focus matters that have not been noted before and that draw us "closer to the ground" of how people experienced and adjusted to changes in their normal circumstances and perspectives, their "rhythms of being" (Trivers 1985), as that ground shifted seismically in the seventeenth century.

It might seem that we already know well enough how people of that day saw "the Ming-Qing transition": as a change of dynasties. This way of regarding the end of one time unit and the beginning of another had a high profile in sinitic temporal thought, since, as is well known, calendrical years were commonly numerated by reigns and reign periods within dynasties, and the monthly calendar was promulgated by dynastic courts. Moreover, the rise, perdurance, decline, and demise of dynasties was seen as a macro-instantiation of the elliptical, yin-yang alternation of "order" (*zhi*) and "disorder" (*luan*). Asia specialists pride themselves on knowing this and on being able, thus, to point out both the Western bias and the presentism of those who make much of the turning points of centuries, temporal spans that, others have shown, were not salient even in Occidental consciousness until the seventeenth century (Cohen 1999: 1619). Sinitic ideas of dynastic cycles and transitions have become so familiar to us, I aver, that we use them to engage in "chop suey pastism." That is, we have taken some simple ingredients from far away in time and space and used them to concoct a "dish" (like "Italian" pizza) that is served when we want to "eat Chinese (or Italian)" or make others do so, neglecting to compare the look and taste of the new dish very closely with the original cuisine. Identification of what occurred in China during the "seventeenth century" as the "Ming-Qing transition" squares us with both the West and the East, and it satisfies our felt obligation to articulate historical change in terms that would be understood by people then and there. In other words, the concept of one dynasty succeeding another, I fear, has become a cognitive plug-in that has relieved us of curiosity about the dynamics of temporal consciousness, about time as lived in such "transitional" periods.[5]

Far be it from me—or any of this volume's contributors—to raise doubt that people in China, and elsewhere in East Asia in the middle of the seventeenth century, knew that a government called the Ming was in dire straits and that during the years we identify as 1644–1645 its chief adversary became a regime called the Qing. Prolonged uncertainty over how the fortunes of those two political entities would turn out (facing not only one another but also other enemies, outside and within) has been characterized by Jonathan Hay, in a study of "remnant subject" (*yimin*) painters, as a "suspension of dynastic time," a period from 1644 to 1662 during which "there were two truly competing frameworks of dynastic time" (1994: 172). However, if we scan a longer interval, the 1620s through the 1670s, and a wider space than that occupied by Hay's painters, and if we consider, in addition to the Qing, other dynastic-wannabe regimes (for instance, those of the rebels Li Zicheng and Zhang Xianzhong or the defector Wu Sangui), we see that dynastic rule could take on many meanings in people's minds, not only in China but in surrounding regions as well. In this perspective, then, the sense of "suspension" as a condition of aporia (marked, in Hay's treatment, by utopian and symbolic expressions) becomes less apt than the sense of temporary cessation in systems of order or control— such as when driving rules are suspended and a traffic jam results—not simply a vacuum but one into which a great rush took place. It was an interval that teemed, in people's rich historical consciousnesses, with thoughts (leading to behaviors) about what kind or quality of dynasty was perhaps ending, at what speed, in what way, and about what kind or quality of dynasty was perhaps taking form in what way. How long would the process take? A few years? A generation? Multiple generations? Would it be a clear-cut case of order-to-disorder and back again and, if so, on the pattern of which interdynastic period in the previous two and one-half millennia? Or would the "disorder" of late Ming come to seem orderly compared to the "order" of a new, alien unifier or patchwork of regional satrapies?

In short, it is not the dynasty-to-dynasty segmentation of time that informs us about that period so much as the texturing, coloring, and shaping of those segments and their joinery, as people drew on funds of temporal thought and practice in their respective cultures to make psychological adjustments and guide action. Among the chapters in this volume, those by Mark Elliott and Roger Des Forges, especially, show us in fascinating detail how those processes ensued, on one hand among the Manchu leaders and, on the other, among the political and intellectual elites of the North China Plain as their fates converged and intersected during six decades of struggle and accommodation.

Of course, dynastic time units were not the only ones available in the sinitic world. In probing the suspension of which he writes, Hay reminds us of the ancient, perpetual sexagesimal (*jiazi*) cycle,[6] in his words, "a calendar transcending the world of affairs which mapped the mortal time of a generation [sixty years] directly onto the immensity of the cosmic process."[7] The potential independence of *jiazi* reckoning from reign dates and of almanacs from courts can be exaggerated—after sixty years, certainty required reference to some non-*jiazi* date (or an event), and some authority eventually had to decide where to insert intercalary months to realign the solar and lunar years. But the coexistence of political and apolitical dating raises the subject of calendrical simultaneity, a common phenomenon in societies past and present the examination of which never fails to be revealing.

When people use more than one calendrical system to regulate their minds and lives, what are the respective meanings and uses of those parallel systems in political, social, economic, and cultural contexts? Paul A. Cohen has pointed out, for instance, that Chinese intellectual and political leaders were responding more to the progressive than to the Christian associations of the Gregorian calendar when they advocated its adoption upon the overthrow of the dynastic system in 1911, but also that Chinese people of all social sectors and classes "still follow lunar dating in the celebration of their birthdays and the New Year and other holidays" (1999: 1626). Perhaps the severe containment and repression of religious practice in mainland China since the communist revolution accounts for Cohen's omission of the fact that, like Jews who have maintained Hebrew-calendar observances while also acknowledging the calendars of the dominant cultures among which they've dispersed, certain Chinese communities have for centuries—with ingenuity and sometimes at their peril—managed to live according to the calendrical rhythms of their religions while not flagrantly violating the temporal demands of majority conventions or the state. The particular difficulties for ordinary Christians in working out such an accommodation with long-established Chinese practices, a process that ensued in the late Ming and reached fruition in the early Qing—a period of especially great openness to Western influences in religion, astronomy, and calendrics—are foregrounded in this volume by Eugenio Menegon, who focuses on the Dominican-led community of Catholic converts in the Mindong region of Fujian.

Simultaneous use of more than one political calendar within a single culturesphere was not unknown. Anyone in seventeenth-century East Asia with even a nonliterate familiarity with history would have recognized many periods during which their ancestors had been politically divided and "followed different calendars." Indeed, the variances between the calendar promulgated by the Qing and the ones followed by adherents of and sympathizers with the Southern Ming courts constituted a recurrence of that situation (Struve 1984: 241n.16). But such times, however extended, had not been the norm and were not considered normative. We are not dealing here with the easy acceptance of spatial and temporal parallelisms that Benedict Anderson has found to be characteristic of the transition to modern nationalisms (1991: 24–25, 192–194). As we see clearly in the chapters by JaHyun Kim Haboush and Johan Elverskog, the perpetuation of pre-Qing systems of dating among the Koreans and the Mongols was a form of resistance, an expression of nonacceptance. Those "nations" were peoples with distinct identities, not independent, sovereign countries, under the Qing imperium. Then, as is the case with many ethnic "minorities" or subjugated peoples today, alternative calendrical usage was a prime means of demonstrating nonacquiescence under hegemonic state and cultural power the assertion of which invariably entailed the dictation of time.

Within China, the inherent quality of resistance in calendrical alterity is shown in this volume by Zhao Shiyu and Du Zhengzhen in their research on the folk practice of celebrating the "Birthday of the Sun" on the 19th day of the 3rd lunar month, the date in 1644 when the last Ming emperor to reign in Beijing committed suicide under siege. In this case, the parallelism lies not literally in the use of dual calendars but, first, in the investment of a certain date—which warranted only a slight historiographical nod under the orthodox, self-legitimating temporal regime of the Qing—with a certain Ming-loyalist countermemory and, second, in the assignment of divergent significances to that date by people of the literati and commoner classes with the passage of generations. Here again we see, in the words of Eviatar Zerubavel, "the intricate relations between schedules and social solidarity" (1981: xiii). And the dynamic again—as in the chapters by Menegon, Elverskog, and Haboush—is intercultural and interreligious, though in this case between cultural levels in Han society and between spiritual traditions in the Han heritage.

The most important simultaneity to contemplate, however, is that all of the temporal consciousnesses revealed in this volume arose and overlapped in continental East Asia during the same space of tumultuous years during which, affecting virtually all other developments, the Ming dynasty faltered and fell and the Qing dynasty clambered into existence and onto firm footing. This transitional period has long fascinated historians and been the subject of excellent scholarship. Yet the full reality of that time, and its consequences for the following two to three centuries, will not be grasped until historians—of art, literature, economic behavior, domestic life, and many subjects beyond the range of this volume[8]—pay greater attention to time itself.

Taking Time

Why should it matter to historians—or to those who study the past from any disciplinary or nondisciplinary standpoint—whether the temporal outlooks of those whom we examine differed from the outlooks represented by the terms we now use to talk about them? Well, aside from the moral imperative to try, as far as possible, to understand other living or once-live things on their own terms, there are two good answers to this question that bear on scholarly practice. First, time and space are fundamental aspects of existence as we know it, so the ways in which people have functioned in, oriented themselves toward, experienced, and perceived those aspects should be primary data in our understanding of their histories—data at least as important as, say, their religious beliefs and practices, economic situations and values, social patterns, or political behavior. Second is the need to heighten awareness of our own temporal biases, which may lead us to characterize the past inappropriately.

Johannes Fabian, writing about the discipline of anthropology, has impugned the "schizogenic" use of time, the privileging of the temporal concepts that we as scholars use to talk about the objects of our study, which "distances those who are observed from the Time of the observer" (1983: 23). Though Fabian is concerned mainly with the interpretation of field reports on subjects who are contemporaries of the researcher, his charge that we "deny coevalness," that we refuse to see the commonality, the intersubjectivity of our temporal outlooks and those of the Other, the people whom we study (1983: 25–35), can also be laid against historians. One might say especially against historians, since "history, arguably the discipline most closely associated with time within the humanities, is notable for its failure to address the question of the ontological, epistemic, and political status of time" (Grosz 1999: 2). While it may be that peace of mind is preserved among historians precisely to the extent that they do not delve into the nature of what defines their discipline,[9] in this respect bliss is ignorance. Despite the example set by Fernand Braudel in posing several "times of history" (those of events, conjunctures, civilizations, and symbol systems) and by others who, inspired by the *Annales* school's attention to mundane regularities in past societies, have made sociotemporalities the focus of or important subjects in their work,[10] outside the sphere of memory studies, few historians think seriously about the multidimensionality of time in structuring their writings or take the temporality of things vis-à-vis the time-consciousness of people as significant data in what they examine. Debates over periodization, in particular, suffer from a lack of fertilization with insights about time from other disciplines, distinctions among "ages" often uncritically perpetuating age-old binary ideologies of order and disorder (Bronstein 1998), and arguments generally turning on where to slice the time-sausage and how to label the slices.

This is especially lamentable since, after more than a century of multidisciplinary research on and discussion of time, inaugurated by

Henri Bergson with his first major work, *Essai sur les données immédiates de la conscience,*[11] published in 1889, a number of dichotomizing problems in our understanding of time have been or are being overcome in ways that could deepen historical insight.[12] Those problems, opened out for us moderns by Bergson's categorical distinction between the uniform, particulate, cumulative instants of (in his view, basically false) scientific time and what was for him the true essence of time, the qualitatively fluctuating human experience of duration, generally boil down to the following questions: Is time a subjective illusion or intersubjective construction, a permutation of individual or collective consciousness, or is it physically rooted in the "outside world"? Either way, is it phenomenal or dimensional—is it something that happens or something that is intrinsic to happening?

Among physicists, whose main business it is to figure out the makeup and dynamic of the universe, time is existent, variable, and delimitable (i.e., it is, but not everywhere, and it is not the same everywhere it is), which might well pass as a basic definition of a kind of phenomenon, notwithstanding our difficulty in grasping time as we do phenomena in the more ordinary sense. Epitomizing that difficulty, Paul Ricouer even despairs that a pure phenomenology of time can ever be developed, taking as his point of departure on "the aporia of the being and non-being of time" the oft-cited complaint of St. Augustine that he knows quite well what time is until someone asks him to explain it.[13] But the doyen of time studies, physicist and philosopher J. T. Fraser, postulates that time is an intrinsic property of mass and, thus, has not only being but also a "natural history," an evolution of ever-increasing complexification since its genesis in the early universe.

Fraser sets forth five "levels of temporality," which correspond, respectively, to the main subjects of special relativity (electromagnetic radiation), quantum theory (atoms and subatomic particles), general relativity (aggregates on the scale of the whole physical universe), the life sciences (living things), and the "sciences of man" (psychology, anthropology, sociology, perhaps history). These distinct but interrelated levels form a stable "nested hierarchy" in the double sense that each more complicated level has evolved from the previous one in the history of the universe. Each also subsumes the simpler one(s) in its current functioning (thus, humans are the most sophisticated of living things, which exist in a certain part of the universe because of contingencies in the aggregations of atoms, which behave in ways dependent on their subatomic constituents, which float in a wavy sea of massless radiation). The simplest level of temporality, the imputed *Umwelt* of photons, actually is atemporal in Fraser's schema, in that photons have only speed, no mass, and only one speed, that of light, which deprives that level of the sine qua non of time, relative motion. On the levels that most elementally involve mass, called by Fraser the eotemporal and prototemporal, there is time because there are different entities (such as protons and neutrons) moving at different speeds, but it is "directionless" time for lack of any "now" point, the compasslike center of the need-meeting and goal-pursuit necessary for the self-maintenance of living things, which thereby exhibit "biotemporality." While many mammals show some capacity for *re*tention and *pro*tention on either side of their forward-flowing *at*tention to now (cats, I learn, can delay expected gratification—for example, they may wait around, unconfined, expecting to be fed—for seventeen hours), humans alone have developed very long, strong, and complex senses of pastness and futurity (including certain, individual death) and a clear consciousness of thickly present selfhood, all highly elaborated with mental constructs. Without this time-sense of the human *Umwelt,* which Fraser calls nootemporality, intentionality would remain limited and civilizations could not be built.

Both bio- and nootemporality have direction, but the human "arrow of time"[14] is much longer than that of any other organism, and its metaphorical tip and tail are vastly better defined. Nootemporality subsumes and thus partakes of the other four levels. For instance, we can know the chaos of the atemporal and, when mentally impaired or in nonwaking or altered states of consciousness such as sleep or trance, we can experience the biotemporal "duration without progression" (a.k.a. time's cycle) in hallucinations, dreams, and visions—major sources of depth psychology, religion, and myth. It is nootemporality that most absorbs humanists and social scientists, who must learn to see it in relation to other temporalities, according to Fraser, to avoid unnecessary mystification.[15]

Fraser's view that time has a natural history is reinforced by Stephen W. Hawking, whose well-known *Brief History of Time* (1988) takes the standpoint of general relativity theory (and *its* history of development in the twentieth century, which has transformed at least scientists' conceptions of time). Here again, the idea that time changes with the universe and that it differs a lot depending on the level of analysis is brought home to the reader. The cognitive separability of space and time, in particular, depends on the speed and distance from us of what we observe. Things relatively nearby, moving at relatively slow speeds on the cosmic scale (collective things such as societies or singular things such as autos—even planets), that is, most of the things directly accessible to human sense perception, can be regarded spatially and/or temporally. But above certain velocities and beyond a certain range of direct observability, the ontological co-dependence of space and time (inseparable from the functional co-dependence of relative motion and time, since the former assumes space) become a mutual identity: location in time and location in space become indistinguishable. Hence, the cosmologists' reference to "space-time."[16] From the perspective of some other galaxy, our world is *in* space-time, but from a much nearer vantage—say, the moon or my front window—our world has both space and time.

Crosscutting the incongruity between time and space, however, Hawking sees a congruity of three arrows of time that embeds the bio-sense of duration firmly in the total, current state of the universe: our "psychological arrow," indicating the direction in which we feel time passes, is as it is because of the "cosmological arrow" of the outward expansion of the universe, which has been going on for some while now (and very probably will continue long after life as we know it ceases). Inherent to that expansion is the "thermodynamic arrow" of entropy, whereby, on the whole, things—such as dynasties—inexorably fall apart. According to Hawking's school of thought, the universe used to be in an unimaginably compacted (ordered), tiny state, the unimaginably great energy of which has been dissipating outward (getting more and more disordered) ever since the "big bang" and will continue to do so until a presumed turn back into the "big crunch." Creatures like ants, honeybees, and humans, however charmingly industrious in their efforts to counteract entropy by forging local spheres of order, always expend more energy in doing so than they trap in their constructions. And all living things combat entropy in trying to stay integral and alive, only to eventually die and dissolve. So fundamentally we are entropic beings. *What* we are is *when* we are, which also is *where* we are, in the history of the cosmos. And only at the present point have conditions, including a strong thermodynamic principle of entropy, been suitable for the existence of beings capable of asking such questions as "What is time?"[17]

Pertinent here is the so-called anthropic principle whereby human intelligence tends to observe that the world (by golly!) is constituted just so for its own existence.[18] Statements about the world turn out to be, at base, statements about the utterer. Timewise, for instance, to say that the big bang occurred about ten thousand million years ago is really to say that it has taken that long for the universe to evolve minds that can wonder about such matters. As Hawking half quips, "Disorder increases with time because we measure time in the direction in which disorder increases. You can't have a safer bet than that!" (1988: 124, quote 147). Reenter Augustine, whose efforts to bridge the gap between the experiential and the theoretical understanding of time now seem to exemplify (besmirched as his soul might be by the heterodoxical association) the quintessential Chan antinomy of one hand trying to clap.

Reenter opposite him J. T. Fraser, who does not share Augustine's felt problem: for him the human experience of time, by virtue of its position in the nested hierarchy, is the prime medium for a comprehensive understanding of time in all its phases. How firm is this positivist stance? Well, John A. Michon (1986) has analyzed Fraser's theory as a system of root metaphors or "world models" and found that they parallel those converged on by theorists of human cognition from Stephen Pepper to Marc de Mey. And Nathaniel Lawrence (1986), eschewing both reification of time as an entity and its reduction to a "spontaneity of consciousness," examines the language of temporality in a wide range of "anthropomorphic" discourses. He comes up with four "master" metaphors of temporality—number, space, activity, and telos—which, in my estimation, can be correlated with Fraser's four levels above the atemporal (as well as with the intertwined modes of interpreting hexagrams in the *Yijing*—with their number-based, spatially positioned lines, associations with action-images, and developmental vectors from incipience to culmination). Correspondingly, the comparative linguist Hoyt Alverson has found in languages as different as English, Hindi-Urdu, Mandarin Chinese, and Sesotho common phrases ("collocations") that consistently fall, by my reading, into four categories—alignable, respectively, with Lawrence's "number," "space," "activity," and "telos"—of expression for the human experience of time: (1) time as a divisible, measurable entity, which can be wasted, saved, used, marked, segmented, et cetera; (2) time as a linear or orbital course, which is ahead/behind, is looked forward/back upon, stretches out, comes around, et cetera; (3) time as a medium in motion, which flows, passes, comes, flies, bears events with it, et cetera; and (4) time as a causal force or effect, which destroys, wears, heals, and befalls (1996). These observations reinforce the suspicion that

Fraser is describing how we apprehend time more than what is apprehended. Michon, moreover, shows that each of Fraser's five temporalities corresponds to one of the five types of measurement scales that scientists find sufficient for quantifying relations among phenomena. Thus, Michon avers, the five "stable integrative levels of nature" about which Fraser purports to speak are actually five "stable integrative levels of *mind*," and the time that Fraser sees as an intrinsic property of matter is not really a feature of internal constitution; rather, it is intrinsic to our few basic ways of interpreting relationality (1986: 56, 62–65). To reuse the Chan metaphor, Fraser, too, is trying to clap with one hand, a hand that indubitably has five fingers.

Of course, the functions of the time-sensing, language-bearing minds studied by analysts like Michon, Lawrence, and Alverson are always socially conditioned, and it is through the prism of social motivation and communal self-definition that Eviatar Zerubavel discerns a few basic structures by which we collectively "shape" the time of the remembered past: unilinearly like a rising, falling, or zigzagging arrow; phyletically with images of ladders and trees; cyclically or resonantly as in visible circles or audible rhymes; topographically, that is, at intervals gaining or losing density or mass; and rhythmically—smooth (legato) or punctuated (staccato) in its pattern of change. Regardless of the root metaphor, he points out, all such shapings involve the emplotment of "sociomnemonic" narratives—whether historically continuous or discontinuous—to situate ourselves in the present as social entities.[19] When that present is one as destabilized as the Ming-Qing transition and the societies striving to establish, maintain, or adjust self-identifications are as complexly engaged with one another as we find in that change of empires, latter-day historians face an especially great but also intriguing challenge. The contributors to this volume have responded by illuminating the multidimensional self-temporalizations and self-historicizations of certain key human collectivities of that age. The apposite, experimental dynastic analogizing of the Manchus and the North Chinese; the divergencies in (re)conceiving national origins (and therefore national essences) among the Koreans and the Mongols; and the tension-fraught choices of calendrical and ritual links to past events of deep religious and emotional significance on the part of Christian converts and Ming loyalists in southeastern coastal China: all these exemplify, in the particularly volatile environment of mid-seventeenth-century East Asia, modes of temporal "bridge"-building between present and past that Zerubavel finds characteristic of viable societies.

Shapes of Time from Ming to Qing

The term "chronotypes" was coined more than a decade ago for modes or patterns, fabricated by people, whereby "time assumes practical or conceptual significance" (Bender and Wellbery 1991: 4). But the idea that time is somehow molded by the existents-in-time "themselves" has been held regarding more existents than the self-aware, human ones. Art historian and anthropologist George Kubler, with his book *The Shape of Time: Remarks on the History of Things* (1962), may have been seminal in introducing the concept of temporal shaping to historiography. Shortly after the publication of this work, Siegfried Kracauer summarized its main thesis as follows:

> Art works, or more frequently their elements ... can be arranged in the form of sequences, each composed of phenomena which hang together inasmuch as they represent successive "solutions" of problems originating with some need and touching off the whole series. One after another, these interlinked solutions bring out the various aspects of the initial problems and the possibilities inherent in them. So it would seem evident that the date of a specific art object is less important for its interpretation than its "age," meaning its position in the sequence to which it belongs. The fact that related consecutive solutions are often widely separated in terms of chronological time further suggests that each sequence evolves according to a time schedule all its own. Its time has a peculiar shape. (1966 [1963]: 67)

Such plotting out of ages according to the solution-fulfillment of discrete phenomena is homologous with the "Typological Time" identified by Johannes Fabian as one of three major uses of time in anthropological discourse. This term, in Fabian's analysis, "signals a use of Time which is measured, not as time elapsed, nor by reference to points on a (linear) scale, but in terms of socioculturally meaningful events or, more precisely, intervals between such events.... In this use, Time may almost totally be divested of its vectorial, physical connotations. Instead of being a measure of movement it may appear as a quality of states; a quality, however, that is unequally distributed among human populations in the world" (1983: 23).

This approach generally has been welcomed as an alternative to the homogenization that often attends the use of chronological time. Synchronically, undue meaning often is attached to the fact that certain events occur in the same calendar intervals (one might say that synchronicity colludes with chronometry to subvert historiography), and diachronically, events are lined up sequentially, with the imputation of some causal relationship. History becomes a single "march" of coordinate bodies of factors and periodization a matter of identifying the change-of-command points. Or, less inspiringly, history becomes a sluice of thrown-together things and periodization a search for the sluice gates. Yet chronology is not dispensable; without it, even Kubler's "cultural bundles" could not be formed. Kracauer was quick to identify the dilemma: "On the one hand, chronological time dissolves into thin air, superseded by the bundles of shaped times in which the manifold comprehensible sequences of events evolve. On the other, chronological time proves indestructible inasmuch as these bundles tend to coalesce at certain moments which then are valid for all of them" (1966 [1963]: 73). Such a "moment," at which all the self-shaping cultural-temporal "bundles" in sinitic civilization coalesced, was the mid-seventeenth-century change of empires at the core of East Asia.

But how are we to conceive the impetus of such movements? The recognition—whether it be in physics, biology, psychology, philosophy, literary studies, or history—that experiences, perceptions, and, deriving from those, beliefs about time constitute actual forces in the *Umwelts* of living things underlies the assertion by some that time is a form of energy.[20] For instance, Chun-chieh Huang describes in the history of Chinese thought a continual interaction and feeding back between two levels of such force: on one hand, the situational timeliness, "vectorial nisus," or, more prosaically, the trend (*shi*) of "Time" within nature and human affairs; and on the other, the normative, paradigmatic "Supertime" of Dao or Li, which gives meaning to Time and can be brought to reign in Time by sagely guidance (2000). That the Chinese often have been influenced in their courses of action, that is, had their history shaped, by how they have apprehended the current or imminent interplay of *shi* and Dao is indisputable.

The complementary chapters in this volume by Elliott and Des Forges can be read as studies in this interplay between how things are going secularly and how they should go cosmically within a certain window of time. We see how the Manchus wished to learn from history as their early state-building and conquest activities met with increasing but also cautionary success, and how the Han Chinese of the central plain, as they tried to find historical moorings in a politico-military tempest, deliberated over various parallels with dynasties and dynastic transitions in the past. The Manchus, we learn, looked principally to frontier-based, non-Han regimes such as the Liao, Jin, and Yuan, which had more or less successfully governed all or large portions of China, and the Henanese looked principally to dynasties claimed by Han-Chinese tradition that were venerated for their success in dealing with problems of rupture, conquest, and multiethnicity: the Zhou, Han, and Tang. It is important for us to understand that such referencing, such shaping and coloring, was not done simply to justify or offer a sop for already-apparent outcomes—as was the early-Qing "Yuan analogy" of cultural perseverance studied by John D. Langlois (1980)—but was done in greater measure to envision and effect certain outcomes.

That time is part of the energy in power relations within the human sphere has been well articulated in political science, sociology, and anthropology. Objectified in calendars, in schedules of work and daily activity, and in the stories told by dominant elites in orthodox religions and philosophies, histories, and schools of academic learning, time becomes an instrument of and an arena of contestation over hierarchic power and governance. From the level of large-scale, long-enduring structures such as empires, religious communities, nation-states, and social science disciplines to shorter-term social entities such as families, kinship organizations, and professional groups, time is an important constituent of every political economy (Rutz 1992; Zerubavel 1981; Fabian 1983). In focusing on groups, however, one should not neglect individuals. In the words of Nancy Munn: "The importance of calendric and related time shifts connected with sociopolitical changes is more than political in the narrow pragmatic sense. It has to do with the construction of cultural governance through reaching into the body time of persons and coordinating it with values embedded in the 'world time' of a wider constructed universe of power" (1992: 109).

In discussing "body time," Munn emphasizes that people do not just perceive or accept temporal structures; rather, they create and adjust time frames continually as they live on in time, accomplishing tasks through succeeding generations. This is well illustrated in the chapters by Menegon, writing on the ambivalent calendrical situation of

Dominican converts, and by Zhao and Du, in their search for the historical roots of a folk practice, commemoration of the Birthday of the Sun. Menegon's missionaries wanted their converts not only to know and observe the sabbath, saints' days, and Christian holidays, but also to experience on those occasions spiritual closure of the constructed temporal distance between the lives and lifetimes of the church's holy figures and their own. So too with the sun's birthday, thought to have begun in Ming-loyalist observance of the anniversary of that fateful day in Chongzhen 17 (1644) when the emperor took his own life. The initiators of that rite apparently hoped that each year in perpetuity a calendrical distance, no matter how long, could be closed—that a "symbolic synchrony of 'now' and 'then'" could be forged (Zerubavel 2003: 47)—through camouflaged commemoration. Although in time the meaning of the rite may have been lost to folk memory, the commemorative principle remained: to subjectively, experientially remove a cumulation of calendrical or generational units to reestablish through the veil of time direct contact with the venerated. To reinforce Munn's point: the cultural implacement and the periodic, bodily removal of time in such practices are codependent.

The fascinating contributions to this volume by Haboush and Elverskog testify that the shape of time is forged in the political processes of appropriation, institutionalization, and legitimation but can also be a medium of resistance to domination (Rutz 1992: 2, 7). In both cases, on the national level, we see again the crafting hand of ritual practice—here in measuring out and texturing different lengths of time and attaching them to the present in different ways—as an essential agent in competing intracultural strategies of self-identification. Their research reveals how the Korean and Mongol nations—both closely engaged with the Ming but in opposite ways, and both subjugated by the Qing but on different terms—were impelled to struggle (among themselves and vis-à-vis Beijing) in the arena of time epistemes. In the case of the Koreans, the struggle was to maintain a civilizing mission—and thus national self-worth—in the world, and in the case of the Mongols, it was to maintain an independent religioethnic identity that could not be wholly subsumed under the one dictated for them by the Qing imperium.

Lifting our horizons to an even higher level than the national, let us ask: what concepts of time-shaping might be useful to us in comprehending the totality of historical change and how it was experienced in seventeenth-century East Asia? Again, physics—leavened by the social sciences—provides a surprisingly applicable suggestion: string theory and its world-sheets. In this method of abstract description, the path of a particle as it moves in space-time is drawn as a string (which may form a loop), and the whole prior existence of that particle at each instant of that movement "hangs down" from that string like a single warp thread in a curtain. The cumulation of instants provides the weft, forming a wavy "world-sheet." The idea is to schematize, in four dimensions, models or histories of cosmic events, which "occur," that is, have reality so far as any other part of the universe is concerned, within "event cones" defined by the speed of light. As such events intersect, world-sheets (or world-tubes) may coalesce or split apart (Hawking 1988: 158–161). This concept has been adapted in the life sciences to track the "world times" of living entities (such as cells, organs, or organisms), that is, the relationships between their times and the times of their inner and outer environments within a system. And it seems eminently adaptable to grasping the intersecting temporalities of the various collective players in the drama of the Ming-Qing transition—the Manchus, Koreans, Mongols (Eastern and Western), Han and non-Han regional populaces of China proper, Tibetans, Europeans, and, more peripherally, the Japanese and Annamese.

Similarly in psychology, subjects' "now lines" are plotted, as later experiences and earlier ones transect through memory and expectation, and, as changes in the speed and intensity at which significant events occur, their individual-psychological time varies in relation to outer-physical time. As the knowledge and moods of people of advancing physical and psychological age intersect with new circumstances, and their now lines cross with those of younger generations, "our time" changes in the course of, but not solely under the dictation of, hour-time. Klaus Riegel, a psychologist, has advocated using the world-line and now-line approach to reduce the unidimensionality of time in social, cultural, and historical studies by treating the times of various event sequences relationally and dialectically, neither privileging sidereal time nor, since it is useful as a standard (like musical bars), leaving it out of the picture (for a synopsis, see Riegel 1977: esp. 65–71).

Have we not begun to do that here? In this volume readers are led to explore the intersections of the discretely undulating world-sheets (each hanging down for centuries) of several sociopolitical "organisms"—the Jurchen/Manchu, Han, Korean, Mongol, even the Catholic. And now-lines, too, are traced through succeeding generations of Manchus, Hans, Koreans, Mongols, Christians, and non-Christians, as their understandings of present situations interacted with those of forebears and as their subjective experiences of the passage of time called for negotiation with the objective systems of time reckoning available to them. A major aim of this volume is to inspire more systematic work in this direction among scholars of East Asian history and culture.

Notes

1. For an elegant contemplation of this meandering, often ironical process, see Zhang 1998. Aside from the move away from binaries, research in cognitive linguistics has found that, contrary to the impression iterated by Peck in the two passages quoted above, the spatio-metaphorical expression of time is basically the same in Chinese and English (Yu 1998: chap. 4).

2. The pioneer, of course, was Joseph Needham. See, in particular, his works of 1959 and 1960 (with Wang and Price) and of 1966 and 1969, as well as Sivin 1966–1967. On the philosophy of timing in human affairs professed in the classic *Lüshi chunqiu*, see Sellmann 2002. For recent works on horological technology and artistry in China and Japan, see Bedini 1994 and Pagani 2001. For collections of writings, see *Time, Science, and Society in China and the West*, ed. Fraser et al. (1986), esp. pt. 3; a special issue of *Philosophy East and West* (24.2 [April 1974]) on "Time and Temporality"; and Huang and Zürcher 1995. A historical comparison of East Asian and Western (Christian) chronology is offered in Sato 1991. For an excellent recent exposition by an anthropologist on the nature of time and how its several dimensions are instantiated in the cultures of China, Han and non-Han, see Huang Yinggui 1999. On time in Japanese and Indian thought, see the issue of *Philosophy East and West* cited above, Nakamura 1966, and Wilson 1980. For comprehensive treatments of time in the history of human thought and culture, see Fraser 1975 and Whitrow 1988.

3. See, for instance, Brook 1998, in which the conceit of "four seasons" in a dynastic life cycle, as articulated by a late-Ming scholar-official, is used to critically set forth material on the development of commerce and commercial culture in the Ming period.

4. Regarding the turn of the twentieth century, though he does not deal solely with temporality, Paul A. Cohen, in *History in Three Keys: The Boxers as Event, Experience, and Myth* (1997), shows what can be gained by juxtaposing latter-day historical narrative with other "zones of consciousness," those of the "immediate participants in different phases of the Boxer experience ... who

did not have the entire 'event' preencoded in their heads, and who therefore conceptualized what was happening to them in ways that differed fundamentally from the retrospective, backward-reading constructions of historians" (xiii).

5. The term "lived time" comes to us through the English translation (1968) of Eugène Minkowski's *Le temps vécu: Études phenomenologiques et psychopathologiques* (1933).

6. Used for sequencing days since the Shang dynasty and for years since the first century BCE (Needham and Wang 1959: 396).

7. Hay 1994: 173. See also the discussion by Haboush in chapter 3. On Inner Asian variants of this system, see chapter 4 by Johan Elverskog.

8. See, for instance, Struve (2004a), on time-consciousness in the memoirs of people who experienced the Qing conquest.

9. See a quotation from Chester Starr in Wilson 1980: 558.

10. For example, Le Goff 1980: pt. 1; Ozouf 1988: chap. 7; and Chaudhuri 1990: chap. 4. Note that Eviatar Zerubavel (*Hidden Rhythms*, 1981) is a sociologist, Anthony Aveni (*Empires of Time*, 1989) is an astronomer, Robert Levine (*A Geography of Time*, 1997) is a social psychologist, Benedict Anderson (*Imagined Communities*, 1991) is a political scientist, and Huang Yinggui (Ying-Kuei Huang) (*Shijian, lishi yu jiyi*, 1999) is an anthropologist. On the vicissitudes of time among sociologists, see Adam 1990. Historically informative works on time in literature and intellectual writings are too numerous to list here. One good example of the former is Stuart 1996 and of the latter, Glasser 1972.

11. The ideas in this work, known in English translation under the title *Time and Free Will: An Essay on the Immediate Data of Consciousness*, were modulated in Bergson's next work, *Essai sur les relations du corps avec l'esprit* (Eng. trans., *Matter and Memory*), of 1896. On Bergson as transitional from nineteenth- to twentieth-century thought on being and time, see Poulet 1956: 34–35.

12. On the "clearly visible tendency [in philosophy and the social sciences] to acknowledge intimate relationships between the study of time as an abstract concept and the study of its concrete experience," see Atmanspacher and Ruhnau 1995. The discipline of history, however, is not represented in that collection of essays.

13. Ricouer 1984–1988: I, 6–7, citing Augustine's *Confessions*, Bk. 11.

14. The common observation that humans tend to regard time as either linear or cyclical, attributed by social scientists to humans' experience of both irreversible duration and seasonal and diurnal renewal, can also be related to physicists' theories: on one hand, time asymmetry or the irreversibility of events in time (unlike in space), and, on the other, the universe as fluctuating

in phases of extension and contraction and of space-time as curving back upon itself. Use of the metaphor "time's arrow" to express time asymmetry dates back to A. S. Eddington's *Nature of the Physical World* (1928). "Time's cycle" as a subject in the humanities and social sciences owes much to Mircea Eliade's *Le Mythe de l'éternal retour: Archétypes et répétition,* of 1949 (Eng. trans., *The Myth of the Eternal Return*). For a study of these root metaphors in the modern discovery of geologic time, see Gould 1987.

15. For outlines of Fraser's levels of temporality and supporting concepts, see Michon 1986: 52–54; and Fraser 1993: 4–8. The most complete presentation is Fraser 1982.

16. In "real" space-time, however, the direction of time and the three directions in space are distinguished. Only in completely abstract, mathematical, "imaginary" or Euclidean space-time does this distinction, also, disappear (Hawking 1988: 134–135).

17. Hawking 1988: 102–103, 145–147, 151–152. For other readable books on time in physics, see Park 1980 and Davies 1995. More dated discussions (by Olivier Costa de Beauregard, Richard Schlegel, G. J. Whitrow, and others) can be found in *The Voices of Time,* ed. J. T. Fraser (1966), and in Whitrow 1980 [1961] and 1972. The general trend of twentieth-century physics was to embed the directedness of time (technically called anisotropy) more deeply in the structure of the universe.

18. The term "anthropic principle" was coined in the middle 1970s to refer to the coincidence of the laws of physics with the prerequisites of human life. This idea has had an active career in theology, where it is taken as reinforcement of the design argument for God. But here Hawking uses it in the sense, common among physicists, that our perspective on the universe is inescapably conditioned by our having an intelligence that has evolved in the history of the very universe whose laws we seek with that intelligence. On the "weak" and "strong" versions of the anthropic principle in physics, see Hawking 1998: 124–127.

19. Zerubavel 2003: esp. chap. 1. Further on the imperative to respond to the "aporias" of time via literary and historical narrative, see Paul Ricouer's monumental *Time and Narrative,* wherein he sets forth the well-known mimesis$_1$, mimesis$_2$, and mimesis$_3$. In the first of these, through memory, groundwork is laid in "a preunderstanding of the world of action," including its temporal character. In the second, using the manifold resources of the preunderstood world and through the creativity of "now," a story is emplotted, shaped into a new temporal whole. When read or heard, this figuration then transforms the recipient's sense of the possibilities in as-yet unknown worlds of action. Succinctly, through this threefold mimesis "we follow the destiny of

a prefigured time that becomes a refigured time through the mediation of a configured time" (Ricouer 1984–1988: I, 54).

20. The relation of time perception to energy in physiology is evident in the fact that temporal judgments correlate with body temperature and metabolic rate. The smaller and warmer we are, the faster our subjective time goes vis-à-vis clock-time. And our experience of time as a seamless continuum, a "flow," has basis in the synthesizing and anticipatory capabilities of our neural makeup. See Davies 1995: 269–278; and Reigel 1977: 69. However, social psychologist Michael Flaherty (1999) has shown that our sense of time as passing rapidly or slowly has more to do with subjective factors of self-in-situation and immediate or retrospective experience than with such objective factors as level of physical activity.

References

Adam, Barbara. 1990. *Time and Social Theory*. Philadelphia: Temple University Press.

Alverson, Hoyt. 1996. "Cross-Language Universals in the Experience of Time: Collocational Evidence in English, Mandarin Chinese, Hindi, and Sesotho." In *Dimensions of Time and Life: The Study of Time VIII*, ed. J. T. Fraser and M. P. Soulsby, 105–119. Madison, Conn.: International Universities Press.

Anderson, Benedict. 1991. *Imagined Communities: Reflections on the Origin and Spread of Nationalism*. Rev. and exp. ed. London and New York: Verso.

Atmanspacher, Harald, and Eva Ruhnau, eds. 1997. *Time, Temporality, Now: Experiencing Time and Concepts of Time in an Interdisciplinary Perspective*. New York, Heidelberg, Berlin: Springer-Verlag.

Aveni, Anthony. 1989. *Empires of Time: Calendars, Clocks, and Cultures*. New York: Basic Books.

Bedini, Sylvio A. 1994. *The Trail of Time: Time Measurement with Incense in East Asia: Shih-chien ti tsu-chi*. Cambridge: Cambridge University Press.

Bender, John, and David E. Wellbery, eds. 1991. *Chronotypes: The Construction of Time*. Stanford: Stanford University Press.

Bronstein, Herbert. 1998. "Time-Schemes, Order, and Chaos: Periodization and Ideology." In *Time, Order, and Chaos*, ed. Fraser et al., 33–49.

Brook, Timothy. 1998. *The Confusions of Pleasure: Commerce and Culture in Ming China*. Berkeley: University of California Press.

Chaudhuri, K. N. 1990. *Asia before Europe: Economy and Civilisation of the Indian Ocean from the Rise of Islam to 1750*. Cambridge: Cambridge University Press.

Cohen, Paul A. 1997. *History in Three Keys: The Boxers as Event, Experience, and Myth*. New York: Columbia University Press.

———. 1999. "*Millennium Review Essay*. Time, Culture, and Christian Eschatology: The Year 2000 in the West and the World." *American Historical Review* 104.5 (Dec.): 1615–1628.

Davies, Paul. 1995. *About Time: Einstein's Unfinished Revolution*. New York: Simon and Schuster.

Fabian, Johannes. 1983. *Time and the Other: How Anthropology Makes Its Object*. New York: Columbia University Press.

Flaherty, Michael G. 1999. *A Watched Pot: How We Experience Time*. New York: New York University Press.

Fraser, J. T., ed. 1966. *The Voices of Time: A Cooperative Survey of Man's Views of Time as Expressed by the Sciences and the Humanities*. New York: George Braziller.

———. 1975. *Of Time, Passion, and Knowledge: Reflections on the Strategy of Existence*. New York: George Braziller.

———. 1982. *The Genesis and Evolution of Time: A Critique of Interpretation in Physics*. Amherst: University of Massachusetts Press.

———. 1993. "Change, Permanence, and Human Values." In *Time and Process: Interdisciplinary Issues*, ed. Fraser and Lewis Rowell, 1–23. The Study of Time, 7. Madison, Conn.: International Universities Press.

Fraser, J. T., N. Lawrence, and F. C. Haber, eds. 1986. *Time, Science, and Society in China and the West*. The Study of Time, 5. Amherst: University of Massachusetts Press.

Fraser, J. T., Marlene P. Soulsby, and Alexander J. Argyros, eds. 1998. *Time, Order, and Chaos: The Study of Time IX*. Madison, Conn.: International Universities Press.

Glasser, Richard. 1972. *Time in French Life and Thought*. Trans. C. G. Pearson. Manchester, U.K.: Manchester University Press.

Gould, Stephen Jay. 1987. *Time's Arrow, Time's Cycle: Myth and Metaphor in the Discovery of Geological Time*. Cambridge: Harvard University Press.

Grosz, Elizabeth. 1999. "Becoming … an Introduction." In *Becoming: Explorations in Time, Memory, and Futures*, ed. Grosz, 1–12. Ithaca and London: Cornell University Press.

Hawking, Stephen W. 1988. *A Brief History of Time: From the Big Bang to Black Holes*. Toronto: Bantam Books.

Hay, Jonathan. 1994. "The Suspension of Dynastic Time." In *Boundaries in China*, ed. John Hay, 171–194. London: Reaktion Books.

Huang, Chun-chieh 黃俊傑. 2000. " 'Time' and 'Supertime' in Chinese Historical Thinking." Paper presented at the International Conference on the Notion of Time in Chinese Historical Thinking, Taibei.

Huang, Chun-chieh, and Eric Zürcher, eds. 1995. *Time and Space in Chinese Culture*. Leiden: E. J. Brill.

Huang Yinggui [Ying-Kuei Huang] 黃應貴. 1999. "Daolun: Shijian, lishi yu jiyi" 導論：時間，歷史與記憶. In *Shijian, lishi yu jiyi* 時間，歷史與記憶 (*Time, History and Memory*), ed. Huang, 1–29. Taibei: Institute of Ethnology, Academia Sinica.

Kracauer, Siegfried. 1966. "Time and History." In *History and Theory: Studies in the Philosophy of History,* vol. 6: *History and the Concept of Time,* 65–78. Middletown, Conn.: Wesleyan University Press. Reprinted from *Zeugnisse: Theodor W. Adorno zum 60. Geburstag,* 50–64. Frankfurt am Main, 1963.

Kubler, George. 1962. *The Shape of Time: Remarks on the History of Things.* New Haven: Yale University Press.

Langlois, John E. 1980. "Chinese Culturalism and the Yuan Analogy: Seventeenth-Century Perspectives." *Harvard Journal of Asiatic Studies* 40.2 (Dec.): 355–398.

Lawrence, Nathaniel. 1986. "The Origins of Time." In *Time, Science, and Society in China and the West,* ed. Fraser et al., 23–38.

Le Goff, Jacques. 1980. *Time, Work and Culture in the Middle Ages.* Trans. Arthur Goldhammer. Chicago: University of Chicago Press. Translation of *Pour un autre Moyen Age: Temps, travail et culture en Occident: 18 essais.* Paris: Gallimard, 1977.

Levine, Robert. 1997. *A Geography of Time: The Temporal Misadventures of a Social Psychologist, or How Every Culture Keeps Time Just a Little Bit Differently.* New York: Basic Books.

Michon, John A. 1986. "J. T. Fraser's 'Levels of Temporality' as Cognitive Representations." In *Time, Science, and Society in China and the West,* ed. Fraser et al., 51–66.

Minkowski, Eugène. 1968. *Lived Time: Phenomenological and Psychopathological Studies.* Trans. and introd. Nancy Metzel. Evanston, Ill.: Northwestern University Press.

Munn, Nancy D. 1992. "The Cultural Anthropology of Time: A Critical Essay." *Annual Review of Anthropology* 21: 93–123.

Nakamura, Hajime. 1966. "Time in Indian and Japanese Thought." In *Voices of Time,* ed. Fraser, 77–91.

Needham, Joseph. 1966. "Time and Knowledge in China and the West." In *Voices of Time,* ed. Fraser, 92–135.

———. 1969. "Time and Eastern Man." In Needham, *The Grand Titration: Science and Society in East and West,* 218–298. London: Allen and Unwin. Originally The Henry Myers Lecture of 1964, abbreviated and adapted in *Cultural Dynamics* 1.1 (1988): 62–76.

Needham, Joseph, with the collaboration of Wang Ling. 1959. *Science and*

Civilisation in China, 3: *Mathematics and the Sciences of the Heavens and the Earth.* Cambridge: Cambridge University Press.

Needham, Joseph, Wang Ling, and Derek J. de Solla Price. 1960. *Heavenly Clockwork: The Great Astronomical Clocks of Medieval China.* Cambridge: Cambridge University Press and the Antiquarian Horological Society.

Ozouf, Mona. 1988. *Festivals and the French Revolution.* Trans. Alan Sheridan. Cambridge: Harvard University Press. Translation of *La fête revolutionaire, 1789–1799.* Paris: Gallimard, 1976.

Pagani, Catherine. 2001. *"Eastern Magnificence and European Ingenuity": Clocks of Late Imperial China.* Ann Arbor: University of Michigan Press.

Park, David. 1980. *The Image of Eternity: Roots of Time in the Physical World.* Amherst: University of Massachusetts Press.

Peck, Graham. 1967. *Two Kinds of Time: Life in Provincial China during the Crucial Years, 1940–1941.* 2nd ed., revised and abridged. Boston: Houghton-Mifflin. 1st ed., 1950.

Poulet, Georges. 1956. *Studies in Human Time.* Trans. Elliott Coleman. Baltimore: Johns Hopkins Press.

Ricouer, Paul. 1984–1988. *Time and Narrative.* Trans. Kathleeen Blamey and David Pellauer. Chicago: University of Chicago Press.

Riegel, Klaus F. 1977. "Toward a Dialectical Interpretation of Time and Change." In *The Personal Experience of Time,* ed. Bernard S. Gorman and Alden E. Wessman, 60–108. New York: Plenum Press.

Rutz, Henry J. 1992. "Introduction: The Idea of a Politics of Time." In *The Politics of Time,* ed. Rutz, 1–17. Washington, D.C.: American Anthropological Association.

Sato, Masayuki. 1991. "Comparative Ideas of Chronology." *History and Theory* 30.3 (Oct.): 295–301.

Sellman, James D. 2002. *Timing and Rulership in Master Lü's Spring and Autumn Annals.* Albany: SUNY Press.

Sivin, Nathan. 1966–1967. "Chinese Conceptions of Time." *Earlham Review* 1: 82–92.

Stewart, Ian. 1995. *Nature's Numbers: The Unreal Reality of Mathematical Imagination.* New York: Basic Books.

Struve, Lynn A. 1984. *The Southern Ming, 1644–1662.* New Haven: Yale University Press.

———. 2004 (a). "Chimerical Early Modernity: The Case of 'Conquest-Generation' Memoirs." In *The Qing Formation in World-Historical Time,* ed. Struve, 335–372. Cambridge: Center for East Asian Studies of Harvard University.

———. 2004 (b). Introduction. In *The Qing Formation in World-Historical Time,* ed. Struve, 1–54.

Stuart, Sherman. 1996. *Telling Time: Clocks, Diaries, and English Diurnal Form, 1660–1785*. Chicago: University of Chicago Press.

Trivers, Howard. 1985. *The Rhythm of Being: A Study of Temporality*. New York: Philosophical Library.

Whitrow, G. J. 1972. *What Is Time?* London: Thames and Hudson.

———. 1980. *The Natural Philosophy of Time*. 2nd ed. Oxford: Clarendon Press. 1st ed., London: Thomas Nelson, 1961.

———. 1988. *Time in History: The Evolution of Our General Awareness of Time and Temporal Perspective*. Oxford and New York: Oxford University Press.

Wilson, George Macklin. 1980. "Time and History in Japan." *American Historical Review* 85.3 (June): 557–571.

Yu, Ning. 1998. *The Contemporary Theory of Metaphor: A Perspective from Chinese*. Amsterdam and Philadelphia: John Benjamins.

Zerubavel, Eviatar. 1981. *Hidden Rhythms: Schedules and Calendars in Social Life*. Chicago and London: University of Chicago Press.

———. 2003. *Time Maps: Collective Memory and the Social Shape of the Past*. Chicago: University of Chicago Press.

Zhang Longxi. 1998. *Mighty Opposites: From Dichotomies to Differences in the Comparative Study of China*. Stanford: Stanford University Press.

I

MANCHU AND HAN
HISTORICAL CONSCIOUSNESS
IN FLUX

CHAPTER ONE

Whose Empire Shall It Be?

Manchu Figurations of Historical Process in the Early Seventeenth Century

Mark C. Elliott

CHARTING THE PASSAGE of time in imperial China was an inherently political act. While in the Western world calendrical matters were mostly left up to the church—Roman rulers fussed about the months but cared little about the year—in China and much of the rest of East Asia the year mattered most, and it was the state that decided what year it was.[1] This was true even for the unlettered sixteenth-century Manchus dwelling on the northeastern periphery of the Chinese ecumene. As Ming subjects whose leaders made regular visits to the Ming capital, Beijing, the Manchus—or Jurchens, as they were known before 1636[2]—were naturally in the habit of thinking of the year (when they thought of it at all) in terms of the length of time the reigning Chinese emperor had been on the throne. That is, for them, as for the Chinese, 1599 (to pick a year at random) was the twenty-seventh year of Wanli, "Wanli" (lit. ten thousand ages) being the reign title of the current Ming ruler. Thus, when the Manchus began entertaining imperial ambitions of their own, one way in which they expressed their rivalry with the Ming was precisely by claiming authority over time. Inherent in this strategy was a general shift in the Manchus' very perceptions of temporality and their place in history.

The Manchus reconfigured themselves temporally in two different ways. First, they declared their own reign titles. Before occupying Beijing (see Map 1)—when others would have to concede that they actually ruled a core area of China and could rightly assume control of the sinitic calendar—the Manchus promulgated four such names:

Tianming, normally dated from 1616; Tiancong, declared in 1626; Chongde, declared in 1636; and Shunzhi, declared in 1643.[3] Graphs such as *tian* (heaven) and *de* (virtue), carefully chosen with the assistance of Chinese advisors, were intended to underscore Manchu legitimacy in Chinese eyes. Their deployment of Chinese-style chrononyms shows that Qing leaders well understood the implications of "changing the era" (Ch. *gaiyuan*) and belies the Manchus' reputation as uncivilized vandals.

The second aspect of the Manchu shift in the organization of time emerged in the latter 1610s, when the political confederation coalescing under Nurhaci named itself the Jinguo (Ma. Aisin gurun, lit. golden nation or golden dynasty). By designating itself with the same Chinese graph as that of the twelfth-century Jin dynasty, which traced its origins to roughly the same region of eastern Eurasia and ruled much of North China between 1115 and 1234,[4] the preconquest Manchu state projected itself as heir to an older imperial legacy. Insisting that the Jin past was literally his past and that Jin history was his history, Nurhaci (1559–1626) sought to inscribe time independently of the Ming state, which he now professed to regard with contempt. But his appeal to history also included generous references to analogies and examples that could legitimate his rivalry with the Wanli emperor, whom he also now professed to regard with contempt. Nurhaci's son and successor, Hong Taiji (1592–1643), inherited this strategic vision and even ordered his scholars to translate the official history of the Jin from Chinese into Manchu. By simultaneously ordering the translation of the official histories of the Liao (907–1125) and the Yuan (1215–1368), he elevated the Manchu link to previous non-Han regimes to a more abstract plane, reinforcing the Qing claim to legitimacy within a broad imperial continuum while continuing to insist that Heaven was impartial and favored the more virtuous contender for the Mandate.

These developments raise a number of questions regarding the Manchu perception of the historical moment. What was the significance to Nurhaci and Hong Taiji of historical parallels? How did the Manchus understand their place in history? What were their sources of information? How strong was the early-Qing self-identification with the Liao, Jin, and Yuan? What sorts of lessons did they hope to draw from history generally and from the experiences of those prior alien dynasties in particular? In putting these questions, I am deliberately bracketing a related set of concerns having to do with how valid certain historical comparisons might have been or how "real" the resemblances are between the Manchu imperial enterprise and those previous ones. The latter problem, which modern scholars began investigating in the 1930s and 1940s, centered on the responses of the Liao, Jin, Yuan, and Qing—often grouped together as "conquest dynasties" or "alien regimes"—to essentially the same political challenge, namely, how to rule China without becoming Chinese. Though they met this challenge in different ways and with different degrees of success, the northern dynasties invite comparison because they shared a number of similarities, among them an emphasis on martial over civil virtues, a reliance on Chinese collaborators, the maintenance of multiple capitals and political centers on the steppe, and the imposition of policies designed to sustain the distinctiveness of the conquest people.[5]

Though it recognizes these similarities, the present essay is not a study in comparative history. Its focus is the matter of contemporary Manchu consciousness of such similarities and the historical perspective the Manchu elite brought to their project of becoming masters of the "Under-Heaven" (Ma. *abkai fejergi*, Ch. *tianxia*), for it is clear from the record that the past thrust itself forcefully upon contemporary awareness and contributed to the sense that a great drama was playing itself out. Like Roger Des Forges in the essay that follows, I am interested in understanding the operation of historical analogies at the time as a means of gauging what people thought they were doing and why. To explore this issue, I begin by considering the references to Liao, Jin, and Yuan history made in conversations conducted "privately" among the Manchus themselves as well as "publicly" with outsiders in the period leading up to the 1644 conquest. The surviving Manchu-language records from the preconquest period show that the Qing reflection on the past, which began early in the seventeenth century under Nurhaci, underwent an important transition under Hong Taiji, who abandoned any pretense that the Qing literally was a reincarnation of the Jin. Instead, Hong Taiji focused on an examination of the historical record to see not just how previous northerners had managed the feat of conquering and holding the realm, but also how they had lost it. This shift is best exemplified by the translation into Manchu of the Liao, Jin, and Yuan histories, commissioned by Hong Taiji in the late 1630s and printed in 1646. Those translations, together with the early Manchu archives, are an excellent source for understanding early Manchu political culture, and they enable us to see the difficult path taken by the Qing—with one foot in the central plain and the other in the steppe—in maintaining a dual basis for their imperial enterprise.

Nurhaci's Historical Rhetoric

The gradual expansion of the early Manchu state in the late sixteenth and early seventeenth centuries depended on a skillful combination of warfare, negotiation, and institution-building. During that process, both Nurhaci and Hong Taiji often took the opportunity to reflect on the precedents for their actions. A careful reading of the chronicles from the period between 1607 and 1643 reveals at least forty-five different historical references to the Liao, Jin, and Yuan in oral and written communications.[6] Ten appear in correspondence with the Korean king, another eighteen in messages sent to various Chinese recipients (either inhabitants of Liaodong, potential defectors, or the Ming emperor), and one in a letter to the Khalkha (Eastern) Mongols. Sixteen more are found in communications with Manchus or non-Mongol allies. In all of these cases, the past functioned as a mirror in which present circumstances were reflected, and precedents were raised to guide decision-making and to illustrate proper (or improper) behavior. But closer examination reveals some obvious differences in the way precedents were used in communications with outsiders as compared to insiders. Broadly speaking, in dealings with those outside the Manchu confederation, on one hand, references to the past and specific historical events or figures were intended to persuade adversaries to cease resistance, to bolster Manchu prestige and legitimacy, or both. Historical allusions used in internal communications, on the other hand, were aimed to stimulate consideration of the risks and rewards of the imperial project.

In trying to establish good relations with his neighbors to the southeast, for instance, Nurhaci found it useful to remind the Korean king of the old friendship between the Jurchen and Korean nations. In a 1619 letter, he wrote as follows:

> After you, Korea, gave troops to the Chinese to come against us, I thought: "It is probably not that the Korean soldiers have willingly come, but that they cannot refuse the Chinese, whom they must repay for their assistance against the Japanese. In days of old, a

Korean official named Jo Wichong, who had rebelled, taking with him over forty cities, came unto our Jin emperor, Dading. Dading responded, saying, 'When we were fighting against the Chinese [Song-dynasty emperors] Zhao Huizong and Zhao Qinzong, the Korean king gave them nothing. Because Korea is a righteous nation, we must send [Jo Wichong] back.'" Considering this, it is not that from the beginning there has been ill will between our two nations.[7]

Emphasizing in this way the historically friendly bonds between Koreans and Jurchens, Nurhaci sought to make common cause against the Ming and to persuade Korea not to give haven to the Ming general Mao Wenlong. The same story, combined with stories of conflict arising over other refugees during fighting between the Liao and the Jin, was used repeatedly in three separate letters sent to the Korean side in July and December of 1621 and January of 1622, urging an end to collaboration between Ming and Korean forces.[8] Similarly, after the fall of Liaoyang in 1621 when the Ming inspector there, Zhang Quan, was taken prisoner and brought before Nurhaci, Hong Taiji employed the following argument to try to coax Zhang into joining the Manchus or at least to kneel before his father: "Once a long time ago two of your Chinese [emperors], Zhao [Song] Huizong and Zhao [Song] Qinzong were captured, but because they knelt in prostration when they met our Jin emperor, they were made princes among us. Why won't you kneel? I am urging you to do so in order to save your life!" But Zhang steadfastly refused, saying, "O Prince, even if I die, I will not forget the lesson you have taught me. It is no doubt the case that you are warning me so that I may live. But those emperors, Huizong and Qinzong, were small emperors who ruled during a time of confusion in the country. I cannot kneel, lest I bring shame to the greatness of my lord's rule."[9]

Speaking in these terms, as Zhang Quan's response shows, was to speak in a language that both Koreans and Chinese could easily understand, even if it did not produce the hoped-for results. It can be argued that an appeal to precedent is a common rhetorical technique found in any argumentation and that such an appeal by no means implies that the person invoking the precedent necessarily sees himself to be in the same situation or acting in the same historical context (strictly speaking, for the argument to be effective, a precedent need only convey an equivalent moral or logical charge). But the deliberate choices Manchu leaders made in selecting which precedents to raise, nearly all of which came from the history of relations with northern dynasties, suggests that they indeed perceived themselves as operating in the same continuum. There were exceptions, such as the April 1625 letter from a group of Han-Chinese officials on the Qing side to Mao Wenlong, then leading a rearguard resistance from near the Korean border. They cited instances not from Liao or Jin history, but from the history of dynasties ruled by Han Chinese, of ministers who had quit their former lords in favor of reputedly more virtuous men, pointing out that in so doing those men had left behind sterling reputations. The examples given were Han Xin, who abandoned Xiang Yu (for his refusal to recognize Liu Bang as Heaven's choice to found a new dynasty, the Han), and Hu Jingde, who abandoned Liu Wuzhou (for his refusal to recognize Li Yuan and his sons as Heaven's choices to succeed the Sui in founding the Tang).[10] But another missive directed at Mao and sent later the same year cited some of the same cases and added one more—that of Liu Zheng, who, significantly, deserted the Song for the Mongol khan, Khubilai.[11]

The examples above involved specific precedents intended to sway an individual in an immediate decision. More commonly, Manchu appeals to history made to outsiders focused on the larger principles by which rulers came to power, aiming thereby to influence overall policy by addressing Chinese or Korean objections that the Manchus were unfit to rule. One of the earliest such arguments that has survived is contained in a long letter of 1620 from Nurhaci to the Khalkha Mongols. After cataloging the outrages committed by the Ming upon his people, the Hada, the Ula, and different Mongol groups, Nurhaci explained that Heaven's favor had enabled the Manchus first to defeat an army of 30,000 led against them by the Koreans and then to defeat an army of 10,000 led against them by the general Jaisai, whom they then captured with his entire family. He went on to tell the following story:

> Long ago, the khan of the Great Liao, having subjugated the
> Chinese emperor Zhao Huizong along with the Mongol, Korean, and
> other nations, went net-fishing on the Ula River in the Jurchen
> country, where, after catching some sturgeon, he held a banquet. He
> had all of the Jurchen officials dance for him. When one official
> named Agūda was told to dance, he would not. The Liao khan,
> Tianzuo, said to his minister, Xiao Fengxian, "Since this Agūda has

refused my order to dance, will he not disobey me again
[someday]?" But Xiao Fengxian counseled [otherwise], saying:
"These people live without refinements. What if it turns out that he
is a good man, without evil intent? I fear that killing him would be
unfounded. He has not committed any crime. Why kill him just
because he won't dance?" So the khan rescinded his command to
kill [Agūda]. Agūda heard this story and, fearing the Liao, built
walled forts and secured the territory. When it came to war, Heaven
approved Agūda. Having completely conquered the Liao, [Agūda]
took the Liao khan, Tianzuo, as his captive and sent him off far away,
demoting him from khan to be Haibin prince.[12]

Nurhaci's point was not, as might be expected, that the Liao emperor had made an error in judgment, but that Heaven chooses those
whom it will favor and that the mighty inevitably fall from grace. As he
observed, this was true even of the Jin-dynasty Jurchens:

In the 5th month of the 6th year of the reign of the Taihe khan
[1206], the khan commanded the leader of the Mongol nation,
Temüjin, to proceed to Jingzhou to pay obeisance and bring tribute,
and sent his uncle, a prince named Yongji [to go receive it]. Yongji
went and, arriving at Jingzhou, met Temüjin, who had brought
tribute from Mongolia. Recognizing that he was a man of unusual
birth, after Temüjin returned home, Yongji reported to the Jin khan:
"This Temüjin is not like the people who have always brought us
tribute. He is someone who is going to cause us trouble some day.
Better to think of some reason having to do with the frontier, accuse
him of a crime, and kill him!" But the Jin khan replied, "If we kill
someone who has come prostrating himself and bearing tribute, why
would the people of the four quarters continue to come to us?" and
he declined Yongji's counsel. When Temüjin got wind of this, he
stopped coming himself and sent officials instead. After the Taihe
khan [i.e., emperor Zhangzong] died, Yongji became the khan and
swore to kill Temüjin. When Temüjin heard [that the Jin khan had
died], he asked the Jin representatives, "As the khan has died, who
has been made the next khan?" The representatives answered,
"Yongji, the khan's uncle, and seventh son of Dading khan, is now
khan." Temüjin replied: "You have been thinking that your central
Jin nation will abide like Heaven. But in making Yongji khan, you are

again only human," and he spat toward the south. "From now on we will no longer go [to pay tribute to the Jin]." Thinking the worst, [the Jin] attacked, but Heaven favored Temüjin, and so the Mongol Chinggis Khan took over from [lit. took the *doro* from] the Jin khan.[13]

Lest his Mongol audience think that they were immune to Heaven's laws, Nurhaci quickly added: "After Chinggis Khan, Khubilai Sechen Khan built and then lived in the city of Dadu. But during the time of Toghon Temür, this was taken away by the Chinese Hongwu emperor, who dwelt there [instead]. These are the stories I have heard about the old days." The grand lesson he drew from these legends was this:

> When one looks at the precedents of earlier generations, once the Heavenly [appointed] time for decline has come, that nation that was seemingly as wise as the spirits loses its wisdom and becomes stupid and confused; forsaking the speech of correct and good people, its people adopt the treacherous speech of evil and false people. Unable to implement propriety, they practice wickedness and destroy the nation. [But] once the Heavenly [appointed] time for arising has come, Heaven raises [them] and the stupid become wise, the evil good. All of you grasping this trajectory of the course of nations, when you speak, you will all speak what is correct and true.[14]

The purpose of this letter was to persuade his audience that the "Heavenly appointed time" had come for the rise of the Manchu nation and that the Khalkhas would do well to throw their lot in with Nurhaci. But the context in which the message was presented, constructed around a retelling of Liao, Jin, and Yuan history, is extremely revealing. Nurhaci appears to have hoped to encourage his audience to associate him not just with the Jin founder, Agūda, but also with the Yuan founder, Temüjin, thereby elevating his prestige among potential Mongol followers. At the same time, he also wished to remind them of the vicissitudes of historical fortune, to make people think that, if the past was any guide, the Ming was indeed on its way out and the state that he was building was the best bet to replace it. A quarter century before a Manchu emperor actually occupied the throne in Beijing, Manchu belief in the logic of historical process lent them the confidence to adopt an aggressive diplomatic stance.

Hong Taiji's Reflections on Virtue

There is no mention of the Wanli emperor by name in the preceding letter, but in letters sent to Chinese recipients with the same goals in mind, Nurhaci and Hong Taiji were by no means above casting aspersions on the fitness of the Ming ruler and classifying him together with notorious figures from ancient Chinese history—a practice that, as the essay following shows, mimicked exactly the habits of Chinese literati, who were forever vilifying their enemies or exonerating themselves with (usually veiled) references to historical precedent. In a letter sent late in 1621 to the Han population living in Liaodong, Nurhaci explained that he intended to implement a fairer policy of corvée and that because his laws were fairer, "Heaven favors me" (Ma. *abka mimbe gosimbi*):

> They say that, in every country, the king's woes come not from outside but from within himself. In ancient times, [rulers such as] King Jie [of Shang], King Zhou [of Zhou], the First Emperor of Qin, Emperor Yang of the Sui, and emperor Wanyan Liang of the Jin all immersed themselves in liquor, women, and wealth and no longer troubled themselves about the country. Having ceased to govern, by themselves they brought ruin to their rule. [Wanli], the emperor of you Chinese, does not rule fairly. He himself allows the eunuchs to take property but exempts the property of the dishonest and crafty from being taken, [instead] causing those with property who are upright and honest to suffer. This is not the enlightened management of internal [affairs]. Moreover, as he interferes in the affairs of other countries outside his borders and confuses right and wrong by blaming rebellions on Heaven, [Heaven] has given me the emperor's lands east of the [Liao] River.[15]

By portraying the Wanli emperor in rather distasteful company, Nurhaci sought to explain his own success in terms that the Chinese inhabitants of the Liaodong region would understand: the enlightened ruler rules in accordance with, and at the pleasure of, Heaven's will, and the hegemon does not. By this logic, because the Chinese ruler was no longer a moral man, the Manchu conquest of Liaodong was not a violation of Heaven's principles but, on the contrary, accorded with them. In other words, in keeping with the most fundamental of all Chinese political formulations, it all came down to virtue. Very much the same line of reasoning is found in a speech made circa 1630 in which the examples of Jie, Zhou, Qin Shihuangdi, and others were used to reproach not only Wanli but also the leaders of erstwhile Jian-zhou rivals, such as Wan Khan of the Hada and Bujantai of the Ula, who "betrayed the Way" in their greed, their love of liquor, and so forth.[16]

Particularly important in such appeals was the notion that the em-pire did not belong to any one person or any one people. As Hong Taiji wrote in 1637 to the Korean king: "An old expression says: 'The Under-Heaven is not one person's realm. The Under-Heaven belongs to all people and goes to him who is virtuous.' Thus the Ming Hongwu emperor, having eliminated the surrounding kingdoms, established his 'great name' [i.e., reign title] at Jinling and later took the realm from the Yuan" (JMD: X, 4631/MBRT: Taizong VI, 2.905–906). In other words, good rulers like the Hongwu emperor were succeeded by bad ones like Wanli; likewise, bad rulers like King Zhou and the First Em-peror of Qin were replaced by good ones like King Wen of Zhou and emperor Gaozu of the Han. This was why dynasties were forever rising and falling. Such was the reasoning in a letter sent ten years earlier to a lama named Li, a priest mediating between the Ming and the Manchus:

> From ancient times on, where are there no instances of rise and decline? As to why this should be so, [one need only think of] the Liao khan Tianzuo, who, without reason, wished to kill the Jin khan Taizu, which led to war; or of the Jin khan Zhangzong, who, without reason, wished to kill the Mongol khan Taizu, which led to war. [Likewise], the Wanli emperor wishes to kill me, and, his having sided with the Yehe, war has broken out between our two countries. (JMD: VI, 2605/MBRT: Taizong IV, 3.29)

Hong Taiji took the same approach in a letter written in 1629 to the Ming field marshal for Liaodong, Yuan Chonghuan, using much the same wording:

> From ancient times on, where are there no instances of rise and decline in your great country? The Under-Heaven is not one person's realm. The Under-Heaven belongs to all people. To whomsoever Heaven gives it, that person must take it. Of old, the Son of Heaven was of the Liao, and Taizu of the Jin was his subject. But then the Tianzuo khan of the Liao lost virtue [lit. *doro*, the way],

and, for no other reason than that the peace-loving Taizu of the Jin
would not dance for him, he sought to kill him. Thus wronged,
Heaven gave the Liao lands in Liaodong to the Jin.... Truly, Heaven
gave the rule of the Liao to the Jin.

This was followed by the additional examples of Chinggis Khan similarly supplanting the Jin khan Yongji and of Zhu Yuanzhang supplanting the Yuan khan Toghon Temür: "[Now], though we are without
fault, it is the Wanli emperor saying he wishes to kill us. How is this
different from what has happened before?... For two years now the letters and emissaries I have sent to the imperial city have been sent back
without even getting through—this is an even greater outrage than
that perpetrated by the Liao upon the Jin! But this is also Heaven's
will" (MBRT: Taizong IV, 17.225–227).

One might well question the judgment of Qing rulers in continually invoking the precedent of northern dynasties in this way. The
Liao and Jin in particular occupied an uncertain place in the procession of dynasties to rule in China, and neither was graced with a standard history (Ch. *zhengshi*) until the Yuan took power in the thirteenth
century. Conceivably, claiming to be part of this line weakened the
Manchu case to be worthy of Heaven's mandate in Chinese eyes and
hurt their chances of being accepted as legitimate Sons of Heaven.
After all, loyalist sentiment had motivated famous patriots like Yue Fei
(d. 1141) to stand up to the Jin, so raising the precedent of the Jin
might resurrect the specter of loyalist resistance to the new "barbarians." As Roger Des Forges observes, the analogy of previous accommodation with non-Han rule was ambiguous for the Chinese, as it furnished examples of resistance as well as of collaboration. The same
was true for the Manchus. But in embracing this "barbarian" past as
their own, the Manchu rulers showed a practical recognition that no
matter what they did or said they would be perceived this way. By dealing as openly as possible with what amounted to Chinese ethnocentric
prejudice against them, it appears, the Manchus hoped to turn the
"outsider" card to their advantage. For in the end, the Jin, along with
the Liao and the Yuan, had become recognized as dynasties in the orthodox imperial tradition. Whatever else one might say, they had evidently enjoyed Heaven's favor, proof that they possessed virtue. So
why not the Qing?

Hong Taiji pursued this line expressly in communications stressing
the point that one did not have to be from the central plain to become

the Son of Heaven and that the Manchus' origins should not be held
against them. In December 1629 he addressed a general proclamation
to the Chinese holding out against the Manchus in Liaoxi. Sketching
the history of Ming offenses against the Manchus, Hong Taiji observed:
"Our country (Ma. *gurun*) is small. So why should you address me as
emperor (Ma. *hūwangdi*)? Of old, [though] the Great Liao, the Jin,
and the Great Yuan were all small nations, yet emperors arose there.
Why were you made to stop calling them emperor? Besides, your
Ming Zhu [Yuanzhang] Taizu was a monk. Heaven valued him and
raised him and he became emperor. Is there a precedent that only
those of one single surname can become emperor?"[17] Seven years
later, writing to the Korean king, he returned to this theme in a slightly
different way. Repeating the adage that the realm does not belong to
any one person, the Manchu ruler underscored the point that he who
possessed virtue would become the Son of Heaven and that, "hence, in
olden times, [though] being barbarians [Ma. *jušen*] from the northeast, the Great Liao became Sons of Heaven; being barbarians from
the east, the Jin took the realm from the Great Liao. They [also] subjugated the Song. The Great Yuan, being Mongols from the north,
took the realm from the Jin. Hongwu of the Great Ming, while being
a monk from the Huangjue temple, took the realm from the Great
Yuan" (JMD: X, 4746–4747/MBRT: Taizong VI, 8.1005–1006). Hong
Taiji's message here was plain: It did not matter where one was from
or how low one's status was in society; if one had virtue and won
Heaven's blessing, the conditions for winning the realm were met.

For this reason also, Hong Taiji added, places were forever changing hands: "Previously our two nations dwelt together in uneventful
harmony. However, not satisfied with the lands of the nine provinces
within your borders, and going beyond the old borders set during the
time of Hongwu and Yongle, [you] stole our meager lands. By erecting
inscribed stone markers every thirty *li* along the frontier, you turned
Jurchen lands into Chinese lands, and so fighting broke out. Heaven
saw this injustice—Liaodong was given [us] by Heaven" (MBRT: Taizong IV, 17.225). Here the unusual argument was being advanced
that the Manchus were heir not only to the imperial tradition of the
Jin, but also to former Jin territory. By the same logic, the Manchu
territorial claim was extended south of the Great Wall as well: "Nanjing, Beijing, and Bianjing [Kaifeng] were not originally the lands of
any one person. They are places that have been exchanged back and
forth between Jurchens and Han" (JMD: II, 1127/MBRT: Taizu II,

41.602)—the last an obvious reference to the Jin occupation of Bianjing in 1127, which marked the demise of the Northern Song.

Indeed, with the situation in the northeast developing ominously,
history was also very much on the minds of the Chinese, and relations
between the Song and the Jin seem to have been a common point of
reference for both sides (although, as Des Forges reports, the betrayal
of Henan by Xu Dingguo in 1645 was lamented by the historian Zheng
Lian in terms of a Tang precedent). Thus, in floating a proposal that
the Ming pay a tribute to the Manchus, Hong Taiji sagely pointed out
that, in their dealings with the Liao and the Jin, the Song in fact had
agreed to such an arrangement.[18] And in rebuffing this, along with
other feelers for peace, the Chinese—who had already made clear
their attitude toward the twelfth-century Jin by desecrating the Jin imperial tombs near Beijing—justified their unwillingness to negotiate
with the Manchus on the grounds that the agreements reached centuries before between the Jin and the Song had not, they said, been respected by the Jurchens (MBRT: Taizong IV, 26.345). Ironically, however, Shi Kefa would propose exactly this arrangement to Dorgon in
1644, when it was already too late (see the essay by Roger Des Forges
in this volume).

The initial Ming response evidently got Hong Taiji thinking. In
mid-1632, he invited three of his Han-Chinese advisors to a meal and
asked them their opinions about whether he should again attempt
negotiations with the Chinese court. In answering, two of the three referred to Song-Jin history. One advisor, Wang Wenkui, noted that "the
Chinese have examined [their actions] in light of the example of the
Song (Ma. *Sung gurun-i songko be buleku obufi*) and are refusing to deal
with us as an entity." Since the Manchu side cannot unilaterally declare peace, he said, it may as well unilaterally declare war. In such a
case, he predicted, "the central plain will be ours" (JMD: VIII, 3837–
3838/MBRT: Taizong V, 58.833–834). Jiang Yun, another advisor,
started off with an allusion to Agūda's seizure of Bianjing and the cap-
ture of the two Song emperors there:

> This was [possible] because the army was strong, an irresistible force
> that could destroy even bamboo. Nonetheless, it was not possible to
> sweep away the chaos and establish unity [across the realm]. That
> things reverted to negotiation was not [the result of] a lack of will or
> a lack of strength. Looking at the way things began, it was because
> the Jurchen people had not planned to unify [things] into one

[whole]. [Recently], when the Chakhar [Mongols] heard that the khan's army was nearing Datong, they fled without even facing our soldiers. Taking the city of Datong was then as [easy as] turning over the palm of one's hand. More than killing and fighting with military power, it is better to proclaim [your] trustworthiness and benevolence by not having the khan's soldiers killing and attacking. This is precisely where a grand strategy (Ma. *amba arga*) for unification has been established. (JMD: VIII, 3839–3840/MBRT: Taizong V, 58.835–836)

This speech urged Hong Taiji to reflect upon the Jin precedent not as a positive, but as a negative example. The Jin had managed to take Bianjing, Jiang was saying, but they could have done more had they planned it better from the start. Since Hong Taiji had a plan, Jiang assured him, he would certainly exceed the Jin, and therefore he ought not place too much hope in negotiations with the Ming.

This advice points to an important difference between the application of historical lessons internally and their application in externally directed propaganda. When intended for domestic consumption, such allusions were restricted almost without exception to other northern dynasties, and they were used more critically.[19] The past here was also a tool, perhaps, but it was a jeweler's pick, not a hammer. The evaluation of historical precedents in communications with Koreans, Chinese, and nonfederation Mongols, because of the rhetorical function such precedents had to fulfill, could not be very objective (though it could be quite inventive). Raising precedents in discussions among themselves, in contrast, was not about persuasion, but about reflection: How do we compare with earlier dynasties? What is our goal? Where do we go from here? These musings show even more powerfully how self-conscious the Manchus were of their Inner Asian roots. They also show how this consciousness changed as the Manchus' imperial ambitions matured under Hong Taiji.

Jin as Edifying Example

As mentioned earlier, one of Nurhaci's great preoccupations was that the Manchus should be seen as the literal descendants of the Jin-era Jurchens. This was probably why he renamed his lineage (a branch of the Gioro *mukūn*) the Aisin, or "Golden," Gioro.[20] This was why, when he decided that the tribal confederation under him needed a name, he chose Jin or, for an interval, "Latter Jin" (Ma. Amaga Aisin gurun, Ch. Hou Jinguo),[21] later amended simply to "Jin." The earliest extant printed account of Nurhaci's reflections on Jin history invariably speaks of "the records of our *gurun*" (Ma. *meni gurun-i kooli*) and even refers to the first Jin emperor, Agūda, as "the man named Agūda of our Manchu country" (Ma. *meni manju gurun-i Agūda gebungge niyalma*"; MG 61626: 30, 34). Similarly, in the early Manchu chronicles, Nurhaci typically refers to any individual former Jin emperor as "our Jin emperor" (Ma. *meni Aisin han*), and on one occasion he speaks of "the ancestor Agūda of our former Jin *gurun*," as if to imply that he looked upon Agūda as a kind of progenitor (JMD: II, 683/MBRT: Taizu I, 22.334). But after becoming khan, and evidently wishing to avoid too close an identification with the earlier Jin state, Hong Taiji never employed this formulation, and on at least one occasion he stated explicitly in a message to the Chinese inhabitants of the coastal city of Dalinghe that the Manchus were different:

[In 1629], when our troops went to Beijing, though I kept on sending letters asking for negotiations, the Chinese emperor and his officials, as usual, reflecting on the [example of] the Song emperor of former times, did not send me one word in response. The emperor of the Great Ming is not a relative of the Song emperor. Nor are we the relatives of the former Jin emperor. That was one time, this is another. Heaven's time and people's minds are entirely different. Why are there no wise men in your great country [who can see this]? In looking at the age and at its people, will it do to remain fixed in one's views like the glued-down bridge of a zither (*qin*), instead of adapting one's thinking?[22]

From this passage it is clear that Hong Taiji saw limits to the value of the Jin precedent. In his opinion, the Chinese would do well to realize, too, that, while the parallels with earlier history were striking, they were still only parallels. They mattered not so much for broad symbolic reasons, but for the lessons they could teach, and for this reason, parallels with the Liao and the Yuan were just as valuable as those with the Jurchen Jin. Thus, in response to the opinion of his ministers that archery was not so very important a skill, Hong Taiji reached back into Liao history for a story to illustrate that it was;[23] and, while he allowed comparison of himself with the second Jin emperor, Ukimai (Taizong), an equally apt comparison could have been made with the

third Yuan emperor, Khubilai (Shizu).[24] Indeed, Hong Taiji's identification with Khubilai seems to have been particularly strong. This is not
surprising, given Hong Taiji's ambitions as a "universal ruler" on the
Mongol model. In 1635, announcing that a new temple was being built
in Mukden to house a golden statue of the Mahākāla Buddha, he took
care to point out that the idol had originally been cast from one thousand ounces of gold by 'Phags pa Lama in the days of Khubilai.[25]

Hong Taiji also recognized the importance of the Jin precedent. In
1629 he sent representatives to perform sacrifices before the spirit tablets of the Jin emperors Taizu and Shizong with the words

> I have always heard that your accomplishments were great and your
> virtue surpassing. No matter how long I thought about this, it always
> still seemed like a dream. Now our army has arrived in Liangxiang,
> and we have discovered the spirit tablets of you two khans. No matter
> how much one age may differ from another, it is indeed the case
> that the fame of truly righteous and virtuous persons is extended
> further when their praise is sung at the spring and autumn
> sacrifices![26]

Hong Taiji raised the Jin as a positive example again in 1638, when
he said: "Of old, in the days when the khans of the three nations of
the Great Liao, the Great Yuan, and the Jin were fighting, they got
as far as India in the west, Korea in the east, the Amur [Sahaliyan
Ula] in the north, and the sea in the south. These men, these horses
are [capable of] the same."[27] Yet, despite such words of praise (the
preceding description of the geographic extent of the Jin empire
was oddly hyperbolic), most of the time Hong Taiji seemed preoccu-
pied with the Jin as a cautionary example, rather than as a model to
be emulated.

This repositioning can best be seen in a famous speech made in
early 1637 to Qing princes and nobles assembled in the multistory
Phoenix Hall pavilion of the Mukden palace. The occasion was the
reading aloud of the official records of the reign of the fifth Jin emperor, Shizong, also known as Wanyan Wulu (the same ruler referred
to in some of the passages cited above by his reign title "Dading
khan"). "Listen well, all of you, to what this says," Hong Taiji addressed his audience. "The emperor Shizong was considered by the
Chinese, the Mongols, and all peoples as having been a good khan.
Thus the wise men of later generations have praised him by calling

him a 'little Yao and Shun.' Ever since I had the record [of his reign] translated into Manchu and read [to me], my eyes and ears have become sharp, like the pricked-up ears of a horse who has seen a wild animal and wishes to dash away." Proceeding to explain what had happened to the Manchus' Jurchen predecessors once they had established their empire, Hong Taiji remarked that the "Old Way" practiced by Agūda (Jin Taizu, 1115–1122) and Ukimai (Jin Taizong, 1123–1134) had been forsaken, as Xizong and his successor, Hailing Wang (1135–1148 and 1149–1160) followed what he contemptuously called the "Chinese way" (Ma. *Nikan-i doro*) of liquor, leisure, and riding in sedan chairs. He then continued:

> After [rule] passed [from Hailing Wang] to Shizong Ulu Khan, he
> repeated over and over again, lest, as from the beginning it had
> previously been feared, children and grandchildren enter Chinese
> ways: "Do not neglect the old ways of the ancestors. Wear Jurchen
> clothing. Learn the Jurchen language. Practice archery and
> horsemanship every day." Although he had thus spoken, the khans
> of later generations entered the Chinese way, putting aside shooting
> and riding. By the time of Aizong [1224–1233], the [Jurchen] Way
> was destroyed. The dynasty had been wiped out. (JMD: X, 5293–
> 5295/MBRT: Taizong VII, 36.1339–1340)

With impressive perspicacity, Hong Taiji saw this aspect of the Jin experience as a powerful warning of the dangers that lay ahead for the Manchus. Having thus laid out the results of forgetting one's origins, Hong Taiji went on to defend his rejection of the proposals put forward by Dahai and Erdeni that the Manchus exchange their own clothing for wide-sleeved Chinese dress on the grounds that this would lessen martial preparedness and lead to eventual ruin.

Such an admonitory tone is entirely absent in Nurhaci's statements. True, he once remarked: "Of old, the Jin khan and the Mongol khan conquered three or four nations and unified them, dwelling as one, but [they] did not dwell as such for many years, generation after generation. This I have completely understood." But his point here (quite possibly disingenuous—he was writing to the Korean king) was that he was being forced into an adversarial position vis-à-vis the Ming and did not seek to emulate the Jin or Yuan, of whose failure, he claimed, he was all too well aware. Hong Taiji, too, was quite conscious of those failures, but his consciousness of the past—and his hunger to become ruler of the known world—led him in the contrary direction, to resolve to avoid repeating them. Therefore, in order to distance himself and his people from the Jurchens, in 1635 he forbade use of the old name Jurchen (in use up to that point) and proclaimed "Manchu" in its place. A few months later he emphasized this break by changing the dynastic name from "Jin" to "Qing."[28] But this did not mean that the past could simply be forgotten or ignored. In October 1636, in an argument with a Ming general surnamed Cen, Hong Taiji reminded him sharply: "You must know, general, that the Great Liao, the Jin, and the Great Yuan ruled successively over China in the past. If you don't know this, you should read the histories of those three nations" (JMD: X, 5109/MBRT: Taizong VII, 28.1300). Hong Taiji obviously already knew this, having taken the trouble to order his best scholars to translate those histories into Manchu—and Mongol—so that everyone else in the Qing state could read them as he had.

Manchu Translations of the Liao, Jin, and Yuan Dynastic Histories

The adaptation of the Mongol writing system, ordered by Nurhaci in 1599, meant that in the early seventeenth century for the first time it was possible to do written translations from Chinese (and other languages) into Manchu. But the generally violent tenor of those years meant that, in fact, relatively little translation was done, as the list of translations accomplished before 1644 is quite short. Among the first ones, begun in the early 1620s, were the Ming penal code (*Xingbu huidian*), the *Mengzi,* works on military science (such as the *Sushu,* the *Sanlüe,* and the *Liutao*), a short Ming-era encyclopedia titled *Wanbao quanshu,* and the *Sanguo zhi yanyi.* Later, portions of the *Daxue,* unknown sections of the Buddhist canon, and the *Gangjian huizuan* (a condensed version of Zhu Xi's *Zizhi tongjian gangmu*) also were begun.[29] As can be seen, the majority of these texts were translated for their perceived practical utility; all were translated at the pleasure of the khan. This work was done more systematically from 1629 onward by a very small cadre of talented men, led by the scholar Dahai, in the so-called Literary Institute (Ma. Bithei yamun, Ch. Wenguan).[30]

In 1636, as part of a general expansion of the Qing bureaucracy, the Three Palace Academies (Ma. Bithei ilan yamun, Ch. Nei sanyuan) were created, one of which was a refurbishment of the Literary Institute, now under a new name, the Palace Academy for the Advance-

ment of Literature (Ma. Kooli selgiyere yamun, lit. "office for promul-
gating precedents"; Ch. Hongwenguan).[31] One of the leading figures
in the Academy at this time was Hife, and it was he who became the
chief translator of the Liao, Jin, and Yuan histories.[32] It seems that
Hife received the charge to translate these histories in 1635. According
to the Chinese-language *shilu* (veritable records), Hong Taiji summoned Hife and his associates in May of that year and spoke as follows:

> Looking at historical works written in Chinese, I have found that a
> great many of them are full of decorative language. There would be
> no point in reading all of them. Now it would be appropriate to
> select from within the four histories of the Liao, Song, Jin, and Yuan
> [sections] concerning important political figures—those who strove
> to rule diligently and under whom the nation flourished; those
> whose reckless rule led to [its] downfall; military geniuses, gifted at
> using men and employing soldiers and armies; as well as loyal
> counselors, and the wicked and crafty who wronged the nation—
> and, for the purpose of reference and reflection, to translate them in
> writing.[33]

According to the preface (which is the same in all three histories),
work on the translation did not begin until more than a year later, in
the 5th month of the 1st year of Chongde, that is, June of 1636 (DLGS:
1.3a). This was probably because the scholars who had been working in
the old Literary Institute were still busy compiling the official records
of Nurhaci's reign, the *Wu huangdi shilu* (presented to Hong Taiji in
December, 1636; Qing *shilu*: Taizong, 32.9a–12b). But, by late 1636,
when Hong Taiji addressed himself to the rest of the Qing leadership,
parts of the *Jinshi* already had been translated.

The entire project—minus the *Songshi,* which was dropped at an
unspecified point—seems to have been finished by July 1639 and was
officially offered to Hong Taiji for inspection at that time. Which Chinese editions they worked from or where they were obtained from is
impossible to say.[34] The translations were presented anew by Hife to
Hong Taiji's successor Fulin, the Shunzhi emperor, in March of 1644,
just three months before Qing forces occupied Beijing. The revised
versions shown to the Shunzhi emperor[35]—who was only four at the
time and certainly could not yet read—evidently met with the approval
of the regents for the throne.[36] Hife and his associates were rewarded
with horses and silver (Qing *shilu*: Shizu, 3.23b–24a), and a decree was

issued that three hundred sets of the three histories should be printed and distributed.[37] The blocks were ready by May 21, 1646. By early 1647, a Mongol translation of the Liao, Jin, and Yuan histories was also completed (Qing *shilu:* Shizu, 30, cited in Kanda 1995: 279).

The common preface to the printed Manchu editions, consisting of the memorial submitted in March of 1644 and the edict commanding their publication, explained the background of and reasons for the translations:

> When one reads the precedents and histories of bygone times, [the causes for] successes and failures are rather secret, [and the reasons behind] peaceful times and troubled times quite hidden. Except for the sage, no one knows them. Thus is it said that, as the successful and unsuccessful points of the rule of emperors are all written down by men of letters, one ought to reflect fearfully on the present and fearfully leave a model for the future. Since ancient times, the principles by which the emperors and princes have ruled have not been lost. They have remained, transmitted for many thousands of years to this age in historical writings. No matter that an order (Ma. *doro*) may have ended; it is right to raise [its example] and speak of it to the [present] generation. No matter that [those] people lived a long time ago; it is right to compare [them] to [the people of] today. Thus it is said that the good is my teacher and the bad is my teacher. Looking one after another at the emperors from ancient times onward, all have done things this way.

The preface continued with an explicit reminder that the precedents for what the Qing itself hoped to accomplish lay in the achievements of the Khitans, Jurchens, and Mongols. Of these, as Hife was at pains to point out, only the Mongols had been completely successful:

> Though the Great Liao and the Jin were unable to unify the Under-Heaven, still, the Great Liao took half of the Under-Heaven, and the Jin took more than half of the Under-Heaven. The Great Yuan unified the Under-Heaven. It is proper to examine their rules, laws, and precedents. Hence the late emperor, who indeed liked to reflect on the past and took it to heart, commanded us specially, saying: "Translate the histories of these three dynasties (Ma. *gurun*), the Great Liao, the Jin, and the Great Yuan, into Manchu. Get rid of anything not useful in them, and include all such things as what they

succeeded at, what they failed at, the battles they fought, and the hunts they went on."[38]

Respecting Hong Taiji's original opinion of the histories as containing too much dross, Hife explained that he and his staff had sifted through the records of the reigns of the fourteen Liao emperors (including those of the Western Liao), the nine Jin emperors, and the fourteen Yuan emperors for items of importance. The Manchu translations therefore are not complete versions of the Liao, Jin, and Yuan histories. Rather, they amount to little more than abridged translations of the imperial annals (Ch. *benji*) in those histories, supplemented by selective borrowing from the biographies of officials (Ch. *liezhuan*) — along with a few additional sections, discussed below.[39]

The basic correspondence between the contents of the translations and the original histories is shown in Tables 1 to 3. Although Hife claimed that the biographies of the Western Liao emperors (of whom there were five) were consulted, they were not included in the finished translation, which was limited to the nine Liao emperors up to Tianzuo (captured by the Jin in 1125). Inasmuch as the translations reflected the political ambitions of the early Qing state, it was the models of prior rule in China by northern peoples that mattered. It is also worth noting that, while many Chinese-language historical works were translated into Manchu later in the Qing, no further translations were ever made of other dynastic histories. This may have been because of rising

Table 1. Correspondence of the Manchu-text *Liaoshi* with the Chinese original

Biography of	Dailiyoo gurun-i suduri		Based on *Liaoshi*	
	Debtelin no.	No. of pages	Juan nos.	Benji nos.
Preface + Taizu (Abaoji)	1	4 + 36	1–2	1–2
Taizong	2	35	3–4	3–4
Shizong, Muzong	3	23	5–7	5–7
Jingzong	4	13	8–9	8–9
Shengzong	5	44	10–17	10–17
Xingzong	6	24	18–20	18–20
Daozong	7	45	21–26	21–26
Tianzuo	7, 8*	24	27–30	27–30
Total: 8 *debtelin*, 248 pages				

*The biography of the Tianzuo emperor begins on p. 21a of fasc. 7. Fasc. 8 also contains additional translations from *juan* 25, 26, 27, 28, 34, 35, 36, and 116 of *Liaoshi*.

literacy in Chinese among the Manchus—although the trend does not seem to have prevented the seventeenth-century Qing court from proceeding with the translation of a number of other Chinese philosophical and historical works.[40] Perhaps those models in themselves were sufficient for the Manchus, and for the same reason the three dynasties

Table 2. Correspondence of the Manchu-text *Jinshi* with the Chinese original

Biography of	Aisin gurun-i suduri		Based on *Jinshi*	
	Debtelin no.	No. of pages	*Juan* nos.	*Benji* nos.
Preface + Taizu (Agūda)	1	4 + 59	1–2	1–2
Taizong	2	25	3	3
Xizong, Hailing Wang	3	40	4–5	4–5
Shizong (to 1178)	4	53	6–7	6–7
Shizong (from 1178)	5	47	7–8	7–8
Zhangzong	6	43	9–12	9–12
Weishao Wang, Xuanzong (to 1215)	7	39	13–14	13–14
Xuanzong (from 1215)	8	40	14–16	14–16
Aizong	9*	48	17–18	17–18
Total: 9 *debtelin*, 398 pages				

*Also contains additional information.

Table 3. Correspondence of the Manchu-text *Yuanshi* with the Chinese original

Biography of	Daiyuwan gurun-i suduri		Based on *Yuanshi*	
	Debtelin no.	No. of pages	*Juan* nos.	*Benji* nos.
Preface + Taizu (Chinggis)	1	4 + 73	1	1
Taizong (Ögedei), Xianzong	2	53	2–3	2–3
Shizu (Khubilai) (to 1266)	3	46	4–6	4–6
Shizu (1266–1275)	4	35	6–8	6–8
Shizu (1275–1278)	5	49	8–10	8–10
Shizu (1279–1294)	6	53	10–17	10–17
Chengzong	7	29	18–22	18–22
Wuzong	8	17	22–23	22–23
Renzong	9	31	24–26	24–26
Yingzong, Taidingdi, Mingzong	10	60	27–31	27–31
Wenzong, Ningzong	11	33	31–37	31–37
Shundi (to 1342)	12	51	38–42	38–42
Shundi (1343–1349)	13	40	42–45	42–45
Shundi (1350–1368)	14	49	45–47	45–47
Total: 14 *debtelin*, 623 pages				

were only evaluated comparatively with one another, not with other dynasties. Whereas the Liao and Jin only managed to conquer half of the realm, the Yuan successfully unified the "Under-Heaven" under its rule. It is not surprising that Hong Taiji preferred to identify himself with Khubilai.

In reading the actual texts, hopes of finding radical differences with the Chinese originals are soon disappointed. By and large, the Manchu translations provide a faithful, if abbreviated, account of the reign of each ruler. Here, for instance, is a passage on the rebel Zhangnu, from the Chinese biography of Tianzuo, the last Liao emperor:

> On the day *yisi* [of the 9th month in the 5th year of Tianqing], Yelü
> Zhangnu rebelled and hastened to the Supreme Capital. He planned
> to welcome and set up the Prince of Wei, Chun, as emperor....
> Zhangnu, on realizing that the Prince of Wei was not acquiescent,
> led his followers to plunder the prefectures of Qing, Rao, Huai, and
> Zu, and also joined up with the many Bohai bandits, so that the
> forces amounted to several tens of thousands in number. They
> rushed to Guangpingdian and attacked the imperial traveling camp.
> But Ahuchuan of the Obedient Nüzhi with three hundred horsemen
> was victorious in a single battle. He captured more than two hundred
> people of [Zhangnu's] noble families, cut off their heads, and
> displayed them publicly. Their wives and sons were punished by
> forced labor in the Embroidery Workhouse or by distribution as
> slaves among the personal attendants of the emperor. Of the rest,
> those who were able to escape all fled to the Nüzhi. Zhangnu tried to
> flee to the Nüzhi by posing as a messenger, but he was arrested by a
> patrol and sent in fetters to the emperor's residence. He was cut in
> two at the waist in the market-place. His heart was cut out and
> offered up at the ancestral temples. He was dismembered and
> displayed on the five routes.[41]

The same section in Manchu reads:

> Having rebelled, the official Yelui Jangnu took over three hundred
> men and, saying he wished to make the Prince of Wei, Yelui Siyūn,
> emperor [Ma. *han*], he returned to the Supreme Capital.... Later,
> when Jangnu learned that the Prince of Wei would not go along, he
> took the troops under him and pillaged the four districts of Cing jeo

[Qingzhou], Zao jeo [Raozhou], Hūwai jeo [Huaizhou], and Dzu jeo [Zuzhou]. Also, joining with the many bandits of the Bohai country, he led several tens of thousands to Guwang ping diyan [Guangpingdian] and attacked the emperor. At this, Agusan, an official of the submissive Jurchens, took three hundred cavalry and defeated them in battle. More than two hundred people of Jangnu's own lineage were killed, and his sons and wives were sent to do sewing and other work in the emperor's court. The rest were given as slaves to the emperor's messengers, and any who remained fled to the Jurchens. Yelui Jangnu disguised himself as an imperial emissary going to the Jurchen country, but the people at the guard post caught him and sent him to the emperor, after which the emperor had him taken into the street and killed. His heart was cut out and displayed at the ancestral temple, and his arms and legs were chopped to bits. (DLGS: 7.33b–35a)

Here, as almost everywhere else in the translations, specific dates are omitted, together with what were considered to be unnecessary "details." This was a version intended for general edification, not for scholarly research.

Despite their fundamental similarity, the original and its translation in a number of respects are quite distinct. One obvious difference is that of packaging. The translators did not respect the original chapter divisions and felt at liberty to divide the Manchu accounts differently. This is most noticeable in longer biographies, such as those of Jin Shizong, Yuan Shizu, and Yuan Shundi. Shorter accounts could also be combined into one fascicle, as with the biographies of Yuan Yingzong, Emperor Taiding, and Mingzong (in fasc. 10), and Wenzong and Ningzong (in fasc. 11). In these cases, pagination within the fascicle is usually done separately for each figure (the biography of the Liao emperor Tianzuo, which continues the pagination from the account of his predecessor, is an exception). Another difference, already noted, is that in translating—one might better say rendering—the biographies into Manchu, the translators (often using the "historical present" tense in Manchu) freely borrowed additional information from elsewhere in the original text, most commonly from accounts of individual officials in the biographical sections of the histories.[42]

Perhaps the most arresting feature of the translations, which reveals the most about what lessons the Qing hoped to learn from history, is the inclusion of what amount to original, specially compiled short appendices to the biographies in the last fascicles of both the *Dai-liyoo gurun-i suduri* and *Aisin gurun-i suduri* (no such appendix is found, however, at the end of the *Daiyuwan gurun-i suduri*—only one sentence noting the length of Yuan rule). At the conclusion of the biography of the Tianzuo emperor, in fascicle 8 of the translated *Liaoshi*, is a short statement, which does not appear in the original history: "The nine khans of the Great Liao ruled [Ma. *tehe*, lit. "sat"] for 219 years. The five khans of the Western Liao ruled for 88 years. Together, the four-teen khans of the Great Liao and the Western Liao [ruled for] 307 years" (DLGS: 7.24b). This statement is followed by approximately eleven pages of miscellaneous additional information about the Liao drawn from different parts of the *Liaoshi*. Included are the rules for ap-pointment of officials (25a–b/LS: III [j. 45]); the geographic extent of the Liao empire ("It is ten thousand *li:* east as far as the ocean, west as far as the Yin Mountains, north as far as the Lugu River, south as far as Begu");[43] the male population (Ma. *alban-i haha*) of the capitals (1,107,300)[44] and the names of fifty-nine subordinate peoples (26a–b/LS II [j. 36]); a list of other outlying tribes (Ma. *aiman*) in the north and south (27a–28a/LS II [j. 34, 35]); the location of the five Liao cap-itals (28b);[45] and a longish essay on the Liao military (28b–35a/LS II [j. 34]), in which the organization of the Khitan army is described in some detail:

> People over the age of fifteen up to fifty are all entered into military registers. For every cavalryman there are three horses, and each soldier has one man[servant] to cut fodder and assist him on campaign. Each wears armor. Individual households provide saddles, *tohoma,* and armor for horses, depending on their means. Also, each is responsible for providing four bows, four hundred metal-tipped arrows, long and short spears, a mace, battle-ax, hammer, awl, flint....[46]

There follows a careful description of the steps in organizing a mil-itary campaign. The reader learns that, in preparation for battle, the khan led the army in the sacrifice of a black ox[47] and a white horse to the spirits (Ma. *enduri*) of the sky, earth, and sun, but not the moon, which was not sacrificed to. Trusted officials were also sent to perform sacrifices at the temple of Taizu and all the tombs, and to the spirit of Mt. Muye.[48] The text then outlines the Liao system of organizing mili-tary forces:

When a command [ordering mobilization] arrives, the soldiers are gathered, and, their household means being examined, registers are surveyed. Then they wait. [Officers] from *syjiyang* (Ch. *shijiang*)[49] on up inspect the soldiers' weapons in turn. After the [other] half of the golden tally arrives, each [officer] sets out leading [the troops] of which he is head. He does not entrust them to any emissary who may come. Once he has inspected the troops together with the military chief (Ma. *coohai ejen,* Ch. *junzhu*), emissaries may only report to the khan. Taking into consideration the relative number of troops, the khan also sends out other officials, who, together with the military chief, supervise [matters]. The military chief also receives a five-colored flag and a drum from the khan. Afterward, the khan personally examines the generals and also the meritorious officials and appoints one [from among them] as commander in chief, one as vice commander in chief, and one as military director in chief to take over general command of the troops. In addition, from among all the soldiers, 30,000 crack troops are selected to be the guard, the soldiers who protect the emperor; another 3,000 heroic men are chosen to be the vanguard, and another hundred or so of the toughest men are picked and sent ahead to man the scout camps.

Further specifics follow on the lines of attack taken against the Song, the methods for assaulting cities, techniques for wearing out the enemy, strategies for advancing against arrayed troops, and the importance of patrols and scouts. The essential secrets of Liao success, which, interestingly, resemble in many points those of guerrilla warfare, are saved for the end:

When it comes time for the troops to move, after the drum is beaten three times, all the soldiers move at once, regardless of whether it is night or day. Before meeting a great enemy, the armored horses [i.e., the horses used in battle] are not ridden. Only once the enemy has drawn nearer are they ridden. If the enemy's formation is complete, there is no attack; pursue only when they return [to their camp]. Lying often in ambush and cutting off the enemy's supply lines; setting fires throughout the night; with the direction of the wind, tying branches to horses' tails to encumber [the enemy];[50] packing dried food to eat while on the move; having the soldiers regroup once they are split up; being strong on the attack and impervious to cold—these [tactics] are why [the Liao] army is so powerful. (DLGS: 8.28b–35a)

This was practical advice on making war that well suited the Manchus' particular needs and their fighting style. Like the Liao, their strength lay in their horsemanship. Also like the Liao, they were frequently outnumbered by the enemy and relied on superior speed and organization in order to win.

These extra selections seem to suggest that, in privately looking to these precedents, the Qing were most concerned with the distinctive practices and strategies that made their predecessors from the steppe militarily strong and enabled them to maintain rule over China. Some of this information could be obtained from the biographies of individual rulers. Useful information was also culled from other parts of the *Histories,* but its exact source in the original was never noted. It is hard to know how much of this information was new to the Manchus in the early 1640s, after almost a half century of warfare. But they may have taken at least one leaf from the Liao book, which was the tactic of tying branches to the tails of their horses "to encumber the enemy." This practice does not seem to make much sense until one reads the full explanation: "When instructed, the troops who gathered grass and food would tie two straw brooms to their horses' tails and, advancing with the wind, ride up and down, raising dust up into enemy lines. Already hungry and weakened, the enemy could no longer open his eyes and would thus be defeated" (DLGS: 8.33b). The day in May 1644 when the Qing army began the formal invasion of China, the enemy forces of Li Zicheng were blinded by dust in just this fashion and went down to defeat (Wakeman 1985: I, 315). One would like to know: was it a storm or hundreds of horse-tail brooms that raised the dust?

The very last page of the *Liaoshi* translation offers an unexpected surprise: a selection of about twenty Khitan words and phrases together with their Manchu equivalents. The items appear to have been chosen entirely at random: *aju sali,* "father, ancestor" (Ma. *ama mafa*); *booli,* "scoundrel, wicked person" (Ma. *ehe niyalma*); *sai i el še,* "it's a nice day" (Ma. *sain inenggi*); *asy,* "really big" (Ma. *yargiyan-i amba*), and so forth.[51] No further explanation is offered on the nature of the language.

The translation of the *Jinshi* also concludes with a brief, five-page appendix. Though it does not include anything on the Jurchen language, an abridged translation of the chapters on Jin administrative geography is presented (44a–45b/JS: II [j. 24–26]), along with a condensed version of the chapter on Jin military organization (45b–48b/JS: II [j. 44]). Here could be found such useful information as the outlines of the *meng-an mou-ke* system and the means of integrating non-Jurchens into the organization, the formation of guard units and the order of military command, the size of the Jurchen herds, and the contests for encouraging excellence in archery. The appendix concludes with a brief passage on the means of using salaries to support soldiers:

> In the third year called *tiyan-juwan* of the Xizong emperor [1140], ten million cash was dispensed annually to the soldiers stationed in Liaodong. If there was not enough money in the public coffers, it was taken from officials and [ordinary] people. The giving of salaries [Ma. *ciyanliyang*] to the troops began from this. Afterward, [a system of] rewards was established. For soldiers, depending on length of service, more [was given] to those who had served a long time and less to recent recruits. Archery continued to be tested, with four taels awarded to first-class men and ten taels each to the most outstanding of all. To the troops guarding the frontiers was given a monthly salary of silver, grain, silk, and cotton. Depending on the remoteness of the post and the difficulty [of its conditions], more was awarded to soldiers at distant, demanding locations and less to soldiers at nearby, less difficult posts.[52]

This reference may have proven worthwhile when the Qing decided to institute a salary system for the support of Eight Banner soldiers soon after the conquest.

The insinuation of the past into Manchu consciousness is readily apparent from the records that have survived from the period. As the foregoing discussion has shown, references to people and events from the Liao, Jin, and Yuan eras pepper their discussions with friends and foes alike and crop up frequently in their own in-house deliberations. By the 1630s, so important had reflecting on the past become that Hong Taiji decided to have the histories of those dynasties translated and to have copies given to everyone in the leadership, from princes down to colonels.[53] Yet, however important the Liao, Jin, and Yuan histories were to reinforcing Manchu historical consciousness, it would be wrong to assume that everything the Manchus knew about the Khitans,

Jurchens, and Mongols they learned from these sources. As demonstrated in the first part of this essay, well before the translations were made, stories about those peoples were already circulating. Accounts of earlier periods were transmitted among the Mongols from the fourteenth through the seventeenth centuries, as we know from texts such as Sagang Secen's *Erdeni-yin tobci* and the "Jewel Translucent Sutra" discussed in Johan Elverskog's contribution to this volume. That this was the case among the Manchus, too, is suggested by the relation of stories concerning figures from the Liao, Jin, and Yuan in the early Manchu archives that are either not preserved or only partially preserved in the standard histories.

The larger significance of the translation of the *Liaoshi, Jinshi,* and *Yuanshi* into Manchu, therefore, is not so much that it introduced new information about a hitherto unknown past, though it no doubt did achieve this. Rather, the project seems most significant because it represented an attempt to integrate the histories of those quasi-orthodox dynasties with the Manchus' own history. Writing—or more accurately, rewriting—those accounts in the Manchu language was one way of saying that the beginnings of the Manchu imperial enterprise lay in the Liao, Jin, and Yuan periods. (As already noted, though guilt by association was a possible result of the deliberate Manchu identification with the Jin and other "invaders," this did not seem to trouble the Manchus unduly.) It was also a way of saying that history—written history—mattered. For at the same time as the translations were being made, the Manchus were becoming more aware of the importance of recording their own history. As noted, the mid-1630s saw the compilation of the first history of Nurhaci's career, along with the first chronicle of Manchu origins (see Matsumura 1988 and 1997). This new preoccupation with the written word was without question the result of Chinese influence, and it would not be out of place to see it as an example of "sinicization," though one might prefer to think of it instead as "civilization," *wenhua*.[54] In fact, the Manchu translations of the three histories can be said to have inaugurated a new beginning in the historiography of the Liao, Jin, and Yuan periods. Later in the seventeenth century, evidential scholars began to take a closer look at earlier periods of non-Han rule. This led to the discovery of new sources and ultimately to a reshaping of the perceptions and awareness of the general structure of Chinese history, in particular its "barbarian interludes," a subject that is beyond the scope of the present essay.

Conclusion: Historical Process and the Right to Rule

One of the problems raised in this volume is the difficulty of characterizing an age such as the Ming-Qing transition and, specifically, the degree to which to include in any such characterization the sensibilities of the people who lived during that age. Is this approach not useful in trying to comb out the temporal positions of contemporaneous actors? Does it not enable us to better negotiate the enormous span of time that separates the modern historian from the middle seventeenth century? From the evidence presented in this essay, the answers to both these questions would appear to be yes. Furthermore, the most recent narratives of the rise of the Manchu state to dominance over most of East Asia, stressing the steppe heritage of the Qing empire, seem largely to accord with the views held by Manchu leaders at the time.

Nurhaci and Hong Taiji were quite conscious of their own epoch-making historicity and habitually framed their enterprise in a long continuum that carried special reference to earlier regimes that had also emerged from the northern frontier. From early in the process of building a regime to rival the Ming for control of China, they and the rest of the Manchu elite (we cannot claim to know what was in the popular mind) demonstrated an acute awareness that what they were attempting had been tried before by other northern peoples. Nurhaci and Hong Taiji made concerted efforts to portray the growth of their political power as a "natural" development that had ample historical precedent as well as the blessing of Heaven. The existence of a prior historical record—available to them in oral as well as written forms— meant that Manchu leaders could refer to the policies and techniques of earlier states to guide their own decision-making in the hope of avoiding the same mistakes and achieving greater success. This record could also be used in diplomacy with various outside parties (Koreans, Chinese, Mongols) to persuade others to cooperate with the Qing as others had cooperated before with the Liao, Jin, and Yuan. All in all, history was a powerful tool in the building of the early Qing state.

Of course, the track record of earlier northern dynasties was in many ways discouraging—either (like the Liao and Jin) they had managed to extend their rule over only part of China and had (in the case of the Jin) lost their distinctiveness, or (like the Yuan) they had not managed to establish a stable system of rule before collapsing. These examples surely gave the Manchus pause. Nurhaci in particular seems to have been undecided as to whether it was worth the risk to try to conquer China. Hong Taiji once cited his father's fears on this score: "After we took Guangning [in 1622], all the princes and military advisors were saying we should enter Shanhai Pass [see Map 1]. To this my father-khan answered, 'Of old, the Great Liao, Great Jin, and Great Yuan ceased to dwell in their own lands and went to dwell among the Chinese. As their ways [Ma. *doro*] changed, all of them became Chinese. Let us live on the other side of Shanhai Pass, in our own Liaodong, with each, the Chinese and the Jurchen, dwelling in his own country'" (JMD: VI, 2605–2606/MBRT: Taizong IV, 3.29–30). Both men, it seems, shared an undeniable consciousness that, whatever might happen, a historical moment—*another* historical moment, they might have said—had arrived and that Heaven's (ineluctable) Time (Ma. *abkai erin*), which brought down the mighty and raised the weak, now seemed to favor them.

But the two leaders' views of history were hardly the same. For Nurhaci, time was cyclically deterministic; it was the dimension in which Heaven manifested its Will to promote the strong and virtuous and remove the feeble and debased. For Hong Taiji, time was a learning medium in which human agency decidedly figured: we can know the choices made by others in analogous situations in the past and make wiser choices in the present. Thus, while Nurhaci was ambivalent about taking over China, Hong Taiji was more bullish on the Manchus' prospects: there can be no question that he was simply waiting for the right opportunity to burst through Shanhai Pass.

That said, the early Manchus' embrace of Liao, Jin, and Yuan precedents provides an outstanding example of the importance of traditionary elements in building a strong Inner Asian state, and it shows the extent to which historical consciousness, the medium by which "traditionary" values were transmitted, was not merely window dressing but assumed real political significance.[55] The previous achievements of Abaoji, Agūda, Chinggis, and Khubilai stood as examples of the possibilities the future held and encouraged an aggressive approach toward the Chinese as well as the Koreans and Mongols. At the same time, the failures of Tianzuo, Wanyang Liang, and Toghon Temür warned of the perils that also lay ahead in the long term.

Yet the Manchus embraced more than just the Liao, Jin, and Yuan pasts. The precedents they invoked—in conversations with themselves as with outsiders—included many examples from Chinese history as well. Famous figures from antiquity (Yao, Shun), the Zhou, Qin, and Han (King Zhou, the First Emperor of Qin, Liu Bang), the Sui

(Emperor Yang), the Song (Huizong), as well as the Ming (the Hong-wu and Wanli emperors) featured prominently in the Manchus' historical vocabulary. The Manchus thus cleared for themselves a place in history that went beyond an exclusive identification with other northern dynasties to include the broader ruling tradition that dominated in East Asia, of which Nurhaci and Hong Taiji were self-consciously seeking to partake. To do so required them to learn and employ the political language proper to the "Under-Heaven," that is, the language of benevolent governance, and to argue in terms of analogies and precedents that could prepare the ground for a new man of virtue to claim Heaven's mandate. These moves suggest that the Manchu elite began thinking of the future in ambitious terms no later than 1619, with the first major military victory over the Ming at Sarhū and the extension of control into territory that had been directly administered by the Chinese. This in turn suggests that as the Latter Jin state was spatially reconfigured, it entered a phase of temporal reconfiguration as well, positioning itself squarely within the historical mainstream.

Finally, it is worth pointing out that, in marked contrast to contemporaneous Chinese consciousness of the moment as outlined by Roger Des Forges, the Tang is curiously absent from early Manchu historical consciousness. The reasons for this are not entirely clear. It is surely not because Nurhaci and Hong Taiji were ignorant of the Tang (as mentioned, the *Gangjian huizuan,* a broad survey of history up to the Song, was one of the first books translated into Manchu). One reason might be that the Tang furnished no outstanding examples of miscreant rulers. For, as this essay has shown, the tendency in the early 1600s was to rely on the Chinese past for negative examples to illustrate the point that simply being Han Chinese was no guarantee of virtue. Inner Asian history, as part of the Manchus' own past, furnished positive as well as negative examples and was perceived as a more relevant guide to action. The major exception to this pattern was the unabashed Manchu admiration for the Ming founder, Zhu Yuanzhang, whose military exploits clearly commanded great respect and whose unification of the Chinese provinces in the mid-fourteenth century was the closest model for what the Manchus hoped to accomplish themselves. The preface to the Manchu translation of Zhu's "Sacred Instructions" (Shengyu) makes it clear that Hong Taiji saw Zhu as someone who "had a profound understanding of the difficulty of making a beginning and clearly understood the nature of the world."[56]

In actively promoting Zhu's exploits as worthy of study and emulation, the Manchus showed the broadening of their historical perspective and their emergence from provinciality to catholicity. Though averse to abandoning their roots in Inner Asia, they saw that creatively combining that past with Chinese historical discourse was essential to realizing their ambition to rule the world.

Notes

1. This legacy is still evident today, as seen in the persistent practice in Taiwan of dating things according to the "*n*th year of the Republic of China" and in the continued use of reign titles in Japan (where 2002 is the "14th year of Heisei").

2. Though the Manchus only became "Manchus" after 1635, I will use "Manchu" uniformly to refer to the early-seventeenth-century Jurchens. I adopt this admittedly anachronistic shorthand in order to minimize possible confusion with the Jurchens of the twelfth-century Jin dynasty.

3. Of these, only Chongde and Shunzhi were reign titles in the orthodox sense. That is, Chongde (Ma. Wesihun erdemungge, lit. acclaimed virtue) and Shunzhi (Ma. Ijishun dasan, lit. submissive rule) were used at the time in noting the year. Before 1636, internal dating was done differently in Manchu than in Chinese. Tianming (lit. heavenly mandate) was used in Chinese-language documents, but its Manchu equivalent, Abkai fulingga (lit. blessed by Heaven) was not; instead, years were counted simply as the "*n*th year of the 'Bright Khan' [Ma. Genggiyen han]." The first year of Tianming was 1616, but the first instance in which it is actually used is in 1619, suggesting that this name was invented after 1616 though no later than 1619 (Yan 1983: 158). Similarly, while Tiancong (heavenly wisdom) was used in Chinese between 1626 and 1635, in Manchu the years were kept not according to the year of Abkai sure (the Manchu translation of Tiancong), but according to the year of the "Wise Khan" (Ma. Sure han). Because the use of the Manchu equivalents (i.e., Abkai fulingga and Abkai sure) for dating these periods was applied only retroactively, Tianming and Tiancong are not quite reign titles.

4. Customarily dated to 1616, the dynastic name Jin, like the era name Tianming, does not appear to have been used until 1619. It seems likely here, too, that its origins were later projected back to coincide with Nurhaci's declaring himself "Bright Khan" in that year (formerly he had been known as Kundulen han, "Respected Khan") (Yan 1983: 158–159). Indications in the

Taebaeksan version of the *Yijo sillok* that "Jin" was used even before 1616 are unconfirmed in the other versions of this source and may represent later interpolations.

5. See, inter alia, Lattimore 1940, Numata et al. 1944, and Wittfogel and Feng 1949. A comprehensive treatment of this issue, though with only occasional reference to the Qing, can be found in the introduction to the *Cambridge History of China*, vol. 6 (Franke and Twitchett 1994).

6. The sources I have consulted include the *Manbun rōtō* (MBRT) and the *Kyū Manshū tō* (KMTTK) (both in transcription), the *Jiu Manzhou dang* (JMD) (in facsimile), and the *Gurun-i suduri yamun dangse* (GSYD) (on microfilm).

7. JMD: I, 424–425. Dading was the reign title of the Jin emperor Shizong (r. 1161–1189). The same passage is found in MBRT: Taizu I, 9.143. Cases such as these are indicated hereafter with a slash mark. In cases where there is no corresponding entry in the JMD, only the entry for MBRT is given.

8. JMD: II, 714–715/MBRT: Taizu I, 24.351–352; JMD: II, 810–811/ MBRT: Taizu I, 28.409–410; JMD: II, 883–884/MBRT: Taizu I, 31.451.

9. JMD: II, 622–624/MBRT: Taizu I, 19.291–292. Zhang was executed immediately after concluding his noble speech. Song Huizong (r. 1100–1126) and his son Qinzong (r. 1126–1127) both were captured when the Jin took Kaifeng in 1127. They were demoted to commoner status and forcibly removed to Manchuria, where they were held captive until their deaths in 1135 and 1156, respectively.

10. JMD: 4, 1868/MBRT: Taizu III, 64.963. The biography of Hu Jingde (Weichi Jingde) is found in *Jiu Tangshu*; see JTS: VIII, 2495–2500 (j. 68). Another instance of examples being drawn from Chinese history is found in a 1629 letter to a group of Ming officials, urging them to be statesmen like Zhang Liang, Chen Ping, Zhuge Liang, and Zhou Yu. See MBRT: Taizong IV, 17.229.

11. JMD: V, 2077–2078/MBRT: Taizu III, 71.1072–1073. Liu Zheng's submission to the Yuan is recorded in the *Yuanshi* in the official annals of Khubilai (YS: I, 71 [j. 4]; a more detailed biography is in YS: IX [j. 48]).

12. JMD: I, 538–539/MBRT: Taizu I, 15.231–233. This basic story is found in the *Liaoshi*; see LS: I, 326 (j. 27). See also Twitchett and Tietze 1994: 140–141.

13. JMD: I, 540–541/MBRT: Taizu I, 15.233–235. Yongji, a.k.a. Wanyan Yunji, was the seventh son of emperor Shizong and hence an uncle of the deceased emperor Zhangzong. He is better known as Weishao Wang (r. 1208–1213). This story does not appear in the *Jinshi*, but part of it is found in the *Yuanshi*. See YS I, 15 (j. 1); also Franke 1994: 251–252. The Manchu word *doro* covers a range of meanings, including doctrine, way, ritual, rule, and morality.

14. JMD: I, 541–542/MBRT: Taizu I, 15.235. Parts of these stories appear again in JMD: II, 1125–1127/MBRT: Taizu II, 41.601.

15. JMD: II, 820–821/MBRT: Taizu I, 28.415–416. Identical wording appears in another letter sent just a week later, in which the Wanli emperor is named explicitly. See JMD: II, 842–844/MBRT: Taizu I, 29.427–429.

16. MG 61624: 39–41. A very similar repertory of negative historical examples is found in MG 61626, a blockprint that appears to date from the early 1620s. The wording of the references to stories from Chinese history ("I have heard …") suggests that these were related orally to Nurhaci, while that of references to stories about Jin history ("I have read …") suggests that parts of the *Jinshi* may already have been translated into Manchu long before Hong Taiji ordered a more systematic translation years later.

17. JMD: VI, 2923/MBRT: Taizong IV, 19.258–259. The reference to Zhu Yuanzhang as "Zhu Taizu" suggests that the Manchus were still not at home manipulating the various personal names, temple names, and such, that designated Chinese emperors.

18. JMD: VI, 2608/MBRT: Taizong IV, 3.31. JMD originally had Daisung for the Song dynasty, but the *dai* (great) was then crossed out and left out in the later MBRT. The agreement referred to here was the Treaty of 1142, which drew the border between the Song and the Jin at the Huai River and committed the Song to substantial annual payments of silver and silk. See Franke 1994: 233–234.

19. The only exceptions I have found are a 1635 reference to Tang Xuanzong and a 1638 reference to Emperor Wen of Han. Both figures are presented in a positive light, as role models. For the first example, see KMTTK: 1, 45; the same passage is found in GSYD Tiancong 9 (Tiancong 9.1.27). Citations of this material adopt the following format: GSYD: reign year.page [if indicated] (date). For the Chinese translation of the GSYD passage, see QNMDY: I, 144. For the second example, see GSYD: Chongde 3.00292 (Chongde 3/7/16)/QNMDY: I, 133.

20. That the mythical Manchu ancestor Bukūri Yongšon was surnamed Aisin Gioro is pure fiction, for the earliest record of the surname Aisin Gioro dates from 1612 (JMD: I, 43/MBRT: Taizu I, 2.20). In his dealings with China and Korea, Nurhaci also sometimes pretended to be descended from the powerful Tong lineage, but this, too, was an invention. A good discussion of Nurhaci's genealogy is found in Xue Hong 1994. See also Zheng 1980, esp. pp. 38–47, as well as an extended discussion of Manchu genealogy in Crossley 1999, esp. 74–84.

21. As pointed out in note 4 above, the proclamation of the Latter Jin name is customarily dated to 1616, but the first documented uses of the name

appear in 1619 correspondence with the Korean throne. Very few contemporary references to the "Latter Jin" can be found in the sources, including only one in the entire preconquest chronicles, where Nurhaci is called the "Latter Jin khan." See JMD: II, 625/MBRT: Taizu I, 19.293. Some have hypothesized that changing Latter Jin to Jin was done to appease Ming sensibilities, but it is hard to see how this would have made much difference to the Beijing court, who in either case could scarcely have overlooked the echoes of the past in the name Jin. It seems more likely that abandoning Latter Jin was the idea of Hong Taiji, who eschewed the idea that the Manchu state represented a literal revival of the earlier Jurchen dynasty. It is worth noting also that, unlike the Liao and the Yuan, which in Manchu were consistently called the Great Liao (Dailiyoo, Dai Liyoo) and Great Yuan (Daiyuwan, Dai Yuwan), the Jin was spoken of as the Great Jin very rarely (only three times in the MBRT, twice as Dai Gin, once as Amba aisin). This pattern is also observed in the Manchu titles given to the translations of the Liao, Jin, and Yuan histories. See below.

22. MBRT: Taizong V, 40.544–545. Unlike the bridge of a violin or violoncello, the bridge of the zitherlike *qin* was permanently fixed to the instrument.

23. JMD: X, 4730/MBRT: Taizong VI, 7.990. Hong Taiji reminded his listeners that as part of the sacrifice to Heaven, Liao Taizong would shoot an arrow into a willow tree. While shooting willow trees does indeed seem to have been part of Liao ritual practice, perhaps with the meaning of rebirth, it seems to have been done primarily with the intent of bringing rain. See Wittfogel and Feng 1949: 216; also LS: I, 84 (j. 7). The only mention of shooting willows that I have found in the biography of Liao Taizong is a reference to the Jurchen presentation of horses for use in the ceremony (LS: I, 51 [j. 4]). It seems possible that this information was part of popular knowledge at the time.

24. KMTTK: I, 46; QNMDY: I, 144. It should be noted that Nurhaci's identification with the Jin was not entirely exclusive, either. In 1621, reflecting on the fact that enterprises begun by the father were often completed by the son, he cited both the example of Agūda (Jin Taizu) and Ukimai (Jin Taizong), as well as of Chinggis (Yuan Taizu) and Ögedei (Yuan Taizong). See JMD: II, 652/MBRT: Taizu I, 21.313.

25. GSDY: Tiancong 9 (Tiancong 9/7/25)/QNMDY: I, 80; KMTTK: II, 216. On the importance of the Mahākāla cult to the early Manchu state, see Grupper 1979; also Crossley 1999: 238–241. In identifying the location of the temple, Grupper relies on the letter of the Korean envoy and so translates "Xingjing" as Mukden (138). But the Manchu text makes it clear that in fact two separate matters were being discussed in turn: first, that a ruined temple in Yenden, the old capital, was being restored, and second, that a new temple

was being built in Mukden to house the Mahākāla statue. Thus Xingjing should be understood as Yenden (i.e., Hetu Ala).

26. JMD: VI, 2940–2945/MBRT: Taizong IV, 20.269–271. These words were followed by a brief narrative outlining the righteousness of Manchu grievances against the Ming and a request for support from the Jin imperial spirits.

27. GSYD: Chongde 3:00256–00258 (Chongde 3/7/6)/QNMDY: I, 326.

28. A letter written by Dorgon to the people of Jinzhou in November 1636, after the proclamation of the name Qing, offers a striking contrast to these apparent efforts to dissociate the Qing from any direct relationship to the Jin. Dorgon announced: "An emperor has come forth. Great Jin is his name. Ruling all under Heaven, he has reestablished the Great Jin khans of five hundred years ago, before the Great Yuan and the Great Ming emperors." JMD: X, 5140/MBRT: Taizong VII, 30.1323.

29. Details of these translations are found in Durrant 1979: 654–656, as well as in Fuchs 1936: 42–43.

30. Dahai (d. 1632) is most famous for having invented a system of diacritical marks (circles and dots) in 1632 to better differentiate the letters of the Manchu alphabet. However, as recent work has shown, this is probably not the whole story. In fact, the script reform movement seems to have begun in the 1620s and to have involved others besides Dahai. Dahai's main achievement in 1632 was to add diacritics to personal names and place names. See Pang 1999.

31. The others were the Palace Historiographical Academy (Ma. Gurun-i suduri yamun, Ch. Nei guoshiyuan) and the Palace Secretariat Academy (Ma. Narhūn bithei yamun, Ch. Nei mishuyuan). Sometimes *dorgi*, "inner" (Ch. *nei*) is prefixed to the names of these institutions in Manchu, sometimes not.

32. More information on Hife, and on Manchu translations in the early Qing generally, can be found in Chase 1979: ch. 2. See also Durrant 1979.

33. Qing *shilu:* Taizong, 23.14a–b. The same event is recorded in KMTTK: I, 144–145.

34. Information on the original compilation of the Liao, Jin, and Yuan standard histories—generally considered to be of rather poor quality—can be found in the bibliographical essays at the end of the *Cambridge History of China*, vol. 6 (Franke and Twitchett 1994).

35. Manuscripts of parts of the Manchu *Jinshi* and *Yuanshi* are extant. Part of the former is in the Zhongguo diyi lishi dang'anguan (First Historical Archives of China, Beijing), where it is stored together with documents from the Palace Historiographic Academy. Titled only "Aisin-i kooli jai" (Records of the Jin, 2), it contains the translation of the biography of Agūda up to the 4th month of the 2nd year of Tianfu (1118) (i.e., JS: I, 19–31 [j. 2]). This work is

a much more literal translation than the biography included for publication in the final version of the *Aisin gurun-i suduri*. The manuscript shows extensive corrections and emendations, which appear to be followed in the final version. Another manuscript fragment of the Jin history is apparently held in the Lüshun Museum (Huang and Qu 1991: 162). A fragment of the draft translation of the *Yuanshi*, purchased in Beijing in 1948, is held in the collection of the School of Oriental and African Studies, London. It represents the translation of two chapters of the annals (*benji*) of Khubilai and contains "many corrections and deletions, which are followed in the final version." See Simon and Nelson 1977: 29, and Kanda 1995. In addition, manuscripts of the Manchu translations of all three histories are believed to be stored in the library of the Imperial Palace Museum in Beijing (Huang and Qu 1991: 162–163). More careful study of these various drafts is sure to reveal more about the process whereby the histories were written. At present, it seems most sensible to assume an initial process of extensive revisions occurring between 1639 and March 1644, and a second, less extensive, revision occurring after March 1644, before publication in May 1646. A detailed discussion can be found in Kanda 1995. Furthermore, it is possible that other fragments of the draft translations may surface in the future. My thanks to Professors Matsumura Jun and Kanda Nobuo for making a copy of the *Jinshi* manuscript available to me and for sharing their views concerning these various textual problems.

36. Dorgon, who led the regents, later cited the *Jinshi* in cautioning against internecine feuding among the nobility (Wakeman 1985: II, 849).

37. The preface notes three hundred each of the Manchu *Liaoshi* and *Jinshi*, and six hundred of the *Yuanshi*, but, as Kanda Nobuo has explained, this probably refers to the number of boxed sets (*tao*). The length of the *Yuanshi* meant that it took up two *tao*. See Kanda 1995: 278.

38. DLGS: I, 1a–3a. The Chinese version of Hife's memorial to the Shunzhi emperor on this occasion, found in Qing *shilu*: Shizu, 3.22a–24a, differs rather significantly in some places from the Manchu original.

39. In this connection, the author of a 1933 catalog of Manchu books in Beijing wrote: "The three books above are the benji of the three histories. I once made a rough comparison of them with the three Chinese histories and found their contents to be mostly identical." See the entries in Li Teh Ch'i 1933. Kanda, however, points out that the translation "is compiled into an annal *[sic]* by selecting from benji and supplementing with accounts from [the] biographical section of the original history." See Kanda 1968: 79.

40. For a list of these translations, see Durrant 1977: 52–54. It is worth noting that Stanislas Julien, in his bibliography of Manchu translations from the Chinese, reports the existence of Manchu versions of the *Shiji* and of the his-

tories of the Han, Zhou, and Southern Song, as well as of the *Lieguo zhuan* (1889: entries 35, 36, 37, 38, and 77). None of these works appears, however, in the modern catalogs of collections of Manchu books I have checked.

41. LS: I, 332–333 (j. 28). The translation is from Wittfogel and Feng 1949: 423, with romanization altered.

42. Some examples are given in Kanda 1995: 280–283.

43. The Yin Mountains (Yinshan) are identified by Wittfogel and Feng as a mountain range along the southern rim of Inner Mongolia (1949: 470); the Lugu (Ch. Luqu) River is the modern Kerulen River, in western Mongolia (62); Begu refers to the Baigou River, then the natural boundary between the Liao and the Song (79n).

44. This figure is from LS: I, 417 (j. 36); see Wittfogel and Feng 1949: 553.

45. I have not been able to find the specific source of this information in the LS.

46. DLGS: 8.28b. A *tohoma* was a special sort of saddle cloth to protect riders' legs. The "small flag" listed in the Chinese original is omitted (LS: I, 397 [j. 34]). Wittfogel and Feng (1949: 560) seem to have mistranslated *huodao shi*, "flint," as "knife."

47. LS: I, 397 (j. 34) says *qing niu*, "blue ox," which Wittfogel and Feng (1949: 561) strangely translate as "grey ox."

48. On this mountain, believed to be the ancient home of the Khitan people, see Wittfogel and Feng 1949: 240.

49. Wittfogel and Feng (1949: 561) translate this as "sergeant."

50. Wittfogel and Feng (1949: 564) understand this passage to mean "to drag brushwood to windward," but see the explanation in the text below. Here, as elsewhere, one is reminded of the general utility of Manchu translations as a means of better understanding the original Chinese text.

51. DLGS: 8.35b. All of these are taken from LS: V (j. 116).

52. AGS: 9.48a–b. This passage is an abstract of JS: III, 1005–1007 (j. 44).

53. Qing *shilu*: Shizu, 29.10a. The edict also states that copies of the "Precious Instructions" (Ch. Baoxun) of the first Ming emperor were also to be distributed to all. This is no doubt the text titled in Manchu *Ming gurun-i hūng u han-i oyonggo tacihiyan* (Important teachings of the Hongwu emperor of the Ming). According to the preface, this translation was completed under the supervision of Garin in the 3rd year of the Shunzhi reign (1646). A complete copy exists in the Bibliothèque Nationale, Paris.

54. Cf. Durrant 1979: 656: "His [Hong Taiji's] emphasis upon the importance of historical example to illustrate the virtues attending a rising state and the vices accompanying decline sounds very Chinese in tone." But see the discussion in Bol 1987: 483–493.

55. On this point, see Di Cosmo 1999, esp. 7, 28.

56. *"Fukjin ilibure mangga babe šumin sahabi. duin mederi banin arbun be ge-tuken ulhihebi."* *Ming gurun-i Hūng u han-i oyonggo tacihiyan:* 2a.

References

AGS. *Aisin gurun-i suduri.* 1646. Trans. Hife [Xifu 希福] et al. 9 fascs. N.p.

Bol, Peter K. 1987. "Seeking Common Ground: Han Literati under Jurchen Rule." *Harvard Journal of Asiatic Studies* 47.2: 461–538.

Chase, Hanson. 1979. "The Status of the Manchu Language in the Early Ch'ing." Ph.D. diss., University of Washington.

Crossley, Pamela Kyle. 1999. *A Translucent Mirror: History and Identity in Qing Imperial Ideology.* Berkeley and Los Angeles: University of California Press.

Daiyuwan gurun-i suduri. 1646. Trans. Hife [Xifu 希福] et al. 14 fascs. N.p.

Di Cosmo, Nicola. 1999. "State Formation and Periodization in Inner Asian History." *Journal of World History* 10.1 (Spring): 1–40.

DLGS. *Dailiyoo gurun-i suduri.* 1646. Trans. Hife [Xifu 希福] et al. 8 fascs. N.p.

Durrant, Stephen. 1977. "Manchu Translations of Chou Dynasty Texts." *Early China* 3 (Fall): 52–54.

————. 1979. "Sino-Manchu Translations at the Mukden Court." *Journal of the American Oriental Society* 99.4 (Oct.–Dec.): 653–661.

Franke, Herbert. 1994. "The Chin Dynasty." In *Cambridge History of China,* vol. 6, ed. Franke and Twitchett, 215–320.

Franke, Herbert, and Denis Twitchett, eds. 1994. *The Cambridge History of China,* vol. 6, *Alien Regimes and Border States.* Cambridge: Cambridge University Press.

Fuchs, Walter. 1936. *Beiträge zur mandjurischen Bibliographie und Literatur.* Tokyo: Deutsche Gesellschaft für Natur- und Völkerkunde Ostasiens.

Grupper, Samuel M. 1979. "The Manchu Imperial Cult of the Early Ch'ing Dynasty: Texts and Studies of the Tantric Sanctuary of Mahākāla at Mukden." Ph.D. diss., Indiana University.

GSYD. *Gurun-i suduri yamun dangse* (*Qing Nei guoshiyuan Manwen dang'an* 清內國史院滿文檔案). 1988. Beijing: Zhongguo diyi lishi dang'anguan. Microfilm.

Huang Runhua 黃潤華 and Qu Liusheng 屈六生, comps. 1991. *Quanguo Manwen tushu ziliao lianhe mulu* 全國滿文圖書資料聯合目錄. Beijing: Shumu wenxian chubanshe.

JMD. *Jiu Manzhou dang* 舊滿洲檔. 1969. 10 vols. Taibei: National Palace Museum.

JS. *Jinshi* 金史. 1975. 8 vols. Beijing: Zhonghua shuju.

JTS. *Jiu Tangshu* 舊唐書. 1975. 16 vols. Beijing: Zhonghua shuju.

Julien, Stanislas. 1889. "Bibliographie tartare: Traductions mandchoues d'ouvrages chinois." *Memoirs de la Société Sinico-Japonaise* 8: 5–19.

Kanda, Nobuo 神田信夫. 1968. "Present State of Preservation of Manchu Literature." *Memoirs of the Research Department of the Tōyō Bunko* 26: 63–95.

———. 1995. "Manbun yaku Genshi no kōhon ni tsuite" 満文訳元史の稿本について. In *Qingzhu Zhaqi Siqin jiaoshou bashi shouchen xueshu lunwen ji* 慶祝札奇斯欽教授八十壽辰學術論文集, ed. Chen Jiexian 陳捷先, 269–287. Taibei: Lianjing chuban shiye gongsi.

KMTTK. *Kyū Manshū tō: Tensō kyūnen* 舊満洲檔：天聰九年. 1972–1975. Trans. and annot. Kanda Nobuo 神田信夫, Matsumura Jun 松村潤, and Okada Hidehiro 岡田英広. 2 vols. Tokyo: Tōyō Bunko.

Lattimore, Owen. 1940. *Inner Asian Frontiers of China*. New York: American Geographical Society.

Li Teh Ch'i 李德啟, comp. 1933. *Union Catalogue of Manchu Books in the National Library of Peiping and the Library of the Palace Museum* (*Manwen shuji lianhe mulu* 滿文書籍聯合目錄). Ed. Yu Dawchyuan 于道泉. Beijing: National Library of Peiping and the Library of the Palace Museum.

LS. *Liaoshi* 遼史. 1974. 5 vols. Beijing: Zhonghua shuju.

Matsumura Jun [松村潤]. 1988. "On the Founding Legend of the Ch'ing Dynasty." *Acta Asiatica* 53: 1–23.

———. 1997. "The Founding Legend of the Qing Dynasty Reconsidered." *Memoirs of the Research Department of the Tōyō Bunko* 55: 41–60.

MBRT. *Manbun rōtō* 満文老档. 1955–1963. Trans. and ed. Kanda Nobuo 神田信夫 et al. 7 vols. Tokyo: Tōyō Bunko.

MG 61624. Musée Guimet manuscript 61624. In Pang and Stary 1998.

MG 61626. Musée Guimet manuscript 61626. In Pang and Stary 1998.

Ming gurun-i Hūng u han-i oyongo tachihiyan (*Hongwu yaoxun* 洪武要訓). 1646. Woodblock print, n.p.

Numata Tomoo 沼田友夫 et al. 1944. *Iminzoku no Shina tōchi shi* 異民族の支那統治史. Tokyo: Kōdansha.

Pang, Tatiana A. 1999. "The Manchu Script Reform of 1632." In *Writing in the Altaic World,* ed. Juha Janhunen and Volker Rybatzki, 201–206. Special issue of *Studia Orientalia,* no. 87.

Pang, Tatiana A., and Giovanni Stary. 1998. *New Light on Manchu Historiography and Literature: The Discovery of Three Documents in Old Manchu Script.* Wiesbaden: Harrasowitz Verlag.

Qing *shilu.* 1937. *Da-Qing lichao shilu* 大清歷朝實錄. Rpt. Taibei: Huawen shuju, 1964. Vol. 2, Taizong 太宗; vols. 5–7, Shizu 世祖.

QNMDY. *Qing Nei Guoshiyuan Manwen dang'an yibian* 清內國史院滿文檔案譯編. 1989. Ed. Zhongguo diyi lishi dang'anguan 中國第一歷史檔案館. 3 vols. Beijing: Guangming ribao chubanshe.

Sagang Secen. 1990–1991. *Erdeni-yin tobci (Precious Summary: A Mongolian Chronicle of 1662)*. 2 vols. Ed. M. Gō, I. de Rachewiltz, J. R. Krueger, and B. Ulaan. Canberra: Faculty of Asian Studies, Australian National University.

Simon, Walter, and H. G. H. Nelson. 1977. *Manchu Books in London: A Union Catalog*. London: British Museum.

Twitchett, Denis, and Klaus-Peter Tietze. 1994. "The Liao." In *Cambridge History of China*, vol. 6, ed. Franke and Twitchett, 43–153.

Wakeman, Frederic E., Jr. 1985. *The Great Enterprise: The Manchu Reconstruction of Imperial Order in Seventeenth-Century China*. 2 vols. Berkeley and Los Angeles: University of California Press.

Wittfogel, Karl, and Feng Chia-sheng. 1949. *The History of Chinese Society: Liao*. Philadelphia: American Philosophical Society.

Xue Hong 薛紅. 1994. "Nuerhachi de xingshi he jiashi" 努而哈赤的姓氏和家世. In *Xue Hong xueshu lunji* 薛紅學術論集, ed. Diao Shuren 刁書仁, 148–156. Changchun: Jilin wenshi chubanshe. Article first published in 1989.

Yan Chongnian 閻崇年. 1983. *Nuerhachi zhuan* 努而哈赤傳. Beijing: Beijing chubanshe.

YS. *Yuanshi* 元史. 1976. 15 vols. Beijing: Zhonghua shuju.

Zheng Tianting 鄭天挺. 1980. "Qingdai huangshi zhi shizu yu xuexi" 清代皇室之氏族與血系. In Zheng's *Tanwei ji* 探微集, 33–63. Beijing: Zhonghua shuju.

CHAPTER TWO

Toward Another Tang or Zhou?

Views from the Central Plain in the Shunzhi Reign

Roger Des Forges

> Given that in the course of history many have acted on
> beliefs in which many others did not believe, we must
> perforce admit that for each, to a different degree, history
> has been largely the Theatre of an Illusion.
>
> Umberto Eco, *Serendipities*

As MARK ELLIOTT points out in chapter 1, the Jurchens (cum Manchus) who spearheaded the founding of the Qing dynasty in the first decades of the seventeenth century sought to legitimate their state primarily by identifying with the Khitans, Jurchens, and Mongols who had established the Liao, Jin, and Yuan dynasties and governed ever larger portions of China several centuries before. This self-identification has reinforced the view that the Qing was another alien, conquest dynasty, distinct from the putatively indigenous dynasties such as the Han and Ming. Although belief in the foreign nature of the Qing contributed to its decline and fall in the early twentieth century, recent studies invoke the very Manchuness of the dynasty as the principal reason for its extraordinary territorial, demographic, and economic growth during the eighteenth and nineteenth centuries.[1] In this view, it is the very non-Han nature of the Qing that best defines its place in Chinese history.

Many Chinese scholars interested in locating the Ming disintegration and Qing formation in world history, meanwhile, continue to operate within the Marxist-Leninist-Maoist paradigm that posits a shift from late feudalism in the Song-through-middle-Ming period to the "sprouts of capitalism" in the late Ming and early Qing.[2] Many Western and some Chinese analysts continue to develop a parallel Weberian-Parsonian-Dengist framework that sees the Ming-Qing transition coinciding with a larger change from late-traditional to early-modern Chinese history.[3] To the extent that these two paradigms take the European experience as normative and anticipate the development of some ultimate society (communism or postmodernity), they have rightly been subject to criticism as Eurocentric and teleological (P. Huang 1991; Wong 1997; Goldstone 1998). Alternatives to them include the early-twentieth-century Japanese (Kyoto school) hypothesis that Song China was the first modern society in the world and the more recent American convention of describing the Ming-Qing period as late imperial.[4] These perspectives are based on the problematic assumptions that modernity can be defined according to standards developed in Europe and that the transition from the Qing to the Republic in the early twentieth century represented an unprecedented and irrevocable institutional breakthrough.

In this essay, I resolutely avoid the terminologies associated with the above paradigms and theories and inquire into the ways in which the vast majority of Chinese thought about their place in time during the beginning of Qing rule over their land. I proceed through an examination of historical analogies stated or implied by representative individuals hailing from three prefectures in northeastern Henan: Kaifeng, Guide, and Weihui (see Map 1). I focus on this region because it lies at the heart of the "central province" (zhongzhou), itself situated in the center of the "central plain" (zhongyuan), a synecdoche for the "central state(s)" (zhongguo), the most common Chinese term for what is known in the West as China. While some participant-observers from this region considered the Manchus to be aliens analogous to the Khitans, Jurchens, and Mongols and regarded the Qing as a conquest dynasty like the Liao, Jin, and Yuan, thus subscribing to a negative version of the Manchus' self-identifications, others emphasized the threat of internal rebellions and sought to restore Ming authority on the model of the Latter Han or late Tang. Still others drew on periods of disunion such as the Warring States, Three Kingdoms, and Wei-Jin-Nanbeichao, or on the preceding unified Ming dynasty, to assume and rationalize various positions vis-à-vis the rising Qing state.

While all three perspectives from the central plain are of interest, I am particularly concerned with another view held by those who were attracted to the culture of the Tang-Song period and to the history of the Tang and Zhou periods as lenses through which to view the incipient Qing. While a few who held this view cited precedents from the Tang and Zhou to explain their refusal to serve the Qing, many more invoked the history of those periods to justify their efforts to turn the Qing into a comparably glorious epoch in the evolution of Chinese civilization. Though they had lived through what might be called "mean" times in the double sense of the hardship and in-between-ness of the rebel Shun interregnum, they also drew on particular experiences of the past in efforts to recover a "mean," a more balanced (*zhongyong*) time characterized by political integration, social order, and cultural confidence. As Felipe Fernández-Armesto has written, "The course of history is influenced less by events as they happen than by the constructions—often fanciful, often false—which people put on them" (1995: 19). If the people of the central plain sometimes placed constructions on events that others may deem fanciful or false, they nevertheless frequently acted on their beliefs and thereby contributed to the resulting Qing formation. Their collective aspirations, activities, and expectations, therefore, provide us with another standard by which to measure the achievements of the Qing. They may even help us to place that polity in larger patterns of Chinese and world history.

The Rise of the Qing

As I have pointed out elsewhere, the people of northeast Henan during the Ming dynasty quite consistently identified that dynasty with the Han, or more precisely with the two Han dynasties, which to them had prefigured the Ming a millennium and a half earlier. In so doing, I have suggested, those residents of the heart of the central plain may have been representative of the Chinese people as a whole (Des Forges 2003). Thus it is not surprising that in the late Ming the Jurchen leader Nurhaci, who was to become the grand progenitor of the Qing, was influenced by the historical novel *Sanguozhi yanyi* (Extended meanings of the *Record of the Three Kingdoms*), which was compiled during the Ming in an effort to dramatize lessons from the rise and fall of the Han.[5] During the late Ming, that novel became a veritable textbook on how regional militarists might bring the dynasty to an end and seek to establish their own authority in the central plain (Des Forges 2001). Indeed, a late-Ming rebel active in the plain, Luo Rucai, adopted the name Cao Cao after the late-Han general who, in the name of defending the Han, had actually brought it to the brink of extinction (Gu

Cheng 1980: 321). Yet, while Nurhaci and Luo may have been inspired by the Han model to take up arms in the late Ming, few people in northeastern China or in northeastern Henan wished to relive the wars that followed the destruction of the Han and ushered in centuries of division.

The Qing founders, therefore, turned to more recent models of frontier states that had governed northeastern and northern China. As Elliott shows clearly from the Manchu records, Nurhaci made the original Jin dynasty ancestral to his own Latter Jin and drew lessons from the Liao and Yuan for his own day. His son, Hong Taiji, intent on incorporating the Mongols and extending his authority to the central plain, focused his attention on the Mongol Yuan, which had succeeded in unifying all of China. Hong Taiji drew on the Mongol model to form a new people, the Manchus, and to establish a new universal state, the Qing. During the early years of the Qing outside the Great Wall, the positive features of those antecedent states (their local origins and eventual legitimation as Chinese dynasties) clearly outweighed their liabilities (their allegedly alien culture and only partial—or evanescent—rule over the central plain).

While inspired primarily by previous frontier states, the Jurchen/ Manchu leaders from the beginning had drawn on other periods of the Chinese past to develop and enhance their claims to the mandate to rule China. For example, Nurhaci himself had adopted as a kind of reign title the "Mandate of Heaven" (Tianming), a concept that had its origins in the founding of the Zhou dynasty in the early first millennium BCE. Hong Taiji invoked the example of Taigong Wang, a semi-legendary advisor to the Zhou founders based in part on a historical figure from the central plain, in an effort to woo the Chinese literati inside the wall. Hong Taiji was reportedly also familiar with Sima Guang's *Zizhi tongjian* (Comprehensive mirror for aid in governance), the famous history of China that celebrated the wise administration of the second Tang ruler, Li Shimin. It was the temple name (Taizong) of the renowned Li Shimin that would ultimately be assigned to Hong Taiji.[6]

Upon Hong Taiji's death in 1643, his younger brother Dorgon faced off against his eldest son Hooge in a struggle for the succession. The Aisin Gioro lineage resolved the conflict by adopting the institution of the regency, made famous by the Zhou founders, and by naming Dorgon regent to Hong Taiji's ninth son, the infant Fulin. Dorgon and Fulin thus shared authority in a reign that was titled Shunzhi, per-

haps in pointed apposition to the Great Shun regime of their enemy Li
Zicheng, who may have found historical significance for his movement
in the Dashun reign of the late Tang. On June 7, 1644, Dorgon was
encouraged by former Ming and Shun officials to mount a carriage formerly used by Ming rulers to enter Beijing. When he demurred on the
grounds that he was a mere regent like the Duke of Zhou, his advisors
insisted that, like the Duke of Zhou, he wielded the ultimate authority
and should take the royal vehicle into the capital city. By the terms of
Dorgon's ostensibly modest demurral, of course, he had boldly
claimed greater charisma for himself by identifying with one of China's
most revered sage rulers. According to the *shilu* (veritable record) of
the Shunzhi reign, he finally agreed to "conform to the opinions of
the multitude" and entered the city in style. This narrative honored
the idea, dating from the Zhou, that the Mandate of Heaven and nature mirrored the support of the people. Four months later an edict
appeared in the name of Fulin stating that Dorgon's achievement in
pacifying Zhong-Xia (Central Xia, i.e., China) actually exceeded that
of the Duke of Zhou (Shunzhi *shilu* 1936: 5.2a, 15a–b; 9.23a–b). Dorgon's personal virtue might not equal that of his illustrious predecessor, the Zhou regent, but his public achievement in ordering an even
larger realm in a much later era might ultimately earn him a similar
place in history.[7]

Taking the Central Plain

The Qing established its principal capital in Beijing, thus following not
only the Jin and Yuan dynasties but also the Ming, which had valued
the city as a link between the steppe and the sown (Naquin 2000:
120). The Qing also followed the example of previous dynasties all the
way back to the Zhou in considering control of the central plain, the
locus of the earliest culture (the Xia) and of the first state (the Shang),
as essential to its claim to rule the central state(s) and pacify the known
world (*tianxia*). During the last years of the Ming, the commoner rebel
Li Zicheng had established his authority there, first by identifying with
the commoner founder of the Han, then by defying Ming efforts at
suppression based on the model of the mid-Han and mid-Tang, and
finally by building on the precedent of the Lis who had founded the
Tang. After proclaiming his Great Shun state in Shaanxi, Li Zicheng
renamed the city of Xi'an Chang'an after the Tang capital. He
then took Beijing and proclaimed himself the Son of Heaven before

abandoning the city and retreating to his original base in Shaanxi. Ming loyalists, meanwhile, rallied around the Prince of Fu at Nanjing, the secondary Ming capital on the southern edge of the central plain. From there they attempted to suppress Li's rebels as the Latter Han had subdued the Red Eyebrows, to use Dorgon's Manchus against the rebels as the mid-Tang had used the Uygurs against An Lushan, or at least to contain both adversaries north of the Huai River as the Southern Song had contained the Liao and the Jin.

The contest for the central plain began in earnest on June 30, 1644, when the erstwhile Ming prefect of Guide in Henan returned to the town and enlisted the support of local government students to arrest the prefect and seven county magistrates appointed by the Shun rebels. He sent them to Nanjing to be punished by the Ming loyalist regime and, in an accompanying report, vowed that he would recover the central province from bandits just as the Latter Han had recovered the region from the Red Eyebrows.[8] The Nanjing government, meanwhile, had appointed Shi Kefa, a Ming metropolitan graduate from Xiangfu County, Kaifeng Prefecture, Henan, minister of troops and Junior Guardian of the Heir Apparent. Shi organized a mission to Beijing, which asked Dorgon to follow the example of the Khitan Liao and withdraw his troops to the northeast (where he could establish a state of his own choosing) in return for annual payments from the Ming of 100,000 taels of silver.[9] Having long since aspired to establish more than a frontier regime like that of the Liao or Jin, Dorgon warned that his forces would advance on Nanjing as soon as they had subdued the Shun. He advised the Nanjing government not to repeat the mistake of others who had negotiated interminably only to have the enemy cross the Yangzi and thrust the "mirror of Yin" upon them, an allusion to Southern Song resistance to the Mongol Yuan couched in terms of the Shang (Yin) defeat by the Zhou.[10] Unfazed, Shi Kefa continued to invoke the restorations by Guangwu of the Latter Han and Suzong of the late Tang as models for Ming resistance against the Shun rebels and Qing interlopers. He supported the Nanjing government's decision to punish erstwhile Ming officials who had made their peace with the rebel Shun regime in Beijing, using the six grades of responsibility devised by the Tang to punish officials who had collaborated with the mutineer An Lushan. He again cited examples from the Han and Tang dynasties to call for severe sanctions against rebel sympathizers, including his own cousin, Shi Kecheng, a provincial graduate from Xiangfu who had survived the rebel tenure in Beijing.[11]

Inspired by the examples of the Latter Han and late Tang, Shi Kefa made two further attempts to restore Ming authority in the central plain. He first sent one of his generals, the one-time rebel Gao Jie, northward to cooperate with the Qing commander Dodo in suppressing the Shun. When Dodo rejected Gao's offer of assistance, Gao turned to a local Henanese militarist, Xu Dingguo, with whom he hoped to ally against the Qing. But Xu nursed an old grudge against Gao and had already secretly surrendered to the Qing. When Gao demanded that Xu place his troops under Gao's command, Xu invited him to dinner and assassinated him. When Shi Kefa learned of Gao's death on February 14, 1645, he exclaimed: "The central plain can no longer be recovered!" When the news reached Beijing, the Qing court congratulated Xu and placed him in charge of troops to "subdue the south." Recording these events, Zheng Lian, an early Qing government student from Shangqiu County in Guide Prefecture, expressed dismay that Gao Jie had not learned from the experience of Li Keyong, a general who had encountered similar challenges at Bianzhou (Kaifeng) in the mid-Tang. Zheng concluded: "No matter how brave a general may be, if he does not read books he will remain a mere commoner."[12] In May 1645 Shi Kefa mounted an all-out defense of Yangzhou from the advancing Qing forces, which brought death to many combatants on both sides, including Shi himself. Angered by Shi's stubborn resistance, the Qing commander Dodo authorized his forces to plunder and rape the city, producing an enormous massacre that became infamous as "the ten days of Yangzhou." Once again the Henanese historian Zheng Lian appraised Shi Kefa's record, arguing that although he was a man of principle he lacked the adaptability exhibited by leading statesmen of the Latter Han and mid-Tang.[13]

Though Ming loyalists were unable to hold the central plain and replicate the Han and Tang restorations, Qing dynasts were able to take the key region on the model of the Zhou victory over the Shang. Meeting little resistance, Dodo's forces took Nanjing on June 7, 1645. Dodo then read an edict drafted by Dorgon in the name of Fulin announcing that the court had "solemnly accepted the Mandate of Heaven and arrayed the six armies to subdue and punish the guilty." Twelve days later, Wang Duo, a metropolitan graduate from Huaiqing Prefecture, Henan, who had been a grand secretary in the Nanjing government, joined one hundred other officials in issuing a response. They referred to previous frontier states such as the Liao, Jin, and Yuan and asked rhetorically: "Did any compare with the Great Qing, which has raised troops to save the world from bandits, driven the Heaven-defying robbers from our central states, avenged the undying griev-ances of former rulers, wiped away disgrace, and purged cruelty, there-by attaining an eminence surpassing that of antiquity?" Noting the Qing victory in the central plain and the orderly seizure of the southern cap-ital, the statement concluded simply: "The armies of the three dynas-ties are to be seen here."[14] The implication was that the Qing might prove to be more civilized than either the rebels or previous frontier states and thus worthy of the hoary legacy of the Xia, Shang, and Zhou.

Views from Northeast Henan in the Shunzhi Reign (1644–1661)

During the wars that attended the Ming-Qing transition, some resi-dents of the central plain had identified themselves or had been com-pared by others with figures from the Warring States period, but as the Qing reestablished order, those analogies became less common. When the unlettered strongman Xu Dingguo from Taikang County had taken power in Guide Prefecture, he had been advised by one Li Zhenyuan, a relative by marriage and a government student, who had modeled himself on the semilegendary Su Qin and Zhang Yi of the Warring States period. But Li had been killed, and Xu, as we have seen, ultimately surrendered to the Qing.[15] When the provincial grad-uate Sun Qifeng had organized militia to oppose Manchu raids on his hometown in Beizhili, he reminded contemporaries of Lu Zhonglian, a strategist of the Warring States period. During the early Qing, however, Sun followed another model, to be discussed below, and retired to Su-men in the hills of Weihui Prefecture, Henan, to pursue a life of schol-arship and teaching (Hummel 1943–1944: 671–672). Hou Fangyue, of Shangqiu County, had been active among Ming loyalists in Jiangnan. After returning home in 1645, he continued to behave in a freewheel-ing fashion, prompting a biographer to compare him with Lu Zhong-lian. But Hou was arrested in 1651 on charges of colluding with the Jin Shenghuan revolt in Jiangxi, and he was executed.[16] Voluntarily or involuntarily, sooner or later, people of the region recognized that the age of warfare was coming to an end and a new era of peace was dawning.

Other scholars and officials of northeast Henan expressed reserva-tions about the early Qing by admiring—and in some cases adopting—the lifestyles of literati of the Wei-Jin period. Xu Zuomei, a Ming met-ropolitan graduate from Weihui Prefecture, held high office in the early Qing, but he later retired to his home and lived out his life in the style of Tao Qian, the famed rustic poet of the Eastern Jin (*Xinxiang xianzhi* 1747: 5.10b, 12a; Li Minxiu 1915: 1.20b). Hou Fangyu, a Ming student from Shangqiu who became a noted prose stylist in the early Qing, alluded to the experiences of Ji Kang and Zhang Han of the Wei-Jin period in a letter urging the scholar Li Wen to quit his post as Dorgon's secretary.[17] Zheng Lian, the above-mentioned Shangqiu historian, became a government student in the early Qing. After failing the provincial examinations ten times, he joined eleven friends to drink and write poetry in conscious imitation of the semilegendary Seven Worthies of the Bamboo Grove (Zhulin qixian). Like those Wei-Jin literati from the central plain, Zheng and his colleagues apparently hoped to camouflage their dissent with eccentricity.[18]

Some residents of northeast Henan continued to hope for the restoration of the Ming on the model of the Latter Han, but they did so in vain. For example, former Ming officials and members of the local elite in six counties of the region supported Li Huajing's Elm Garden Army (Yuyuan jun) with the idea that it might lead, on the analogy of the Green Wood uprisings during the reign of Wang Mang, to the overthrow of the Qing and the restoration of the Ming. In 1648, however, the Elm Garden Army was suppressed by the Qing without any visible benefit to the Ming-loyalist cause.[19]

Under these conditions, others drew on the Ming experience to proffer advice to the Qing. Further encouraging interest in the Shang-to-Zhou model, the Qing state initiated the practice of invoking Ming precedents by acknowledging the continuing relevance of the Ming system. For example, in 1652 court officials concerned about tax arrears in Henan and elsewhere cited the example of the Ming founder in recommending that fallow land, with or without certifiable owners, be reallocated to others, including the landless and the floating population (FHA, *tunken lei* 53, 63, 97; Guo 1980: 126–127). Members of the local elite therefore naturally invoked Ming precedents in support of various policy proposals. Zhang Wenguang, a 1628 metropolitan graduate from Xiangfu who had helped defend Kaifeng from Li Zicheng's rebels before surrendering to the Qing, had become a supervising secretary in the new government. In a daring proposal, given Qing identification with the Yuan, Zhang recommended that the Qing stop using the official titles for Kongzi derived from the Yuan and revert to "purer" designations of the sage used by the Ming.[20] Xu Zuomei, introduced above, who had risen to be a supervising secretary in the new government, invoked the experience of the late Ming to warn Fulin against using eunuchs in the Thirteen Offices of the Directorate of Ceremonial.[21] In the next generation, Tang Bin, a 1652 metropolitan graduate from Guide Prefecture, served the Qing as governor of Jiangsu and Supervisor of Instruction for the Heir Apparent. He cited early Ming historiographical practice to argue that the official Qing history of the Ming (the *Mingshi*) should include biographies of men who had served the Ming and later joined the Qing (Li Minxiu 1915: 2.11a).

Since the Qing had invoked the Yuan as a precedent for its rule over all of China, literati from Henan naturally alluded to experiences under that dynasty to articulate their positions vis-à-vis the Qing. Xue Suoyun, a Ming metropolitan graduate from Huaiqing Prefecture who had held office under both the Ming and the Shun before rallying to the Qing in Beijing, served as head of the Directorate of Education in the new government. Xue repeatedly urged Sun Qifeng to accept a post on the model of the scholars Xu Heng and Wu Cheng who had served the Yuan.[22] But the Yuan analogy continued to be a double-edged sword, providing models of resistance as well as of cooperation. Hou Fangyu, an erstwhile Ming government student from Shangqiu, steadfastly refused to seek office under the Qing, citing the example of Zheng Sixiao, who had gone into retirement and painted unrooted flowers to protest the loss of the central plain to the Mongol Yuan.[23]

Sun Qifeng, the Beizhili man who had resisted Manchu raids in his home province, split the difference between Xue Suoyun and Hou Fangyu by refusing to serve the Qing but teaching others who would eventually hold important posts in the state. Sun's model was Shao Yong, a leading scholar of the Northern Song period who declined any post so as to pursue his scholarship and make a long-term contribution to civilization. Shao, who hailed from Luoyang in western Henan, had gone into retreat at Sumen, in Hui County. It was there that Sun Qifeng established his own Baiquan Academy, which attracted students to engage in physical labor as well as to study the classics and histories. Sun soon developed his own capacious Way, including ideas from Shao Yong and Wang Yangming that had previously fallen somewhat outside the main line of Kongzian thought. Sun also transmitted his syncretic ideas through his writings, including the *Zhongzhou renwu kao* (Personalities of the Central Province), which treated scholars from his adopted province of Henan, and the *Lixue zongchuan* (Core transmitters of the School of Pattern), which included scholars from the entire realm. The strengths and weaknesses of Sun's latter work stimulated Huang Zongxi to compile the *Mingru xuean* (Record of Ming scholars), which provided a similarly broad overview of inherited scholarship.[24]

Other scholars from northeast Henan also looked back to the early Song and to the preceding Tang to get their bearings in the early Qing. Song Quan, a Ming metropolitan graduate from Shangqiu who had served briefly under the Shun before rallying to the Qing in Beijing, assumed the posts of grand secretary and chief examiner in the Dorgon regency. He presided over reforms in the examination system that emphasized merit but effectively favored the wealthy and cultured elite of Jiangnan. During a visit home in 1649 to mourn his mother's death, Song commissioned Hou Fangyu to draft an encomium for a shrine honoring the scholar Yan Zhenqing of the mid-Tang. He also had him compose an inscription for a school named after the reformer Fan Zhongyan of the Northern Song. By involving Hou in honoring these earlier scholar-officials active in the region, Song hoped to enlist Hou's talents in transmitting Tang-Song culture without requiring him to become actively involved in the state. When the Qing governor of Henan threatened to arrest Hou for maintaining contacts with Ming loyalists, Song persuaded him to desist by arguing that the talented young writer was for the Qing what the famous poets Li Bo and Su Dongpo had been for the Tang and Song.[25]

The comparison was appropriate because Hou Fangyu, although often depicted as a Ming loyalist, actually had more complicated views. For example, in a letter congratulating a friend in nearby Xiayi County for passing the first Qing provincial examination in 1645, he wrote that scholars of the Tang and Song periods provided models for serving the state without violating the Way. Although Hou did not elaborate, he implied that the Tang and Song had also shown imperfections, so scholars of those eras had been forced to make hard choices about public service that remained relevant under the Qing.[26] Like Hou, Song Quan's son Song Luo admired the Song poet Su Dongpo, and he was delighted when his first post turned out to be in Huangzhou, Hubei, where Su had once served. Unlike Hou, however, the young Song Luo became a guard to the Shunzhi emperor and emerged as one of the leading officials of the Kangxi reign. Other Qing scholar-officials from northeast Henan, such as Liang Xi from Yanling and Geng Yinggeng from Xiangcheng, strongly supported the cultural legacy they associated with the Tang and Song.[27]

While the Tang and Song were noted for their glorious cultural achievements, they could also be mined for negative models when such were needed. Zhang Jinyan, a 1631 metropolitan graduate from Xinxiang County, had served the Ming as a censor and written a series of impressive reports on military conditions in the 1640s. He subsequently made offers to serve the Shun and the Qing that were so poorly timed they were widely regarded as opportunistic. Zhang eventually secured minor posts under the Qing, but, when under consideration for a major promotion, he was impeached by an ambitious censor on the grounds that he had served and betrayed both the Ming and the Shun and could hardly be expected to be loyal to the Qing. When Zhang defended himself as a hero who was being victimized by slander, his critics compared him with Lu Qi of the Tang, who was infamous for intriguing against upright colleagues, and Jia Sidao of the Southern Song, who was often blamed for the defeat by the Mongols. Coming on top of personal and factional animosities, these historical associations were sufficiently damaging that Zhang was stripped of most of his property and exiled to Heilongjiang.[28]

The Tang, of course, was more than just the first phase in the renewal of Kongzian scholarship that reached new heights in the Song. It was also a golden age—perhaps *the* golden age—of Chinese poetry. As such it provided numerous illustrious benchmarks against which Qing writers could measure themselves and be appraised by others. In northeast Henan, Lian Zhenji of Yongcheng County belonged to the literary Snow Garden Society (Xueyuanshe) along with Hou Fangyu, but Lian departed from Hou's path by becoming a Qing tributary student in 1651. Lian explicitly modeled himself on poets of the high Tang.[29] Zhang Wenguang of Xiangfu was reputed to have begun writing poetry at the same age as the prodigy Gao Shi of the Tang, prompting some to suggest that he was a reincarnation of that earlier master,[30] using a Buddhist concept to explain the striking affinities between Tang and Qing poetry. Wang Zishou, a Xiangfu scholar who had passed the last Ming provincial examination and the first Qing metropolitan one, became a companion to the heir apparent. He also wrote poetry that critics compared to that of the high Tang.[31] Even Zhang Jinyan, who served the Qing only briefly before being cashiered, exemplified the Qing fascination with Tang literary achievements by editing, in exile, a collection of Du Fu's poetry.[32] Song Luo argued that Qing poetry might go with the current as it had in the Yuan, but it should also trace its source to the Tang (Langlois 1980: 381). Even Zhou Lianggong, a Ming metropolitan graduate who became one of the leading officials, writers, and art collectors of the early Qing, only to be impeached and posthumously disgraced, wrote poetry that was highly regarded and compared with that of the Tang.[33] If, as Pauline Yu has suggested, the emulation of Tang poetry in the Ming was part of a larger project to reproduce all possible aspects of the Tang achievement (1997: 91), then it apparently was even more the case in the Qing.

Other early Qing observers reached for Tang precedents to describe the status of certain court women and the achievements of certain local officials. Bumbutai, a Mongol concubine of Hong Taiji, had become Empress Dowager Xiaozhuang when her son Fulin succeeded to the throne in 1643. She worked closely with her brother-in-law Dorgon during his regency, and she helped establish a regency for her young grandson Xuanye when he assumed the throne in 1661 as the Kangxi emperor. Xiaozhuang was less successful in arranging Fulin's marriages, including those to two of her relatives, from whom he became estranged. Fulin instead devoted himself to a concubine named Xiaoxian, and his mourning for her when she died was compared with Tang Taizong's distress over the death of his favorite concubine.[34] In northeast Henan, Hou Fangyu's elder brother Fangxia, who had won his provincial degree in the Ming, broke ranks with the rest of his family to take and pass the first metropolitan examinations given in the Qing. He assumed a judicial post in Zhejiang, where he was said to be widely admired. According to one biography, contemporaries compared him with Xu Yougong and Du Jingguan, two exemplary prison officials who had served under empress Wu Zetian in the Tang period.[35] Whether or not the comparison was accurate in detail, it reflected a common aspiration in the early Qing—to restore the "good government" of the early Tang.

If the Tang was an attractive model for many in the early Qing, it is also true that the early Tang had fashioned itself in part on the much earlier model of the Zhou. While it might have been conceivable that Dorgon could surpass the Duke of Zhou by replicating his achievements on a larger scale in a later age, it was also widely assumed that the finest achievements of human beings could be found among the sages of early times. Among high Qing officials from northeast Henan, Xu Zuomei articulated that view most explicitly. When he was summoned to Beijing in 1645 to serve in the Ministry of Works, he called on the young ruler Fulin to follow the example of King Cheng of the Zhou. In Xu's words,

> The learning of rulers is different from the learning of scholars, and our August Superior's learning is different from the learning of the average ruler. The Duke of Zhou initiated methods for cultivating a minor on the throne that were further developed in later dynasties. He indicated that the first responsibility was education. Cheng Yi of the Song said that living members of the royal clan should nurture their virtue, but our August Superior, being intelligent and empowered by Heaven, has already surpassed the Song philosopher and can be compared with [King] Cheng of Zhou.[36]

Xu dismissed the idea that adolescence was a time for play and cited the *Yijing* (Book of changes) to the effect that the youthful years should be devoted to nourishing the capacity for sagehood. He stated frankly that study was particularly important because of differences in language and culture between Manchu and Han, and he urged Fulin to select scholars from among both old and young, Manchu and Han, to guide his intellectual and moral development.

Eight years later, while serving as a supervising secretary in the capital, Xu once again drew on the Zhou model, this time in developing river policy. The Yellow River, which had flooded disastrously in 1642 as a by-product of the Ming and rebel struggle over Kaifeng, continued to breach its banks almost every year during the Shunzhi reign, despite the best efforts of officials and residents to direct it back into the single course it had followed in the late Ming. After a flood in 1653, Xu and others suggested the need to investigate the location, described in the *Shangshu,* of the original nine beds of the Heshui, which were later guided into a single course and named the Huanghe (Yellow River). They called for surveys to determine the feasibility of allowing the river to return to its original Zhou distributaries. This radical proposal was embraced by Xu's fellow provincial, Liu Chang, a 1625 metropolitan graduate from Xiangfu. Liu had supported the Ming in its stalwart defense of Kaifeng from the rebels, but he blamed the dynasty for the destruction of the city by flood. Like Xu, Liu had subsequently surrendered to the Shun and then to the Qing. He had assumed several high posts in the new state and was now strategically positioned as president of the Ministry of Works. Local officials in charge of river conservancy in Shandong and Henan, however, opposed the surveys, arguing that a single course was essential if the river was to flow rapidly enough to scour its bed and supply water to the Grand Canal. They also pointed out that shoring up the existing dikes along a single course would be easier and cheaper than building new ones along multiple courses. Censors meanwhile impeached Liu Chang on the grounds that he had approved the surveys to cover up his subordinates' failure to secure the existing course by diking and dredging.[37] In the end, the proposal to return the Yellow River to the multiple courses of the Zhou came to nothing, but the fact that it got as far as it did reflects the appeal of the Zhou model at the Qing court.

While those two officials from northeast Henan failed to persuade the Qing to return to the Zhou approach in managing the Yellow River, the Qing was unable to win over another leading scholar-official from that region on the model of Shang officials who had transferred their allegiance to the Zhou. Hou Fangyu's father, Hou Xun, had been a vice-minister of war in the Ming before being jailed as a result of factional conflicts and military setbacks. He may subsequently have come to terms with the Shun in Beijing and, as a result, encountered threats to his life in Nanjing. Unlike Xu Zuomei and Liu Chang, however, Hou Xun remained loyal to the Ming. In the words of his biographer, he returned to his country estate in Shangqiu and refused repeated calls to "go out and pour libations and assist in the capital." This phrase, taken from the *Shijing* (Book of poetry), referred to virtuous Shang officials who had ultimately served the Zhou.[38]

Other literati from the region were inspired by the examples of Bo Yi and Shu Qi, Shang officials who accepted the existence and perhaps even the legitimacy of the Zhou but who starved themselves to death rather than serve it. Fu Tingxian, a 1643 metropolitan graduate from Kaifeng Prefecture, threatened to jump into the Yangzi rather than surrender to Dodo. He later retired to the hills of his home county, where he became known as the Old Dreamer of the Pepper-Cedar Grotto (Jiaobodong Mengweng), named for the flora he planted next to his abode. Since the characters for pepper and cedar resemble those for Shu and Bo (in the names Shu Qi and Bo Yi), by choosing them in naming his grotto, Fu signaled his desire to emulate those hermits who had refused to serve the Zhou. (The signal would have been picked up more readily by the literate elite than by the partially acculturated Manchus and the nonliterate masses.) In any case, Fu apparently ate his peppers, among other things, for he died a natural death, rebuking the Qing more mildly than his heroes had rebuked the Zhou (Li Minxiu 1915: 34.14a).

Others followed the example of Bo and Shu less consciously but more closely. In one case, Wu Yingji's death in the course of resisting Qing forces in Anhui reminded his Fushe associate Hou Fangyu of the early Zhou martyrs.[39] In another, Peng Zhican, a Beizhili provincial graduate of 1600 who, like Sun Qifeng, had lost his property to Bannermen in the early Qing, retreated with Sun to Sumen in the early Qing. In 1658, after years of despair over the loss of his family estate, Peng finally stopped eating and soon died, reminding at least one observer of Bo and Shu (Zheng 1984: 178; Li Minxiu 1915: 34.4a–b). In resembling the early-Zhou hermits, these early-Qing literati expressed a range of attitudes toward a polity that, like the Zhou, seemed destined to last and make major contributions to civilization.[40]

Hou Fangyu himself pursued a more central path between service and suicide, refusing to prepare for holding office but often citing classical texts in an effort to hold the Qing to the Zhou standard. During a drought in 1650, he drafted an essay calling for rain on behalf of the governor-general of Zhili, Shandong, and Henan. Therein he adopted the literary style of the *Shangshu* and the *Zhouli* (Rites of Zhou) to dignify his almost shamanistic role. The following year, when congratulating a young townsman for passing the newly regularized provincial military examinations, Hou emphasized that the *Shangshu* and the *Shijing* had recognized the need for martial as well as civil talent in consolidating a state. That same year he praised the son of the Qing regional commander of Guide, who happened to be a Manchu, for cutting flesh from his thigh to nourish his ailing father. Hou conceded that some people considered the custom extreme, but he insisted that it exemplified the same filial piety that had led the Duke of Zhou to offer to sacrifice himself for his elder brother. In 1654, on the eve of his death, Hou called for strict measures to limit the number of clerks in the bureaucracy. He cited the "Zhoushu" (Declaration of Zhou) in the *Shangshu* to the effect that regulations should be harsh or lenient according to the times.[41]

Under great duress from both family and state, Hou Fangyu finally agreed to take the Qing examinations, but he apparently failed them on purpose. He thereby held to a middle path between his father, Xun, who withdrew completely from politics, and his patron Song Quan, who held high office in the Qing. Hou was thus free to work with friends to develop his own brand of ancient culture (*guwen*) in which literature and statecraft were closely related. In one essay he formulated a pattern of history in which the Way had been observed in the Zhou and lost in the Six Dynasties, regained in the Tang and lost again in the Five Dynasties, recovered again in the Northern Song and lost yet again in the Southern Song. In another essay he made a similar argument that the Way had prevailed for a thousand years in ancient times before falling into desuetude from the Qin through the Six Dynasties, reviving again in the Tang. In his view, the Tang came close to re-creating the humane and just rule of the Three Dynasties. In the Zhenguan era of Taizong's reign, for example, "grain was abundant, prisons were empty, doors were left unlatched at night, people traveled 10,000 *li* without weapons—it was an era of great peace." Hou noted that some people said it was because the trusted counselor Wei Zheng had offered sagely advice, but he insisted that it was Taizong's having acted on that advice that was key (Hou Fangyu 1992: 19–20, 330). Hou never served the Qing in any official capacity, but he probably hoped that his Snow Garden associate Song Luo would convey his ideas to the throne. In Hou's view, after all, the ruler had it within his power to determine whether the Qing would recover the Way attained in the Zhou and Tang, or persist in error as had so many lesser dynasties.

A Key to Two Puzzles of the Ming-Qing Transition?

The appeal of the Zhou and Tang models in the early Qing may help to explain two long-unsolved puzzles in the historiography of the Ming-Qing transition in northeast Henan. The first involves the date of the arrival of a small community of Jews in Kaifeng. According to the inscription on a stele erected at the synagogue in that city in 1489, the ancestors of the community had arrived in Kaifeng in the Song dynasty, when it was the capital of China and one of the largest and most prosperous cities in the world. A subsequent inscription of 1512 dated the arrival of the Jews in China to the Han dynasty. While there is an apparent discrepancy between these two accounts, it virtually disappears if we adopt the reasonable hypothesis that the authors of the second inscription considered the Jews of Kaifeng to be part of a larger community of Jews who had begun arriving in China in the Han. In any case, by judicious strategies of endogamy and intermarriage, preservation of Jewish customs, and compromise with Han culture, the Chinese Jews of Kaifeng continued to flourish during the Ming, when

Jewish enclaves elsewhere in China disappeared. Owing to its relatively large size and strong solidarity, as well as to hard struggle and good luck, a community of some two hundred families survived the flood of 1642 and reconstituted themselves in Kaifeng in the early Qing.[42]

In 1658 the Qing granted the Jews of Kaifeng permission to reconstruct their synagogue and bestowed on it two tablets featuring phrases from the *Shijing.* When the new temple was completed in 1663, the rabbis asked Liu Chang, a local metropolitan graduate then on leave from his post as president of the Ministry of Works, to draft an inscription. Liu's inscription followed the earlier Ming ones in emphasizing the commonalities between Judaism and Chinese thought, but it made two significant changes, one in theology and one in history. It asserted that the Chinese original "man," the legendary giant Pan Gu whose body ultimately produced all fauna, including humans, was not identical to the first Jewish man, Adam, but was instead Adam's ancestor who had lived fourteen centuries earlier. By this maneuver, the primordial Chinese human suddenly enjoyed much greater antiquity—and in Chinese eyes, presumably, greater value—than his Jewish counterpart. As if to balance this claim, however, Liu also innovated by pushing the date of the arrival of the Jews *in Kaifeng* back to the Zhou, over a millennium and a half earlier than had been claimed in the Ming inscription. The Zhou date resulted, I suggest, not simply from a misreading of previous inscriptions or from a confusion between the date of the origins of the Jewish people in the Middle East and the date of their arrival in China.[43] Instead, Liu Chang probably came up with the Zhou date to enhance the antiquity and legitimacy of the Kaifeng Jews by associating them with an order (the Zhou) that was increasingly accepted as the ultimate model for the Qing.[44]

The second puzzle involves the identity of Li Yan, the supposed chief advisor to the rebel Li Zicheng. According to the story, Li Yan was a literatus from northeast Henan whose early advice to Li Zicheng propelled the Shun to victory and whose later murder by Li Zicheng's henchmen precipitated its fall. As I have explained elsewhere, the story appears to have originated in rumors in and around Henan in 1643 and to have been incorporated in diaries, novels, and histories composed by Ming loyalists in Jiangnan in 1644–1645.[45] The early chroniclers apparently wished to use the story to implicate Henanese who had surrendered to the Shun in Beijing while exonerating Jiangnanese who had made similar compromises before fleeing to Nanjing. Subsequent novels and histories transmitted the story, which had the value of attributing the demise of the rebellion more to its internal contra-dictions than to forcible suppression by the Ming and Qing military. The story became part of the official *Mingshi*, printed in 1739, and appeared in later plays and novels to dramatize the moral that upright literati should remain loyal to the state and not get involved in rebel-lions. It persisted into the Republic and the People's Republic, first as a warning to revolutionaries not to become conceited in the flush of victory, then as a reminder that, whereas intellectuals may embrace re-bellion in their own interest, they typically stop short of revolution on behalf of the masses. Most recently, the Li Yan story has been affirmed by local historians and putative descendants in northeast Henan who remain proud of their ancestor's role in the late-Ming rebellions.

Henanese scholars who lived through the late-Ming rebellions were the first to challenge the historicity of the rebel advisor Li Yan. They argued that there was no literatus, let alone provincial graduate, by that name from Qi County or any other county of northeast Henan who rallied to Li Zicheng in Henan or played an important role in the movement. Others pointed out that the late-Ming official who was sup-posed to be Li Yan's father had no son by that name or any who partici-pated in the rebellion. Moreover, the Ming magistrate who was sup-posed to have been killed by Li Yan in Qi County was not serving there at the time. In the critics' view, the storied Li Yan was a creation of Jiangnan fiction writers and should never have been included in his-tories of the rebellion. More recently, Chinese historians operating under the banner of "seeking truth through facts" have argued that there was no one named Li Xin or Li Yan from Qi County, Kaifeng Pre-fecture, or anywhere else in Henan who played any important role in Li Zicheng's movement in Henan, Hubei, Shaanxi, or Beijing. Roles as-signed to that hero were actually played by other figures including Li Zicheng, Niu Jinxing, and several obscure generals surnamed Li. Con-tradictions between the time and place of Li Yan's supposed murder at the hands of Li Zicheng make it impossible that the event occurred as described in the story. In previous work, I have accepted and devel-oped the view that the Li Yan matter can no longer be regarded as straight history.[46]

At the same time, I believe we must go beyond the surface mean-ing of the Li Yan story, question the dichotomy between history and myth assumed by some of its critics, and focus on its function in histo-riography, which inevitably involves both fact and fiction.[47] In this per-spective, the Li Yan story becomes a powerful allegory that superficially conceals—but more profoundly reveals—many of the forces at work in the Ming-Qing transition. Since the story became part of the official Qing history of the Ming, it can tell us something about the place that the Qing wished to assume in the pattern of Chinese history. The history behind the story may be relevant to our own efforts to examine temporalities of the Ming-Qing transition.

Building on the findings of Chinese scholars, I have argued elsewhere that the hero of the story, Li Yan, also known as Master Li, was a composite figure. His persona was based on the actual lives of the Shaanxi rebel leader Li Zicheng, who was also known as Master Li, his chief advisor Niu Jinxing, who was a provincial graduate from Henan, and a historical Li Yan, a metropolitan graduate from Shandong who served as the last Ming prefect of Kaifeng before returning home in 1643 to mourn the death of his father. The heroic scholar-rebel, once created in rumors and novels, soon grew to absorb many elements from the lives of other officials, scholars, students, clerks, and commoners who joined Li Zicheng in Henan and Beijing.

Writers in Jiangnan identified the hero as a provincial graduate from Qi County, knowing that the county had fallen to Li Zicheng without a fight and that a local provincial graduate, He Yinguang, had surrendered to the rebels in Beijing. They wrote that Li Yan had quarreled with a magistrate named Song over famine relief and had rallied to Li Zicheng's rebel band, knowing that there were many such incidents in the region at that time and that a magistrate named Song Mei, noted for his ambition and greed, had once served in Qi. The historical Song Mei had returned home to Laiyang and died in the same Manchu raid of 1643 that took the life of the historical Li Yan's father. The same writers had the storied Li Yan extend his protection to scholars who surrendered to the rebels because, according to the earliest sources, a Henanese rebel advisor named Song Xiance had intervened on behalf of literati from Jiangnan and enabled them to survive the Shun administration in Beijing. Those who had the storied Li Yan mount a conspiracy against Li Zicheng to take advantage of a prophecy—that an "eighteenth son" (*shibazi*, three characters that combine to form the character Li) would take the throne—knew that a *shibazi* had rebelled in Qi County in 1638. They were also aware that the prophecy had circulated widely in Henan and that Song Xiance had reportedly used it in the central plain to encourage Li Zicheng to establish his own state. The same writers had the rebel leader Li Zicheng authorize the assassination of his scholar-advisor knowing full well that he had killed several historical subordinates, including Luo Rucai and Yuan Shizhong, whom Li suspected of competing with him for authority in the central plain. The murder, in turn, helped to explain the defection of many literati from the rebel movement on grounds more respectable than sheer opportunism.

While some historians such as Tan Qian and Gu Yingtai circumspectly reduced the saga to its core elements, others boldly expanded the hero's persona to include more personalities and make it more credible, useful, and popular. Ji Liuqi dated the storied Li Yan's supposed provincial degree to 1627 to conform to the date of Niu Jinxing's degree, and he dated Li Yan's revolt to 1641 to coincide with the time of Niu's decision to join Li Zicheng. Wu Weiye gave Li Yan an original name, Li Xin, for reasons still unclear, but he made Li Xin's father a member of the "eunuch party" in an apparent effort to divert attention from the participation of Donglin and Fushe partisans in Li Zicheng's rebellion. Wu had his antihero Li Xin kidnaped by a woman rebel, Hong Niangzi, perhaps on the basis of accounts of several female rebels at the end of the Ming, but also possibly to discredit the scholar-rebel even while romanticizing and popularizing his story. Zha Jizuo added "equal fields" to Li Yan's reform proposals to symbolize the currency of that ideal in the late Ming and to dramatize (and discredit?) the Shun (and early Qing?) efforts to redistribute land. Scholars who worked on drafts of the *Mingshi* were probably aware of local misgivings about and objections to the Li Yan story, but they may have suspected that the Henanese, many of whom had supported the Shun regime, protested too much. They may also have wished to appeal to former rebels and former Ming loyalists who were involved in the origins and development of the story or could benefit from its acceptance and spread. Even well-informed local historians who openly denied Li Yan's historicity, such as He Yinguang in Qi County and Zheng Lian in Shangqiu, had personal reasons to value the story as a popular romanticization of—as well as an effective cover for—their own or their kin's participation in what they may well have thought was a just but failed rebellion.[48]

While the immediate origins, development, and persistence of the Li Yan story can be explained in terms of the history of the Ming-Qing transition and later times, its ultimate genesis, power, and significance may have owed something to the Tang, Zhou, and other models that shaped the Qing formation. The rebels Li Yuan and Li Shimin had been inspired by a *shibazi* prophecy to found the Tang dynasty, the very polity that had stimulated Li Zicheng to found his Great Shun state. According to a famous Tang tale, a woman with a red fly whisk, Hong Fuji, had played a role in the Tang founding, providing a literary precedent for Wu Weiye's female rebel Hong Niangzi. A Henanese rebel named Li Mi had first rallied to Li Yuan's and Li Shimin's rebellion but had later returned to his home and been killed, providing ample precedent for those who had the storied Li Yan return to Henan with a similar result. A certain Li Yan*, whose personal name was homophonous with Li Yan's, although written with a different character, had appeared along with a prophecy regarding a *shibazi* at the time of the founding of the Latter Han, an event that had encouraged some Ming loyalists to hope for a full Ming restoration. Li Shiqi, whose surname was homophonous with Li Yan's and who was a native of the region later included in Qi County, had rallied with his brother to the banner of Liu Bang, the founder of the Han, offering yet another reason to locate the storied Li Yan in Qi and to give him a younger brother. Taigong Wang, who had served as an advisor to the early Zhou monarchs and was invoked, as we have seen, by Hong Taiji as a model for officials who would serve the Qing, was himself a composite figure whose persona included a historical figure from the central plain.[49]

Given this long and rich heritage of rebel advisors and prime ministers, including some named Li and one named Li Yan*, some from areas that had become Henan Province and one from Qi County, it was highly plausible, if not exactly predictable, that Li Zicheng's rebels and/or their opponents or bystanders would invent a chief advisor named Li Yan from Qi, and that former rebels, Ming loyalists, and Qing dynasts would accept, develop, and transform that persona for their own purposes. The Qing and its supporters, at least, could use the Li Yan story to explain the fall of the Ming and the fortunes of the Shun leadership in a way that put them in line to inherit the legacy of the Zhou and Tang and perhaps even that of the Han and Ming.

Implications of the Zhou-Tang Discourse

Such historical analogies played an important part in shaping the Ming-Qing transition because Chinese officials were trained to use history in administration much as Euro-American politicians have been socialized to use law to manage public affairs. History writing and reading were two of the official responsibilities of several of the figures discussed in this essay. Song Quan, the first prominent member of the local elite of northeast Henan to rally to the Shunzhi court, was asked to help compile the records of the preceding Chongde reign (Song n.d.: 17; Wakeman 1985: II, 891). Wang Zishou, the prominent poet from Xiangfu, assumed his first post in the Academy for the Advancement of Literature, where he was charged with collecting materials for the history of the first two Qing reigns (Li Minxiu 1915: 24.4a–6b; Hummel 1943–1944: I, 95). Xu Zuomei, from his high position in the Ministry of Works, advised the young Shunzhi emperor to select worthy officials to serve as tutors and lecturers on the classics and histories (Li Minxiu 1915: 1.17a). Tang Bin, who served as governor of Jiangsu, participated in planning and drafting the official history of the Ming (ibid.: 2.11a). Zheng Lian, who remained a government student, wrote a private history, the *Yubian jilüe* (Brief record of the changes in Yu), which differed substantially from the official history. With such members of the elite engaged in writing history, with emperors and others busy studying it, and with the rest of the population hearing tales or viewing dramas about it, the discipline naturally exerted considerable influence over their thought and action.

Since northeast Henan lay at the heart of the central plain, which had been an important site for the development of Chinese civilization from earliest recorded times, its residents may have been particularly aware of the relevance of past polities in the making of the Qing. As inhabitants of North China, whose forebears had been ruled more frequently by peoples originating on the northern frontier than had their neighbors to the south, they may have been more receptive to the Zhou and Tang models, while others admired such polities as Chu, the Eastern Jin, and the Southern Song. At the same time, as residents of the central province in the heart of the central plain, which often stood for the central state(s), the people of this region may also have been more representative of the Chinese people as a whole than were inhabitants of any other single region.

Many officials at the early Qing court resorted to the Zhou-Tang discourse to articulate their views on contemporary issues. Feng Quan, a Beizhili scholar-official who was associated with the "eunuch party" in the late Ming, became a powerful grand secretary in the early Qing. In 1645 Li Senxian, a former Ming official from Shandong, took advantage of the open atmosphere at court, which he explicitly compared to the ethos of the early Tang, to impeach Feng for his former association with the eunuch Wei Zhongxian and his son's alleged acceptance of bribes. In the course of his indictment, Li asserted that Feng and fils were "just like Fei Lian and Elai of the Shang, who could scarcely have attained rank in the Zhou." The allusion was to one of the last ministers of the Shang and to his son, whose corruption had precluded their use by the Zhou, whereas Feng Quan and his son had found favor with the Qing. In the ensuing court conference, Gong Dingzi, an Anhui man who had associated with the Shun regime, also charged Feng with having colluded with the eunuch Wei Zhongxian. When Feng countered with the accusation that Gong had taken office under the bandit Li Zicheng, Gong replied that he was not the only one, and, anyway, had not the upright scholar Wei Zheng "gone over" to Tang Taizong? At this point Prince Regent Dorgon intervened, scolding Gong for presuming to compare himself with Wei Zheng and for equating Li Zicheng with Tang Taizong. Dorgon warned that factional squabbling would be severely punished. Gong's intent may indeed have been to compare Li Zicheng with the Tang monarch on whose state, after all, Li Zicheng had modeled his own. But he also may have been suggesting that he, like Wei who had served Li Mi before rallying to Li Shimin, had once served the rebel Li Zicheng but had subsequently gone over to—*Dorgon!* Indeed, Dorgon may ultimately have interpreted Gong's point in that way, for he soon promoted him to a higher post.[50]

A similar case involved the impeachment of Zhang Jinyan, who, as we have seen, had tried to serve the Ming, the Shun, and the Qing in quick succession. In the course of excoriating Zhang for his lack of loyalty, the censor Wei Yijie called on the Qing to honor those who had died for the Ming, just as the Zhou had honored Bi Gan, the trenchant critic of Shang court abuses who was cruelly executed by the last Shang ruler. The analogy was hardly perfect, since most Ming loyalists had not been killed by the Ming, but it was quite pertinent because Bi Gan's grave was located in Ji County adjacent to Zhang's home county of Xinxiang.[51] Bi Gan was thus a particularly apposite figure with whom to rebuke Zhang Jinyan, who had curbed his tongue in an effort to serve three different political orders. Meanwhile, Zhang Jinyan's patron, Hong Chengchou, the high-profile Ming official who became a powerful Qing governor-general, also alluded to Zhou and Tang precedents in his efforts to shape Qing policies in the Shunzhi reign.[52]

The Zhou model could also serve as a sop to dissidents who only reluctantly made their peace with the Qing. In the 1660s the leading scholar Huang Zongxi, whose father *had* died at the hands of the Ming, was inspired by the model of the former Shang official Jizi, who had refused to serve the Zhou but had reputedly drafted a "Great Plan" to guide its policies. Like Jizi, Huang declined to take office in the Qing but wrote the "Record of 'Waiting for the Dawn'" (*Mingyi daifang lu*) to assist the dynasty, or some successor regime, in striving to live up to the Zhou standard (De Bary 1993; Struve 1998a). Similarly, in a poem written on the third anniversary of the Chongzhen emperor's death in 1647, the leading scholar Gu Yanwu had invoked the image of the Shang ruins (Yinxu) as seen by Jizi as he passed through on his way to enter the service of the Zhou (Hay 1999: 46). Like Huang Zongxi, Gu Yanwu remained loyal to the Ming and refused to serve the Qing, but he also gradually realized that the Ming epoch was over, and he worked to enhance the cultural life of the succeeding era.

Interest in the Shang-Zhou transition may also help to explain some other phenomena of the Ming-Qing transition discussed elsewhere in this volume. While the Shun honored the early Zhou precedent of enfeoffing a Shang heir by promising to enfeoff an heir to the Ming, the Qing failed to do so. This may illuminate Chosŏn Korea's continued loyalty to the Ming ruling house and its preference for systems of time inscription that did not require use of Qing reign titles—as discussed by JaHyun Kim Haboush in chapter 3. The Qing's inability to replicate that long-standing Zhou symbol of generosity toward the vanquished may also help to elucidate the practice among some people along the southeast coast—as explained by Zhao Shiyu and Du Zhengzhen in chapter 6—of worshiping the sun on the 19th day of the 3rd month, the day in 1644 when the last effective Ming ruler hanged himself in Beijing. In other scholarship, we see that early Qing officials cited Zhou and Tang astronomical science to justify their reforms of the calendar (Henderson 1999). The Zhou model appears to loom behind an early-Qing Yangzhou scholar's decision to pattern his *Poetic Survey* on the *Shijing,* and the Tang model was implicit in Yangzhou litterateurs' romantic emulation of the ninth-century poet Du Mu (Meyer-Fong 1999: 77; 2003: 13–14). The Zhou model was invoked during the Kangxi reign to justify lenience toward Ming loyalists who eventually accepted the Qing, and it was reinvoked during the Yongzheng reign to emphasize the legitimacy of a frontier people establishing their authority over the central plain (Struve 1998b: 36, 54–55; Spence 2001: 128–129). Kangxi also cited Zhou and Tang expeditions on the northwestern frontier to legitimate his wars against the Zunghars (Perdue 2004). In most of these cases, the Zhou and Tang models provided structures within which issues were addressed, and they influenced, without determining, the outcomes. In short, they functioned as discourses that allowed for diversity as well as commonality in the formation of the Qing state and culture.

Preoccupation with the history of their own polity did not preclude Chinese interest in the viewpoints of peripheral peoples. On the contrary, insofar as China by definition aspired to be the central state(s) of the known world, it had to take account of what was happening on its frontiers and even, occasionally, well beyond.[53] That was particularly true for multiethnic and far-flung dynasties like the Zhou, Tang, and Qing. In the early Qing, for example, Wu Qi, a 1658 metropolitan graduate from Suizhou who studied the Zhou-period *Yijing* and wrote commentaries on Tang poetry, also took account of the Western learning transmitted by the Jesuits.[54] Information about the outside world remained limited in northeast Henan, as in China as a whole during the Shunzhi reign, but it was perhaps commensurate with Qing ambitions, which in that early phase remained largely confined to what had been Ming China and some of the adjacent steppe inhabited by Mongols. Contrary to what is often assumed or asserted by scholars operating under Marxian, Weberian, and other paradigms, it is unlikely that more knowledge about the outside world in the early Qing period would have prepared China any better for the different world system the West was then beginning to construct and would only later try to impose on China and the rest of the world.[55] Instead, Qing efforts to replicate the Zhou and Tang experiences under new conditions in the seventeenth and eighteenth centuries resulted in a polity that was admired in much of the rest of Asia as well as in Europe and America.[56]

From our present perspective, the Zhou and Tang discourses seem to have functioned in a manner similar to what others have called *habiti*, robust processes, or path dependencies.[57] They provided guidance for the peoples of China as they adjusted to changing circumstances at the end of the Ming and sought to influence the emerging new order. The Zhou and Tang were more attractive than the Liao or Yuan, founded by steppe peoples who acculturated less fully to the plain, or the Han or Ming, founded by plains people who adjusted less creatively to the steppe. They were more appealing than the Qin or Yuan, which had tried to impose central control over large territories and suffered relatively short lives, or the Spring and Autumn/Warring States or Liao/Song/Jin eras, which endured rapid social change and were plagued by civil wars. The Zhou and Tang had avoided the harsh authoritarianism of the late Shang and Sui and the extreme populism of the early Han and Ming. Of course, the two polities had their own imperfections, which resulted in internal disorder and foreign encroachment followed by brief restorations and eventual disintegration. In the nineteenth century, the Qing approximated that pattern, causing people of the central plain to turn to other historical models in an effort to retain some influence over their destiny. Although time would continue to accelerate and space to broaden, the people of the central plain and of the "central state" (Zhongguo) would continue to use various pasts, including those of other peoples, in their quest to maintain or recover their "rightful place" in the world (Des Forges and Xu 2001).

Notes

I am grateful to Jack Goldstone, Lynn Struve, Richard von Glahn, and other participants in the conference on "The Qing Formation in World and Chinese Time" for comments on an earlier version of this essay.

1. See, for example, Rawski 1996 and 1998; Crossley 1999. For reiteration of the previous consensus that the Manchus became Chinese, see Ho 1998. For some middle views, see Elliott 2001; Guy 2002; and Sen 2002. For reservations about the trend to ascribe Qing success in Inner Asia to "Manchuness," see Swope 2003: 85.

2. See essays in Wakeman and Wang 1997, as well as Wei 1998.

3. Duara 1995; Fairbank and Goldman 1998; Spence 1999; Roberts 1999; Hsu 2000. See also several essays in Struve 2004.

4. For a succinct summary of the "Naitō hypothesis" and its influence on Western scholarship, see Zurndorfer 1995: 16–22. The concept of late imperial has been widely accepted but is rightly described as undertheorized (Brook 1998: 12, 264–265).

5. See the essay by Moss Roberts in Luo 1991: 961–971; Crossley and Rawski 1993: 93–94; Wang 1999: 128; Hsu 2000: 21.

6. Sun and Li 1983: 266–267, 408–412; Li and Xue 1991: 56, 106–107; Zhang 1998: 12, 18; Dennerline 2002: 109.

7. Dorgon's reputation was sullied after his death, so any analogy between him and the Duke of Zhou, regarded by Master Kong (Confucius) as a paragon of virtue, might be thought fanciful. But recent research suggests that the Zhou king, Cheng, for whom the duke served as regent, was actually a healthy adult. This raises some doubt about the duke's ethics in becoming regent (Loewe

and Shaughnessy 1999: 311). In addition, the Duke of Zhou had killed two of his brothers in his rise to power, a precedent invoked by Tang Taizong to justify similar fratricide in the name of good government. For reasons to use "Master Kong" (Kongzi), rather than the Latinate form "Confucius" introduced by the Jesuits, see Jensen 1997.

8. Zheng 1984: 181–182; Liu 1983: 247–248; He 1987.

9. Tan 1958: VI, 6130, 6199 (j. 102, 103); Shi Yuanqing 1979: 173, 181, 186–187; Shi Kefa 1984: 27–28; Wakeman 1985: 405–411.

10. Shi Yuanqing 1979: 189, 190; Shi Kefa 1984: 89–90, 190; Wakeman 1985: I, 550–551; Mote 1999: 830.

11. Tan 1958: VI, 6094–6095, 6099, 6103–6105, 6109 (j. 101), 6123–6124, 6130, 6162 (j. 102, 103); Shunzhi *shilu* 1964: 14.7b; Shi Yuanqing 1979: 230; Shi Kefa 1984: 31–40; Wakeman 1985: 512, 552.

12. Tan 1958: VI, 6176 (j. 104); Zheng 1984: 194; Shunzhi *shilu* 1964: 14.7b; Shi Yuanqing 1979: 230; Wakeman 1985: I, 512.

13. Tan 1958: VI, 6204 (j. 104); Zheng 1984: 201; Wakeman 1985: I, 549–569; Struve 1993: 28–48; 1998a: 110–113.

14. Quotation from Wen 1964: II, 185. See also Tan 1958: VI, 6209 (j. 104); Shunzhi *shilu* 1964: 15.17b–26a, 16.19b–22b; Wakeman 1985: II, 570, 582–583; Struve 1993: 55–72; Mote 1999: 831.

15. Tan 1958: VI, 6147 (j. 103); Zheng 1984: 182–184; on Su and Zhang, see Crump 1964: 13–14.

16. *Shangqiu xianzhi* 1705: j. 8 (rpt. pp. 258–259), j. 10 (rpt. p. 322); FHA, *qitalei, han* 464; Zheng 1984: 178.

17. *Shangqiu xianzhi* 1705: j. 9 (rpt. p. 311); Hou Fangyu 1992: 601–603.

18. Zheng 1715: autoepitaph, and biography by Tian Lanfang; Li Minxiu 1915: 25.7b–8a.

19. *Qingshi gao* 1976–1977: XXXII, 9540 (j. 240); Xie 1956: 90–101; *Qingdai nongmin* 1984: 195; Wakeman 1985: II, 788–795; *Qingshi liezhuan* 1987: XX, 6499 (j. 78). On the collapse of a Ming-loyalist conspiracy in Kaifeng and Guide prefectures the following year, see FHA, *panni* 103/0151; *Xiayi xianzhi* 1920: 8.9a.

20. The recommendation was approved. See Li Minxiu 1915: 9a–b.

21. The warning was ignored. See Li Minxiu 1915: 1.18a–20a; Wakeman 1985: II, 931, 1013–1016; *Qingshi liezhuan* 1987: XX, 6557 (j. 79).

22. Sun Qifeng n.d.: 2.3a; Li Minxiu 1915: 19.3a. On Xu, see Mote 1960; on Wu, see Gedalecia 1982; for Xu and Wu as positive and negative models, respectively, in the early Qing, see Langlois 1980: 358, 367.

23. Langlois 1980: 376. On Zheng, see Mote 1960: 234–236.

24. Sun Qifeng 1844; Hummel 1943–1944: II, 671–672; Langlois 1980: 376; Sun Jurong 1986: *shixi*.1b; *Qingshi liezhuan* 1987: XVII, 5240 (j. 66). On Shao Yong, see Wyatt 1996. On Huang Zongxi, see Huang Tsung-hsi 1987: 4, 45; and Struve 1988.

25. Song n.d.: 16a–19a; *Shangqiu xianzhi* 1705: j. 5 (rpt. pp. 103–104), j. 16 (rpt. pp. 497–501); *Qingshi gao* 1976–1977: XXXII, 9494–9495 (j. 238); *Qingshi liezhuan* 1987: XX, 6486, 6591–6592, 6595–6597 (j. 78); Hou Fangyu 1992: 604–608. On Su, see Egan 1994.

26. Hou Fangyu 1992: 7, 11–14, 77–82, 271–274, 486–487, 601.

27. Song n.d.: 20a–21a; *Shangqiu xianzhi* 1705: j. 9 (rpt. p. 292), j. 10 (rpt. p. 312); Li Minxiu 1915: 1.4–5a, 23.43a–45b; Hummel 1943–1944: II, 689–690; Langlois 1980: 385–386; *Qingshi liezhuan* 1987: XX, 6486 (j. 78). For additional evidence of Su's popularity in the early Qing, see Meyer-Fong 1999: 55–56.

28. Hummel 1943–1944: II, 848–850; Wakeman 1985: II, 944; *Qingshi liezhuan* 1987: XX, 6623 (j. 79). On Lu, see Twitchett 1979: 582, 583, 586; on Jia, see Franke 1962.

29. *Mingshi* 1974: XXIII, 6740 (j. 280); *Yongcheng xianzhi* 1903: 12.17b, 23.3a, 24.1b; Hou Fangyu 1992: 597, 613.

30. *Xinxiu Xiangfu xianzhi* 1898: 16.35a; Li Minxiu 1915: 24.9a–10a.

31. Zheng 1984: 139–140; *Xinxiu Xiangfu xianzhi* 1898: 15.62a–63b; Li Minxiu 1915: 24.4a–6b; Hummel 1943–1944: I, 95.

32. *Qingshi liezhuan* 1987: XX, 6624 (j. 79); Li Xingsheng 1984: 91–96; Wakeman 1985: II, 1000.

33. *Xinxiu Xiangfu xianzhi* 1898: 16.28a–29a; Li Minxiu 1915: 23.20–22; Hummel 1943–1944: I, 173–174, 551–552; Kahn 1971: 49, 128; Langlois 1980: 366–368; *Qingshi liezhuan* 1987: XX, 6574–6575 (j. 79); Woodside 1991: 12; Kim 1996; Hay 1999: 32; Di Cosmo 1999: 25.

34. *He'nan tongzhi* 1735: 67 and passim; Shunzhi *shilu* 1964: 40.14b; Wakeman 1985: II, 897; Zhou and Zhao 1986: 409; Rawski 1991: 170–203; 1998: 128–130, 135–136. On Tang Taizong's infatuation, see Wechsler 1974: 198–199.

35. *Shangqiu xianzhi* 1705: j. 9 (rpt. p. 287); Hou Fangyue 1908: 3.23; Hou Fangyu 1992: 594, 596, 602.

36. Li Minxiu 1915: 1.17a. In addition to playing on the homophonous names "Cheng," Xu here seems to intimate that Song learning might become the orthodox school of thought in the Qing but that Zhou history should be the ultimate guide for political actors.

37. Li Minxiu 1915: 1.18a–20a; *Qingshi gao* 1976–1977: XXXIV, 10110 (j. 279); *Qingshi liezhuan* 1987: XX, 6584, 6596 (j. 79); Zhou et al. 1990: 497.

38. *Shangqiu xianzhi* 1705: j. 8 (rpt. p. 256), j. 16 (rpt. pp. 494–497); Hou Fangyu 1992: 596, 602. The Kangxi emperor later praised the Zhou practice of welcoming former adherents of the previous dynasty to its ranks as an obvious model for the Qing. See Struve 1998b: 36, 54–55.

39. Hou Fangyu 1992: 11–14, 77–82, 271–274, 486–487, 601.

40. For Kongzi's own mixed feelings about Bo Yi and Shu Qi, see Hall and Ames 1987: 125–127.

41. Hou Fangyu 1992: 26–29, 215–218, 488–489, 536, 538.

42. Chen 1923: 3, 6–9, 22; W. C. White 1942: II, 42–46, 51–54; Leslie 1972: 5; Wei 1993: 37.

43. For such explanations, see Chen 1923: 9–10; Pollak 1980: 70; Wei 1993: 37.

44. For data consistent with this interpretation, see W. C. White 1942: II, 19, 62, 82; Plaks 1999: 39. For those in the early Qing who preferred to keep their history more distinct from myth, there was a second inscription on the back of the same stele that once again dated the Jews' arrival in Kaifeng to the Song dynasty and that concentrated on the reconstruction of the synagogue in the early Qing. In 1679, moreover, the Zhaos, a leading scholar-official family among the Kaifeng Jews, erected another stele, focusing on their own ancestors, which reverted to the Han date for the arrival of the Jews in China (W. C. White 1942: I, 16, 43, 52; II, 87–97, 100, 104, 105, 110–111, 121–134; Leslie 1966: 14; 1971; 1972: 28–29, 40, 46). Assuming, once again, affinity between the Jewish community of Kaifeng and other Jewish communities in China dating from the Han, the Zhaos may have altered (or corrected) the record out of a simple concern for accuracy. But their decision was also consistent with their determination, evident in their increasing intermarriage with Han Chinese, to acculturate—and perhaps even assimilate—to the Han majority among whom they lived.

45. For an early review of the story, see Des Forges 1982; for more recent scholarship accepting and developing the story, see Xing and Du 1983; Fan and Li 1985; Li Xiaosheng 1986, 1987a, and 1987b.

46. For early reviews of the evidence, see Luan 1983 and Des Forges 1984; for more recent studies, see Luan 1986 and Qin 1995, 1996a, 1996b.

47. For some recent studies of the interrelationships between history and myth and between fact and fiction, see Hayden White 1973, 1978; McNeill 1982, 1986; Appleby, Hunt, and Jacob 1994; Lewis and Wigen 1997; Dirlik 1998.

48. Tan 1958: VI, 6070; Gu Yingtai 1977: 1340, 1389; Ji 1671: 13.10b–12b, 23.5b–6a; Wu 1804: 9.5b; Zha 1962: II, 223; *Qixian zhi* 1693: 13.*renwu, zhonglie* sec.; Zheng 1984: *fanli* 1–2.

49. On the *shibazi* prophecy in the Tang founding, see Bingham 1941: 272. On Li Mi, see Wechsler 1974: ch. 2. On the homophonous Li Yan in the Latter Han, see Seidel 1969–1970: 272. On Li Shiqi in the Former Han, see Watson 1968: 269–275; *Qixian zhi* 1693: 14.1a–3b. On Taigong Wang, see Allan 1972–1973: 57–99. In addition, Yi Yin, the primordial prime minister of the Shang dynasty, invoked as a model by the late-Ming grand secretary Zhang Juzheng, was honored as an ancient sage in a biography in the Kangxi-period edition of the *Qixian zhi* (1788: 13.3a–4b).

50. Shunzhi *shilu* 1964: 20.7–9a; Wakeman 1985: II, 865–870; Zhou and Zhao 1986: 361–365; *Qingshi liezhuan* 1987: XX, 6556, 6594 (j. 79).

51. Wakeman 1985: II, 944–945, 967; Shi and Hou 1988: 247. In 1993, on a visit to a temple to Bi Gan in Ji County, I found numerous stele inscriptions in memory of the outspoken Shang minister. Most of them date to the late Ming and early Qing.

52. Wang 1999: 90, 125, 138, 180, 247–248, 253–254. Two of Hong's early-Qing admirers, the Shunzhi emperor and a local scholar, likewise invoked Zhou and Tang models in praising and defending him (ibid.: 177, 232–233).

53. For recent texts inspired by this theme, see Waley-Cohen 1999, and, at least up to the Ming, Hansen 2000.

54. Li Minxiu 1915: 2.11a–26a, 23.29b–30a; 24.8a–9a, 11a–12a, 18a–19b; Hummel 1943–1944: II, 690, 709–710.

55. Frank 1998; Pomeranz 2000. This perspective is quite different from that developed by Ray Huang in 1988 and 1999.

56. Adshead 1988: ch. 5.

57. For these concepts, see Bourdieu 1990: 54–55; Goldstone 1991: 54–60; Wong 1997: 3.

References

Adshead, S. A. M. 1988. *China in World History*. London: Macmillan.

Allan, Sarah. 1972–1973. "The Identities of Taigong Wang in Zhou and Han Literature." *Monumenta Serica* 30: 57–99.

Appleby, Joyce, Lynn Hunt, and Margaret Jacob. 1994. *Telling the Truth about History*. New York: W. W. Norton.

Bingham, Woodbridge. 1941. "The Rise of Li in a Ballad Prophecy." *Journal of the American Oriental Society* 61: 272–280.

Bourdieu, Pierre. 1990. *The Logic of Practice*. Stanford: Stanford University Press.

Brook, Timothy. 1998. *The Confusions of Pleasure: Commerce and Culture in Ming China*. Berkeley: University of California Press.

Chen Yuan 陳垣. 1923. *Kaifeng Yicileye jiaokao* 開封一賜樂業教考. Dongfang wenku, 72. Shanghai: Shangwu yinshuguan.

Crossley, Pamela. 1999. *A Translucent Mirror: History and Identity in Qing Imperial Ideology.* Berkeley: University of California Press.

Crossley, Pamela, and Evelyn Rawski. 1993. "A Profile of the Manchu Language in Ch'ing History." *Harvard Journal of Asiatic Studies* 53.1 (June): 63–102.

Crump, J. I., Jr. 1964. *Intrigues: Studies of the Chan-kuo Ts'e.* Ann Arbor: University of Michigan Press.

De Bary, Wm. Theodore. 1993. *Waiting for the Dawn: A Plan for the Prince: Huang Tsung-hsi's Ming-i Tai-fang Lu.* New York: Columbia University Press.

Dennerline, Jerry. 2002. "The Shun-chih Reign." In *The Cambridge History of China,* vol. 9, pt. 1: *The Ch'ing Empire to 1800,* ed. Willard Peterson, 73–119. Cambridge: Cambridge University Press.

Des Forges, Roger. 1982. "The Story of Li Yen: Its Growth and Function from the Early Qing to the Present." *Harvard Journal of Asiatic Studies* 42.2 (Dec.): 535–587.

———. 1984. "The Legend of Li Yen: Its Origins and Implications for the Study of the Ming-Ch'ing Transition in 17th Century China." *Journal of the American Oriental Society* 104.3 (July–Sept.): 411–436.

———. 2001. "The Concept of the Central Plain in the History and Literature of the Three Kingdoms." Paper delivered at the Sino-American Colloquium on the Historical, Fictional, Theatrical, and Artistic Three Kingdoms, in Chengdu, Sichuan.

———. 2003. *Cultural Centrality and Political Change in Chinese History: Northeast Henan in the Fall of the Ming.* Stanford: Stanford University Press.

Des Forges, Roger, and Luo Xu. 2001. "China as a Non-Hegemonic Superpower? The Uses of History among the *China Can Say No* Writers and Their Critics." *Critical Asian Studies* 34.4 (Dec.): 483–507.

Di Cosmo, Nicola. 1999. "State Formation and Periodization in Inner Asian History." *Journal of World History* 10.1 (Spring): 1–39.

Dirlik, Arif. 1998. *What's in a Rim? Critical Perspectives on the Pacific Region Idea.* Oxford: Rowman and Littlefield.

Duara, Prasenjit. 1995. *Rescuing History from the Nation: Questioning Narratives of Modern China.* Chicago: University of Chicago Press.

Eco, Umberto. 1998. *Serendipities: Language and Lunacy.* Trans. William Weaver. New York: Harcourt, Brace, and World.

Egan, Ronald C. 1994. *Word, Image, and Deed in the Life of Su Shi.* Cambridge: Harvard University Press.

Elliott, Mark. 2001. *The Manchu Way: The Eight Banners and Ethnic Identity in Late Imperial China.* Stanford: Stanford University Press.

Fairbank, John K., and Merle Goldman. 1998. *A New History of China.* Cambridge: Belknap Press.

Fan Peiwei 範沛瀟 and Li Xiaosheng 李肖勝. 1985. "Qixian 'Li shi zupu' yu Li Yan" 杞縣"李氏族譜"與李巖. *Shixue yuekan* 史學月刊 1985.6 (June): 27, 42–46.

Fernández-Armesto, Felipe. 1995. *Millennium: A History of the Last Thousand Years.* New York: Scribner.

FHA. Zhongguo diyi lishi dang'an guan 中國第一歷史檔案館 [First Historical Archives of China], Beijing. Shunzhi tiben 順治題本 archive.

Frank, Andre Gunder. 1998. *Re-Orient: Global Economy in the Asian Age.* Berkeley: University of California Press.

Franke, Wolfgang. 1962. "Chia Ssu-tao (1213–1275): A 'Bad Last Minister'?" In *Confucian Personalities,* ed. Arthur F. Wright and D. C. Twitchett, 217–234. Stanford: Stanford University Press.

Gedalecia, David. 1982. "Wu Ch'eng's Approach to Internal Self-Cultivation and External Knowledge-Seeking." In *Yuan Thought: Chinese Thought and Religion under the Mongols,* ed. Hok-lam Chan and Wm. Theodore de Bary, 279–326. New York: Columbia University Press.

Goldstone, Jack A. 1991. *Revolution and Rebellion in the Early Modern World.* Berkeley: University of California Press.

———. 1998. "The Problem of the 'Early Modern' World." *Journal of the Economic and Social History of the Orient* 41.3 (Aug.): 249–284.

Gu Cheng 顧誠. 1980. "Lun Luo Rucai" 論羅汝才. In *Zhongguo nongmin zhanzheng shi luncong* 中國農民戰爭史論叢, ed. Zhongguo nongmin zhanzheng shi luncong bianji weiyuanhui 中國農民戰爭史論叢編輯委員會, 321–336. Zhengzhou: He'nan renmin chubanshe.

Gu Yingtai 古應泰. 1977. *Mingshi jishi benmo* 明史紀事本末. 4 vols. Beijing: Zhonghua shuju.

Guo Songyi 郭松義. 1980. "Qingchu fengjian guojia kenhuang zhengce fenxi" 清初封建國家墾荒政策分析. In *Qingshi luncong* 清史論叢 2: 111–138. Beijing: Zhonghua shuju.

Guy, R. Kent. 2002. "Who Were the Manchus? A Review Essay." *Journal of Asian Studies* 61.1 (Feb.): 151–164.

Hall, David L., and Roger T. Ames. 1987. *Thinking through Confucius.* Albany: State University of New York Press.

Hansen, Valerie. 2000. *The Open Empire: A History of China to 1600.* New York: W. W. Norton.

Hay, Jonathan. 1999. "Ming Palace and Tomb in Early Qing Jiangning: Dynastic Memory and the Openness of History." *Late Imperial China* 20.1 (June): 1–48.

He Xinzhen 何心貞. 1987. *Heshi zupu* 何氏族譜. Supplementation of Guangxu-period edition. Qi County, Henan: N.p.

He'nan tongzhi, xu tongzhi 河南通志, 續通志. 1735. Comp. and ed. Tian Wenjing 田文鏡, Sun Hao 孫灝, and Asiha 啊思哈. 5 vols. Rpt. Taipei: Huawen shuju, 1969.

Henderson, John. 1999. "Seventeenth-Century Reconceptualizations of Astronomical History and Time." Unpublished paper, cited with author's permission.

Ho, Ping-ti. 1998. "In Defense of Sinicization: A Rebuttal of Evelyn Rawski's 'Reenvisioning the Qing.'" *Journal of Asian Studies* 57.1 (Feb. 1998): 123–155.

Hou Fangyu 侯方域. 1992. *Hou Fangyu ji jiaojian* 侯方域集校箋. Ed. He Fazhou 何法周 and Wang Shulin 王樹林. Zhengzhou: Zhongzhou guji chubanshe.

Hou Fangyue 侯方岳. 1908. *Shangqiu Houshi jiasheng* 商邱侯氏家乘. Shangqiu, Henan: N.p.

Hsu, Immanuel C. Y. 2000. *The Rise of Modern China.* London: Oxford University Press.

Huang, Philip. 1991. "The Paradigmatic Crisis in Chinese Studies: Paradoxes in Social and Economic History." *Modern China* 17.3 (July): 299–341.

Huang, Ray. 1988. *China: A Macro History.* Armonk, N.Y.: M. E. Sharpe.

———. 1999. *Broadening the Horizons of Chinese History.* Armonk, N.Y.: M. E. Sharpe.

Huang Tsung-hsi. 1987. *The Records of Ming Scholars.* A selected translation edited by Julia Ching and Chaoying Fang. Honolulu: University of Hawai'i Press.

Hummel, Arthur, ed. 1943–1944. *Eminent Chinese of the Ch'ing Period, 1644–1912.* 2 vols. Washington: United States Government Printing Office.

Jensen, Lionel. 1997. *Manufacturing Confucianism: Chinese Traditions and Universal Civilization.* Durham: Duke University Press.

Ji Liuqi 計六奇. 1671. *Mingji beilüe* 明季北略. 3 vols. Rpt. in *Zhongguo fanglüe congshu* 中國方略叢書, ser. 1, no. 12. Taibei: Chengwen chubanshe, 1968.

Kahn, Harold. 1971. *Monarchy in the Emperor's Eyes: Image and Reality in the Ch'ien-lung Reign.* Cambridge: Harvard University Press.

Kim, Hong-nam. 1996. *The Life of a Patron: Zhou Lianggong (1612–1672) and the Painters of Seventeenth-Century China.* New York: China Institute of America.

Langlois, John D. 1980. "Chinese Culturalism and the Yuan Analogy: Seventeenth-Century Perspectives." *Harvard Journal of Asiatic Studies* 40.2 (Dec.): 355–398.

Lanyang xian xuzhi 藍陽縣續志. 1747. Comp. Tu Guangfan 涂光範 and Wang Ren 王壬. Lanyang, Henan: N.p.

Leslie, Donald. 1966. "The Chinese-Hebrew Memorial Book of the Jewish Community of K'aifeng." Pt. 2. *Abr-Nahrain* 5: 1–28.

———. 1971. "Chao." In *Encyclopedia Judaica*, vol. 5, ed. Cecil Roth, 333–335. New York and Jerusalem: Macmillan.

———. 1972. *The Survival of the Chinese Jews: The Jewish Community of Kaifeng.* Leiden: E. J. Brill.

Lewis, Martin W., and Kären E. Wigen. 1997. *The Myth of Continents: A Critique of Metageography.* Berkeley: University of California Press.

Li Minxiu 李敏修. 1915. *Zhongzhou xianzhe zhuan* 中州先哲傳. [Kaifeng]: Jingchuan tushuguan.

Li Xiaosheng 李肖勝. 1986. "Cong Qixian 'Li shi zupu' kan Li Yan qi ren" 從杞縣"李氏族譜"看李巖其人. *He'nan daxue xuebao* 河南大學學報 1: 53–55.

———. 1987a. "Cong xiangtu ziliao kan Li Yan qiren" 從鄉土資料看李巖其人. Paper delivered at the Second National Conference on the Study of Peasant Wars at the End of the Ming 第二次全國明末農民戰爭史學術討論會, Xi'an.

———. 1987b. "The Question of Li Yan as Seen from *The Genealogical Records of the Li Clan* of Qi County." *Ming Studies* 24 (Fall): 39–57.

Li Xingsheng 李興盛. 1984. "Zhang Tan gong ji qi 'Ningguta shanshui ji,' 'Yuwai ji'—liangbu yinmo sanbai yu nian de Heilongjiang lishi wenxian" 張坦公及其'寧古塔山水記,' '域外集'一兩部湮沒三百餘年的黑龍江歷史文獻. *Qiushi xuekan* 求是學刊 5: 91–96.

Li Xun 李洵 and Xue Hong 薛虹. 1991. *Qingdai quanshi* 清代全史. Vol. 1. Shenyang: Liaoning renmin chubanshe.

Liu Yi'nan 柳義南. 1983. *Li Zicheng jinian fukao* 李自成紀年附考. Beijing: Zhonghua shuju.

Loewe, Michael, and Edward L. Shaughnessy, eds. 1999. *The Cambridge History of Ancient China, from the Origins of Civilization to 221 B.C.* Cambridge: Cambridge University Press.

Luan Xing 欒星. 1983. "Li Yan chuanshuo de yubo" 李巖傳說的餘波. *Zhongzhou jingu* 中州今古 4: 10–14.

———. 1986. *Li Yan zhi mi: Jiashen shi shang* 李巖之迷: 甲申史商. Xuchang, Henan: Zhongzhou guji chubanshe.

Luo Guanzhong 羅貫中. 1991. *Three Kingdoms: A Historical Novel.* Trans. with notes and afterword by Moss Roberts. Berkeley: University of California Press; Beijing: Foreign Languages Press.

McNeill, William. 1982. "The Care and Repair of Public Myth." *Foreign Affairs* 61.1 (Fall): 1–13.

———. 1986. *Mythistory and Other Essays.* Chicago: University of Chicago Press.

Meyer-Fong, Tobie. 1999. "Making a Place for Meaning in Early Qing Yang-zhou." *Late Imperial China* 20.1 (June): 49–84.

———. 2003. *Building Culture in Early Qing Yangzhou.* Stanford: Stanford University Press.

Mingshi 明史. 1974. Comp. Zhang Tingyu 張廷玉 et al. 28 vols. Beijing: Zhong-hua shuju.

Mote, Frederick W. 1960. "Confucian Eremitism in the Yuan Period." In *The Confucian Persuasion,* ed. Arthur F. Wright, 202–240. Stanford: Stanford University Press.

———. 1999. *Imperial China, 900–1800.* Cambridge: Harvard University Press.

Naquin, Susan. 2000. *Peking: Temples and City Life, 1400–1900.* Berkeley: University of California Press.

Perdue, Peter. 2004. "The Qing Empire in Eurasian Space and Time: Lessons from the Galdan Campaigns." In Struve 2004, 57–91.

Plaks, Andrew. 1999. "The Confucianization of the Kaifeng Jews: Interpretations of the Kaifeng Stelae Inscriptions." In *The Jews of China,* vol. 1: *Historical and Comparative Perspectives,* ed. Jonathan Goldstein, 36–49. Armonk, N.Y.: M. E. Sharpe.

Pollak, Michael. 1980. *Mandarins, Jews, and Missionaries: The Jewish Experience in the Chinese Empire.* Philadelphia: Jewish Publication Society of America.

Pomeranz, Kenneth. 2000. *The Great Divergence: China, Europe, and the Making of the Modern World Economy.* Princeton: Princeton University Press.

Qin Xinlin 秦新林. 1995. "Shilun *Chao Chuang xiaoshuo* yu Li Yan xingxiang de guanxi" 試論《剿闖小說》與李巖形象的關係. *Beijing shifan daxue xuebao, Shehui kexue ban* 北京師範大學學報, 社會科學版, supplemental issue: 70–75.

———. 1996a. "Li Yan zai jing shishi zhiyi" 李巖在京史實質疑. *Shixue yuekan* 史學月刊 1996.3: 29–33.

———. 1996b. "Qixian *Lishi zupu* zhi Li Yan yibian" 杞縣《李氏族譜》之李巖疑辨. *He'nan daxue xuebao, Shehui kexue ban* 河南大學學報, 社會科學版 36.2: 77–82.

Qingdai nongmin zhanzheng shi ziliao xuanbian 清代農民戰爭史資料選編. 1984. Vol. 1, pt. 2, ed. Zhongguo renmin daxue lishixi 中國人民大學歷史系 and Zhongguo diyi lishi dang'an guan 中國第一歷史檔案館. Beijing: Zhong-guo renmin daxue chubanshe.

Qingshi gao 清史稿. 1976–1977. Comp. Zhao Erxun 趙爾巽 et al. 48 vols. Beijing: Zhonghua shuju.

Qingshi liezhuan 清史列傳. 1987. Ed. Wang Zhonghan 王鍾翰. 20 vols. Beijing: Zhonghua shuju.

Qixian zhi 杞縣志. 1693. Comp. and ed. Li Jilie 李繼烈 and He Yiguang 何彝光. Qi County: N.p. Nanjing University Library rare book collection.

———. 1788. Comp. and ed. Zhu Xuan 朱璿 and Zhou Ji 周璣. Qi County: N.p.

Rawski, Evelyn S. 1991. "Research Themes in Ming-Qing Socioeconomic History—the State of the Field." *Journal of Asian Studies* 50.1 (Feb.): 84–111.

———. 1996. "Presidential Address: Reenvisioning the Qing: The Significance of the Qing Period in Chinese History." *Journal of Asian Studies* 55.4 (Nov.): 829–850.

———. 1998. *The Last Emperors: A Social History of Qing Imperial Institutions*. Berkeley: University of California Press.

Roberts, J. A. G. 1999. *A Concise History of China*. Cambridge: Harvard University Press.

Seidel, Anna. 1969–1970. "The Image of the Perfect Ruler in Early Taoist Messianism." *History of Religions* 9.2–3: 216–247.

Sen, Sudipta. 2002. "The New Frontiers of Manchu China and the Historiography of Asian Empires: A Review Essay." *Journal of Asian Studies* 61.1 (Feb.): 165–177.

Shangqiu xianzhi 商邱縣志. 1705. Comp. and ed. Liu Dechang 劉德昌 and Ye Yun 葉澐. Rpt. Zhengzhou: Zhongzhou guji chubanshe, 1989.

Shi Kefa 史可法. 1984. *Shi Kefa ji* 史可法集. Ed. Zhang Chunxiu 張純修 and Luo Zhenchang 羅振常. Shanghai: Shanghai guji chubanshe.

Shi Xiaosheng 石小生 and Hou Qin 侯琴. 1988. *He'nan mingsheng guji cidian* 河南名勝古跡辭典. Zhengzhou: He'nan renmin chubanshe.

Shi Yuanqing 史元慶. 1979. *Shi Kefa xiansheng nianpu* 史可法先生年譜. Taibei: Huaxin wenhua shiye zhongxin.

Shunzhi *shilu* 順治實錄. 1964. *Da Qing Shizu Zhang (Shunzhi) huangdi shilu* 大清世祖章(順治)皇帝實錄, vol. 1. In *Da-Qing lichao shilu* 大清歷朝實錄. Rpt. Taibei: Huawen shuju.

Song Luo 宋犖, ed. N.d. (Kangxi). *Song Wenkang gong nianpu* 宋文康公年譜. In *Shangqiu Songshi sanshi yiji* 商邱宋氏三世遺集. Shangqiu: N.p.

Spence, Jonathan D. 1999. *The Search for Modern China*. New York: W. W. Norton.

———. 2001. *Treason by the Book*. New York: Penguin.

Struve, Lynn A. 1984. *The Southern Ming, 1644–1662*. New Haven: Yale University Press.

———. 1988. "Huang Zongzi in Context: A Reappraisal of His Major Writings." *Journal of Asian Studies* 47.3 (Aug.): 474–502.

————. 1993. *Voices from the Ming-Qing Cataclysm: China in Tigers' Jaws.* New Haven: Yale University Press.

————. 1998a. "Enigma Variations: Huang Zongxi's 'Expectation of a New Age.'" *Ming Studies* 40 (Fall): 72–85.

————. 1998b. *The Ming-Qing Conflict, 1619–1683: A Historiography and Source Guide.* Monograph and Occasional Paper, 56. Ann Arbor: Association for Asian Studies.

————, ed. 2004. *The Qing Formation in World-Historical Time.* Cambridge: Council on East Asian Studies, Harvard University.

Sun Jurong 孫居容. 1986. *Sunshi zupu* 孫氏族譜. N.p.: N.p.

Sun Qifeng 孫奇逢. N.d. (Kangxi). *Zhengjun Sun xiansheng nianpu* 徵君孫先生年譜. N.p.: N.p.

————. 1844. *Zhongzhou renwu kao* 中州人物考. Rpt. Taibei: Guangwen shuju, 1977.

Sun Wenliang 孫文良 and Li Zhiting 李治亭. 1983. *Qing Taizong quanzhuan* 清太宗全傳. Changchun: Jilin renmin chubanshe.

Swope, Kenneth M. 2003. "All Men Are Not Brothers: Ethnic Identity and Dynastic Loyalty in the Ningxia Mutiny of 1592." *Late Imperial China* 24.1 (June): 79–129.

Tan Qian 談遷. 1958. *Guoque* 國榷. 10 vols. Beijing: Guji chubanshe.

Twitchett, Denis, ed. 1979. *The Cambridge History of China,* vol. 3, *Sui and T'ang China, 589–906,* pt. 1. Cambridge: Cambridge University Press.

Wakeman, Frederic, Jr. 1985. *The Great Enterprise: The Manchu Reconstruction of Imperial Order in Seventeenth-Century China.* 2 vols. Berkeley: University of California Press.

Wakeman, Frederic, Jr., and Wang Xi, eds. 1997. *China's Quest for Modernization: A Historical Perspective.* Berkeley: University of California Press.

Waley-Cohen, Joanna. 1999. *The Sextants of Beijing: Global Currents in Chinese History.* New York: W. W. Norton.

Wang, Chen-main [王成勉]. 1999. *The Life and Career of Hung Ch'eng-ch'ou (1593–1665): Public Service in a Time of Dynastic Change.* Monograph and Occasional Paper, 59. Ann Arbor: Association for Asian Studies.

Watson, Burton, trans. 1968. *Records of the Grand Historian of China: Translated from the Shih-chi of Ssu-ma Ch'ien.* 2 vols. New York: Columbia University Press.

Wechsler, Howard J. 1974. *Mirror to the Son of Heaven: Wei Cheng at the Court of T'ang T'ai-tsung.* New Haven: Yale University Press.

Wei Qianzhi 魏千志. 1993. "Zhongguo Youtairen dingju Kaifeng shijian kao" 中國猶太人定居開封時間考. *Shixue yuekan* 史學月刊 (Kaifeng) 1993.5: 36–41.

———. 1998. *Ming-Qing shi gailun* 明清史概論. Beijing: Zhongguo shehui kexue chubanshe.

[Wen Bing 文秉]. 1964. *Sheng'an benji* 聖安本紀 [*Jiayi shian* 甲乙事案]. 2 vols. Taiwan wenxian congkan 台灣文獻叢刊, 183. Taibei: Taiwan yinhang.

White, Hayden. 1973. *Metahistory: The Historical Imagination in Nineteenth-Century Europe.* Baltimore: Johns Hopkins University Press.

———. 1978. *Tropics of Discourse: Essays in Cultural Criticism.* Baltimore: Johns Hopkins University Press.

White, William Charles. 1942. *Chinese Jews: A Compilation of Matters Relating to the Jews of K'ai-feng Fu.* 3 vols. Toronto: University of Toronto Press. Rpt. Paragon Press, 1966.

Wong, R. Bin. 1997. *China Transformed: Historical Change and the Limits of the European Experience.* Ithaca: Cornell University Press.

Woodside, Alexander. 1991. "Emperors and the Chinese Political System." In *Perspectives on Modern China: Four Anniversaries,* ed. Kenneth Lieberthal, Joyce Kallgren, Roderick McFarquhar, and Frederic Wakeman, Jr., 5–30. Armonk, N.Y.: M. E. Sharpe.

Wu Weiye 吳偉業. 1804. *Suikou jilüe* 綏寇紀略. N.p.: Zhaokuangge. Rpt. in 3 vols., Ming-Qing shiliao huibian 明清史料彙編, pt. 3. Taibei: Wenhai chubanshe, 1969.

Wyatt, Don J. 1996. *The Recluse of Loyang: Shao Yung and the Moral Evolution of Early Song Thought.* Honolulu: University of Hawai'i Press.

Xiayi xianzhi 夏邑縣志. 1920. Comp. and ed. Li Defen 黎德芬 and Jin Zhong 金鍾. Bo County, Anhui: Fuhua.

Xie Guozhen 謝國楨. 1956. *Qingchu nongmin qiyi ziliao jilu* 清初農民起義資料輯錄. Shanghai: Xinzhishi chubanshe.

Xing Shuen 邢樹恩 and Du Baotian 杜寶田. 1983. "Qiren Li Yan bing fei 'wuyou xiansheng'" 杞人李巖并非"烏有先生." *Zhongzhou jingu* 中州今古 1983.1: 17–20.

Xinxiang xianzhi 新鄉縣志. 1747. Comp. Zhao Kaiyuan 趙開元 and Chang Jun 暢俊. Xinxiang, Henan: N.p.

Xinxiu Xiangfu xianzhi 新修祥符縣志. 1898. Comp. and ed. Shen Chuanyi 沈傳義 and Huang Shubing 黃舒昺. N.p.: N.p.

Yongcheng xianzhi 永成縣志. 1903. Comp. and ed. Yue Tingkai 岳廷楷, Hu Zanlai 胡贊來, and Lü Yonghui 呂永輝. Yongcheng, Henan: N.p.

Yu, Pauline. 1997. "Canon Formation in Late Imperial China." In *Culture and State in Chinese History: Conventions, Accommodations, and Critiques,* ed. Theodore Huters, R. Bin Wong, and Pauline Yu, 83–104. Stanford: Stanford University Press.

Zha Jizuo 查繼佐. 1962. *Zuiwei lu xuanji* 罪維錄選集. Comp. Taiwan yinhang jingji yanjiushi 台灣銀行經濟研究室. 2 vols. Taiwan wenxian congkan, 136. Taibei: Taiwan yinhang.

Zhang Jinfan. 張晉藩. 1998. *Qingchao fazhishi* 清朝法制史. Beijing: Zhonghua shuju.

Zheng Lian 鄭廉. 1715. *Liuxiatang yiji* 柳下堂遺集. Henan Provincial Library rare book collection, Zhengzhou.

———. 1984. *Yubian jilüe* 豫變紀略. Ed. Wang Xingya 王興亞. Hangzhou: Zhejiang guji chubanshe.

Zhou Kuiyi 周魁一 et al., annot. 1990. *Ershiwu shi hequ zhi zhushi* 二十五史河渠志注釋. Beijing: Zhongguo shudian.

Zhou Yuanlian 周遠廉 and Zhao Shiyu 趙世瑜. 1986. *Huangfu shezheng wang Duoergun quanzhuan* 皇父攝政王多爾袞全傳. Changchun: Jilin wenshi chubanshe.

Zurndorfer, Harriet T. 1995. *China Bibliography*. Leiden: E. J. Brill.

II
TEMPORALITIES OF NATIONAL SUBJUGATION AND RESISTANCE

CHAPTER THREE

Contesting Chinese Time, Nationalizing Temporal Space

Temporal Inscription in Late Chosŏn Korea

JaHyun Kim Haboush

WITH THE MANCHU CONQUEST of China, there was a shift in the epistemological strategy of perception of the world and of self in the Korean intellectual community that encompassed both spatial and temporal dimensions. From the fourteenth century, the operative concept with which Koreans ordered the world was the binary opposition of "civilized" and "barbarous." Chosŏn Koreans had accepted the sinocentric view that China was the center of the civilized world, in which they eagerly claimed membership among the civilized. This concession had been based on an acknowledgment that Ming China's political, cultural, and ethnic identity qualified it to be the rightful heir to Confucian civilization and thus the leader of the civilized world. China's position as the spatial center was inextricably embedded in the perception that it was the legitimate transmitter of Confucian civilization. Although Koreans increasingly viewed their civilization as more authentically Confucian than Chinese civilization, this did not lead them to believe they could challenge Ming China's historical role or its place as the center of civilization.

With "barbarian" Manchus in China proper, the sinocentric world view was no longer viable, and the conceptual remapping of center and periphery emerged as an urgent issue.[1] Koreans believed that Confucian civilization had been lost or at least greatly compromised in a barbarian-dominated China and that this civilization, consequently, had to be safeguarded and transmitted in Korea. In transferring the role of culture-transmitter to Korea, they were rejecting the sinocentric world view. This ideological rejection, however, was not accompanied by changes in Sino-Korean power relations. Despite Korea's contempt for the Manchus, it remained under the hegemony of the Chinese empire, performing the same diplomatic rituals of tributary deference to the Qing court that it had performed to the Ming court (Chun 1968).

Those tributary rituals connoted something completely different, however. During the Ming, the tributary rituals had been seen as signifiers of peaceful relations between two who shared a commitment to Confucian civilization and of their respective roles within it. After the Qing conquest, the same rituals signified the disrupted world order in which the hierarchy among nations did not correspond to their degrees of civilization and in which power was separated from legitimacy. Even worse, those rituals were reminders, etched into the collective psyche, of miserable defeats inflicted by the Manchus—the determined but ineffectual Korean refusal to negotiate with the Manchus having resulted in invasions in 1627 and 1636–1637, the latter having concluded with King Injo's humiliating personal obeisance to the Qing ruler Hong Taiji who had led the invasion.

This dilemma—of regarding the Qing as illegitimate usurpers while having to render them the rituals of subservience—led Koreans to an intense search for a new episteme through which to view the new world order. While there was a general consensus in the Korean intellectual community to reconfigure the world by drawing a dichotomy between geographic and cultural centers, relegating Qing China to the former and elevating Korea to the latter, this was accompanied by an intense disagreement over the meaning and source of authority for Korea's new role. If Korea was to be the caretaker of Confucian civilization, should it claim to be a center? If so, the center of what? Was it a discrete, self-contained center or the center of a greater entity or region? Was it unique or one among many?

Elsewhere, I have written about the discourse on the Korean search for a new identity (Haboush 1999), so I will not discuss it in detail here. Suffice it to say that differing modes of repossessing the past emerged as crucial signifiers of differing visions of Korea's identity. There were two opposing camps that disagreed on the question of how the past should be rendered into history to suit their respective visions. In one view, Korea, as the de facto spiritual heir to Ming China, became a unique center and assumed the Chinese historical identity as the transmitter of culture. An alternative approach was to seek a more autonomous link to the source of tradition by constructing a separate tradition of transmission.

In this essay, I will discuss the Korean practice of temporal inscription and its meaning in the context of the Korean search for a new identity. The sinocentric world order was imagined as a politico-cultural universe suspended in temporal and geographic space. The symbolic and physical center of this universe was the Chinese emperor residing in a capital,[2] who mediated between the natural and supernatural worlds and between the human and cosmic worlds. The Korean belief in the illegitimacy of the Manchu emperor denied him this symbolic role. It led Chosŏn Koreans to reject Qing-Chinese time and to search for a way to repossess time. Hence, time inscription was an important constituent in the discourse of constructing a new center.

I will concentrate on two sites in this discursive formation. One is the practice of ritual sacrifice to Ming emperors. The Yi royal house erected an altar to several Ming emperors, and Yi rulers offered sacrifices to them. This act was paralleled by the erection of another shrine to those same Ming emperors at which scholar-officials sacrificed. I feel that through these activities the boundary between civilization and nation was redrawn, and the past was remapped in history. Another discursive site is the use of Chinese reign titles and its signification. Koreans used the reign titles of the Qing emperors, but they also continued to use the reign title of the Chongzhen emperor, that is, the last Ming emperor, on certain occasions. I believe that these uses of past China and present China encoded different visions of the Korean cultural and political self. Lastly, I will discuss modes of inscribing nonpolitical time and the ways in which concepts of self and gender interacted with one another and also with concepts of time.

The Ming and the Tributary Structure

Despite the widely held notion that Korea had been a model tributary of China through the ages, most of the time the Sino-Korean relationship had been anything but peaceful. In the early period when "Korean" peoples were forming themselves into states and consolidating their statehood, China was a source of both inspiration and threat. The first direct encounter between these proto-states and China was the Han-dynasty establishment of the four commanderies in the first century BCE, the last of which was expelled by Koguryŏ in the early fourth century. During the period of disunity in China from the third to the sixth centuries, when states in "Korea" and "China" were in constant flux, Sino-Korean relations were characterized by rapidly fluctuating and extremely complex multidirectional negotiations among Korean and Chinese states, on the one hand, and equally complex dealings among Korean states and among Chinese states, on the other. As soon as China was unified, the Chinese view of "Korea" as belonging within territorial perimeters that should be subjugated and conquered reasserted itself in large-scale invasions of the Koguryŏ state— by Sui Yangdi in 612 CE and again in 613, and then by Tang Taizong in 644–645. None of these attacks was successful, although they seriously depleted Koguryŏ's resources.

It was only under the Silla, one of the Korean Three Kingdoms that would conquer the other two states and bring the peninsula under one polity in 668, that the semblance of a mutually accommodating relationship was forged. The Silla state was eager to ally with the Tang to vanquish its Korean rivals, and in 650 it accepted the status of a tributary state to Tang China. Tributary status, both in its operative mechanisms and in later historiographical assessments, is an extremely complex matter. It is often described as holding a subordinate status in the Chinese cultural universe while maintaining political autonomy. The tributary relation, however, was neither fixed nor monolithic and was subject to negotiation. For example, when it became apparent that the Tang Chinese forces, which had joined the Silla campaign against the other Korean states, intended to stay on in Korea after the victory of 668, the Silla successfully expelled them.

Notwithstanding its complexities, the forging of a Korean tributary relationship with China opened a new era. For the first time, a concept of East Asia emerged in which the three countries in the region, China, Korea, and Japan as well, were on good terms and in which they shared a certain compatibility in written language, religion, and world view. Moreover, Han-Chinese dynasties did not once invade Korea thereafter.

Tributary status also signified that "colonization" or "globalization," however one wishes to see it, had shifted from a spatial to a temporal phenomenon. I have mentioned the symbolic role of the Chinese emperor as the center of geotemporal space. The first recorded politicization of time in China was in 163 BCE, when Emperor Wen of the Han dynasty initiated the practice of declaring reign titles (*yŏnho*, Ch. *nianhao*) with the choice of "Houyuan." This proclamation signified an occupation of temporal space, a transformation of time from commodity into political currency.[3] The use of reign titles continued in China and by the Ming dynasty had evolved into a custom of coterminous reign titles—that is, a new emperor upon his accession proclaimed a new reign title that continued for the duration of his reign. The practice of proclaiming reign titles was emulated in Korea, albeit briefly. According to the *Samguk sagi* (History of the Three Kingdoms), the oldest extant history of the period, in Silla the reign title Kŏnwŏn was adopted in 536, and subsequently six more reign titles were adopted until the practice was discontinued in 650.[4] Of the three states, only Silla is described as having adopted such titles. Perhaps this is attributable to the Silla-centered perspective of the *Samguk sagi,* but the *Samguk yusa,* compiled by the Buddhist monk Iryŏn a century later, which is viewed as representing the Korean nativist tradition, repeats the same information.[5] In any case it is noticeable that, unlike in China where rulers often proclaimed more than one reign title, the Silla anachronic reign titles tended to last longer than the rulers' tenures on the throne.[6] Fragmentary evidence suggests that Koguryŏ and Paekche on occasion may have adopted reign titles of their own, but this is not certain.[7]

By accepting the Chinese emperor's reign title in 650, Korea entered the Chinese imperium, which was marked by the dominance of temporal space. In 674, several years after the Silla conquered Paekche and Koguryŏ, it adopted the Tang calendar (*Samguk sagi:* 1977: I, 75), thereby accepting the sinocentric construction of cosmic temporal space.[8] Koreans did calibrate their own time but within the frame of the Chinese calendar. This continued until 1894, when they adopted the Western calendar (Pak 2000). Depending on the power structures in China proper and Korea, however, Sino-Korean relations constantly fluctuated. Given the independent ethos of early Koryŏ, which had risen in Korea during the power vacuum between the Tang and the Song dynasties in China, and the military weakness of the Song, the Koryŏ-Song tributary relation was strained most of the time. King T'aejo, the founder, upon his accession proclaimed the reign title Ch'ŏnsu (918–933). Kwangjong proclaimed reign titles on two occasions: Kwangdŏk in 950, which he discarded in the following year under bureaucratic pressure, and Chunp'ung in 960, which lasted to 963. The rise of "barbarian" peoples on the eastern steppes and in the Sungari-Liao region—that is, the Khitan and the Jurchen—with whom both China and Korea had to cope, shattered the traditional structures of tributary relations (Rogers 1983). The Mongol conquests of China and Korea in the thirteenth century, though they resulted in only about a hundred years of Mongol rule, had a profound psychological impact insofar as they embodied the worst fear of the Chinese and the Koreans: not just part, but all of their territory could be brought under "barbarous" alien rule or domination.[9] Thus, the Ming dynasty and the Chosŏn dynasty exulted in their respective roles as rescuers of the cultural universe from near annihilation, as redeemers of civilization from the grip of barbarity, and as reclaimers of ethnic identity and tradition.

The founding of the Chosŏn dynasty in 1392 was not merely a victory of pro-Ming forces over residual pro-Yuan forces, but also the emergence of a Confucian state that assertively adopted Neo-Confucianism as its state ideology (Deuchler 1992). In this formation, the Chosŏn-Ming tributary relation was an integral factor. It signified to Korean Confucians the restoration of a well-ordered cultural universe in which Korea was a full-fledged member (Haboush 1988: 21–25). Despite unavoidable tensions between the two neighboring countries of unequal power, size, and status, strains in the political sphere were masked under a rhetoric of shared commitment to Confucian civilization. Perhaps for the first time—and, as it turned out, the last—the rituals of the tributary structure corresponded with its rhetoric: peace between the two states and order in the larger world.

The history of Chosŏn-Ming relations, however, would not be complete without reference to the Ming dispatch of troops during the Japanese invasions of Korea from 1592 to 1598. After Sino-Korean relations were normalized, the Chosŏn state had reduced its army of defense, keeping the military as a means of maintaining internal order. This action derived from a national security policy that historically understood external threats as originating from the north. The sense of security that prevailed now that the northern border was under a Chinese protective umbrella lasted for two hundred years, until Japan invaded Korea for the first time in Korean historical memory.

When the Japanese army, 150,000 strong, landed on the southern coast and advanced to and took the capital, Hansŏng, in three weeks, the Korean court, driven to a northern border region, had to muffle its misgivings and request military assistance from China, which responded swiftly (see Map 1). Chinese troops played a crucial role in expelling the Japanese invaders and, although they caused an array of problems and conflicts, left promptly after the war (Ledyard 1988–

1989). Feeling that the Chinese had translated a common bond into a blood commitment, the Koreans were imbued with an undying sense of indebtedness to the Ming. This gratitude acquired an element of regret and sadness in subsequent periods, as Koreans realized they could not do for the Ming, in its struggle against the Manchus, what the Ming had done for them and as they watched the Ming demise in helpless dismay and horror.

The Historicization of the Past and the Appropriation of History

Rendering the past into history was never a simple matter in the Confucian world; it was both imperative and complex. The past acquired meaning only through its role in human history: an unhistoricized past was unimaginable and unacceptable.[10] Because of the importance attached to the moral evaluation of any period, historical judgments of given periods were often contested. As the Ming passed into history, that history became a site of serious contention in two different ways among the ruling and intellectual elite in Korea.

One concerned how to view the role of the Ming as the erstwhile transmitter of Confucian civilization. This question was debated by intellectuals as they constructed Korea's new identity as the last bastion of civilization. On the question of the definition of civilization, two drastically different views emerged. One, held by the scholars of the dominant Sŏin faction, was that human civilization had achieved its pinnacle in the correlation of Zhu Xi philosophy and Ming civilization. Hence, the best way for Korea to fulfill its mission was to adhere faithfully to Zhu Xi scholarship and, within the limits of possibility, to Ming civilization (Haboush 1999).

A contending view, subscribed to by members of the Namin faction, who were mostly out of power, vested authority in the Confucian classics and the classical era. It held that no dynasty after the Xia, Shang, and Zhou had yet recaptured the ideals of the classical age, but that each period should be evaluated for its own distinct character and achievement. This view placed Zhu Xi and the Ming in a respectable but not unique place in the evolving history of civilization. The ritual controversy of the seventeenth century centered on this issue. Here, I will not go into the details of this controversy. Suffice it to say that the Sŏin defined the Korean mission as inheriting and continuing Ming civilization, while the Namin defined it as carrying out Korea's own destiny while trying to embody the spirit and institutions of the classical age.

Another contest concerning the Ming was over who should inherit the Ming tradition and in what fashion. Was the Yi royal house, representing the Chosŏn state, to be entrusted with the mission of safeguarding civilization in Korea, or was it the community of scholars who saw themselves as the heirs of Zhu Xi and Ming civilization? As the Ming had both political and cultural aspects, both the state and the scholarly community competed for a superior claim to stewardship. Their competition began to take concrete form in the late seventeenth and early eighteenth centuries. By that time, the Ming was no longer a living polity and had joined the historic dynasties of China; it was no longer a potentially menacing force at Korea's northern border. Thus, it was transformed from a spatial to a temporal entity.

In a Confucian society, commemorative ritual sacrifices signified the most visible link between the living and the dead, and in Korea both the state and the scholarly community sought to formalize their claims to civilizational heirship through commemorative rituals to several Ming emperors. But those rituals presented extremely delicate problems for both parties. For the Yi royal house, it was a question of ancestry: while they customarily offered sacrifices to the rulers of past Korean dynasties, they had never performed any to a foreign ruler (Haboush 1988: 47–48). No matter how revered the Ming had been, it was a foreign dynasty. The challenge was to claim spiritual heirship while circumventing issues of ethnic descent.

Appropriating the symbols of Ming authority also presented thorny issues to the scholarly community. The main question was the appropriateness of scholars' offering sacrifices to symbols of political power. There had long existed a well-defined structure of ritual sacrifice that recognized their heirship to Confucian scholarship. On an official level, sacrifices were offered to the pantheon of canonized Confucian sages, both Chinese and Korean, at the Confucian temple (Munmyo) at Sŏnggyun'gwan, the Royal Confucian Academy, and at smaller shrines at the state-run county schools (*hyanggyo*). In addition, private academies had shrines (*sau*) that were dedicated to specific luminaries (Ch'oe 1999). Hence, crossing the boundary between the scholarly and political spheres required circumspection and justification.

The scholarly community took the first step. Song Siyŏl (1607–1689), the charismatic leader of the Sŏin, a staunch Ming loyalist and faithful Zhu Xi scholar, proposed it. Citing the precedent of earlier scholars' sacrifices to the legendary sage-emperor Shun, he expressed a desire to establish a shrine to the Wanli emperor (r. 1573–1620), who had sent Ming troops to Korea during the Japanese invasion. Song's subsequent execution almost terminated the plan, but Kwŏn Sangha (1641–1721), Song's student who had gone to see his famous teacher in his place of exile, was able to communicate and carry out Song's wishes after the Sŏin faction was restored to power. A shrine called Mandongmyo was established in 1704 at Hwayangdong in Ch'ŏngju city, Song's birthplace, to which he frequently retired from political life, and sacrifices were regularly offered there to the Ming emperors Wanli and Chongzhen (r. 1628–1644).[11] These sacrifices, known as the "four baskets and four footed dishes of offerings" (*sabyŏn sadu*), symbolized Korean Confucian legitimacy.[12] The name refers to a passage in the *Hanshu* (History of the [Former] Han) in which the great Han historian Ban Gu praised the peoples of the Korean Peninsula saying that they observed beautiful customs based on the Eight Prohibitions, which they had received from Kija but which had been lost in China, and that those customs were symbolized by the baskets and footed dishes.[13]

The Mandongmyo shrine served as a potent symbol of Korean scholars' heirship to Ming civilization. It was also a reminder of Sŏin hegemony. The Hwayang Academy, which was associated with Mandongmyo, grew increasingly powerful.[14] Many tales circulated concerning the Hwayang Academy's abuse of scholars and local officials who did not offer cooperation. Even if we regard such stories as skewed, it seems probable that continuing Sŏin power made possible the convergence of the political and scholarly spheres and brought about an extremely unusual situation in which a "private" community appropriated public symbols. All this embodied and was embedded in a new epistemological structure. As a way of maintaining a viable cultural identity while accepting political subservience to the Qing, Sŏin scholars devised an episteme in which they constructed individual as well as national selves with distinct and functionally separate political and cultural selves. Hence, they could claim that their sacrifices to the political rulers of a bygone, alien dynasty were a confirmation of cultural continuity.

The Yi royal house's appropriation of ritual heirship to the Ming posed considerably more problems. Because of the institution's public nature and because of the extremely delicate question of the nation's ethnic identity, that appropriation had to be implemented cautiously and in several steps. The first ritual formally symbolizing the transformation of the Ming from a spatial to a temporal entity was performed in 1704, the first sexagesima of that dynasty's demise in 1644. King Sukchong (r. 1674–1720), ever a zealous champion of the monarchy, proposed that the Chosŏn court perform a sacrifice to the Chongzhen emperor on the sexagesimal anniversary date of the end of the Ming dynasty. Because this was proposed as a one-time sacrifice to the soul of a tragic emperor "whose gaze upon his old home cannot find his descendants," it elicited relatively few objections, although some officials voiced a certain discomfort with the absence of precedent and thus of a proper ritual protocol (SS: 39.20a–21a).

On the appointed day in the 3rd month, the sacrifice was performed in the manner of the great offering (*taesa*),[15] the grandest ceremony in the hierarchy of rites in the Chosŏn court, with the king as the first officiant. The eulogy was full of laments for the collapse of civilization in China, the deep shame Koreans felt at their continued existence without having avenged the Ming, and their resolve to carry out their mission to perpetuate civilization. It ended with a heartfelt supplication specifically to the spirit of the Chongzhen emperor:

> How can we requite this sorrow and bear this deep pain? We have
> constructed a ritual altar and we offer our sacrifices. Although the
> texts do not specify this ritual, righteous principle enables us to
> perform it in the right manner. Because your old country fell into
> ruin, even when the bright spirit of Your Majesty descends to this
> earth, who will offer you a sacrifice? Although our country is a distant
> land, our devotion is unparalleled. We pray that you come to us and
> accept and enjoy these offerings. (SS: 39.24a–b)

The next step was the erection of a permanent altar to the Wanli emperor to ritualize the court's "gratitude for [his] having saved Korea from the brink of ruin." Sukchong had already broached this matter very early in 1704, but a number of his officials expressed apprehension. They pointed out that the ritual texts made no provision for it. Moreover, the matter would present exceedingly complex problems since both the shrine and the rituals for the Wanli emperor would have to be grander than those for the Yi royal ancestors (SS: 39.2a–5b). There were supporters as well, however. About 160 students at the Royal Confucian Academy, for example, sent a joint memorial requesting the erection of the shrine (SS: 39.6b–7a). Buoyed by this support, and exploiting the momentum created by the sacrifice to the Chong-zhen emperor, Sukchong ordered the erection, effectively shutting out the opposition (SS: 39.26b–27a).

When the shrine was completed at the end of the year, it was given the name Taebodan, the Altar of Gratitude. Symbols of ancestry were everywhere. The Taebodan was located within the palace precinct, and its shape and size approximated those of the Sajiktan (Altar of Land and Grain) of the Chosŏn, though it was one *ch'ok* higher than the latter. The ritual protocols, including even the music and the offerings to be used in the sacrifices, also mostly followed those prescribed for the Sajiktan (SS: 40.50b–51a). The sacrificial utensils as well as the placement of the offerings followed those used at the Chongmyo, the Yi ancestral temple (SS: 40.50b–51a). The sacrifice was to be performed annually in the 3rd month.

When Sukchong performed the first sacrifice to the Wanli emperor at the Taebodan in 1705, the rhetorical trope of the eulogy had certain conspicuous themes: it is necessary to offer a sacrifice to our benefactor since, after the fall of the Ming, there is no one in China who can perform it; and the sacrifice is not an ancestral offering but a commitment to uphold and continue the Confucian tradition that began in the Eastern Zhou period (SS: 41.31b–32b). Clearly, Sukchong was eager to claim for the Yi royal house spiritual heirship to the Ming as the rightful successor to the Confucian tradition embodied by the Zhou dynasty. Nonetheless, the Chosŏn court was aware that this ritual, the protocols of which consisted of a mixture of Ming Chinese and Chosŏn Korean elements, created a certain symbolic ambiguity and that there was no effective means of resolving it.[16]

Claiming heirship to a previous ruling house during the Chosŏn period required performing appropriate rituals—in particular, sacrifices to the founder of that dynasty. The Chosŏn court performed sacrifices to the founders, mythical as well as real, of the previous Korean states starting from Tangun, the legendary founder of Tangun Chosŏn, the earliest Korean state, down to Wang Kŏn (r. 918–943), the first ruler of the preceding dynasty, the Koryŏ. These rituals signified the status of the Yi royal house as the legitimate successor to these native dynasties. When Yŏngjo (r. 1724–1776), Sukchong's ambitious son, came to the throne, he was eager to appropriate for the Yi monarchy the potential benefits of a direct link to the Ming. His campaign, however, should be understood in the context of his overall symbolic politics.[17] Ever the inventive and tireless politician availing himself of the symbols and emblems of his throne, he tapped those associated with Ming authority among many others. In 1727 he extended the taboo on using the personal names of Yi royal ancestors to include those of the Ming emperors (YS: 11.5a). He laid much groundwork for two decades before broaching this topic. The bureaucrats, astute practitioners in the minutiae of symbolic politics in their own right, responded to the royal proposal with apprehension. It took considerable maneuvering by Yŏngjo to accomplish what he wished.

Yŏngjo first suggested the inclusion of the Chongzhen emperor in the sacrifice to the Wanli emperor at Taebodan. The rhetorical trope accompanying this suggestion was the same as had been used in the case of the Wanli emperor—military assistance to Korea, though in this case unrealized. Yŏngjo claimed that when Korea was invaded by the Manchus in 1636–1637, the Chongzhen emperor had wished to send troops, but this had been obviated by the Korean capitulation. He also insisted that, had his father Sukchong known of this—it is not clear how Yŏngjo himself knew—he surely would have offered sacrifices to Chongzhen as well as Wanli. Yŏngjo's elaborately constructed rationale won the day (YS: 69.22a; Haboush 1988: 40–41). His reference to the Chongzhen emperor's unfulfilled wish to send troops, whether the bureaucrats believed it or not, probably evoked their own unfulfilled wish to avenge the Ming. After all, who could object to making an offering to this ill-fated last emperor whose soul might forever wander in loneliness?

Within a week Yŏngjo suggested, almost as an afterthought, that perhaps they should also include the Hongwu emperor (r. 1368–1399), the founder of the Ming dynasty, in the sacrifice. He pointed out that the Hongwu emperor had bestowed the dynastic name Chosŏn upon them, and, hence, they were indebted to him for his confirmation that the Chosŏn state was the heir to Kija Chosŏn. Kija was a semihistorical figure who linked Korea to China and Confucianism in Korean prehistory. He was supposed to have come from China and to have founded Kija Chosŏn, a legendary Korean state that was believed to have succeeded Tangun Chosŏn. Not only was he credited with having been a civilizer of the Korean people, he also became a pivotal figure through whom Koreans traced their own independent genealogy to ancient Confucian civilization.[18]

However, Yŏngjo's strategy of invoking Korea's cultural heirship, both its own and that which came through Ming China, did not persuade his officials. They went to the heart of the matter—the connotation of ancestry. They pointed out that sacrifices to the Ming emperors at the Taebodan were specifically for their military assistance to Korea but that the rituals he was proposing to the Hongwu emperor were appropriate to one's parents or ancestors, not to one's superiors. Yŏngjo, for his part, argued on the basis of the fact that sacrifices to Hongwu were no longer performed in China: "Incense and paper money for the imperial house have long since been extinguished. That is why we want to offer sacrifices to the three emperors at the Taebodan. If there were to be a restoration [of the Ming dynasty] in the central plain, of course our country would not sacrifice to them. If incense and paper money had not stopped and we were still to sacrifice to the three emperors, it would be a sacrilege."[19]

This rhetoric only confirmed the connotation of ancestry. Realizing that he had reached the limits of what rhetoric could accomplish, Yŏngjo resorted to the politics of filiality and self-flagellation. The *Yŏngjo sillok* (Veritable records of Yŏngjo) have a rather detailed account of his performance: Yŏngjo summoned his officials at night, telling them that his father had appeared before him. Then he had a royal secretary read aloud four poems that he claimed had been spectrally composed by his father. The third one reads:

> The lofty emperor conferred upon us the name Chosŏn;
> Who could reproduce the dragons and snakes of his brush?
> For three hundred years we have been in his debt.
> How can we repay his heavenly kindness?

The fourth one reads:

> To uphold the Way in a solitary castle by the aura of the moon year
>   upon year,
> Each year unable to renew the Court of Heaven.
> Alas! Sadness! The sixth sexagesima of the *sin* year[20] draws near,
> Yet no one recommends sacrificial vessels.

The king thereupon threw himself to the ground and cried for quite some time. Then he declared that, since he was unable to obey the explicit wishes of his father, conveyed in the poems, he had to consider himself unfilial. He was even being made to commit a disloyal act, since his officials' opposition to a sacrifice to the Hongwu emperor amounted to nothing less than forgetting and rejecting the three hundred years of gracious beneficence that the Ming house had bestowed upon them. In view of all this, Yŏngjo's officials could not further resist his wishes (Haboush 1988: 42–43; YS: 69.26b–27a).

The sacrifices to the three emperors, which were performed in the 4th month of that year, were redolent of ancestral ritual. Each of the three emperors received a separate eulogy: the Hongwu emperor was honored for having restored order and for having extended that benefit even to the Eastern Country, on which he had conferred a dynastic name; the Wanli emperor for having sent military assistance; and the Chongzhen emperor for his righteous act of committing suicide when the Ming dynasty came to an end. Particularly interesting is the clause included in the eulogy to the Hongwu emperor, which said that, because of the proximity of the "parental country" (*pumo chi kuk*), Koreans had received unique benefit from it. All this was expressed with repeated references to the absence of proper sacrifices in China, which had made this performance imperative. The ritual protocols of the sacrifices, which required Yŏngjo to perform obeisance to the three emperors in chronological order, seems to have completed the ritual confirmation of Chosŏn's heirship (YS: 69.30b–31a, 69.31b–32b). Although this was intended as a spiritual rather than ethnic inheritance, at least ritualistically there was a blurring of boundaries.

The Politics of Time Inscription

If it was unimaginable to have an unhistoricized past, it was also extremely difficult to historicize unpoliticized time in Korea. There were different modes of inscribing time. Personal time, which was relatively unmediated by political time, conjoined as it was with cosmic time,[21] was inscribed by sexagesimal years. Each sexagesimal cycle began with the *kapcha* year and ended with the *kyehae* year, but each person had his or her own cycle beginning with his or her year of birth. Inasmuch as the sexagesimal cycles themselves did not have markings to distinguish one from another, they did not lend themselves to being located in historical time.

It is not that Koreans or Chinese did not have any concept of linear time.[22] Although they subscribed to a cyclicity to describe certain kinds of recurring patterns in nature and the human world, in the sphere of imagining and constructing human history, the concept of linear time functioned as a principal ingredient (for a discussion of this duality, see Aveni 1989: 321–322). In this sphere, however, time came in blocks of political time—the reign of a ruler within the span of a dynasty. Because sexagesimal cycles were by themselves linearly non-specific, they were historicized through political time. The *muo* year, for example, referred equally to all of those years that fell at that point in the sexagesimal cycle—418, 1078, 1798, to name a few. It entered history and gained specificity and meaning when it was mapped against political time. The *muo* year of Chŏngjo's reign was 1798, while the *muo* year of the Yuanfeng era referred to 1078. Certain sexagesimal years also acquired specific historicity when they were defined by a major political or social event. The Literary Purge of the Kapcha Year (Kapcha sahwa), for example, referred to King Yŏnsan's wholesale purge of literati in 1504, while the Rebellion of the Musin Year (Musin nan) meant the major rebellion of 1728 in the southern part of Korea. Though these sexagesimal years were taken out of the anonymity of cyclicity and rendered historic, this occurred through their identification with events.

Inscribing time was a mode of possessing time. It was not merely historicizing impersonal cosmic time, but inscribing one's vision of history. In Confucian societies, inscriptions of political time signified specific moral qualities of an era. A reign or a dynasty was marked with different signs of morality and stability ranging from the virtuous and well-ordered to the corrupt and chaotic, with various combinations in between. Sometimes there was more than one mode of inscribing political time, and the choice seems to have represented an ideological stance. In Korea, where different ways of inscribing historical time were possible—international (universal) as well as national—this was frequently true. Different modes of time inscription were used by different agents in different spheres.

Inscribing the present, however, imposed a greater constraint on Korea, which held tributary status in the sinocentric world. A Chinese ruler was known by two kinds of appellations. Upon accession, he proclaimed a reign title with which he occupied and sinicized temporal space, not just for his Chinese subjects but for other peoples in the sinocentric world as well. Upon death, a temple name was bestowed on him to insure his place in the pantheon of his own imperial house.[23] Although there were sporadic uses of reign titles during the Three Kingdoms and Koryŏ, by the Chosŏn dynasty Korean rulers did not have their own reign titles; the Korean court used the Chinese one, acknowledging the universality of sinicized time. There were exceptions. King Kwangjong (r. 949–975), the famous Koryŏ ruler who pushed the power of his monarchy to the limit,[24] for example, took reign titles on two occasions, once in 950, when he acceded, and again in 960, before he reverted to using the Song emperor's reign title in 963. From the time when the Silla took the reign title of the Tang emperor in 650, however, the Korean court generally adhered to using the reign titles of concurrent Chinese emperors.

When it came to temple names, the situation was different. Beginning with the founder, the Koryŏ rulers upon their deaths were bestowed with temple names that ended with *cho/jo* (Ch. *zu*) or *chong/jong* (Ch. *zong*), denoting ancestry. This practice was discontinued when the Koryŏ state came under Mongol dominance in the thirteenth century. Then Korean kings instead were given names that ended with *wang* (prince).[25] When the Chosŏn dynasty was founded, the practice of conferring temple names ending in *cho/jo* or *chong/jong* was revived, and it continued until the demise of the Chosŏn in 1910.

It is interesting that earlier Koryŏ rulers as well as the Chosŏn kings, who shied away from proclaiming reign titles, insisted on receiving *cho/jo* or *chong/jong* temple names. It was not as though such temple names were to be had for the asking. China regarded the conferral of *-zu/-zong* temple names as a prerogative denied to its tributary states. Thus the conferral of these temple names was an act of defiance on the part of the Korean state, kept secret from their suzerain state. One reason the Chosŏn court hesitated to request the dispatch of Chinese troops in 1592 as it fled the Japanese army, sending for them only when the court reached the northernmost Korean town at the Chinese border, was their fear that, once in Korea, the Chinese might discover this practice. One wonders why the Korean court did not do the same with reign titles. Vietnam did exactly that—they proclaimed their own reign titles, which they kept secret from China. Perhaps the Koreans saw reign titles as indicators of an independent universe, which the Korean ruling house did not venture to assert, while temple names connoted for them an ethical commitment to perfect Confucian rule, which the Chosŏn rulers felt they could seek within the hierarchy imposed by the tributary structure.

This meant that the Korean present was "colonized" by sinicized time in the political sphere. There was no formal way to inscribe the present except by the reign title of the Chinese emperor. Only when inscribing the past was it possible for Koreans to nationalize time by using deceased kings' temple names. The date of publication of the

Kyŏngguk taejŏn (National code), 1469, for instance, was inscribed as the 5th year of Chenghua, the reign title of the concurrent Ming emperor.[26] In publications that collected the edicts and legal decisions of past Chosŏn kings, however, time was inscribed by reign years using the Korean kings' temple names.[27] This pattern continued when the Ming was replaced by the Qing, for whom Koreans had nothing but contempt. When the *Sok taejŏn*, fifteenth-century additions and modifications to the *Kyŏngguk taejŏn,* was published in 1744, it was dated the 9th year of the Qianlong emperor (see the preface to the *Sok taejŏn* 1964: i–ii).

The contrast between the colonized time of the present and the nationalized time of the past was vividly displayed by the time inscriptions used in day-to-day record keeping at the court and in official historiography. In the *Sŭngjŏngwŏn ilgi,* the daily records that the Royal Secretariat kept of the king's public activities, including his written and verbal communications with officials, entries were made under dates with the Qing emperor's reign title: for example, "the *kapcha* day of the 3rd month, the *kyŏngjin* year, the 39th year of Kangxi [1700]." In the *sillok,* the official annals of a reign compiled after the death of each king, the dates were inscribed with the temple name of the Korean ruler. The same date above, for example, was inscribed as the "*kapcha* day of the 3rd month, the *kyŏngjin* year, the 26th year of Great King Sukchong." We might view this situation as ironic in that the *Sŭngjŏngwŏn ilgi,* which was an unedited and rather intimate record of the daily events of the court, was dated with the Manchu emperors' reign titles, while the *sillok,* the most official form of historiography, was dated with the Chosŏn rulers' temple names. These may be cases in which Chosŏn Koreans, finding the Manchu's infiltration of temporal space untenable, sought alternative means of inscribing the present.

As most of the Korean ruling-intellectual elite became engaged in this search, solutions largely fell into two modes. One was to continue using the title of the last Ming emperor's reign, Chongzhen, which began in 1628 and ended in 1644. In the sexagesimal cycle, the year 1644 was a *kapsin* year, the 17th year of the cycle. After 1644, rather than change to the Qing emperor's reign title, some Koreans continued to inscribe time with the Chongzhen reign title. When that sexagesimal cycle came to an end in 1683 and a new cycle began with the *kapcha* year in 1684, they designated it the *kapcha* year of the new first cycle after the Chongzhen era. By designating repeat cycles—as the second, third, and so on—they were able to inscribe time using the Chongzhen reign title throughout the Chosŏn dynasty.

This practice apparently was widespread in both government circles and the scholarly community. It appears that the Chosŏn government continued to use the Chongzhen reign title in the identification plaques (*map'ae*) that they issued to the populace. In 1730 a Korean ship, driven by a storm, landed on the China coast. In the course of investigating the sailors, Chinese officials discovered that their identification plaques bore dates with the Ming reign title. Deeply offended by this symbolic resistance to their authority, the Qing government sent to the Chosŏn court a letter of inquiry demanding an explanation. Yŏngjo was forced to submit a formal apology and to order that identification plaques thereafter be issued using only Qing reign titles (YS: 26.16a–17b).

Scholars, working in the privacy of their studies, fared better. One of the most visible indications of their use of Ming reign titles is in how they inscribed their writings and dated their books. While their use of Ming reign titles in dating their own works was merely occasional, it appears frequently in annotations, prefaces, introductions, or other supplements to the works of others—"paratextual" space, to use Gerard Genette's term. Though Genette points out that paratexts render a text into a book (1997: 1–2), in the case of the writings of Chosŏn scholars, not all texts that received paratextual treatment by later scholars became books in the sense of commodities in the public domain. Nevertheless, those paratexts carried with them an implied historicization of the work. In writing a postscript (*pal*) to the *Hwayang chi* (Record of Hwayang),[28] for example, one scholar inscribed 1861 as "the *sinyu* year, the 234th year of Chongzhen" (*Sungjŏng ibaeksam-sipsa nyŏn sinyu*) ("Hwayang chi pal," in *Songja taejŏn*: 8.689). Writing another postscript to the same book, another scholar dated the same year as "the *sinyu* year of the 4th [cycle after] Chongzhen" (*Sungjŏng sa sinyu*) (ibid.: 8.690). In a less formal text describing the life of a private scholar, 1661 was rendered as "the *sinch'uk* year, the 34th year of Chongzhen" (*Sungjŏng samsipsa nyŏn sinch'uk*). Thereafter, the reference to Chongzhen was omitted; thus 1785 was inscribed as "the *ŭlsa* year, the 158th," while 1788 became "the *musin* year, the 161st."[29] Of note here is that the writings and books produced by nameless scholars living in rural areas frequently bore this kind of time inscription.

One wonders what the significance of the ubiquity and duration of

Ming time inscription is. It appears that, in the beginning, it signified conscious resistance to the new China, based on the Korean view of the Qing as illegitimate usurpers. But over many years, Ming inscription appears to have changed in its signification. It no longer symbolized Ming loyalism or nostalgia for a bygone age. By inscribing the present with a signifier of the past, Koreans were constructing a separate temporal universe paralleling that of the contemporary China. The convolutedness of Ming time inscription underscored the defunct status of China-past and the illegitimacy of China-present. It highlighted the central and unique role that Chosŏn Korea had come to play as the carrier of civilization. Interestingly, as were the sacrifices to the three Ming emperors, Ming time inscription was a Korean appropriation of Ming authority and tradition for the purpose of constructing a separate non-Chinese temporal and cultural universe.

Alternative Time Inscription

Koreans also employed modes of inscribing the present that did not involve the use of Chinese political time signifiers, either past or present. There were mainly two usages: one according to the reign year of the Korean king (e.g., the 3rd year of the present king), the other by unadorned sexagesimal dating. These modes of inscription were not considered complete, since their immediate comprehensibility was limited to the writer's contemporaries. When the inscription of the present was to mark a specific moment in the span of continuous time and thereby to historicize the present, this method did not suffice. Several questions can be raised about these modes of inscription. For instance: Did they become more common in the later Chosŏn period? How are we to interpret them?

The practice of sexagesimal inscription was neither new nor limited to Korea—it long had been in wide use in the rest of East Asia. One sometimes finds this usage in the paratextual space of "official" publications of an earlier period. The earliest Chosŏn edition of the *Samguk sagi*, for example, was dated with the sexagesimal year in its postscript: the *kapsul* year (1394) (*Samguk sagi:* 1.463). This was rather unusual. Most other official or semiofficial historiographical works published in the early Chosŏn period came with Ming reign titles: the *Koryŏsa* (History of Koryŏ), published in 1451, was inscribed Jingtai (*Koryŏsa* 1963: 1.12); the *Samguk yusa*, published in 1512, was inscribed Zhengde (*Samguk yusa:* 1.175). Nonetheless, it shows that even during early Chosŏn, sexagesimal dating was not confined to temporal inscriptions of a personal nature. This mode of dating, however, became conspicuously more prevalent in the later Chosŏn period. In view of the antiquity of these usages, one wonders whether the increased use was deliberate and whether it acquired a different meaning after the mid-seventeenth century.

Cursory examination suggests that, at least in some cases, these inscriptions were matters of deliberate choice. They seem to have been another marker of ideological division in the scholar-intellectual community. A scholar's life or writing was historicized after his death when descendants or students wrote about his life and collected his writings. The scholar's original writings, most often inscribed with sexagesimal years, were in this way given political time inscriptions, situating personal time within history. Of interest in this practice is inscription by the Korean king's reign year. In referring to 1856, one scholar used "*pyŏngjin*, the 7th year of Our Sagacious King" (*sŏngsang ch'ilnyŏn pyŏngjin*); another scholar used "the 10th year of the king" (*sang chi sipnyŏn*) in referring to 1844.[30] This "nationalization" of the present appears to have begun in the later Chosŏn period and to have become common thereafter. Although this practice deserves a more extensive investigation, I have not found it before the eighteenth century. It is tempting to view the prevalence of inscriptions referring to "Our Sagacious King" as an emergent consciousness of national identity. This mode of inscribing time occasionally was used in conjunction with the Ming reign title but very seldom with the Qing reign title. In fact, it is difficult to find inscriptions of Qing reign titles except in official publications.

Most intriguing, however, are the texts or publications that do not bear political time inscriptions. To cite an example, the *T'aengni chi*, a famous eighteenth-century human geography by Yi Chunghwan, bears sexagesimal dating not only in the author's own postscript, but also in those by later scholars (Yi 1999: 202–207). This dating can be interpreted as a subversive use of paratextual space. Writings by Hŏ Mok (1595–1682), Yun Hyu (1617–1680), Yi Ik (1681–1763), and Chŏng Yagyong (1762–1836) are also in this mode. Yun and Hŏ were seventeenth-century scholars who were opposed to the Sŏin faction's Zhu Xi supremacism, while Yi and Chŏng were scholars of the practical-learning school who, in their construction of the world order, rejected the long-established binary opposition of the civilized and the barbarous, and searched for a different episteme. One can argue that these scholars rejected not only the legitimacy of the Qing but the sinocentric world order itself. To replace its absoluteness and hierarchy, they seem to have searched for a framework that would allow for the autonomy of different societies.

The difficulty of interpreting these scholars' publications is that we must base our analysis on the absence of political time inscription rather than on the presence of signs. Why did the descendants and students of these scholars leave their writings unhistoricized? Inasmuch as this contravened the prevalent practice of the time, it should be read as a deliberate gesture. In some cases, these scholars remained unhistoricized because their writings were not published until the modern era. Yun Hyu's collected writings, for example, were not published until 1973.[31] However, even if their marginalized status precluded historicization, we can still see them as constituting an alternative tradition.

There also appeared what can be construed as an even more subversive use of paratextual space. Sometimes certain "popular" texts eschewed temporal inscriptions altogether. Kim Sohaeng's *Samhan sŭbyu* (Remains and fragments from the Three Hans), a late-seventeenth- or early-eighteenth-century historical Daoist novel and thus a completely nonofficial text, for example, bears no dating in paratexts except at the end, where the author's abbreviated vitae are given. His dates of birth and death are indicated in sexagesimal dating combined with Korean kings' reign years: the *ŭryu* year of Yŏngjo's reign (1765) and the *kimi* year of Ch'ŏlchong's reign (1859), respectively. The popularity and meaning of date omission, however, remains to be further investigated.

In this connection, let me briefly consider gendered time inscription. Women used sexagesimal years to inscribe time, and in their letters they used even smaller units of time, such as the 12th day of the 6th month.[32] This was also true of men, but sometimes men also used political time inscription in their personal writings. In a letter to his child written in Korean in 1603, King Sŏnjo (r. 1567–1608), for example, used the Ming reign title (Kim Ilgŭn 1986: 259). Women not only eschewed the use of political time inscription, they were far less frequently historicized by their descendants. Those who received historicization did so through illustrious male descendants who wrote some form of necrology. Thus, it was their lives, lived as members of a particular family, rather than their writings that were historicized. Their writings were seldom published and thus remained in the sphere of personal time: unhistoricized, they were also unpoliticized.

How to interpret plain sexagesmal inscription among Koreans remains a daunting question, since properly it requires comparison with this practice in other East Asian cultures—a task beyond the scope of this essay. If plain sexagesimal inscription was a deliberate alternative to inscription in political time, as it seems to have been in some Korean cases, should we see this as a desire to historicize the self in nonpolitical time or as something more neutral? Does this signify the emergence of a different, more autonomous concept of the person and his or her relationship to society and the cosmos? If so, this could have been a significant expression of a subversive temperament. Even if use of plain sexagesimal inscription was not a deliberate act, the existence and perpetuation of unpoliticized time inscription evinced an alternative consciousness of time, albeit one underarticulated and almost invisible.

Concluding Remarks

There were multiple spheres of time conceptualization and inscription in premodern Korea—personal, cosmic, and historical. It appears that changes in concepts of time were manifested mostly through views on how these different spheres of time—especially the personal and the historical—were related. From the mid-seventeenth century onward, there appears to have been an extensive examination of this relationship.

One of the ways in which the Chinese imperium maintained the sinocentric world order was by occupying temporal space. When the Silla accepted being a tributary state to Tang China, it was by entering the temporal universe defined by China. Thus, Chinese hegemony was transformed from the conquest of space to that of time. How Koreans perceived their relationship with China was a major ingredient in their sense of identity. At no time was this more evident than when the Ming dynasty was replaced by the Qing and Chosŏn Korea was forced to redefine its cultural and political identity by revising the way in which it viewed past and present China. As Koreans redrew the imaginary map of civilization and barbarity, they also had to reconfigure temporal space. Thus, time inscription became a site for expressing both political ideology and meaning in history. It also seems to have been a signifier for gender.

The difficulties involved in reading meanings in historical discourse, however, are not confined to decoding signs that are explicit and obvious. In post-Ming Korea, the rituals of sacrifice to the three Ming emperors and the continued use of the Chongzhen reign title, unprecedented and conspicuous, resonate with obvious meaning. But the difficulties lie in interpreting the less articulated, less obvious markers. Incomplete dating—plain sexagesimal inscription and dating only with a certain year of "Our Sagacious King"—provides cases in point. Since sexagesimal dating had been in use for a long time, should we view it as ordinary and without specific meaning? Undoubtedly, many dates inscribed in the incomplete mode fall into this category. And what about the apparently new practice of nationalizing the present? In some cases, this was done in conjunction with, rather than in contradistinction to, Ming time inscription.

As different modes of inscribing time became more widely practiced, none was seen as the correct mode: one's mode of temporal inscription became a choice. In this sense, when sexagesimal dating and a nationalized present were used independently, each seems to have signified a hidden discourse in search of alternatives. We now can see their meaning only through a glass darkly; it remains elusive, as contemplations of time frequently prove to be.

Notes

1. Parallel activities to "decenter" China recurred in late-nineteenth-century Korea. See Schmid 2000.

2. For the Chinese emperor's ritual activities of this nature, see Aveni 1989: 313.

3. I am indebted to Jack Goldstone for drawing my attention to a distinction between currency and commodity.

4. See "Yŏnp'yo," in *Samguk sagi* 1977: I, 288–295 (*kwŏn* 30).

5. Ibid. The second reign title, Kaeguk, was adopted in 551, the 12th year of King Chinhŭng; the third, Taech'ang, in 568, Chinhŭng's 29th year; the fourth, Hongje, in 572, Chinhŭng's 33rd year; the fifth, Kŏnbok, in 584, King Chinp'yŏng's 6th year; the sixth, Inp'yŏng, in 634, Queen Sŏndŏk's 3rd year; the seventh, T'aehwa, in 647, Queen Chindŏk's 1st year (*Samguk sagi*

1977). See also the record of these reign titles in the *Samguk yusa* 1972: 14–17.

6. Chinese emperors sometimes adopted more than one reign title. In fact, they frequently did so before the Yuan dynasty. In the case of Korea, rulers usually continued to use the reign title that was in effect when they acceded to the throne.

7. The stele of King Kwanggaet'o of Koguryŏ, for instance, bears the inscription "5th year of Yŏngnak [395 CE]," which might indicate his reign title. Pak 2000: 174.

8. Subsequently, the calendar the Koreans used contained minor variations, at times, from the Chinese. Pak 2000: 175–178.

9. Because the Mongols did not directly rule Korea, as they did China, and kept the structures of the Koryŏ state intact under the Wang royal family, Korean historians characterize this period as the "time of foreign interference."

10. The Chinese even historicized their mythical time. See Aveni 1989: 311–313.

11. See the entry on Kwŏn Sangha in the *sillok* at the time of his death, *Kyŏngjong sujŏng sillok:* 2.17a.

12. For details of these rituals, see the *Hwayang chi,* in Song 1985: VIII, 603–690.

13. Ban Gu 1995: II, 1657–1658. I am grateful to Professor Gari Ledyard for identifying this passage.

14. For the complete history of Hwayangdong, including the Mandongmyo and the academy, see the *Hwayang chi,* in Song 1985.

15. The sacrificial rites of the Chosŏn court were divided into three categories: great offerings, medium offerings (*chungsa*), and lesser offerings (*sosa*). The great offerings included regular sacrifices at the Yi Ancestral Temple (Chongmyo) and the Altar of Land and Grain (Sajiktan). See Haboush 1988: 36.

16. For a discussion of the appropriate relationship between ritual and principle, and the blending of Chinese and Korean ritual protocols, see SS: 43.8b.

17. For a discussion of Yŏngjo's use of symbols, see Haboush 1988: 29–82.

18. For a discussion of the historical symbolism of Kija, see Han 1985.

19. Haboush 1988: 42; YS: 69.25a–26b. Incense and paper money were burned in ancestral sacrifices.

20. That is, 1728, 360 years after 1368, when the Ming dynasty was founded.

21. The way I use "personal" time here is different from Eviatar Zeru-

bavel's use of "private" time. For his discussion of private time and public time, see Zerubavel 1981: 138–166.

22. On Chinese concepts of linear time, which were shared by Koreans, see Needham 1981; and Fraser 1990: 39–41.

23. For a discussion of the Chinese emperor's dual roles, see Wechsler 1985.

24. Kwangjong, for instance, instituted a civil service examination system, overriding intense opposition from the aristocracy (Kang 1974).

25. Wŏnjong (r. 1260–1274) was the last Koryŏ king to receive a temple name ending with *jong*. He was succeeded by Ch'ungnyŏl-wang (r. 1274–1308).

26. See the preface by Sŏ Kŏjŏng to the *Kyŏngguk taejŏn* (1962: 3, 6).

27. See the entries in *Yukchŏn chorye* 1966, *Sugyo chipnok, sasong yuch'wi* 1964, and *Sugyo chŏngnye, yullye yoram* 1970. The entries are the 10th year of Injo (*imsin*), the 37th year of Yŏngjo (*sinsa*), and so on.

28. Hwayang was where the Mandongmyo was located.

29. *Kim Ch'ungjang kong yusa* 1843: 2.14; 2.19; 2.20. The scholar concerned here is Kim Tŏngnyŏng.

30. These appear in the 1904 edition of the *Sarye p'yŏnnam,* a book on the four life-cycle rituals compiled by Yi Chae (1680–1746). See in particular Cho Inyŏng's postscript from an 1844 edition.

31. See Yun 1973. As far as I know, this was the first time the collection was published.

32. For examples, see the letters contained in Kim Ilgŭn 1986: 180–331.

References

Aveni, Anthony F. 1989. *Empires of Time: Calendars, Clocks and Cultures.* New York: Basic Books.

Ban Gu 班固. 1995. *Hanshu* 漢書. 4 vols. In *Ershisi shi* 二十四史, vols. 4–7. Beijing: Zhonghua shuju.

Ch'oe, Yong-ho. 1999. "Private Academies and the State in Late Chosŏn Korea." In *Culture and the State in Late Chosŏn Korea,* ed. JaHyun Kim Haboush and Martina Deuchler, 15–45. Cambridge: Harvard University Asia Center.

Chosŏn wangjo sillok 朝鮮王朝實錄. 1955–1958. 48 vols. Rpt. Seoul: Kuksa p'yŏnch'an wiwŏnhoe.

Chun, Hae-jong. 1968. "Sino-Korean Tributary Relations in the Ch'ing Period." In *The Chinese World Order,* ed. John K. Fairbank, 90–111. Cambridge: Harvard University Press.

Crossley, Pamela Kyle. 1999. *A Translucent Mirror: History and Identity in Qing Imperial Ideology.* Berkeley: University of California Press.

Deuchler, Martina. 1992. *The Confucian Transformation of Korea: A Study of Society and Ideology.* Cambridge: Council on East Asian Studies of Harvard University.

Fraser, J. T. 1990. *Of Time, Passion, and Knowledge.* 2nd ed. Princeton: Princeton University Press.

Genette, Gerard. 1997. *Paratexts: Thresholds of Interpretation.* Cambridge: Cambridge University Press.

Haboush, JaHyun Kim. 1988. *A Heritage of Kings: One Man's Monarchy in the Confucian World.* New York: Columbia University Press.

————. 1999. "Constructing the Center: The Ritual Controversy and the Search for a New Identity in Seventeenth-Century Korea." In *Culture and the State in Late Chosŏn Korea,* ed. Haboush and Martina Deuchler, 46–90. Cambridge: Harvard University Asia Center.

Han Young-woo. 1985. "Kija Worship in the Koryŏ and Early Yi Dynasties: A Cultural Symbol in the Relationship between Korea and China." In *The Rise of Neo-Confucianism in Korea,* ed. Wm. Theodore de Bary and JaHyun Kim Haboush, 349–374. New York: Columbia University Press.

Kang, Hugh. 1974. "Institutional Borrowing: The Case of the Chinese Civil Service Examination in Early Koryŏ." *Journal of Asian Studies* 34.1 (Nov.): 109–125.

Kim Ilgŭn 金一根. 1986. *Ŏn'gan ŭi yŏn'gu* 諺蕳의 研究. Seoul: Kŏn'guk taehak-kyo ch'ulp'anbu.

Kim Ch'ungjang kong yusa 金忠壯公遺事. 1843. Kwangju.

Koryŏsa 高麗史. 1963. Ed. Kim Chonggwŏn 金鍾權. Seoul: Pŏmjosa.

Kyŏngguk taejŏn 經國大典. 1962. 2 vols. Seoul: Pŏpchech'ŏ.

Kyŏngjong sujŏng sillok 景宗修正實錄. 1955–1958. In *Chosŏn wangjo sillok,* vol. 41.

Ledyard, Gari. 1988–1989. "Confucianism and War: The Korean Security Crisis of 1598." *Journal of Korean Studies* 6: 81–119.

Needham, Joseph. 1981. "Time and Knowledge in China and the West." In *The Voices of Time,* ed. J. T. Fraser, 92–135. 2nd ed. Amherst: University of Massachusetts Press.

Pak, Songnae 박성내. 2000. "Han'guk chŏn'kŭndae yŏksa wa sigan" 한국전근대역사와시간. *Yŏksa pip'yŏng* 여사비평 50: 171–183.

Rogers, Michael. 1983. "Medieval National Consciousness in Korea: The Impact of Liao and Chin in Koryŏ." In *China among Equals: The Middle Kingdon and Its Neighbors, 10th–14th Centuries,* ed. Morris Rossabi, 151–172. Berkeley: University of California Press.

Samguk sagi 三國史紀. 1977. Ed. Yi Pyŏngdo. 2 vols. Seoul: Ŭryu munhwasa.

Samguk yusa 三國遺史. 1972. Ed. Yi Pyŏngdo. Seoul: Kwangjo ch'ulp'ansa.

Sarye p'yŏnnam 四禮便覽. 1904. Comp. Yi Chae 李縡. Privately published, apparently by the family of Cho Inyŏng 趙寅永 (1680–1746), retaining prefaces and postscripts from successive nineteenth-century editions.

Schmid, Andre. 2000. "Decentering the 'Middle Kingdom': The Problem of China in Korean Nationalist Thought, 1895–1910." In *Nation Works*, ed. Barbara Brooks and Andre Schmid, 83–107. Ann Arbor: University of Michigan Press.

Sok taejŏn 續大典. 1964. Seoul: Pŏpchech'ŏ.

Song Siyŏl 宋時烈. 1985. *Songja taejŏn* 宋子大典. 8 vols. Seoul: Pogyŏng munhwasa.

SS. *Sukchong sillok* 肅宗實錄. 1955–1958. In *Chosŏn wangjo sillok*, vols. 38–41.

Sugyo chipnok, sasong yuch'wi 授教輯錄, 詞訟類聚. 1964. Seoul: Pŏpchech'ŏ.

Sugyo chŏngnye, yullye yoram 授教定例, 律例要覽. 1970. Seoul: Pŏpchech'ŏ.

Wechsler, Howard J. 1985. *Offerings of Jade and Silk: Ritual and Symbol in the Legitimation of the T'ang Dynasty*. New Haven: Yale University Press.

Yi Chunghwan 李重煥. 1999. *T'aengni chi* 擇里志. Seoul: Ŭryu munhwasa.

YS. *Yŏngjo sillok* 英祖實錄. 1955–1958. In *Chosŏn wangjo sillok*, vols. 41–44.

Yukchŏn chorye 六典條例. 1966. Seoul: Pŏpchech'ŏ.

Yun Hyu 尹鑴. 1973. *Paekho chŏnsŏ* 白湖全書. 3 vols. Taegu: Kyŏngbuk taehakkyo.

Zerubavel, Eviatar. 1981. *Hidden Rhythms*. Chicago: University of Chicago Press.

CHAPTER FOUR

Mongol Time Enters a Qing World

Johan Elverskog

ON THE AFTERNOON OF February 15, 1894, a powerful explosion ripped asunder the seeming tranquility of the Greenwich Observatory. The intention of Martial Bourdin, the twenty-six-year-old French anarchist who carried out this chronological terrorist attack, was never explained; it was generally seen as an act of complete madness, devoid of any ideological value. The novelist Joseph Conrad went so far as to proclaim that it was a "bloodstained inanity of so fatuous a kind that it was impossible to fathom its origin by any reasonable or even unreasonable process of thought," and he proceeded to write *The Secret Agent* on this very premise (Burnett 2000: 37–38). Comprehensible or not, the attack gave the British authorities an excuse to round up and deport foreign radicals and lower-class dissidents from the isle. But was this attack indeed beyond our comprehension?

Nowadays, the location of the prime meridian in Greenwich is generally taken for granted, a fact brought into consciousness perhaps most often through the worldwide broadcasts of the BBC and its six-pips time signal informing us of "Greenwich Mean Time." In 1894, however, the concept of Greenwich, England, being at the center of the world's spatiotemporal framework was relatively new. Only twelve years earlier, twenty-five delegates from different countries to the International Meridian Conference in Washington, D.C., had agreed on Greenwich as the location of the prime meridian. This choice was far from self-justifying. A Louisville newspaper asked why the United States should "concede to John Bull's dull Greenwich the position of time dictator? Now what is Greenwich to us? A dingy London suburb" (Burnett 2000: 44). Similarly, the French contingent argued the necessity for a scientific and specifically "nonnational" location for the line, certainly not one in the center of the British Empire. Instead, other "neutral" yet still meaningful sites were suggested: the top of the pyramids in Egypt, the island of Ferro, the summit of Teneriffe, the Bering Strait. Another group had earlier suggested, in view of medieval Christian cartography and eschatology, drawing the line through Jerusalem or Bethlehem. None of these was accepted, though the controversy reflects the difficulties inherent in mapping an abstract notion of time onto the reality of a world with competing centers.

The twenty-five delegates in Washington did not have to be familiar with the now large corpus of theoretical interpretations of time as a social reality—from Marx, Weber, and Durkheim to Bloch and Le Goff—to understand that control of time with its cultural implications entailed power. As is evident in our contemporary world, the Western construction and understanding of time is one, perhaps the most, effective framework for organizing society and human experience across cultural boundaries. And the importance of structuring and maintaining time for the purpose of creating communal identification was also not lost in the practice of ruling imperial China. A fundamental role of the emperor was to control the flow of time properly by creating the calendar and propitiating its cultural force through ritual and ceremony. This inclusion of time within the domain of imperial control made for a discursively powerful incorporation of state subjects within an "encompassed hierarchy" of rulership. The production and ritualization of imperial calendars linked the emperor and the people of the realm in a relationship intended to "include them [the people] in a whole that embodied simultaneously his [the emperor's] own power and their relative importance vis-à-vis that power.... This mode of social engagement ... acts not to overcome Others by force but to include them in its own project of rulership" (Zito 1997: 29).

As a result, the Chinese imperial production of time and its manifestation in the polity through ritual and ceremony needs to be recognized as an important facet of statecraft operations. In interpretations of Asian polities—most notably in Stanley Tambiah's idea of the "galactic polity" (1976) and Ronald Inden's of the "imperial formation" (1990)—the state is basically defined as a symbolic and ritual entity, which ultimately is framed within a discourse of time. The production of a communal identification, which entails a chronological and cosmological framework, is embedded in the rituals of the nation and its production of "ritualized agents" inscribed with the national identity. The internalization of these narratives occurs through engagement with these rituals. Because the dominant imperial rituals become accepted by communities as coherent structures of identity, and because they engender in individuals a sense of "personal empowerment in accordance with what that agent regards as his or her goals and intentions, the process of ritualization is generally not experienced as a coercive technique for social conformity" (Trainor 1997: 138–139). The power of rituals in the formation of the state and its attendant constructions of identity and chronology is such that they "do not function to regulate or control the system of social relations, they *are* the system" (Bell 1992: 130). While this theoretical interpretation offers a framework within which to explore the creation of an encompassed hierarchy of identity and time, one still needs to examine that creation as something that occurred within a certain passage of time. In other words, the importance of ritualizing the nation in shaping identity and its attendant conceptions of time is not in doubt, but a further question is how such ritualization is internalized and negotiated over time. Does a new dynasty become "the system" almost immediately, or is there an extended period of contestation when differing narratives and representations are employed?

While the answer I intend to offer to this question may seem evident from its phrasing, we should emphasize that the theoretical model outlined above tends to be temporally static and, thus, does not fully engage such a question. It accords with the dynastic master narrative but obscures other historical processes. Occluded is the important question of what happened in the interstice of the Ming and Qing "systems" when dynastic time was suspended and contested. As is readily evident in the essay by Haboush on Korean resistance to the Qing through ritual and temporal inscription, the Qing system did not go unchallenged. Analogously, the standard presentation of the Mongol submission to the Qing as a near inevitability through the Manchus' adoption of a Buddhist structure of legitimacy is widely accepted without much critical analysis. Because Ligdan Khan (r. 1604–1634) had been recognized as the Daiyuwan (Ch. Daiyuan) Khan by a Tibetan lama, it is taken for granted that the Manchus could therefore simply project themselves as Buddhist Cakravartins and the Mongols would cordially accept Qing rule. This idea has become entrenched in our understanding of the incorporation of the Mongols within the Qing imperium: by adopting the "well-established" Buddhist principle of fusing religion and state (Mo. *qoyar yosu*), the Manchus were able to conquer and control the Mongols. In other words, simply by being Buddhist patrons, the Manchu emperors could re-create themselves as Chinggis or Khubilai Khan, thereby claiming legitimacy as the proper rulers of the Mongol nation. But was the matter that simple?

We need to recall that the authority ritualized through the bestowal of rank by a Tibetan hierarch in the seventeenth century was a relationship that lay outside any Manchu ruler's control. At the time, the Tibetans and large groups of Mongol and Oirad peoples were not incorporated within the Manchu dominions, as they would come to be by the end of the reign of that well-known Buddhist Cakravartin, the Qianlong emperor. Before his rule, Tibetan hierarchs, the Great Fifth Dalai Lama in particular, were an independent and international source of legitimate power within the Oirad and Mongol realms as well as within that of the Manchu emperor. None of the recognized relations of Buddhist imperial legitimacy created a single hierarchy wherein any one of those realms was incorporated by any of the others. An analogy can be drawn with the Roman Catholic Church's endowment of emergent European nations with a theory of sovereignty and bestowal of legitimacy "without at the same time obliging them to achieve a universalizing empire." This was possible, according to Duara, "because of the separation of temporal from spiritual authority or, in other words, the source of legitimacy from actual exercise of power" (1995: 70). Thus, the Mongol, Oirad, and Manchu leaders were fundamentally equal in being recognized as the rulers of their respective nations within a Buddhist discourse based exclusively on the ritualized authority of Tibet. The reality of this international leveling of legitimacy is evident in the Dalai Lama's investiture and bestowal of seals upon Mongol and Oirad rulers during the seventeenth and early eighteenth centuries. If the Manchu emperors were the legitimately recognized universal rulers, then their power ought to have superseded the others, but in truth it was only after the Dalai Lama recognized a Mongol ruler that, in response, the Qing reconfirmed the bestowal of title (Ishihama 1992). Thus, Buddhist patronage gave the Manchus no inherent authority on an international level, still less on a local level. If the Dalai Lama recognized the Manchu emperor as a Cakravartin or an incarnation of Mañjuśrī, he received no more authority than Galdan of the Oirad received as the Boshugtu Khan, the incarnation of the first Tibetan Buddhist emperor Srong bstan sgam po.

In the master narrative of the Qing, however, this reality invariably has been suppressed, and unfortunately, its uncritical acceptance has colored all subsequent scholarly representation of Mongol incorporation into the Qing order. This narrative also has instilled a static or reified notion of Buddhism—easily grafted onto the concept of a Qing "Great Enterprise"—a Buddhism the adoption of which straightaway produced legitimacy and hegemony for the Qing. As noted above, Buddhist religiopolitical relationships were multiple. Moreover, other factors need to be explored, especially how the narratives and rituals of the Qing succeeded in transforming the boundaries of Mongol communal identification—in particular, how the Mongols of a Mongol nation became inscribed as Mongols-of-the-Qing.

Numerous aspects of this transformation need to be explored in order to understand it fully, but the representation of time during that period of change is particularly revealing. As the Meridian conference delegates, the Chinese emperors, and Martial Bourdin all knew, the control of time and its refraction in the creation of identity is of paramount importance. Thus, an investigation of Mongolian sources and their shifting narratives—that is, temporalities—from pre-Qing to Qing allows us to reenvision the Mongol response to the Manchu conquest, especially in terms of Mongol perceptions of time and space. By elucidating a small segment of the arena of contestation that was the Qing formation, that segment in which time was negotiated, we can bring back to memory a time that the Qing and its narrative wished to forget.

A Nation in Two Times

One of the standard requirements in a nationalist enterprise is to prove its ideological claim that the nation being created has always existed. If the process of narrativization is successful, with its transformation of the historical narrative and its remapping of time, the desired nation can be forged. Of course, such re-presentations can be challenged, and the modern world is perpetually filled with fervent counter-formulations of ethnic, cultural, and national histories aimed at "exposing" or "demythologizing" prospective national monologues.

Many times, however, the new narratives acquire legitimacy and inherently function to shape the new conceptions of national identity.

In the case of the Mongol submission to the Manchus, the Qing narrative of Buddhist imperial rule was so successful that it has been carried into the discourse of the twenty-first century. It is, succinctly put, that the Manchus adopted a Mongolian form of Buddhist religiopolitical rule and therefore initiated relations with Tibetan Buddhist hierarchs, producing legitimacy for themselves in the images of Chinggis and Khubilai Khan. In this way they produced an encompassed hierarchy, in which the Mongols accepted Manchu hegemony because the Manchus had appropriated a discourse of rule with which they were familiar. As Angela Zito notes in her study of Qing imperial ritual, "The throne's relations with its Mongol and Tibetan subjects proceeded in the idiom of Buddhist practice" (1997: 23).

Although this cannot be denied, can one readily assume that from the first submission of the Mongols to their complete incorporation within the Qing there was a straight, full-scale, reduplicative transfer of the rituals and narratives of legitimacy from an independent Mongol people to the Qing imperial state? More important, why should we think that such a reduplication secured the submission of the Mongols, since we know that the Khalkhas and Oirads, both Buddhist, did not submit? Actually, the "Buddhist practice" that is thought to have been adopted from the Mongols by the Manchus was being created as the Mongols submitted. This process is hard to recognize because the sources that have shaped the post-Qing understanding of this development were all written during the Qing and present a linear history that conforms with the narrativization and ritualization of the Qing. Thus, we must question how the rituals and narratives of the Mongol-Buddhist nation were transformed to coincide with the Buddhist-Qing dynasty's mythic structures of legitimacy.

If we look at the pre-Qing Mongolian sources, we find that they constitute totalizing representations of a Mongol nation, ritualized through a Buddhist discourse and headed by various members of the Borjigid nobility, who traced their ancestry from Chinggis Khan. But what happens when the Mongol nation is made part of the Manchu-Qing empire? How are the narratives of communal identification represented in order to create the boundaries of the new community, and what is the impact of this representation on the national boundaries of time? The standard Qing narratives and their refractions in modern studies allow no gap in the cultural logic of the Mongols between the pre-Qing and Qing states of affairs. Yet, precisely because we are presented with a seamless, coherent picture of an interval that had profound social consequences, we must question the narrative.

The histories written after the advent of the Qing were intended to generate a cohesive narrative that held in suspense the Mongols' previous independent history and what in fact had been their submission to the Manchus. A fundamental aim of those histories was to engage in the formation and reproduction of socialized beings, in this case Mongols-of-the-Qing, which entailed creating shared realities that transcended the immediate context (Comaroff 1994: 304–305). Such "shared realities," or totalizing representations, create a nation with its inherent national identity through narratives and rituals of community, usually in the medium of political authority. Therefore we need to reevaluate the dominant narrative as found in Qing sources in order to enhance our understanding of the process of becoming a part of the Qing. In particular, we need to examine the different narratives and strategies deployed between the period of the independent Mongol nation and that of the Qing-created linear trajectory, focusing our attention on the nation in time.

A logical place to start this excavation is at "the sanctification of the starting point," to borrow Adrian Hastings' phrase from his study of Christianity's effects on national formations (1997: 187–190). In the case of the Mongols, Buddhism was first introduced during the reign of Chinggis Khan, but it was not given credence until the Mongol Prince Köden, in his attempt to conquer Tibet, invited Sa skya Paṇḍita to meet with him in 1247 (Wylie 1977). This was followed by the visit of the Bka' brgyud lama Karma Pakshi to the court of Möngke Khan. Subsequently, the influence of Tibetan Buddhism among the Mongol elite flourished and reached its apogee during the reign of Khubilai Khan, who established an important relationship with Sa skya Paṇḍita's nephew, 'Phags pa Lama (Petech 1993). Throughout the Yuan dynasty, the Mongols continued to support and be interested in Tibetan Buddhism and developed relations with all the major Tibetan schools. After the fall of the Yuan, however, the presence of Buddhism among the Mongols waned, though it never fully disappeared (Serruys 1962). A turnabout then occurred in the 1570s, when Altan Khan (1507–1582), the most powerful ruler on the Mongolian plateau, grew increasingly interested in Buddhism and eventually invited the Third Dalai Lama to meet him near Lake Kökenuur in 1578 (see Map 1). After that, Bud-

dhism again became a fundamental element in the representation of
the Mongol nation.

As has been shown in the construction of narratives for religions in
which group conversion is formative, histories of the conversion process are produced to define the newness of the religious community
or nation. A fundamental aspect of these narratives is the representation of the group's ethnogenesis, wherein there is a fusion of the legendary founder of the group with the new religion. Among the Mongols, this is evident in the well-known link made between Chinggis
Khan and the Sa skya Lama Kun dga' snying po. Although modern
scholarship has shown that Kun dga' snying po died before Chinggis
Khan was born (Ratchnevsky 1954), the fiction played a vital role in
creating a powerfully linear narrative of the Mongol-Buddhist nation.
It is clear in the rhetorical structure of all pre-Qing Mongol sources
that the Mongol nation began with Chinggis Khan and his conversion
to Buddhism.

Yet in all the Qing-period Mongolian chronicles, the starting sanctification point of the Mongol nation shifts. Instead of seeing themselves as originating with Chinggis Khan, the Mongols then imagined
their genealogy as stretching back to India. While this representation
often is regarded as reflecting the Mongols' sincere adoption of a Buddhist identity, in none of the pre-Qing sources is such a connection
made. Instead the sanctified community is understood to be solely
Mongols and thus begins with Chinggis Khan. This fact is corrobo-
rated in Cogtu Taiji's inscription written expressly for Ligdan Khan,
his ally and head of the Mongol nation, wherein the nation is defined
in terms of the Buddhist pantheon and the divinely blessed Borjigid
lineage.

> Homage to Samantabhadra and Amitabha and the Buddha
>   Sakyamuni.
> Homage to Hevajra and Mother Varahi and Vajrapani.
> Homage to Heaven the Superior, to the emperor and empress, and
>   to all benevolent people....

> By the order of Cogtu, Prince of Khalkha, offspring of Chinggis Khan
> and grandson of Emperor Ocir, this was, for the Holy Emperor of
> the Mongols [Ligdan Khan], written on the rock like a gem of jade
> by Page Daicing and Güyeng the Valiant on the great white day, the
> 15th of the fire-tiger month, which is the first of the months [cycle],

in the wood-mouse year [1624], which is the first of the years [cycle],
when 464 years had elapsed since the water-ox year [1160] in which
Chinggis Khan was born.[1]

In this inscription there is no attempt to link the Mongols to anything
beyond the temporal boundaries of Chinggis Khan's initial formation
of the Mongol nation.

The same temporal structure is also found in a recently published
early history of Chinggis Khan, the *Cinggis qagan-u altan tobci ner-e-tü
cadig* ([History entitled the] golden summary of Chinggis Khan), in
which the standard Qing-period Buddhist genealogy is absent.[2] Instead
of providing an extensive history and genealogy of the Mongols
stretching back to India and Tibet as found in Qing-period sources,
this early source recognizes the history of the Mongols as originating
with Chinggis Khan. Similarly, a stele inscription of 1594 from Olon
Süme in Inner Mongolia, which briefly describes the history of Buddhism among the Mongols and its vicissitudes, also notes that Buddhism begins with Chinggis Khan. "From among the descendants of
Genius Chinggis Khan for fifteen generations the Buddha Dharma
was built. After this enlightened age, the ocean of Chinese subjects destroyed the jewel of the peaceful Great Yuan ... [until] Supreme Altan
Khan invited the Limitless Ocean Majesty" (Heissig 1966: 9). In this
narrative there is a coupling of Chinggis Khan with the creation of
the Mongol-Buddhist nation. This also occurs in the opening passage
of the longest extant pre-Qing Mongolian history, a biography of
Altan Khan and his descendants, the *Erdeni tunumal neretü sudur orosiba*
(Jewel translucent sutra), in which Chinggis Khan, the founder of the
Mongol nation, is also the initial propagator of the Mongol-Buddhist
nation.

> Born by the fate of the Supreme God,
> Creating the supreme customs of the state from its beginning,
> Causing all those of the world to enter his power,
> Temüjin became famous as Genius Chinggis Khan.

> He caused the Five-Colored Nations to enter his power,
> Miraculously set into order the world's customs of state,
> And invited Kun dga' snying po the Supreme Sa skya Lama.
> He was the first to propagate the Buddha's Dharma.
>
> (Elverskog 2003: 63–64)

In none of these narratives is any genealogical link inserted within the larger Buddhist continuum; they exclusively narrativize the Mongol nation. A similar description is found in the Chagan Baishing (White House) inscription commemorating the building of monasteries at Prince Cogtu's city, in which Chinggis Khan is said to have been born purely on account of the accumulation of his own Buddhist merit. There is no appropriation of other genealogies, and Mongol history and nation begin with this narrative of Buddhist ethnogenesis:

> Having accumulated an enormous amount of merit
> Through endless kalpas,
> [Chinggis Khan] was born miraculously in this great Mongol land
> And became the khan of the ten directions.
>
> (Huth 1894: 31)

Genealogical links between India, Tibet, and Mongolia are found, however, in all the seventeenth-century Mongol chronicles written after the Manchu conquest. In these works the "ancestral figure of Börte Cino—the 'blue-grey wolf' named as Chinggis Khan's first ancestor in the thirteenth-century *Secret History*—was transformed into a Tibetan prince with [genealogical] links to the sacred centers of Buddhism in India" (DeWeese 1994: 443–444). As a result, in the course of the incorporation of the Mongol nation within the Buddhist discourse of the Manchu empire, Chinggis Khan's role as the initiator of the Mongol Buddhist nation was denationalized. Instead, he was understood as a Buddhist ruler within a universal continuum.

In a certain sense, one can argue that the creation of the Qing empire and its incorporation of the Mongol nation worked in a reverse manner to the collapse of the Holy Roman Empire. The Holy Roman Emperor's legitimacy to rule over a multiethnic Christian world rested on links to Constantine and the ideal of universal Christian rule. However, with the empire's collapse, different groups appropriated the same discourse while producing different narratives. Thus, the French traced their descent as a collectivity from the baptism of Clovis at Reims by St. Remigus in 496. In the case of the Qing, this process occurs in the opposite direction. No longer is Chinggis Khan the founder of the Mongol-Buddhist nation; rather, he becomes but one transnational avatar of a Buddhist ideal within a Buddhist cosmological continuum.

The inception of this temporal shift in the origins of the Mongol nation is unclear, but it certainly draws on the Tibetan historical tradition wherein the three Buddhist groups—Indians, Tibetans, and Mongols—are presented as consecutively but not actually linked genealogically, as in 'Phags pa Lama's *Shes bya rab gsal* (What is to be known). This format is also found in Shireetü Güüsi's early-seventeenth-century compilation the *Ciqula kerelegci* (What is to be known). But only in the Qing-period Mongol histories are the Mongol khans portrayed within a genealogy originating with the first Buddhist ruler Mahasammata—then come the Cakravartins of Tibet, then Chinggis Khan in Mongolia, culminating with the Manchu emperor. Although this universalizing Buddhist discourse may seem to be inherent to the "Lamaist-Caesaropapist" model, it is important to recognize that this temporal transformation in the origins of the nation was historically tied to a form of Buddhist rule institutionalized by the Manchus and to the creation of a new Mongol identity that was related not to the independent Mongol-Buddhist nation but to the Manchu-Buddhist empire.

The Mongol nation as an integral part of the Qing order was forged through this reformulation of the Mongols' conception of time and origins. During the Qing period, Mongol authors recognized themselves, and presumably all Mongols, as being situated firmly within the Qing narrative. And their national identity was seen as bound to that of the Qing empire, consistently referred to in Mongol sources as "Our Great Qing" (Mo. Manu yeke Cing). However, while this shifting of temporal boundaries dispersed, so to speak, the Mongol *nation* within the structure of the Manchu-Qing, the same cannot be said for conceptions of a distinct Mongol *identity,* an identity that was divorced from the independent Mongol nation but maintained boundaries of differentiation for the Mongols within the Qing.

Rather, a particular Mongol identity was reasserted through a similar temporal discourse. As Buddhism coalesced with the Qing, a new narrative that remythologized the Mongol-Buddhist past was produced among the Mongols. Whether or not this new appropriation of a primordial Mongol-Buddhist identity arose in relation to the eighteenth-century imperially sanctioned Manchu ethnicity project, a point that is unclear, the remythologization produced a new narrative for the Mongols. The first example of this narrative is found in the well-known *Rgya nag chos 'byung* (History of Buddhism in China; GC), written by Qing loyalist and Beijing resident Gombojab around 1740.[3] In this work, as implied in Gombojab's earlier *Gangga-yin urusqal* (Flow of the Ganges), the primordial nature of Mongol Buddhist history is reaffirmed through the use of Chinese historical materials.

In this endeavor, Gombojab makes a historiographical supposition that still resonates today, in both nationalist discourse and academic inquiry: all the nomadic peoples north of the Great Wall are identified historically as Mongol; more important, since the Han dynasty they have been Buddhist. The first evidence used to support this narrative is from the *Hanshu* (History of the Former Han), which records that a Chinese general saw at the court of the Xiongnu khan a statue of a "gold man" (Ch. *jinren*, T. *ston pa'i gser sku*), which is interpreted as having been a Buddha statue (GC: 37; see also AE: 74–75). This observation is followed by evidence culled from Tang-dynasty sources that record that an Indian monk, Prabhakaramitra (T. Pra'dza ka ra mi' tra), with ten companions, spread the Dharma in the north during the era of the Turk empires. The Turk ruler of Prabhakaramitra's day is identified in the Chinese sources as Tong Yehu Kehan, which enables Gombojab to argue that Yehu is a Chinese distortion of the Mongolian term *yeke*, "great," and that Kehan is "khan" (GC: 128). With the above suppositions, Gombojab brought plausibility to etymologies that purported to show that the Turk empire in fact had been Mongol. Gombojab also used the same idea in his later work on Xuanzang's travels to India, *Chen po Thang gur dus kyi Rgya kar zhing gi bkod pa'i kar chag bzhugs so* (Outline delineating the area of India in the time of the great Tang dynasty), based on Xuanzang's own *Xiyu ji*.[4] He similarly argued that the nomadic inhabitants of Inner Asia whom Xuanzang met were actually Mongols (Atwood 1992/1993: 19). In this way Gombojab, through historical and philological studies of Chinese sources, was able to generate a mythology of Mongol-Buddhist identity, which in turn was adopted in the *Bolur erike* (Crystal rosary) by Rasipungsug, who went so far as to say that the Mongols had existed and had fought the Chinese since the Zhou dynasty (BE: 8). While this new narrative generated prestige within the narrative of the multiethnic Buddhist-Qing, in that the Mongols could claim the longest Buddhist history, it did not challenge the current state of Mongol integration with the Qing. By blindsiding the past reality of an independent Mongol-Buddhist nation and its implications for what should be in the present, this vision reaffirmed Mongol-Buddhist identity through a new historical genealogy, one that did not challenge the multiethnic Buddhist-Qing narrative.

A similar phenomenon is found in Mergen Gegen's *Altan tobciya* (Golden summary) of 1765, which uses material from the Tibetan historical tradition rather than from Chinese sources. In two works on which the author drew, the *Deb ther Sngon po* (Blue annals) and the *Rgyal rabs Gsal ba'i Me long* (Clear mirror), it is recorded that during the reign of Glang darma in the mid-ninth century, three monks fled Tibet with scriptures in order to preserve the dharma from the king's persecution. While in neither of these sources do they flee to Mongolia, this idea is presented in Mergen Gegen's work.

> At the time when Tibet's [Glang]darma was destroying the religion, three monks, Mar Obogtu Sakyamuni Gelong, Wi Obogtu Buyandalai Gelong, and Chang Obogtu Geyigülügci Gelong, fled from Tibet. When they came, [the Mongols'] Tamaji Khan became a disciple and was named Sa skya Shes rab. Tamaji's twenty-first son, Qurca Mergen, became khan and received initiations and teachings from those lamas. While he was still on the throne, he became fully accomplished and attained magical powers. Finally, because he abandoned his body and flew into the sky, he became famous as an emanation of Padmasambhava. After having gone to and stayed in Mongolia, those three lamas went to a place called Sergüleng in Amdo. (ATMG: 57)

In the presentations of both Gombojab and Mergen Gegen, the Mongol nation and Mongol identity are no longer linked to the Ur-Mongol Chinggis Khan and the empire he created. Instead, Mongol identity is shaped through a new narrative that originates not in relation to the Mongol nation, but in relation to a lengthy history of pure Buddhism.

On the basis of this later narrative, which reaffirms Mongol identity within the parameters of the Qing narrative, it is evident that although Qing rule was not questioned, its powerful monologue of imperial rule was neither as all-encompassing nor as stationary as earlier studies have implied. From the above Mongol sources we can see that narratives of the Mongol nation and Mongol identity were often adjusted and readjusted in shaping new boundaries of communal identification. An important element in all of these was temporal spacing. It is clear that the "sanctified starting point," so efficacious in defining community, changed radically with the Qing formation. The representation of identity bound to the independent Mongol nation was transformed within the narrative of the Qing, and Mongol identity was reaffirmed through the setting of new temporal bounds within a Buddhist discourse. These changes in the Mongols' conceptions of time and their relation to it, with its confirmation of a Mongol temporality outside the Qing discourse, raises the question of how much effect the Qing imperial control of time had on the Mongols—put another way, did the Mongols live in Qing time?

Mongol Being-in-Time and Calendrical Inscription

Because imperial rule was tied to the control of time—through astronomy, astrology, and their ritualization in the imperial calendar—it can be imagined that the new imperial time would superscribe any preceding models. For it was through this project that a new meaning was imposed, in terms of both time and space, a meaning that emanated from the new centers of power. And from the narratives discussed above and the abundant evidence of Mongol support for the Manchu rulers throughout the Qing, it may also be easy to imagine that the Qing enterprise entailed a remapping of Mongolian concepts of time. In the case of the Mongols, the imperial calendar in question was tied to the Buddhist discourse that had generated the encompassed hierarchy of Qing rule. "Qing time" in this sense can perhaps be more aptly referred to as "Tibetan time" so far as Inner Asia is concerned, since the Dge lugs pa and their Buddhism had become the medium of discourse and identification.

Indeed, the success of relations between the Qing and the Dge lugs pa in maintaining rule among the Mongols is readily visible in the process of Tibetanization that occurred throughout the Qing. It is most notable in the Mongols' abandonment of their own language in favor of Tibetan as a liturgical language, even though the entire Buddhist canon had been translated into Mongolian. The success of this process and its cultural implications were never seriously questioned. Even when it was questioned by Mongol monks like Mergen Gegen— who, in the mid-eighteenth century, attempted to "reconstruct the model of Buddhism's relation to Mongolia, first by providing a rich array of [religious] services in the Mongolian language, and second by reinterpreting the relation of the Buddhist church with native religious powers"[5]—the process of Tibetanization proceeded unhindered. This is reflected in the fact that even though Mergen Gegen's four-volume Mongolian national liturgy was printed in Beijing in 1783 during the heady Qianlong reign (Heissig 1954: 151–154), it did not have any lasting impact. Only two monasteries within the Qing realm were recognized as using a ritual corpus in Mongolian, neither one of which included Mergen Gegen's liturgy. Rather, they used the work of the Beijing-connected First Lcang skya Khutugtu (Pozdneyev 1978). It was through the Manchu-sponsored Tibetan religious "language," broadly conceived, that Mongol identification with previous narratives and rituals ultimately was destroyed and the Mongols became entirely ritualized into melding their identity with Qing identity.

With this transformation of the Mongol world, new ritual and social networks based on new spatial and temporal orders were created, which broke previous patterns of Mongol identity. Through the replacement of earlier practices with ones bound to the imperial and Buddhist calendars and sacred sites, the Mongols were socialized as members of the Buddhist-Qing imperium.[6] The most striking example of the fusion of sacral praxis with the symbolism of Qing rule was the Mongols' religious fervor regarding Wutai Shan in Shanxi (see Map 1), the mountain revered for its connection with Mañjuśrī, whose manifestation was believed to be none other than the Manchu emperor. The Mongols' desire to be buried at that mountain reached such epic proportions that the Qing authorities eventually, in the nineteenth century, banned the burial at Wutai Shan of any Mongols other than local residents.[7]

Ironically, even though the early Manchu ruler Hong Taiji was privately contemptuous of the Mongols' adoption of Buddhism because it "vitiated their cultural identity" (Wakeman 1985: I, 203), in order that the rhetoric of Buddhist imperial rule be employed, Mongolian culture was fully reengineered within the Buddhist structure mandated by Qing rule. As outlined above, this involved the temporal respacing of the Mongol nation. Yet, as we also have seen in the Mongol narratives of ethnoreligious primordialization, the Mongols continued to assert a special identity within the Qing narrative by employing, yet simultaneously challenging, that same Qing temporal spacing of the Mongol nation. Time became an arena of contestation not only over the matter of community ethnogenesis, but also over the passage of time as demarcated by the calendar. One of the emperor's mandates was to regulate the calendar and, through its ritualizing force, shape the temporal conceptions of nation and community. But throughout the social and cultural upheavals of establishing and extending Qing rule—and the extensive process of Tibetanization this entailed—the Mongols persisted in living by Mongolian time.

Here, my discussion of "Mongolian time" is confined to the calendar system, particularly the ways in which the Mongols named the months and years and used them to mark time. This choice of focus is induced, first, by the lack of extensive Mongolian materials that deal directly with other aspects of time in Mongol culture and, second, by the importance of calendars in shaping the boundaries of communal identification. Just as the transnational celebration of Chinese New Year reinforces concepts of identity through temporal marking, so the acceptance or rejection of particular modes of time reckoning operates as a fulcrum on which tips differentiations of ethnicity and power. The persistent Mongolian avoidance of both the Tibetan and Sino-Manchu imperial systems of timekeeping reflects an effort to assert Mongol identity outside the Qing discourse.

In order to understand these developments during the Qing, it is necessary to outline the development of Mongolian calendrical usage and its relation to that of other traditions. The earliest recorded evidence is found in Zhao Gong's *Mengda beilu* (Complete record of the Mongol Tatars), a description of Zhao's trip among the Mongols in 1221. A Song-dynasty military commissioner of the Huaidong circuit, Jia She, had dispatched Zhao Gong to investigate the emerging Mongol threat and see whether a Song-Mongol rapprochement could be forged to defeat the Jurchen Jin state. One of the reasons for this project was that, although the Jurchen were understood to be "barbarians," over time the Jin order had become so Confucianized that it presented nearly a mirror image of the Song itself and therefore raised issues of Han-Chinese imperial legitimacy. The Mongols, in contrast, were completely beyond the pale of "civilization" and therefore supposedly could be coopted into the Song enterprise against the Jurchens. An important factor in Song considerations was the calendar, a fundamental symbol of Sino-imperial rule. In his report, Zhao Gong emphasizes that the Mongols did not possess a calendar of their own, that they only understood the passage of time by the "greening of the pastures." (This later became a standard trope in Chinese sources, reinforcing the notion that the Mongols were "backward" and "childlike.")

The present Emperor Chinggis was born in a *jiaxu* year [1154].
Originally in their customs they had no sexagesimal dating, so now it
is easier to [just] record what they say than to determine their

[actual] ages. In their custom, each time the grass grows green is one year, so if someone asks one of them his age, he says how many times the grass has greened. Once [I] asked one of them what month and day he was born. He laughed and replied, "I've never known, nor can I remember how many springs and autumns it has been." Whenever they see a full moon, they consider it one month, and when they see that the greening of the grass is very delayed, then they know that this year has an intercalary month.[8]

But Zhao Gong goes on to record, in consternation, that under the influence of intellectual refugees from the Jin and the Uygurs, the Mongols had begun to employ a calendar.

In the last two years, officials of the [Jurchen] Jin dynasty who had either deserted or surrendered had nowhere safe to go, thus they willingly took service with [the Mongols] and began to teach them writing for intercourse with the Jin—actually using Han characters. In the spring of last year, whenever [I], Gong, saw [any of] their documents in circulation, they still used "Great Court" and named the year simply "rabbit year" [1219] or "dragon year" [1220]. Only last year did they change the designation and call it *gengchen* year [1220], and what they now call *xinsi* year [1221] is this one. In addition, [an earlier people known as] the Mong were admired as a brave nation, so the title "Great Mongol State" was adopted—this also having been taught them by the fugitive Jurchen officials. (Atwood 2000a: 4)

For the Song envoy this was an abomination. In Zhao's opinion, so long as the Mongols lacked a calendrical system, it was possible to bring them into the temporosphere of Song civilization and to forge a Song-Mongol alliance against the Jurchen Jin. To his dismay, however, exiles from the Jin had already ingratiated themselves with the Mongols and provided them with important elements to create their own imperial rule—a dynastic title (*guohao*), a writing system, and a calendrical system. As a result, the formerly "pristine" Mongols were becoming "civilized," yet unfortunately for the Song, the process was taking place beyond their control.

The same point of view, highlighting the dangers of this transformation, is also found in the *Heida shilüe* (Sketch of the Black Tatars)

compiled by Xu Ting and Peng Daya of the Song, who had visited the
Mongols in 1233 and 1235–1236 respectively.

> Their calendar formerly used the [animal] correlates of the twelve
> branches (for example, the *zi* branch they called the mouse year,
> and so on), but now they use the cycle of six *jias* (for example, they
> say the 1st or 13th day of the 1st moon of the *jiazi* year). All this was
> taught to them by Hans, Khitans, and Jurchens. In original Tatar
> customs, they had no [such] orderly calculations; they could only
> take the greening of the grass as one year and the birth of the new
> moon as one month. So if someone asked them their age in
> sexagesimal terms, they would count back on their fingers how many
> times the grass had greened. (Atwood 2000c: 7)

Xu Ting adds that the famous Khitan advisor to the Mongols Yelü
Chucai had personally created a calendar and had it printed and promulgated throughout the Mongol realm without the knowledge of the
Mongol ruler (Atwood 2000c: 7). It is highly unlikely that Ögedei, the
successor to Chinggis Khan, was completely oblivious to the fact that
the Mongol empire had adopted a new calendar, printed and disseminated under the orders of Yelü Chucai. This unlikelihood is reinforced
by an entry in the *Yuanshi* (Yuan history), which informs us that in
1235 "the ministers of the Secretariat requested that a Daming calendar be revised and adopted, and the emperor agreed to it."[9] Thus,
early in the empire period the Mongols began appropriating elements
of Chinese imperial rule, including the regulation of time and the calendar. Exemplifying this is the 1260 edict of Khubilai Khan announcing the reign year Zhongtong, "Central Unification," recorded in the
Yuanshi:

> To establish new periods and announce years makes visible the
> tradition of men and rulers for ten thousand generations; to record
> the time and inscribe the ruler manifests the rightness of the whole
> world as one family. This follows the proper commencement [of a
> reign, as seen in] the *Chunqiu* (Spring and autumn annals) and
> embodies Heaven as the fundament [as found in] the *Yijing*
> (Classic of changes). It is a bright and shining, august plan which
> commences the way of rule. From the 19th day of the 5th moon of
> *gengshen* [June 29, 1260], let a new period be established as the first
> year of Zhongtong. (YS: I, 65 [j. 3]; Atwood 2000b: 53)

The first evidence of Khubilai acting on his prerogative of maintaining time for parts of the empire outside Yuan China occurred two years later, when he sent a calendar to the Koreans (YS: I, 81 [j. 5]).

Reading these Chinese sources, one might easily imagine that the Mongols, in adopting Chinese modes of rule, also adopted and exclusively used the Chinese calendrical system. The two earliest works about the Mongols cited above, however, record that they also counted time by "animal years." And indeed the earliest date recorded in a Mongolian source, the *Secret History,* is "the hen year," or 1201.[10] This date reflects the Mongol adoption, most likely from the Uygurs, of the well-known Inner Asian model of a twelve-year cycle based on the animals of the zodiac (rabbit, dragon, snake, horse, sheep, monkey, chicken, dog, pig, rat, ox, tiger). The exact origin of this system is unclear, but it probably derived from the Turks' adoption and transformation of the Chinese cycle of ten "heavenly stems" (*tiangan*) and twelve "earthly branches" (*dizhi*) (Bazin 1991). This Chinese system matches the first heavenly stem (*jia*) with the first earthly branch (*zi*), and then the second (*yi*) with the second (*chou*), continuing until the first heavenly stem and earthly branch match up again, creating a sixty-year (sexagesimal) cycle. The heavenly stems repeat six times, and the earthly branches repeat five times.

Among the Uygurs, this system was slightly modified, most notably in that the twelve earthly branches were replaced by the twelve animals, and two variations were created involving the ten heavenly stems. In one approach, the Uygurs paired the Chinese heavenly stem with the animal—for instance, "*ding* ox" or "*wu* monkey." This system also was adopted by the Mongols during the Yuan, as seen in a Sino-Mongolian stele inscription from 1338, where a date is given as the "*wu* tiger year" (Cleaves 1951: 104). The same format also is found in a Mongolian calendar fragment discovered in Turfan, which reads "*gi taulai,*" that is, "*ji* rabbit," for the year 1324 (Franke 1964: 33). However, the more common method was to replace the ten heavenly stems with five colors (red, yellow, white, black, and blue), so that two red years were followed by two yellow years. This generated confusion, and eventually the two consecutive colors were differentiated by a case ending that signified gender, a yellow (*sira*)–dragon year, for example, being followed by a female-yellow (*siragcin*)–snake year.[11] The differences among these forms of calender reckoning and those used in the Qing are summarized in the following list of ordinal combinations for months and years:

Mongol	(gender-) color–animal
Uygur	stem-animal
Tibetan	element-animal
Chinese	stem–branch and/or reign number
Tibeto-Qing	element–animal and reign number

In addition to the gendered color–animal schema of year reckoning, the Mongols also had their own designations for the twelve months:

1. Qubi sara (destiny moon)
2. Qujir sara (soda moon)
3. Ögeljin sara (hoopoe moon)
4. Kökei-kökege-köküge sara (cuckoo moon)
5. Ularu sara (heath cock moon)
6. Üjürü sara (crow? moon)
7. Ghuran sara (roebuck moon)
8. Bughu sara (stag moon)
9. Quca sara (ram moon)
10. ?
11. Itelgü sara (falcon moon)
12. Kögeler sara (? moon)[12]

These specific names for the months, however, were lost over time (except for the initial and last months, which were preserved in certain texts and dialects), beginning with the calendar reform of 'Phags pa Lama that was launched during the reign of Khubilai. One part of his reform was the standardization of months. Instead of using the above Mongolian terms or the combinations of animals with the "five elements" (earth, metal, water, wood, and fire) used in Tibet, 'Phags pa Lama introduced the so-called Mongol months (hor-zla), naming months solely by ordinal numbers: 1st month, 2nd month, and so on. Eventually this became the accepted standard among the Mongols, until it was replaced by the system used in official Qing correspondence, which identifies months in a series of three in relation to the four seasons (e.g., 2nd month of winter, 3rd month of winter, 1st month of spring).

The main aim of 'Phags pa Lama's new calendar for the Yuan was to coordinate the different Chinese and Tibetan calendrical systems. In particular, the Tibetan and Chinese calendars were to coincide in both beginning the year and numbering the year (Schuh 1973: 6). This exact alignment, which was to begin in the year 1264, the first of the reign period Zhiyuan, "Reaching the Prime," reflected the sincere attempt of Khubilai to unite his disparate empire temporally. One measure of his success was that under Hülegü, the new year in the region of present-day Iran was not celebrated at the vernal equinox according to Islamic calendars, but was celebrated six weeks before the spring equinox in keeping with the Chinese calendar (Melville 1994).

The changes that occurred during the Yuan shaped Mongolian dating up to and through the Manchu conquest. To what extent this imperial recalculating took effect locally, however, is another question. In the case of Tibet, 'Phags pa Lama's new calendar created a "king's new year" (*rgyal po lo gsar*) to accord with the Chinese calendar, but it never displaced the old "farmer's new year" (*so nam lo gsar*) (Stein 1972: 117). And even today the political overtones of this temporal imposition are played out among Tibetan religiopolitical entities: the Karma Bka' brgyud monastery of Rumtek in Sikkim, seat of the Karmapa, celebrates the new year according to the older calendar, while Dharamsala, seat of the Dge lugs pa's Dalai Lama and the Tibetan government in exile, celebrates it according to the newer calendar. Here we find evidence that the power asserted by religiopolitical and national authorities in controlling and ritualizing time is not necessarily heeded. While there was intense bureaucratic pressure for the Mongols to adopt Chinese modes of time, this adoption also never extended beyond official usage.

In Mongolian sources from the pre-Qing period, the two systems developed by the Uygurs as well as 'Phags pa Lama's ordinal reckoning of months were employed. The longest text from this period is a biography of Altan Khan, the above-mentioned *Jewel Translucent Sutra,* throughout which the color-animal calendar is used, though in one case the author identifies an event using the Uygur system of heavenly stems and animals. The passage in question describes the Third Dalai Lama sending back Altan Khan's envoys in order to arrange the famous meeting of 1578, during which the two met and ushered in the "second conversion" of the Mongols.

> The Dalai Lama said to Dayan Khiya and the translator Bombu
>   Sanding,
> "When you arrive at the Supreme Great Khan speak my words thus:
> 'My sign of us two meeting one another with pleasure,

Shall be that we meet together on a good day, the 15th day of the
   5th month.' "
Then [he] sent them off.
When the dispatched envoys came they explained fully to the majesty
   of the Khan the words of the Clear Holy Dalai Lama.
The Perpetual Khan and Queen, leading the Great Nation, approved
   [meeting]
On a good day, in particular, the 15th day of the 5th month of the
   wu tiger year [1578].
To the east of Kökenuur and west of Cabciyal Monastery,
Reverently the All-knowing Meritorious Dalai Lama and the
   incarnation of Bsod nams grags pa,
Together with all of the Buddha Sangha, arrived as desired.
                                                    (Elverskog 2003: 155)

Why the author chose to use the older form specifically in this case, and only in this case, is unknown. Yet it shows that both of these systems were still in use and understandable to the Mongols at the beginning of the seventeenth century.

The majority of other Mongol texts from this period use the more standard color-animal schema. For example, the Sino-Mongol inscription from Bayuud Monastery informs us that it was written on the "15th of the 4th month of the white-dragon year."[13] Also, Prince Cogtu's famous poem written for his aunt begins with the date "the white-hen year [1621]" (Damdinsüreng 1982: 920), and the record of an animal sacrifice performed at the Manchu-Khalkha union of 1620 notes that it took place in a "yellow-sheep year" (Weiers 1987: 137). Even some Buddhist monuments, instead of employing the Tibetan mode of year counting as might be expected, continued using the Mongolian system, as seen in this inscription from Ligdan Khan's White Stupa: "As decreed by the Khan and carried out by his younger sister Suravati Dayisun Huangdi, the construction was magnificent, filled with majestic light and, having a beautiful shape, it was surrounded by a blessed halo. It was completed on an auspicious day ... in the red-tiger year [1626], 3759 years after the Buddha passed into Nirvana" (Pozdneyev 1977: II, 240–262).

We also can see through this sort of evidence, however, that the influence of Buddhism and the Tibetan dating system started well before the Manchu conquest and its consequent religio-calendrical institutionalizations. This is most clear in Prince Cogtu's inscription, cited above, which was composed in honor of the then recognized ruler of the Mongol nation, Ligdan Khan. The inscription informs us that it was "written on the rock like a gem of jade by Page Daicing and Güyeng the Valiant on the great-white day, the 15th of the fire-tiger month, which is the 1st in the months [cycle], in the wood-mouse year [1624], which is the first in the years [cycle], when 464 years had elapsed since the water-ox year [1160] in which Chinggis Khan was born."[14] This is the first Mongol text to incorporate the Tibetan elements of calendrical reckoning, wherein the months and years are identified by the five elements and twelve animals of the zodiac. The text itself reveals that this system was not familiar to the Mongols, since it must be explained that the fire-tiger month is the first of the cycle of months. And even though the use of the Tibetan calendar may indicate a certain level of Buddhist piety, the passage is firmly situated within the temporal spacing of the Mongol nation in that the "year zero" is that of the birth of Chinggis Khan.

That use of the Tibetan Buddhist calendar was not the norm among Mongols during the pre-Qing period is evident in other kinds of sources as well. Even in Mongolian translations of Tibetan Buddhist texts, where one might expect that Tibetan time would be used, colophons reveal the continued use of Mongolian time. For example, in Toyin Güüsi's translation of the *Vajracchedika* (Diamond sutra), the colophon states that it was completed in the "female-blue–chicken year" (Sárközi 1972: 88), showing use of the Mongol color-animal schema. And the colophon to the famous translation of the *Suvarnaprabhasa* (Golden beam sutra), prepared by the descendants of Altan Khan, records that it was completed in the "*wu* sheep year" and written out in the "*ding* red-ox year" (Heissig 1971: 205), exemplifying persistent use of the old Uygur calendar system among the Mongols, even after their conversion to Tibetan Buddhism.

Other pre-Qing materials also offer evidence that Buddhist conversion did not necessarily mandate Tibetanization—for instance, the persistent use of the five colors instead of the five elements in the calendar system. Though the two practices are different, they are congruent in that the Mongol colors accord with the Tibetan elements (yellow = earth, white = metal, black = water, blue = wood, red = fire), and thus on a functional level the choice of one or the other is arbitrary. By continuing to use the colors rather than the Tibetan elements, the Mongols maintained their identity in this medium of time inscription. Materials from the Qing period, in contrast, reflect that Tibetanization of Mongol time was an integral aspect of the imperial enterprise.

The calendrical effects of the Qing formation among the Mongols were not slight, but neither were they totally transforming. Not surprisingly, all of the Mongol chronicles from the seventeenth century reflect influence from the Tibetan system of calendrical reckoning. There is one glaring exception, however: the best-known chronicle of all, Sagang Secen's *Erdeni-yin tobci* (Precious summary; ET), written in 1662. Instead of the Tibetan method of dating or the more widely used color-animal schema, Sagang Secen used the old Uygur combination of heavenly stem and animal. This choice was not accidental but a clear assertion of Mongolian time in a Qing world. This is not to say that Sagang Secen was a rebel against Manchu power, as his immortalization in the nineteenth century claims, but within the Qing narrative as maintained in his work, resistance to Qing hegemony was exercised in certain ways. For one thing, he never mentioned the Manchu conquest; for another, he asserted independence from Qing time. It is not known whether Sagang Secen's use of the old Uygur system in the face of Tibetanization was the reason why, as the *Erdeni-yin tobci* was being prepared for an imperial edition in the latter part of the eighteenth century during the Qianlong emperor's literary inquisition, several sections were deemed anti-Manchu and deleted (Morikawa 1995). But the work certainly opens a perspective on the other chronicles' use of the Tibetan system.

Although the other chronicles do use the Tibetan calendar, it is employed neither consistently nor coherently. The anonymous author of the *Sira teüke* (Yellow history; ST) uses just an animal to date most events; only in regard to certain important ones, such as the births of 'Phags pa Lama and Dayan Khan and the death of Khubilai Khan, is the full combination of element and animal employed. A similar approach is also found in Lubsangdanjin's *Altan tobci* (Golden summary; ATL), where only a few important events, such as the birth of the fourth Dalai Lama (ATL: 644), are made temporally specific with the assignment of both an element and an animal. The same approach is also found in the anonymous *Altan tobci* (ATA), where, for the history of the Yuan and post-Yuan periods, years are only distinguished by an animal. For the history of Chinggis Khan, whose birth in accord with the Qing narrative is dated to the Buddha's parinirvana (ATA: 128), the author uses both the Mongolian color-animal form and the Uygur system. In his description of Chinggis Khan's enthronement he writes: "The blessed Chinggis Khan was born in a black-snake year. When he was forty-five years old, in a *bing* tiger year, he raised up his nine-pointed white banner at the head of the Onon River and sat on the great throne of the khans" (ATA: 129). In one case, the death of Chinggis Khan is identified only by the Uygur system: "He died in the *bing*-pig year, on the 12th of the 7th month, being sixty-seven years old" (ATA: 143). The duality of time in the work reflects the dislocation implied in the adoption of the Tibetan system within the narrative of the Qing.

If the Mongols had rejected their system in favor of the Tibetan one, it would have signified their complete acceptance of the Tibeto-Qing narrative of rule. Yet the Mongols' persistent deviation from the standard framework implies that within the larger discourse of Qing hegemony, which could not be challenged without severe repercussions, the Mongols wished to assert their own history and identity. One mode of resistance was time. Instead of adopting the Tibetan calendrical system, the Mongols used it in a perfunctory manner, challenging the parameters of the Qing representation of time and its embedded marginalization of Mongol identity.

The postulate that this superficial use of the Tibetan calendar in the seventeenth-century Mongolian chronicles was a way of circumventing the incorporation of the Mongols within the Qing is supported by the *Asaragci neretü-yin teüke* (Asaragci's history; ANT) of 1677. This work was composed for and about the Khalkha Mongols, who at the time still had not submitted to the Qing. But the Khalkhas had converted to Buddhism, and the ruling Tüshiyetü Khan had even recognized his son as the spiritual head of the Khalkha Buddhists, the Jebdzundamba Khutugtu. This development unmistakably threatened the relationship that had been forged between the Manchu emperors and the Dge lugs pa order, since it circumvented both of them while not reducing the importance of Tibet as a center of Buddhist authority. Its author, Byamba Erke Daicing, used the same perfunctory Tibetan calendar system that is found in the other Mongol chronicles, identifying most years solely by an animal and in certain important cases adding the Tibetan element. There is just one aberration from this pattern, but it is a big one: the account of Geresenje, the son of Dayan Khan who was regarded as the progenitor of the Khalkha ruling lineages, in which the author uses only the Mongol color-animal dating system (ANT: 116–117). That this was simply a result of the composite nature of this work seems unlikely, since the color-animal dates occur only in this one passage describing the origin of the Khal-khas. I believe that this shift in the temporal markers of the narrative signifies that the Khalkha Mongols remained outside of the Tibeto-Qing discourse that was integral to the narratives and rituals of Qing rule.

These Mongol authors thus employed systems of temporal mark-ing as codes to signal the boundaries of communal identification. Sagang Secen and Byamba Erke Daicing did so most dramatically, while the other authors, by adopting an almost nonsensical (in terms of historical writing) Tibetan dating convention, recognized Qing rule and its Buddhist narrative but on their own terms. Only two Mongolian authors fully adopted both the Tibetan and Qing representations of time. One of these is the Jarud lama, Dharma, whose work of 1739, the *Altan kürdün minggan kegesütü* (Thousand-spoked golden wheel; AKMK), includes the history of the Qing and incorporates the Mongols within the Tibeto-Qing time frame. Thus, in describing the submission of the Khalkhas and their division into Qing banners, Dharma, unlike Byamba Erke Daicing, identifies this event specifically within the Qing frame of reference: it took place in the "29th year of Kangxi, an iron-horse year" (AKMK: 239). In this way, unlike the seventeenth-century authors who played with the notions of time and their boundaries, Dharma, through his use of Tibeto-Qing time, represented the Mon-gols as an inalienable part of the Qing.

A similar representation is found in the work of Gombojab—not surprising since he was close with the court and a resident of Beijing, where he was an instructor at the Tibetan School. In his short work of 1725, the *Gangga-yin urusqal* (Flow of the Ganges; GU), Gombojab consistently used the Tibetan calendrical system—not, however, the ordinal number of months introduced by 'Phags pa Lama but the Sino-Manchu classification of the months by season. A typical entry thus begins: "in the last month of winter in the fire-tiger year" (GU: 49). Interestingly, he dates pre-Qing events among the Mongols in re-lation to the Ming rulers, thereby associating Mongol history with the legitimate political power in China and foreshadowing Mongol inclu-sion in the Qing enterprise. The death of Buyan Secen Khan thus is dated to the "31st year of Wanli" (GU: 98–99), and the death of Lig-dan Khan, the last Mongol ruler before the fall of the Ming, is re-corded as follows: "At the age of forty-three, in a wood-dog year, the 7th year [1634] of the Chinese Great Ming Emperor Chongzhen, [Lig-dan Khan] destroyed his empire and died on the Yellow Steppe" (GU:

99). Significantly, Gombojab does not attribute the fall of Ligdan Khan to any actions undertaken by the Manchus; instead it was his own doing, and Qing rule therefore is legitimate. Use of the Tibetan dating system here goes hand in hand with writing the pre-Qing history of the Mongols within the time frame of the Ming, precursor of the Qing.

This chronological shift bears on whether or not the Mongols had been in "Chinese time" since the fall of the Yuan. In Gombojab's representation it clearly is understood that the Mongols have been a part of "China" since the fall of the Yuan in 1368. The Mongol submission to Manchu rule and Qing time is therefore a natural development, because China and Mongolia had always been under one regime, which had gone through three phases—the Yuan, the Ming, and the Qing. This interpretation radically transformed earlier Mongol views of their history and its relation to China. In the seventeenth-century chronicles it is the view, never explicitly stated, that the Yuan dynasty did not collapse with the expulsion of the Mongols from China in 1368 (Mostaert 1959: 12–15). Indeed, throughout the Ming period Mongol rulers continued to identify themselves as the emperors of the Yuan. For instance, in 1453 when Esen Tayisi of the Oirads defeated the Mongols and deposed their ruler, he proclaimed himself the "Heavenly Saintly Emperor of the Great Yuan" (Da Yuan Tiansheng Kehan) (Serruys 1977b: 364), a title that Dayan Khan again assumed, in modified form, after he defeated the Oirads and reclaimed leadership of the Mongols. After his death, the mantle of rule over the Mongol-Yuan dynasty passed to his descendants by primogeniture. The last Yuan ruler therefore was Ligdan Khan, and the dynasty only came to an end with his defeat by the Manchus.

Gombojab's chronological assumption, however, departed from this narrative of a legitimate and independent Mongol nation by temporally placing the Mongols within the Ming, and then within the Qing, a departure that did not go unchallenged. The most vociferous critic of Gombojab's narrative and its framework of Ming and Qing historiography was Rasipungsug. In his 1775 work, mentioned above, Rasipungsug directly criticized the supposition that the Yuan ended in 1368. Citing Chinese sources, mainly a Manchu translation of the *Xu Zizhi tongjian gangmu* (Continuation of the "Summary of the *Comprehensive Mirror in Aid of Governance*"), he argues that Chinese dynasties had also gone into exile yet remained legitimate: the Mongol-Yuan was no different.

When I, Rasipungsug, look, [I see that] in the Chinese books they have made a decision that in the reign of Emperor Shun the rule of the Yuan dynasty was extinguished. I, the foolish one, say it was not extinguished.

Some say, "As Emperor Shun thus had his state completely taken away, and as he himself barely escaped, how would it be right that still it was not extinguished?"

I say, "The First Ruler [Liu Bei] of the Shu-Han dynasty, Emperor Yuan of the [Eastern] Jin dynasty, and Gaozong of the Song in Jiangdong [(south)east of the Yangzi] sat [on their thrones] by a succession [that came to them] from distant [times]. In the *Gangmu,* they busy themselves with making them all central dynasties in the [legitimate] line. Now, the [Mongol] emperor did not abdicate like Emperor Xian of the Han, nor was he captured by enemies like Emperors Huai and Min of the [Western] Jin, nor was he handed over to others like Song Huizong and Qinzong. Since he escaped and reigned as lord in Mongolia, how shall we say the Yuan dynasty was extinguished?" (BE: 792–793)

Rasipungsug in this way challenges the assumption in Gombojab's work that the Mongol nation had been a part of the Ming, and thus that it naturally had become a part of the Qing. He asserts, instead, that the Mongol nation had been independent for most of its history and that its current union with the Qing is a historical aberration. The independence of the Mongol nation is thereby asserted through temporal spacing: it had only been a part of China since 1636. And Rasipungsug demanded, in accord with this logic, that the Mongols and their history from 1368 be recognized as the "Latter Yuan." He further accentuated this difference by reverting back to the original Mongolian calendar of colors and animals. Even though he was greatly influenced by Chinese historiography and even divided his history into dynasties and reign periods, within that framework he continued to use the Mongolian dating system.

Thus, the adoption of Qing time as found in the work of Gombojab and Dharma cannot be considered the norm; it was more an anomaly. Mongolian authors continued to use the Mongolian calendrical system throughout the eighteenth century, as seen in Mergen Gegen's *Altan tobciya* (Golden summary; ATMG). Similarly, in the composition of Mongolian Buddhist histories, such as the *Bilig-ün jula* (Light of wisdom; BJ) of 1757, which drew its inspiration from the Tibetan *chos 'byung* (history of the dharma) tradition, instead of adopting the Tibetan calendrical system as one might expect, the authors trace the transmission of Buddhism within a Mongolian calendrical matrix.

The continued assertion of Mongol time, however, was not limited to historical sources; it also was manifested in the copious production of Mongolian Buddhist manuscripts. While it is well known that the Qing appropriated the production of Buddhist literature as part of the imperial project, it may be less known that, in spite of that enterprise, the Mongols continued to make their own manuscript versions of the same texts produced under imperial patronage. Because such versions were turned out locally, for local consumption and use, the discord between them and the imperial xylographs provides a unique window on how the Mongols understood the Qing. In particular, it shows how the Tibeto-Qing time frame found in the imperial editions was transformed in the manuscript versions. To cite one example, in the 1720 Beijing Kanjur version of the *Dologan ebügen sudur* (Big Dipper sutra), the initial auspicious day for worshiping the stars of the Big Dipper is identified using a Tibeto-Qing way of indicating days of the month: "the 7th day of the first month of spring" (Ligeti 1963: 111). In two late manuscripts, however, the same date is given in the Mongolian way: "the 7th of the destiny moon (Qubi sara)" (DESa: 10v; DESb: 12v).

From these historical sources it is evident that during the incorporation of the Mongols into the Qing order, time was an arena of negotiation the outcome of which was that the Mongols maintained Mongolian time. This is most manifest in a passage from a nineteenth-century Mongolian text of astrology and divination, which informs practitioners about how to deduce the time, so crucial to divination: "According to the Kalacakrists of India [at a certain point] it is the *citra* month, the middle month of spring. For the peasants it is the first month of summer. For the mathematicians of Black China it is the final month of spring. In Tibet it is the dragon month. In Mongolia it is the 3rd month."[15] Thus for the diviner, and the Mongols as a whole, it was of crucial importance to know the time, and of all the competing systems, the most important was Mongolian time.

Conclusion

The temporal withholding of complete submission by the Mongols is something the Qing narrative wished to forget, and that it has been forgotten reflects the Qing success. Fortunately, extant Mongol sources afford us a rich picture of this transitional period outside the monologue of stationary Manchu-Buddhist imperial rule. In the process of imperial consolidation we can see an ongoing dialog in which narratives and representations of identity were continually being renegotiated and communal boundaries were continually being transformed. This is the case not only through narratives outside the official discourse, but also when we examine how the "Qing" itself was envisioned as time went by. And it is only at the interface of these representations that a clearer understanding of the Qing idea can emerge.

In the case of the Mongols and their change in status from adversaries of the Ming to junior partners in the Qing empire, we can see from their concepts of time that the Mongols' understanding of their nation and of the Qing was constantly shifting. Ritual, narrative, history, and time invariably are linked with individual and collective identity; in that linkage they are instruments not only of power, but also of resistance to marginalizing representations by others (Le Goff 1992: 98). Thus, within the narrative of the Qing, the Mongols continued to assert their own identity through the discourse of time. Just as present-day Uygurs reject "Beijing time" and assert their religious and ethnic identity by living in "Xinjiang time," the Mongols of the Qing employed time as a means of differentiation. By rejecting or manipulating the Tibeto-Qing framework of time and asserting instead Mongolian time, with its power to shape the social and cultural matrix, the Mongols deflected the marginalizing representations of the Qing imperial narrative—a tactic that the French anarchist and chronological terrorist Martial Bourdin understood well.

Notes

1. The text of Cogtu Taiji's inscription is found in Damdinsüreng's collection of Mongolian literature (1982: 922). Translation prepared by György Kara, with some alterations here.

2. This manuscript was discovered in 1958 in a cave near Khara Shorong, located in the Darkhan Moominggan Banner of the Ulaanchab League of Inner Mongolia. In his study of this text, Kesigtogtaqu (1998) argues that it was written at the same time as the *Cagan teüke* (White history), sometime between 1260 and 1330, on account of the two having the same geospatial arrangement of the Five-Colored Nations and the Four Subjects. The manuscript, however,

probably dates from the late sixteenth or early seventeenth century. Although Kesigtogtaqu's early dating of the work's composition is problematic, the text in its present form is probably one of the oldest extant Mongolian histories.

3. The date of this work has been disputed by Walther Heissig, J. W. de Jong, and S. Bira, but it probably was composed around 1740, plus or minus five years (Kämpfe 1983: 204).

4. Gombojab's work *Chen po Thang gur dus kyi Rgya kar zhing gi bkod pa'i kar chag bzhugs so* is reprinted with a preface by S. Bira (in Bira 1974: 141–209).

5. Atwood 1994a: 137. Use of the Tibetan language by Mongolian Buddhists continues today. However, during the past decade in independent Mongolia the use of Tibetan has come under question. Leading the call for a return to Mongolian is the Association of Buddhist Lay Believers (Khar Burkhany kholboo) in Ulaanbaatar. This group argues that Mongols do not understand Buddhism because it is practiced in Tibetan, so a return to Mongolian is called for (Bareja-Starzynska 2000: 5). Another reflection of this sentiment is that the Beijing blockprint of Mergen Gegen's four-volume collected works (see Heissig 1954: 150–154) has recently been published in Inner Mongolia (MGB) with four cassette tapes of the liturgy performed in Mongolian.

6. See, for example, studies of the rituals of mourning mandated for Qing emperors in Mostaert 1961 and Serruys 1977a.

7. Miller 1959: 82–84. The development of the cult of Wutai Shan and its relation to national identity can be paralleled with today's cult of Mao Zedong and pilgrimage to Mao's mausoleum in Beijing (on the latter, see Wagner 1992).

8. I thank Christopher Atwood for providing me with his translation of Zhao Gong's work (this quote, 2000a: 2–3). In addition, I thank him for extensive suggestions and information on Mongol calendrical reckoning during the Mongol Empire period.

9. YS: I, 34 (j. 2). "The Daming calendar, devised by astronomer Zu Congzhi in the 6th year of the Daming period of the Liu Song dynasty (that is, in 462 CE), was the second major revision of the Chinese calendrical system. Zu based his calendar on the calculation of the year as 365.2428 days.... This calendar remained state of the art in China until the end of the twelfth century" (Atwood 2000b: 28).

10. The passage in the *Secret History,* §141, reads "te'ün-ü qoyina takiya jil" (Rachewiltz 1972: 61). For a translation of this passage see Cleaves 1982: 68, and for extensive commentary on this date see Bazin 1991: 390–403.

11. For a concordance of the different calendars—Chinese, Mongol, and Tibetan—see Everding 1982.

12. Baumann 2000: 55–56. My thanks to Brian Baumann for making avail-

able his material on Mongolian astrology and concepts of time. A fine example of how these month designations were used in the early seventeenth century can be found in the newly discovered "wedding calendars" from Xarbuxyn Balgas (Chiodo 2000: 216).

13. The Mongolian text reads "cagan luu jil-ün dörben sar-a-yin arban tabun-a," and the parallel Chinese reads "Wanli banian siyüe shiwuri" (15th of the 4th month of the 8th year of Wanli) (Altan'orgil 1989: 3).

14. The Cagan Baishing inscription in Cogtu Taiji's city also uses the Tibetan elements in its date, "temür öker jilün kögege sara-yin arban tabun-aca egüscü" (Huth 1894: 32).

15. Mostaert 1969: folio 10r. This translation is based on Baumann (2000: 21) with slight modifications.

References

AE. Na-ta. 1989. *Altan erike.* Ed. Coyiji. Kökeqota: Öbör Monggol-un arad-un keblel-ün qoriy-a.

AKMK. Dharma. 1987. *Altan kürdün mingan kegesütü.* Ed. Coyiji. Kökeqota: Öbör Monggol-un arad-un keblel-ün qoriy-a.

Altan'orgil. 1989. *Kökeqota-yin teüke monggol surbulji bicig,* vol. 6. Kökeqota: Öbör Monggol-un soyul-un keblel-ün qoriy-a.

Anderson, Benedict. 1991. *Imagined Communities: Reflections on the Origins and Spread of Nationalism.* London: Verso.

ANT. Kämpfe, Hans-Rainer. 1983. *Das Asaragci neretü-yin teüke des Byamba Erke Daicing alias Samba Jasag (Eine mongolische Chronik des 17. Jahrhunderts).* Wiesbaden: Otto Harrassowitz.

ATA. Bawden, Charles. 1955. *The Mongol Chronicle Altan Tobci.* Göttinger Asiatische Forschungen, 5. Wiesbaden: Otto Harrassowitz.

ATL. Lubsangdanjin. 1983. *Altan tobci.* Ed. Coyiji. Kökeqota: Öbör Monggol-un arad-un keblel-ün qoriy-a.

ATMG. Lubsangdambijalsan. 1998. *Altan tobci.* Ed. Cimeddorji, Möngkebuyan, and Gerel. Kökeqota: Öbör Monggol-un soyul-un keblel-ün qoriy-a.

Atwood, Christopher. 1992/1993. "The Marvellous Lama in Mongolia: The Phenomenology of a Cultural Borrowing." *Acta Orientalia Hungarica* 46: 1–30.

———. 1994a. "Buddhism and Popular Ritual in Mongolian Religion: A Reexamination of the Fire Cult." *History of Religions* 36: 112–139.

———. 1994b. "Revolutionary Nationalist Mobilization in Inner Mongolia, 1925–1929." Ph.D. diss., Indiana University.

———. 2000a. "*A Complete Record of the Mong Tatars* by Zhao Gong of the Song." Unpublished manuscript.

———. 2000b. "*The History of the Yuan.*" Unpublished manuscript.

———. 2000c. "*A Sketch of the Black Tatars* by Peng Daya and Xu Ting of the Song." Unpublished manuscript.

Bareja-Starzynska, Agata. 2000. "Revival of Buddhism in Mongolia after 1990." Unpublished paper, presented at the Seventh Annual Central Eurasian Studies Conference, Indiana University, March 25.

Baumann, Brian. 2000. "Theory and Practice: The Occult Ways of Buddhist Mathematics as Found in an Anonymous Source from Ordos Published by Rev. Antoine Mostaert as *Manual of Mongolian Astrology and Divination.*" Unpublished manuscript.

Bazin, Louis. 1991. *Les systèmes chronologiques dans le monde turc ancien.* Budapest: Akademiai Kiado; Paris: Éditions du CNRS.

BE. Rasipungsug. 1985. *Bolor erike.* Ed. Kökeöndür. Kökeqota: Öbör Monggol-un arad-un keblel-ün qoriy-a.

Bell, Catherine. 1992. *Ritual Theory, Ritual Practice.* New York: Oxford University Press.

Bira, S. 1974. "'Da Tan si yui tszi' Syuan' Tszana v tibetskom perevode Guna Gombozhava." In *Mongol ba Töw Aziin ornuudin tüüxend xolbogdox xoyor xowor surbalj bicig.* Ulaanbaatar: Shinjlex Uxaani xüreelen (Academy of Sciences).

BJ. *Bilig-ün jula.* Manuscript held by the Neimenggu shehui kexueyuan 內蒙古社會科學院 (Inner Mongolia Academy of Social Sciences), cat. no. 22.912 125:1.

Burnett, D. Graham. 2000. "Writing the History of Time: Greenwich Village." *New Republic,* Sept. 1, 37–45.

Chiodo, Elisabetta. 2000. *The Mongolian Manuscript on Birch Bark from Xarbuxyn Balgas in the Collection of the Mongolian Academy of Sciences,* part 1. Wiesbaden: Harrassowitz Verlag.

Cleaves, F. W. 1951. "The Sino-Mongolian Inscription of 1338 in Memory of Jiguntei." *Harvard Journal of Asiatic Studies* 14: 1–104.

———. 1982. *The Secret History of the Mongols.* Cambridge: Harvard University Press.

Comaroff, Jean. 1994. "Defying Disenchantment: Reflections on Ritual, Power, and History." In *Asian Visions of Authority: Religion and the Modern States of East and Southeast Asia,* ed. C. Keyes, L. Kendall, and H. Hardacre, 301–314. Honolulu: University of Hawai'i Press.

Damdinsüreng. 1982. *Monggol uran jokiyal-un degeji jagun bilig orosibai.* Rpt. Kökeqota: Öbör Mongol-un arad-un keblel-ün qoriy-a.

DESa. *Dologan ebügen neretü odun-u sudur orosiba.* Manuscript held by the Nei-menggu shehui kexueyuan, cat. no. 49.328 1403:1.

DESb. *Dologan ebügen-ü sudur.* Manuscript held by the Neimenggu shehui kexueyuan, cat. no. 49.328 1403.2.

DeWeese, Devin. 1994. *Islamization and Native Religion in the Golden Horde: Baba Tükles and Conversion to Islam in Historical and Epic Tradition.* University Park: Pennsylvania State University Press.

DO. Antoine Mostaert. 1968. *Dictionnaire ordos.* 2nd ed. New York: Johnson Reprint Corporation.

Duara, Prasenjit. 1995. *Rescuing History from the Nation: Questioning Narratives of Modern China.* Chicago: University of Chicago Press.

Elverskog, Johan. 2003. *The "Jewel Translucent Sutra": Altan Khan and the Mongols in the Sixteenth Century.* Leiden: Brill.

ET. Sagang Secen. 1990. *Erdeni-yin tobci (Precious Summary: A Mongolian Chronicle of 1662),* vol. 1. Ed. M. Gō, I. de Rachewiltz, J. R. Krueger, and B. Ulaan. Canberra: Australian National University.

Everding, Karl-Heinz. 1982. "Die 60er-Zyklen: Eine Konkordanztafel." *Zentrala-siatische Studien* 16: 475–479.

Franke, Herbert. 1964. *Mittelmongolische Kalendarfragmente aus Turfan.* Philosophisch-Historische Klasse, 2. Munich: Bayerische Akademie der Wissenschaften.

GC. Mgon po skyabs. 1983. *Rgya nags chos 'byung.* [Chengdu?]: Si khron mi rigs dpe skrun khang.

Gellner, Ernest. 1983. *Nations and Nationalism.* Ithaca: Cornell University Press.

GU. Gombojab. 1984. *Gangga-yin urusqal.* Ed. Coyiji. Kökeqota: Öbör Monggol-un arad-un keblel-ün qoriy-a.

Hastings, Adrian. 1997. *The Construction of Nationhood: Ethnicity, Religion and Nationalism.* Cambridge: Cambridge University Press.

Heissig, Walther. 1954. *Die Pekinger lamaistischen Blockdrucke in mongolischer Sprache.* Göttinger Asiatische Forschungen, 2. Wiesbaden: Otto Harrasso-witz.

———. 1966. *Die mongolische Steininschrift und Manuskriptfragmente aus Olon süme in der Inneren Mongolei.* Göttingen: Vandenhoeck and Ruprecht.

———. 1971. *Catalogue of Mongol Books, Manuscripts and Xylographs.* Copenha-gen: Royal Library.

Hobsbawm, Eric. 1990. *Nations and Nationalisms since 1780.* Cambridge: Cam-bridge University Press.

Huth, Georg. 1894. *Die Inschriften von Tsaghan Baišiṅ: Tibetisch-Mongolischer Text.* Leipzig: F. A. Brockhaus.

Inden, Ronald. 1990. *Imagining India.* Oxford: Basil Blackwell.

Ishihama, Yumiko. 1992. "A Study of the Seals and Titles Conferred by the Dalai Lamas." In *Tibetan Studies: Proceedings of the Fifth Seminar of the International Association of Tibetan Studies, Narita 1989*, ed. Ihara Shōren and Yamaguchi Zuihō, vol. 2, 501–514. Narita: Naritasan shinshoji.

Kämpfe, H. R. 1983. "mGon po skyabs' rGya nag chos 'byung als Quelle des Cindamani-yin erikes." In *Documenta Barbarorum: Festschrift für Walther Heissig zum 70. Geburtstag*, ed. K. Sagaster and M. Weiers, 203–209. Wiesbaden: Otto Harrassowitz.

Kesigtogtaqu. 1998. "Cinggis qagan-u altan tobci ner-e-tü-yin cadig." In *Cinggis Qagan-u takil-un sudur orosiba*, ed. Durungga, 1–17. Kökeqota: Öbör Monggol-un arad-un keblel-ün qoriy-a.

Le Goff, Jacques. 1992. *History and Memory*. New York: Columbia University Press.

Ligeti, Lajos. 1963. *Preklasszikus Emlékek. Jüan-és Ming-kori szövegek klassikus átirábsan*. Budapest: ELTE Belsó-ázsiai Intézet.

Melville, Charles. 1994. "The Chinese-Uighur Animal Calendar in Persian Historiography of the Mongol Period." *Iran* 32: 83–98.

MGB. Lobsangdanjin [Mergen Gegen]. 1783. *Vcir dhara mergen diyanci blam-a-yin gegen-ü gbum jarlig kemegdekü orosiba*. Rpt. in Mergen Gegen Sudulul, 5. Kökeqota: Öbör Monggol-un surgan kümüjil-ün keblel-ün qoriy-a, 1999.

Miller, Robert James. 1959. *Monasteries and Culture Change in Inner Mongolia*. Asiatische Forschungen, 2. Weisbaden: Otto Harrassowitz.

Morikawa Tetsuo 森川哲雄. 1995. "'Mōko genryū' no shahon to sono keitō" 「蒙古源流」の写本とその系統 (Manuscripts of *Erdeni-yin tobci* and Their Connections). *Ajia, Afurika gengo bunka kenkyū* アジア・アフリカ言語文化研究 (*Journal of Asian and African Studies*) 50: 1–41.

Mostaert, Antoine. 1959. "Critical Introduction." In *Bolor Erike: Mongolian Chronicle, by Rasipungsug*. Scripta Mongolica, 3. Cambridge: Harvard University Press.

———. 1961. "Annonce de la mort de l'Empereur Te-tsoung et de l'Impératrice douairière Ts'cu-hi aux Mongols de la bannière d'Oto (Ordos)." In *Studia Sino-Altaica: Festschrift für Erich Haenisch zum 80. Geburtstag*, ed. Herbert Franke, 140–155. Wiesbaden: Otto Harrassowitz.

———. 1969. *Manual of Mongolian Astrology and Divination*. Cambridge: Harvard University Press.

Olbricht, Peter, and Elisabeth Pinks, trans. 1980. *Meng-Ta pei-lu und Hei-Ta shih-lüeh: Chiniessche Gesandtenberichte über die frühen Mongolen 1221 und 1237*. Wiesbaden: Otto Harrassowitz.

Petech, Luciano. 1993. "'P'ags-pa (1235–1280)." In *In the Service of the Great Khan: Eminent Personalities of the Early Mongol-Yüan Period*, ed. Igor de Rachewiltz et al., 646–654. Wiesbaden: Harrassowitz Verlag.

Pozdneyev, Aleksei M. 1977. *Mongolia and the Mongols.* Trans. William H. Dougherty. Uralic and Altaic Series, 61–62. Bloomington: Indiana University.

———. 1978. *Religion and Ritual in Society: Lamaist Buddhism in Late 19th-Century Mongolia.* Ed. John R. Krueger, trans. Alo Raun and Linda Raun. Publications of the Mongolia Society, Occasional Papers, 10. Bloomington: Mongolia Society.

Rachewiltz, Igor de. 1972. *Index to the Secret History of the Mongols.* Uralic and Altaic Series, 121. Bloomington: Indiana University.

Ratchnevsky, Paul. 1954. "Die mongolischen Grosskhane und die buddhistische Kirche." In *Asiatica: Festschrift Friedrich Weller zum 65. Geburtstag gewidmet,* ed. J. Schubert and U. Unger, 489–504. Leipzig: Otto Harrassowitz.

Sárközi, Alice. 1972. "Toyin Guisi's Mongol Vajracchedika." *Acta Orientalia Hungarica* 27.1: 43–102.

Schuh, Dieter. 1973. *Untersuchungen zur Geschicte der Tibetischen Kalenderrechnung.* Verzeichnis der orientalischen Handschriften in Deutschland, 16. Wiesbaden: Franz Steiner Verlag.

Serruys, Henry. 1962. "Early Lamaism in Mongolia." *Oriens Extremus* 10: 181–216.

———. 1977a. "Mourning Regulations in Ordos, 1909." *Bulletin of the School of Oriental and African Studies* 40: 580–581.

———. 1977b. "The Office of Tayisi in Mongolia in the Fifteenth Century." *Harvard Journal of Asiatic Studies* 37: 353–380.

Sperling, Elliot. 1987. "Lama to the King of Hsia." *Journal of the Tibet Society* 7: 31–50.

———. 1994. "Rtsa-mi Lo-tsā-ba Sangs-rgyas grags-pa and the Tangut Background to Early Mongol-Tibetan Relations." In *Tibetan Studies: Proceedings of the Sixth Seminar of the International Association of Tibetan Studies, Fagernes 1992,* ed. Per Kvaerne, 801–824. Oslo: Institute for Comparative Research and Human Culture.

ST. Anon. 1983. *Erten-ü Mongol-un qad-un ündüsün-ü yeke sir-a tuuji orosiba.* Ed. Öljeyitü. Kökeqota: Ündüsüten-ü keblel-ün qoriy-a.

Stein, R. A. 1972. *Tibetan Civilization.* Stanford: Stanford University Press.

Tambiah, Stanley. 1976. *World Conqueror and World Renouncer: A Study of Buddhism and Polity in Thailand against a Historical Background.* Cambridge and New York: Cambridge University Press.

Trainor, Kevin. 1997. *Relics, Ritual, and Representation in Buddhism: Rematerializing the Sri Lankan Theravāda Tradition.* Cambridge and New York: Cambridge University Press.

Wagner, Rudolf G. 1992. "Reading the Chairman Mao Memorial Hall in Peking: The Tribulations of the Implied Pilgrim." In *Pilgrims and Sacred*

Sites in China, ed. Susan Naquin and Chün-fang Yü, 378–423. Berkeley: University of California Press.

Wakeman, Frederic, Jr. 1985. *The Great Enterprise: The Manchu Reconstruction of Imperial Order in Seventeenth-Century China.* 2 vols. Berkeley: University of California Press.

Weiers, Michael. 1987. "Die Vertragstexte des mandschu-khalkha Bundes von 1619/20." *Aetas Manjurica* 1: 119–165.

Wylie, Turrell. 1977. "The First Mongol Conquest of Tibet Re-interpreted." *Harvard Journal of Asiatic Studies* 37: 103–133.

Xu Ting 徐霆 and Peng Daya 彭大雅. 1926. *Heida shilüe jianzheng* 黑韃事略箋證. Annot. Wang Guowei 王國維. In *Menggu shiliao jiaozhu sizhong* 蒙古史料校注四種. Rpt. Taibei: Zhongzheng shuju, 1962. Trans. in Olbricht and Pinks 1980.

YS. *Yuanshi* 元史. 1995. 5th ed. [1976]. 15 vols. Beijing: Zhonghua shuju.

Zhao Gong 趙珙, attrib. 1926. *Mengda beilu jianzheng* 蒙韃備錄箋證. Annot. Wang Guowei. In *Menggu shiliao jiaozhu sizhong*. Rpt. Taibei: Zhongzheng shuju, 1962. Trans. in Olbricht and Pinks 1980.

Zito, Angela. 1997. *Of Body & Brush: Grand Sacrifice as Text/Performance in Eighteenth-Century China.* Chicago: University of Chicago Press.

III
ALTERITIES IN FOLK CULTURE
AND
THE SYMBOLICS OF CALENDAR TIME

CHAPTER FIVE

The "Teachings of the Lord of Heaven" in Fujian

Between Two Worlds and Two Times

Eugenio Menegon

IN AN EXTRAORDINARY POEM, the seventeenth-century painter, poet, and eventually Jesuit father Wu Li describes his sense of dislocation upon waking in unfamiliar surroundings:

> At the tips of red lichee branches
>   the moon again goes west;
> I rise and watch
>   the wind-swept dew,
> My eyes still all confused.
> Before the lamp, this place is not
>   a scholar's studio:
> I only hear the sound of bells,
> I hear no rooster's crow.[1]

In the deep south, where lichee abounds, he opens his eyes after a night's rest with his senses still heavy and confused. It is the new moon. In the flickering light of a lamp, he realizes that the usual objects and the walls of his scholar's studio, which he perhaps expected to find at his rise, are not there. Neither is the comforting, certainly familiar sound of the rooster's crow. Instead, he has been awakened by the striking of "self-sounding bells," that is, by a mechanical Western clock.

Religious Temporality in China and Europe

Indeed, Wu Li was not in his scholar's studio in his native Changshu (Jiangsu Province) when writing this poem between 1681 and 1688. Rather, he was residing in the Jesuit residence of Macao, where, as a member of the Society of Jesus, he was taking courses in Western philosophy and Catholic theology in preparation for his priestly ordination. This rare Chinese observer of Western lifestyles in Macao was clearly struck by the lack of natural time markers (roosters) and by the presence in their stead of mechanical devices (chiming clocks) to measure the hours. He must have been familiar with the tolling of bells or the beating of drums to mark time in Chinese cities, but probably the scholar's studio he referred to, as the poetic topos required, would have been in some rustic retreat where life flowed easily and slowly, and where such sounds normally would not be heard. In contrast, he elsewhere noted how his daily life of study as a Jesuit novice in Macao was rigidly disciplined by the clock.[2]

Wu Li's reflection on his waking stupor reminds us, as David Landes has noted, that the subdivision of time in hours, minutes, and seconds is far from being "natural." Indeed, more stringent conceptions of time were mainly limited to urban centers, both in China and the West, where mechanical time-keeping devices were required for security night watches and the precise measurement of labor. In fact, scheduling in hours, minutes, and subminutes, as well as a need and desire for precision, diffused beyond urban centers only after the introduction of railways in the West in the 1840s.[3]

In the countryside of China or Europe, where the vast majority of people lived in premodern times, the meaning of time was rather different from ours. In rural Europe, until the mid-sixteenth century most people contented themselves with identifying the middle of the day, either by looking at the sun or by listening to the bells of a nearby church. Similarly, in the countryside of China the sun dictated the daily rhythms of activity and rest, while the occasional tolling of the bell of a Buddhist monastery or the sound of the night watch in a walled county seat would mark the passing of time only for those people residing in the vicinity.[4] What truly mattered to most rural folk was not so much the micromanagement of time but knowledge of important dates in the annual cycle. That cycle, it is important to underline, was mainly a cultic one. While people at large were aware of the linear progression of time, from the birth of Christ or the creation of the world in Europe, the date of the al-Hijra in the Muslim world, or the beginning of a reign in a given dynasty in China, what they experienced in daily life was the temporal circularity of rituals, calendrically linked to the lunations.[5]

In Western Christendom, the main orientation through the year was offered by the celebration of major feasts like Easter or Christmas, by the weekly recurrence of the *dies dominica* (Lord's Day), and by the feasts of saints, whose position in time was often linked to important agricultural moments of the season. Besides these landmark dates, precise dating linked to the astronomical year remained the preserve of a small literate public of clerics, government officials, and urban dwellers, who could read and employ books of hours or astrological almanacs. In fact, absolute astronomical dates, as opposed to relative recurrences linked to the liturgical year of the church, did not become commonly used until the second half of the sixteenth century, when printed almanacs began to have wide distribution. However, most people in the countryside continued to mark their time through the liturgical calendar well into the eighteenth century (Maiello 1994: chap. 8). The prominence of the liturgical calendar in Europe clearly indicates the pivotal role the church had as the keeper of time. Benedictine monks, following the Roman system, introduced the division of time in "hours" to mark their rhythm of work, study, and prayer, and it was a pope who issued in 1582 the calendar that we still use today. Starting in the Middle Ages, secular powers vied with the church for control over time but with limited success. Even the radical attempt of French authorities, in the period from 1793 to 1806, to introduce a new non-Christian calendar based on *décades* and thus to erase any influence of the church on the collective mind of the people, failed in no small measure because of resistance by staunch Catholic peasants and urban women, who would not renounce the weekly rhythms and the recurrent liturgies they had grown up with (Le Goff 1980; Zerubavel 1981: 82–97).

Also in the countryside of China, the toils of agriculture were punctuated by festivals in the rich cycle of the lunar year—some of empirewide import, others local.[6] As observed by Jean DeBernardi, this cycle still provides the "primary temporal framework which orders the practice of Chinese religious culture," offering a rhythm of reunion, fostering communal identity, and structuring a cosmological framework for human experience (1992: 261). Being a cycle of celebrations in honor of gods, spirits, and ancestors, it can be compared to the Christian liturgical calendar of celebrations, although it would be improper to call it a liturgical cycle, since, unlike in Christianity, the Chinese cycle is a composite and all-inclusive one, not depending on any one set of liturgical texts or rites.[7] Emperors, divinized imperial officials, Buddhist and Daoist deities, folk deities, and ancestral spirits—all are celebrated at some point in the year. There is no single authority that decides who should be included. Instead a centuries-long stratification of different local religious traditions has yielded a calendar rich in regional variations, which in this respect is similar to the local religious calendars of the medieval West before uniformity was ordered by Rome in the sixteenth century.

However, unlike in Europe, calendrical and astronomical matters in China were tightly controlled by the imperial state, not by any "church." Astronomy was a science monopolized by the court because of its important cosmological function, and the private compilation of calendars was formally forbidden (Smith 1991: 39, 74–75). The early Qing period was in fact a very important moment in the history of Chinese astronomy and the imperial calendar. For the Manchu dynasty, a precise calendar was not only a crucial sign of legitimacy, but also a matter of proper cosmological ordering of the world (*tianxia*). It is thus not surprising that in the early years of the Kangxi reign control over the calendar and its mantic dimensions became an area of contention between indigenous astronomers and the Jesuits charged with astronomical reform.[8]

Starting in the late Ming period, the Jesuits introduced new astronomical computation methods, which had great impact on the way experts calculated calendrical time. However, as the disputes in which the Jesuit astronomer Adam Schall von Bell (1592–1666) became entangled demonstrate, such computational astronomy only increased the accuracy of the Chinese calendar; it did not change its cosmological rationale or its basic structure. Indeed, as was the case in Europe with the liturgical calendar, the function of almanacs (an elaboration on the basic structure of the imperially sanctioned calendar) in Chinese daily life was not so much the measuring of absolute time but, on one hand, the selection of auspicious and inauspicious days for agricultural work or conducting business and family functions (hemerology) and, on the other, the classification of the days on which rituals to ancestors, gods, or spirits should be celebrated. In other words, almanacs were in some sense the most basic "liturgical texts" of the Chinese: they not only were the ordering instruments of the ritual cycle but also, by virtue of the mantic arts they expounded and encouraged, were a compass to rely on in the complicated geomantic and cosmological landscape of daily life, inhabited as it was by spiritual entities and forces.

It was particularly the mantic component of almanacs that provoked disputes and debates among early Christian missionaries. Schall, who became employed in the Qing Imperial Directorate of Astronomy, was forced to rebuff accusations from opponents in the Catholic camp that he was helping in the production of a "superstitious" calendar, which would have been used by millions of Chinese to mark auspicious and inauspicious days. The Jesuit argued that he was responsible only for the mathematical accuracy of the calendar and that he could not prevent the imperial government from employing the native cosmology in its "superstitious parts" to dictate appropriate times for activities. Although Chinese divination and hemerology occasionally had been employed by Schall out of expediency, such practices were definitely opposed by the Jesuits and their literati converts.[9] Schall felt obliged, around 1662, to compose a treatise on popular calendars (*Minli puzhu jiehuo*) to clarify his position, and in 1670 Ferdinand Verbiest SJ (1623–1688), Schall's successor in the Directorate of Astronomy, authored at least three short books against the "superstitious" practices of geomancy (or, more precisely, siting), hemerology, and astrology, all of which were connected to the calendar.[10] Moreover, a number of works by Chinese converts, especially in the early Qing period, attacked divination and hemerology.[11] It might not be happenstance that most of these treatises remained unpublished: in the end, in spite of crucial postings at court, the Jesuits were unable to challenge native divinatory practices.

As observed by Richard J. Smith, institutional religious groups were in no position to undermine such ancient traditions: "Chinese monks and priests did not have the institutional power to challenge longstanding mantic traditions, even if they had the will, for the Buddhist and Daoist establishment in China remained ever subordinate to the imperial Confucian state" (1991: 270). To the contrary, the Daoist and Buddhist establishments probably endorsed mantic practices and were instrumental in having important religious festivals of their respective traditions included in the almanacs. Even when political power was used to force the adoption of a new calendar and the shedding of mantic practices, as happened with the radical introduction of a new Christian-inspired calendar (including a sabbath day and devoid of connection to the old astrology and deities) by the Taiping regime in the 1860s, popular reaction was negative.[12] The Jesuits indeed had no hope of influencing the popular use of the calendar, and even the rejection of any relation between the calendar and native mantic practices by some rationalistic Chinese scientists like Mei Wending (1633–1721) in the late Kangxi period did not hinder their flourishing.[13]

While missionaries and some converts attempted in their writings to undermine the authority of Chinese mantic practices, they did not show any interest in challenging the Chinese way of reckoning daily time. After all, the Chinese luni-solar calendar could be seen as a simple "shell" that by itself did not engender any superstitious practices. Thus, Christian converts were never asked to reject "Chinese time" in favor of "Western time." In spite of official prohibition, popular calendars were privately produced all over China, and the ubiquity of almanacs could hardly be reduced by the imperial government, let alone by a handful of Christian astronomers in Beijing.[14] The solution for missionaries was not to try to suppress popular almanacs but to assure that converts would not follow their superstitious prescriptions. Thus, Chinese Christians were asked to undertake a subtle shift in temporality, which potentially had important implications for their lives. Although the Chinese luni-solar calendar continued to mark the days for converts, Christianity superimposed on the old calendar a new temporal rhythm: the rhythm of the Christian liturgical calendar. Thus, while at the court the Jesuit control over time was disputed by native scholars, in the countryside of China, where Christian communities existed, a new set of liturgical occurrences, determined by neither imperial sanction nor native tradition but by an alien tradition and a calendar calculated in Rome, subjected the native ritual calendar and its associated social processes to a series of contestations and negotiations.

The Sociology of Time: Liturgical Calendars as Social Markers in the West and in China

To illustrate the importance of this novelty in the Chinese context, it is instructive to look at the function of liturgical calendars in creating separate communities of believers in the Mediterranean and to contrast that to what happened in the adoption of those same calendrical cycles in late-Ming and early-Qing China. As will become clear below, the exclusivist claims of the Christian calendar over the ritual life of the Chinese village resulted in partial segregation of converts from current social practices, but it also generated a wide range of negotiations between Christian and Chinese temporal practices.

The "sociologist of time" Eviatar Zerubavel has pointed out how religious calendars in the three great Religions of the Book (Judaism, Christianity, and Islam) performed an extremely important role in separating the minority group of believers from the vast numbers of unbelievers at first, while becoming the deep structure of daily life once minority became majority. The foundational unit of the Christian calendar, the week (a nonastronomical and absolutely unnatural unit), in the main is a Jewish invention, and some major feasts in the Christian calendar (such as Easter from Passover) are indeed of Jewish derivation. In the Jewish tradition, respect for the sabbath, the day of rest that memorializes the end of creation by God, is in fact so strict that any work or activity is absolutely forbidden on that day. It is easy to understand how powerful such religious prohibitions of time use can be in shaping the daily life of believers. Christians first, in the Roman empire, and Muslims later, in early-Islamic Arabia, decided to adopt the week in their fight against pagan rhythms. However, they also selected as their sabbath a different day than had the Jews: Sunday—that is, the *dies dominica*, the Lord's Day—for the Christians, and Friday for the Muslims. The Christians, moreover, starting probably around 120 CE, set the date of Easter on a different day from the Jewish Passover, declaring heretical those who would continue the celebration on the same day.

These choices in distancing the holy days of the three religious traditions historically meant that whenever the three communities, which had many tenets in common, came into contact, they were obliged by the temporal rhythm of their own liturgical calendars to segregate themselves from each other (Zerubavel 1981: 71; and 1982). In the Mediterranean monotheistic traditions the separation between sacred and profane, a concept sanctioned by Durkheim and Eliade, seems indeed quite stark. Perhaps for this reason the classical sociology of religion has shown little interest in exploring areas of negotiation. In the case of China, foreign religions had to reach compromises between their sacred pretensions and the surrounding world, and thus to engage in an array of ritual and social negotiations. In the Chinese context, this phenomenon was more pronounced for Judaism and Islam, while for Christianity it appears to have been more limited.

Jewish and Muslim enclaves existed in the territory of China proper (that is, apart from the large Muslim populations of the North-west and Yunnan) at least from the Song dynasty onward (see chapter 2 in this volume by Roger Des Forges). Although I am not aware of the survival of a Sino-Judaic calendar, it is clear from extant scriptures that the calculation of liturgical time was of utmost importance to the Jewish community of Kaifeng, which wished to celebrate the various festivals at the appropriate time.[15] In a 1663 stele Jewish leaders noted the way in which Yom Kippur, the most holy day, was celebrated: "At the end of autumn [the Jews] close their doors for a whole day, give themselves up to the cultivation of purity, and cut themselves off entirely from food and drink in order to nourish the higher nature. On that day the scholar interrupts his readings and studies; the farmer suspends his work of ploughing or reaping; the tradesman ceases to do business in the market; and the traveler stops on his way" (quoted in Pollak 1980: 293). This is an apparent manifestation of the sabbath law prescribing religious celebrations that clearly set the Jews apart from their Han neighbors. Scholars believe that the schedule of annual worship in Kaifeng was the same as that adopted by the Persian Jews. But important changes occurred in China. Between the sixteenth and seventeenth centuries, ancestral rituals were introduced in the Jewish liturgy, and they were performed exactly at the time of the seasonal rituals performed by Chinese at large, in particular at Qingming (3rd month) and at the Festival of Hungry Ghosts (7th month). Meanwhile, in ways that became more accentuated in the eighteenth century, numerous Jewish observances were slowly abandoned. Andrew Plaks observes, for instance, that on Jewish stelae of the sixteenth and seventeenth centuries, the weekly sabbath is no longer emphasized.[16]

Written liturgical calendars were certainly used in Islamic communities.[17] In 1730 the Yongzheng emperor himself, while defending Muslims from the accusations of a high Han official, observed that "the Hui people have always followed the orthodox [i.e., imperial] calendar, but the official accuses them of doing otherwise merely because they have their private method of reckoning time."[18] From this statement we learn that the emperor, while recognizing that the Muslims had their own ways of measuring time (i.e., mainly liturgical/religious time), also understood that they accepted the framework offered by the imperial government and kept their own calendars as a "private matter" for internal circulation. Indeed, especially in the seventeenth and early eighteenth centuries, that is, before the rise of the so-called New Teaching "heresy" in the late Qianlong reign, the Muslim leadership in China proper showed a great eagerness to adjust to Chinese ways, as attested both by their writings in Chinese and by their participation in the civil and military examination systems. Hui people in relatively isolated Muslim enclaves like Quanzhou (Fujian), which have only recently been re-Islamized, always maintained a remembrance of their ancestry and some core elements of their identity, but until the 1980s they ate pork and celebrated Chinese festivals and ancestor reverence on the same dates as their non-Muslim neighbors.[19]

These examples indicate that Jewish and Muslim religious calendars did not exist in isolation from the larger temporal framework imposed by the Chinese lunar calendar. As minority communities vis-à-vis the Han populace, Jews and Muslims could not cut themselves off from their social surroundings. For example, a Muslim calendar would attach to the corresponding Arabic names of the months the precise times of the beginnings of the meteorological and astrological dates of the Chinese luni-solar calendrical periods (see Farjenel and Bouvat 1908). Thus, it was the case that the Chinese luni-solar calendar, not the Muslim lunar calendar, was the pivot of time for Muslims in Han-dominated society. Moreover, the dates of major Chinese festivals became the ones on which important Jewish festivals were celebrated, and both Jews and Muslims living amidst Han majorities started forgetting their own customs and ritual cycles and adopting Chinese festivals. The lack of an effective clerical leadership conversant in the sacred languages and knowledgeable about rituals and scriptures was certainly a factor in the loss of ethnic and religious memory.

Christian Calendars in Ming and Qing China

Like Jews and Muslims, Christian converts remained part of Chinese society and shared some of its religious conventions. However, unlike in the isolated Jewish and Muslim communities referred to above, foreign missionaries emphasized the capital importance of the Christian liturgical cycle and the attached obligations of believers. In turn, this emphasis determined changes in the temporality of the converts' lives and had a definite impact on their social interactions with society at large. The Christians, like others, went through a shift from one dynasty to another and thus experienced both Ming and Qing time— politically. But in addition, the religious experience of Christians became located at the sociocultural intersection of "two worlds," and Christians found themselves positioned between two times in that sense as well. To the time organized around the agricultural year and the festivals and ritual cycles in honor of ancestors, gods, and spirits that marked rural life, Chinese Christians added—more often substituted—a new set of church devotions organized in a fixed temporal order, disciplined not only by liturgical calendars but also by fasting schedules.

In the following pages I will examine how this positioning between two worlds and two times affected the lives of Christians in a locale of southern China, Fuan (Fujian Province; see Map 2, inset), where a strict form of orthodox Catholicism was introduced by Spanish Dominican friars in the seventeenth century. More specifically, I will try to show through my case study how Chinese Christians in their daily lives negotiated between the religious and social beliefs temporally structured by the indigenous cycle of the lunar year and the new Christian obligations and devotional practices ordered according to the liturgical time introduced by missionaries. I will concentrate on some devotional practices—penance, fasting, and the recitation of the rosary—that, although disciplined by the Christian calendar and new to China, resonated with long-established, native religious traditions. These devotions introduced to the lives of Christians new temporal rhythms, but at the same time, in their contents, they resembled practices found in Buddhism and popular religion.

By exploring the range of negotiations over religious practice and religious time in the Christian community of Fuan during the formative years of the Ming-Qing transition, I aim to show how Fuan Christians concretely shaped their familial and religious practices within the framework of a "Chinese-Christian time" in the climate of general religious tolerance of the Kangxi reign and how, once it took root, Christianity continued to influence converts' "lived time" into the period of anti-Christian prohibition (the Yongzheng and Qianlong reigns). In doing so, I hope to contribute to a better understanding of the ways Christian converts in a popular milieu and in a local context "acted out" their religious faith, an area of investigation that has been little explored.[20]

Christianity in Fuan

The Christian experience in Fuan was a distinctive one. While most of the Christian communities of China in the late Ming and early Qing were under the control of Jesuits, Fuan was a Dominican mission. Missionaries who had reached China by the 1630s exclusively belonged to the Jesuit order, but after 1632, owing to a reversal of papal policy in

1600, other Catholic religious groups started to evangelize in China. Thus, in the final decade of the Ming dynasty, friars of the Dominican and Franciscan orders reached the province of Fujian, where they began to spread their faith. Unlike the Jesuits, who directed their activities at both the elite and non-elite levels, Dominicans and Franciscans mainly worked among commoners and the lower strata of the gentry (government students and lower degree holders).

In the late Ming period, the spread of Christianity in China had mainly followed a two-step sequence. The Jesuits would initially attach themselves to literati in official positions who moved from one administrative post to the next. In the process they would visit a number of localities, and they would finally find a place suitable for the establishment of a residence, usually a locale that was under the protection or influence of one of their patrons and that was strategically positioned both in the administrative hierarchy and in the transportation network. They would purchase a residence for a Jesuit priest in a major administrative center. This then would become the center of a web of missionary stations (in general consisting of a small chapel and a dwelling), which the priest would visit periodically (Standaert 2001: 534–575). Thus, Jesuit Christianity was built on a network of friendly scholar-officials and on a web of local communities in which the vast majority of converts resided—men and women of all ages and of highly varied social composition, including artisans, schoolmasters, farmers, and so on. The Jesuits would visit rural villages, but they remained based in urban centers, usually situated at the administrative core of a certain region. This distribution of Jesuit missionary residences established in the late Ming period, though it was affected by the turmoil of the dynastic change, remained largely unaltered into the Qing period. However, in Fujian, the regional focus of this study, the network of communities set up by the "apostle" of the province, Giulio Aleni SJ (1582–1649), was dramatically curtailed by the Ming-Qing fighting and the policy of coastal evacuation.[21] When a missionary was lacking, local communities would try to sustain their faith through simple devotional practices, and conversion of whole families assured that the faith became part of the heritage of a family or a locality.[22]

The friars' mode of evangelization differed somewhat from that of the Jesuits. Because of their small number and the effective Jesuit monopoly of the China missionary field, the friars, mainly of Spanish origin and based in the Philippines, had to content themselves with areas outside of Jesuit control. Since they initially could not enter China from Macao, an entrepôt of the Portuguese, who only allowed the transit of trusted Jesuits, the Dominicans and Franciscans decided to enter the Chinese empire from the maritime province of Fujian. To reach the Fujianese coast, the friars could count both on the support of the Spanish colonial government (which occupied northern Taiwan from 1626 to 1642) and on the network of contacts they had developed in Manila among the local immigrant community of southern Fujianese.[23]

While the Franciscans maintained only a sporadic presence in Fujian, deciding at the beginning of the Qing to concentrate their efforts on Shandong, the Dominicans selected a cluster of rural villages in Fuan County in northeastern Fujian—a region known as Mindong (see Map 2)—as their main missionary territory.[24] This region uninterruptedly remained under their ministration from the early 1630s until the early 1950s. Today, Catholics in Fuan township are still a sizable group, constituting at least 8 to 9 percent of the population according to 1990 official statistics.[25] In the seventeenth and eighteenth centuries, apparently, the percentage was even higher: alarmed officials in the early Qianlong reign, when Christianity had been prohibited for over twenty years, claimed that 20 to 30 percent of the local population was still actively practicing the Religion of the Lord of Heaven. Over 3,000 families—totaling probably at least 10,000 people—were identified as Christian by authorities in the wake of a 1746 anti-Christian campaign.[26]

No doubt the most flourishing period for the community of Fuan before the nineteenth century was the Kangxi reign, when imperial toleration allowed for unprecedented growth.[27] A string of Dominican missionary posts extended from Guangzhou (Guangdong) to Jinhua (Zhejiang). The main residences were in Fuan, Ningde, Luoyuan, Funing (all in Mindong), and Zhangzhou (in southern Fujian), while outposts were established in Lanxi (Jinhua Prefecture, Zhejiang) and Guangzhou. The distances between the farthest posts in Fujian-Zhejiang were considerable: thirteen days of travel between Zhangzhou and Fuan, another twelve between Fuan and Lanxi.[28] The Dominicans would occasionally travel long distances to far-flung outposts, but they mostly resided in a central place, visiting the neighboring rural hamlets frequently. This was particularly true of the Fuan region, always the most densely evangelized. There, villages could be easily reached in one day or less. A surviving 1719–1721 baptismal record-book owned by a single missionary shows that over the span of one month at least two or three villages were visited by the priest, who would administer baptisms, mostly of children from Christian families. He would probably reside for longer periods in localities where a residence-cum-church was available, while he would only visit briefly localities that merely had an "oratory" (Sierra 1719–1739: passim). The county seat of Fuan and the important nearby fortified village of Muyang had the largest numbers of Christians.

Sociologically, most of these converts belonged to the lower echelons of society, although some of them were literate. The story of the Jesuit dialog with late-Ming literati and the toils of Catholic priests who had become clockmakers and painters at the Qing court are well-studied subjects. However, no matter how important and influential the contact of the Jesuits with the elites had been, the vast majority of Catholic converts in China (who probably never exceeded 200,000) were not *jinshi* or Manchu noblemen but simple villagers and local students in the smaller towns and in the countrysides of the Chinese provinces. From the Wanli reign in the Ming until the Yongzheng reign in the Qing, these local Christians benefited from the influential contacts of missionaries in high government circles. However, they led lives that were far removed from the glitter of the philosophical debates among Ming literati or the courtly rituals of Beijing.

This was indeed the case for Mindong Christians. The region, unlike the culturally and economically advanced areas of Fuzhou and Minnan, had seen its heyday before the Yuan period. From the Tang to the Song, the major commercial venue for the agricultural products of the region and the home base of the lineages producing higher degree holders had been the Mushui valley (*Fujian Liancun* 1997: 3). Liancun, together with the other villages of Muyang in the upper reaches of the valley and Suyang on Baima harbor, formed a commercial axis that controlled the flow of people and merchandise between the coast and the interior. From the eleventh through the thirteenth century, out of the seventy-six *jinshi* holders from Fuan, fifty-six were members of the important lineages of the Mushui valley, such as the Xues and Chens of Liancun, the Lius of Suyang, and, in lesser numbers, the Miaos of Muyang, among whom many eventually became—and still are—Christian (Miao 1996?: 1; Liu and Zhuang 1996: 7–8). Fuan became the main commercial and political center of Mindong only in the Ming-Qing period. Overall, the region underwent a gradual decline in importance from the Song period on, and it was a backwater by late-imperial times.

A measure of this marginality is the fact that during the period from the Wanli through the Chongzhen reign (1573–1644), only five *jinshi* and seventeen *juren* came from the whole subprefecture of Funing, the lowest rate of success in all of Fujian. And this trend worsened during the Qing period.[29] This cultural marginality was reflected in the social standing of Dominican converts during the Chongzhen reign: while some were lower degree holders (mainly *gongsheng* and *shengyuan*), only one, Miao Shixiang, would eventually earn a *juren* degree. In the first decade of Dominican presence, a number of local government students (*shengyuan*) converted. Some, in fact, had been baptized by the Jesuits in Fuzhou while trying to pass the provincial examinations. In a local government document of 1637, we find a list of sixteen Fuan lower degree holders and a few male commoners, some clearly close relatives bearing the same surname, bringing the total to twenty-nine male Christians in positions of some leadership in the community (Xu Changzhi 1855: 2.30a–34b). Domingo Navarrete mentions in his *Controversias* that by 1649, during a period in which Christianity enjoyed the favor of the local Ming-loyalist military commander Liu Zhongzao, 5,400 people had been baptized and that between 1632 and 1671 there had been among them four *mandarines militares,* three *gongsheng,* one *juren* (probably a reference to Miao Shixiang), seventy *shengyuan* (thirty-four were still alive in 1671), and twelve *beatas* (blessed virgins) from prominent families.[30]

The region was deeply affected by the Qing conquest: between 1647 and the early 1650s, Fuan and the surrounding subprefecture of Funing, like many other coastal prefectures of Fujian, were repeatedly attacked by the troops of different Ming-loyalist regimes and by Qing forces, becoming the temporary stronghold of one side or the other.[31] Even later, with the continuation of military confrontation between the Qing and Zheng regimes and the outbreak of war between the Qing court and the feudatory Geng Jingzhong, Mindong continued to suffer from the dynastic upheaval: the coastal evacuation entailed enormous dislocations, and bandits or unruly troops continued to pillage the region, as is testified in Chinese and missionary sources.[32] In spite of this, Christianity flourished. The number of *beatas* continued to increase: 24 in 1695, 50 in 1714, between 130 and 200 in the 1740s through 1760s.[33] Also, the overall number of converts grew continuously. However, the percentage of Christian degree holders seems to have decreased during the Qing, since missionary documents stop boasting about the number of such converts. We know that two brothers from a prominent lineage of Muyang, Wang Daoxing and Wang Daosheng, who both earned *engongsheng* degrees in the 1690s (*Fuan xianzhi* 1884: 20.6b), were probably active leaders in their religious community, since they provided prefaces to some devotional works of the missionaries that were published in Fuan in the Kangxi period. At the beginning of the Yongzheng reign, in 1724, a government report denounced the presence of over ten *jiansheng* and *shengyuan* among the hundreds of converts in Fuan, while missionary sources give details on a number of Christian literati involved.[34] However, the Qianlong-period male leaders arrested by the imperial authorities were mostly *shengyuan* and more often just commoners. Clearly, the illegal status of Christianity would bar degree holders with any ambition for an official career from openly associating with the missionaries.[35]

Times of the Lord of Heaven: Calendars of Devotion

Since the vast majority of Fuan Christians were lower degree holders and commoners, among them a large number of women, it is not too surprising that they had little penchant for reading doctrinal-philosophical arguments or scientific tracts, unlike the late-Ming Jesuit converts and sympathizers in the Jiangnan area, in the capital, or in the learned circles of Fuzhou. This is confirmed by the surviving Christian literature from Fuan. Eleven Chinese books confiscated in 1746 by Qing authorities from the minuscule library of the church of Fuan reflect the range of religious interests of local Christians.[36] Those books were all published during the late Ming and the Kangxi period. Written by missionaries of various religious orders with the help of their converts, they fall into the categories of catechisms in differing degrees of sophistication (three titles), Marian devotions (three titles), the lives of saints (one title), the sacraments (one title), meditation and prayer (one title), scriptural commentary (one title), and Scholastic philosophy (one title). This subdivision of topics indicates that the two priorities for Dominican missionaries were the elementary teachings of the faith and the dissemination of devotional practices linked to the liturgy of sacraments and to the saints' calendar. Local Christians' religious interests lay in daily practices pertaining to spiritual salvation and physical healing: prayers for one's spiritual well-being and the souls of the departed; use of holy water and blessed images and objects to safeguard the spirit and body; confession of sins; rituals for the sick, dying, and dead; and so on. For many rural people, the most crucial and thorny problems of life were illness, death, and personal salvation after death, so it is only natural that some of them were attracted by the rituals and devotions of the Teachings of the Lord of Heaven.[37] As Erik Zürcher observes in regard to the Jesuit Christian communities of Fujian in the late Ming, "Christianity was not just an intellectual construct, but a living minority religion, a complex of beliefs, rituals, prayer, magic, icons, private piety, and communal celebration. In that whole sphere of religious practice Christianity was by no means a semi-Confucian hybrid [as it was in the realm of doctrine]; in fact it came much closer to devotional Buddhism than to Confucianism" (1997: 650).

Among the novelties brought to China by Western missionaries were liturgical calendars, which, as we have seen, were pivotal in ordering ritual life. Such calendars introduced to new converts the organization of "Christian time." This new structure of time, organized in the unit of seven days familiar to us in the West, was previously unknown in late-imperial China. The most important day in Christian calendars was the "Day of the Lord" (*zhuri*), and the remaining days were numbered from two through seven, revolving around that most important day.[38] Daily devotions—such as the Fifteen Mysteries of the Rosary—were to be practiced according to a specific weekly schedule, which was calculated around feastdays, that is, Sundays. Moreover, attendance at mass on the Day of the Lord was in principle a religious obligation for all believers, and according to church rules nobody should work on that day or on other religious holidays. Thus, for any Christian, calculating the occurrence of Sundays was of paramount importance in ordering religious life.

Another important aim of the liturgical calendar was to mark the celebration of the church saints. In China, new Christians would often take the name of the saint celebrated on the day of their baptism. As a consequence, the new convert gained a powerful protector in Heaven, to whom he or she could direct prayers for special favors, especially on the day when his or her patron saint was remembered in the calendar (see Couplet n.d.: 1a).

The missionaries did not attempt to introduce the Western calendar in China and substitute it for the current lunar calendar. Although such an unrealistic proposal was aired, it was rejected at a missionary conference in 1668 (see Metzler 1980: 27). Instead, following the ex-

ample of the pioneer of the mission, the Jesuit Matteo Ricci, missionaries produced adaptations, or concordances, between the Gregorian
and the Chinese lunar calendar. In a 1605 letter, Ricci referred to a
manuscript translation of the Gregorian calendar he had done:

> I have translated into Chinese the Gregorian calendar, adapted to
> their [lunar] year, so that Christians can see by themselves all the
> movable and fixed feasts of the year. Moreover, [they can] also
> [check] their moons and periods of the year, which are twenty-four,
> and do so more precisely than by using their own calendar, which
> they issue every year at much expense. Even the non-Christians
> are surprised [at our calendar's accuracy], as I have given good
> explanations [of the method in it]. Some wanted to print it; but I did
> not let them do so, since to issue new calendars is a suspect thing in
> China.[39]

Since 1589 all Ricci had done was to circulate simple one-sheet
liturgical calendars for internal use by converts.[40] Only in 1625 did
Nicolas Trigault in Xi'an dare to print a full calendar with instructions,
apparently offering a trilingual edition in Chinese, Latin, and Syriac.[41]
But fear of incurring the displeasure of officials and literati for producing an unofficial calendar must have continued to limit publication of
such works. The oldest specimen related to the liturgical calendar that
I have found (which probably derived from Trigault's prototype) is
indeed a late-Ming printed *Tuiding linian zhanliri fa* (Method to calculate the [Christian] calendrical feastdays) of 1636.[42] In the preface, the
authors observe that "since the Days of the Lord fall on the days of the
constellations *fang, xu, mao,* and *xing* [i.e., every seventh day] according to the basic calendar of the Great Ming, there is no need to describe the Western calendar."[43] The *Method* continued by explaining
the difference between the Western solar calendar and the Chinese
lunar calendar, and by suggesting ways to calculate Christian feastdays
based on the lunar cycle (Standaert and Dudink 2002: V, 303–306).
Thus, for Chinese Christians the cycle of the lunar year remained the
underlying reference structure to measure time, and it was to this that
the new liturgical rhythm was grafted.

While Sundays could be easily marked because of their astronomical regularity, other recurrences had to be calculated in relation to the
important astronomical dates of the Chinese lunar year. For example,
Christmas (*Yesu shengdan,* December 25) was usually marked as "four

days after the winter solstice [*dongzhi*, December 21]," and Epiphany (January 6) was then calculated by counting twelve days after Christmas. As explained in Christian calendrical tables, some feasts (like Easter) were "movable" according to the cycle of the moon: "Movable feasts must be calculated first by looking at the spring equinox (*chunfen*). In determining the date of Easter, [for example], if the equinox is in the first half of the month, then Easter will fall on the Sunday after the full moon (*wang ri*) [of that month]. If the equinox is in the second half of the month, then [Easter] falls on the Day of the Lord after the full moon of the following month" (Couplet n.d.).[44] Perpetual calendrical tables (*yong zhanli dan/biao*) thus allowed one to calculate feastdays for any given year. While perpetual calendars in the West were mainly used by the clergy for the recitation of the Divine Office (Bonniwell 1945: 296–297), it appears that in the China mission— including the Dominican communities that followed the usages introduced by the Jesuits—they were also employed by converts.

Following in the steps of the Jesuits, the Dominicans also produced their own liturgical calendars. An eighteenth-century perpetual calendar printed in Fuan, titled *Shengjiao zhanli zhaiqi lüeyan*, states that it was "especially created for people receiving baptism, so they could choose the name of a saint for themselves, remember easily the day on which their soul had been born in the church of God, and thank the Lord of Heaven for the grace of baptism. Moreover, there is no lack of people who, out of devotion, invoke and take saints as their patrons to obtain some grace, and such people will be able to exercise their piety as they wish [using this calendar]."[45] Fuan Christians often bore names linked to the martyrology of the Dominican order or to the devotion of the Virgin Mary.[46]

It is likely that different segments of the community had varying degrees of familiarity with such liturgical calendars. Perpetual calendars could be rather complex and required a certain level of literacy and education for proper use. Thus, in Fuan they probably circulated especially among the leadership or the most devout members of the Christian community: Chinese and Western priests, catechists and *jingtou* (prayer leaders), members of the Dominican Third Order (San hui), and *beatas*. Such individuals needed to calculate with precision the dates of religious festivals in order to lead rituals and prayer sessions when a priest was lacking, to recite the appropriate prayers, and to follow the correct fasting schedule. Also, some of them, that is, priests and—when none was available—catechists, had to administer baptism, and they had to be able to choose the right baptismal name recurring on a certain day. However, converts less involved in the devotional life of the community would probably own the simpler calendrical tables (*zhanli zhaiqi biao*)—usually consisting of one leaf—that were printed every year and specified only the main feastdays and the prescribed fasting and abstinence days (see Figure 1). Christians were not the only religious group in China using such calendars: for example, Chinese Muslims had a similar tradition of printing a calendar specifying the customary abstinences mandated by the Qur'an (see Farjenel and Bouvat 1908).

Thus a new set of Christian recurrences was superimposed on the regular time frame by means of some simple calculations, and this new cycle helped Christians to structure their religious lives. The more pious would have an intense devotional and ritual routine, but even semiliterate converts, less involved in active worship, would know when major Christian feasts had to be celebrated.

Christian Time and Chinese Time: Elements of Change and Incompatibility

As I observed in the introductory part of this essay, Christian time principally affected two important aspects of Chinese time: the selection of auspicious and inauspicious days, and the ritual cycle in honor of gods and ancestral spirits.

Almanacs were widely employed as hemerological tools as well as to determine the days on which rituals to ancestors or gods and spirits should be celebrated.[47] Fujian, one of the major printing centers of unofficial almanacs and calendars, was the home of innumerable cults, and ancestral rituals were celebrated there with great pomp and pride. Thus, a myriad of religious experts and ritual masters of ceremonies in the family cults were interested in charting time, and almanacs enjoyed the widest sales among the reading items of popular consumption (Huang 1996; Smith 1991: 77–82; Rawski 1979: 142).

Although popular almanacs and calendars could still be used by Christian converts to locate the calendrical correspondences between the lunar cycle and their liturgical calendar, the "superstitious" side of such instruments had to be ignored.[48] The practice of selecting auspicious days and times to offer sacrifices was forbidden. In the *Shengjiao mingzheng*, a catechism written by the Dominican Francisco Varo in Fujian between the early 1660s and 1677, for example, much effort is

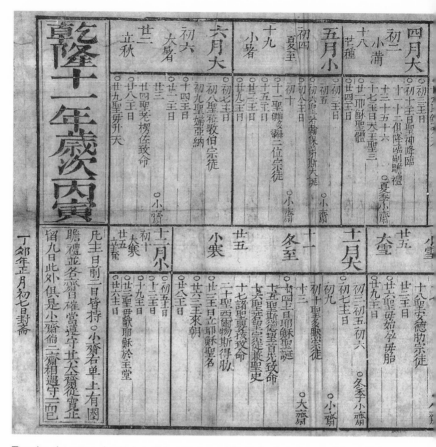

Tianzhu shengjiao zhanli zhaiqi biao (A timetable of the feastdays and fasts of the Holy Teachings of the Lord of Heaven), 1746, preserved in AMEP, Chine, vol. 434: 1069r. Courtesy of Archives des Missions Étrangèrs, Paris.

spent in refuting the belief in auspicious and inauspicious days: "The numerologists say … that the auspiciousness of a certain day and hour depends on the influence of a certain star, so that such a day is auspicious, and such an hour is good. Likewise, to avoid what is inauspicious and a diminution of fortune, one has also [to look at the stars' influence]. [However] … the sun, the stars, and the moon have all been created by the Lord Creator to benefit humankind.… Thus fortune and misfortune are all decided by the power of the Great Lord."[49]

Varo also observes that atmospheric phenomena depend on changes in temperature according to the astronomical seasons and not on astral influences. As to the selection of days for weddings and

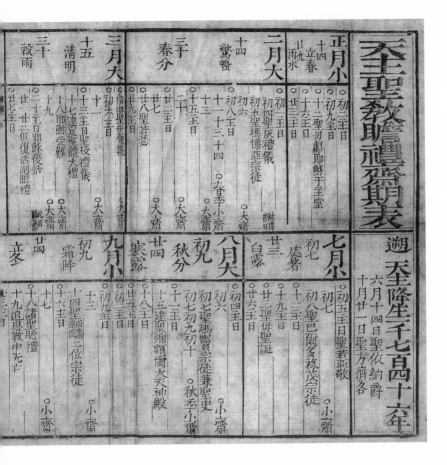

other ceremonies, he adds that the numerous Chinese who converted "do not select the days, and their joy or grief comes from the Supreme Lord" (Varo 1720: 63a). He nevertheless comments that the Holy Teachings do not forbid peasants from following the rhythms of the seasons, since to take advantage of the weather is the duty of their profession. Thus, the traditional festivals marking the agricultural year could still be retained as time markers but purged of their "superstitious" contents.

Similarly, three decades later (in 1706) Varo's confrère Francisco González de San Pedro criticized the selection of auspicious days in his catechism *Shengjiao cuoyao,* on the grounds that "human will is highly superior to the stars." In a preface to that catechism, Wang Daoxing, the converted, lower-degree-holding literatus from the village of Muyang near Fuan, mentioned earlier, endorsed the position of González by joining him in an attack on the "heterodox theories" (*xieshuo*) of Chinese divination.[50]

However, the most important consequence of conversion, entailing acceptance of the Christian liturgical cycle, was the change provoked in the temporal cycle of communal festivals and domestic ceremonies. Christians were strictly forbidden to worship local gods or Buddhist and Daoist deities, or to use the services of shamans, healers, fortune-tellers, or other religious experts. In fact, one of the first acts required of converts was to surrender to the missionary all the statues and images of gods in the house, as well as any scriptures, so that such items could be destroyed.[51] Although common to most missionary orders in China by the seventeenth century, this iconoclastic practice had first been implemented by Dominicans and Franciscans in the New World in vast campaigns to eradicate "idolatry" among the natives.[52] In the Dominican communities of the Fuan region, moreover, the removal of ancestral tablets was required, although enforcement was not always possible, and missionary positions changed over time. Clearly, the calendar of communal and domestic celebrations in honor of the gods would lose significance for those Christians who truly forsook previous beliefs.

Communal Rituals

A case reported by Varo shows the significant consequences of conversion for the celebration of traditional communal ritual events. In 1678 a conflict over participation by a Christian in a local temple cult developed in Luoyuan (Fuzhou Prefecture), a coastal town on the road between the provincial capital and Fuan, where the Dominicans had a church connected to their missionary center up north in Mindong. Varo reports the case as follows:

> In that town there is one idol among others to which the gentiles are extremely devout, and every year they celebrate a procession and a festival [in its honor], spending a large amount of money. Every year, eighteen [ritual] masters (*maiordomos*) are selected, in order to make sure that the festival is celebrated with [due] solemnity. It so happened that in that year, the father of a Christian was selected to be one of the masters. [However, that man] died before the festival,

and thus the gentiles wanted to oblige his son Jacobe to fulfill the obligation of his father. He said that he was Christian and that he could not occupy such a position.[53]

The reference here is apparently to the celebrations held in honor of the local "god of the earth" (*tushen*) in Luoyuan during the third moon (mid-April), around the time of the Qingming festival. On that occasion, a local cultic association (*she*) would bring the image of the god out of the temple and would conduct a procession in the god's territory. The Daoguang edition of the Luoyuan gazetteer records that "in previous times, each family would contribute to the expenses, and they would dress in ceremonial robes, have music played, and bring the god around in a procession.... Among all the god's festivals (*hui*), the most lavish, the one that thus was called 'the great procession' (*daying*), used to be that of the Vanguard Temple" (*Luoyuan xianzhi* 1831: 27.5a). For the festival of that temple—continues the gazetteer—the local people would be divided into eighteen groups (*dui*), called "the eighteen tents," since each group set up a colorful temporary structure (*caipeng*) with musicians and banners. It thus appears that this festival is the one described by Varo. The gazetteer adds that the expenses borne by the "gathering heads"—Varo's *maiordomos* (in Chinese *huishou,* presumably one for each *dui*)—were very high, especially on the occasions of the communal banquets (*chahui*) and the feast for the appeasement of the god (*anshen*). The text also adds that "no matter whether someone among those on the roster of names [selected on a rotating basis to support the festival] is dead or alive, or whether he has transferred his residence elsewhere, his son and nephews cannot back out from it" (ibid.) This statement indicates that attempts to avoid the responsibilities involved in the festival were not uncommon, and our 1678 incident falls squarely among those attempts. However, evidence from research on temple cults also indicates that it was very difficult to avoid one's duties.[54] In spite of this, the Christian Jacobe probably felt that his justification to avoid what others in Luoyuan perceived as his ritual duty was strong and did not warrant any counterclaim from non-Christians. By his conversion to Christianity, he had pledged allegiance to a different set of spiritual entities—the Lord of Heaven, the Holy Mother, the saints—and *their* ritual cycle.

The development of this case seems to confirm that Christians—whose loyalty rested with their new god, the Lord of Heaven—did not feel obliged to respect the local ritual cycle honoring other gods. The gathering heads, in an attempt to force Jacobe to contribute to the festival, left the statue of the earth god in the entrance hall of his house, perhaps in the hope that the god would scare him into compliance or punish him. At night, however, the mother and the mother-in-law of Jacobe, both Christians, went out and emptied a bucket of garbage on the statue. All this happened without the intervention or advice of any missionary, since none was residing in Luoyuan at the time, as Varo himself points out. The outcry that followed this sacrilegious act can easily be imagined.

> The [ritual] masters,... filled with fury and anger for the irreverence shown to their idol, immediately went to the main military mandarin of that town, who was very devout toward the idols, in order to get his consent to demolish the Church of the Lord. After he learned what the Christians had done to the most venerated idol of that place, his answer was not what they expected, but what the Lord wished, since *Cor regis in manu Domini* [the heart of the king is in the hands of God (Prov. 21:1)]. He thus told them: "If you knew that the Christians do not venerate our idols but that on the contrary they disapprove of them and defame them, you did something truly bad in bringing [the idol] to their house. I do not judge or care for things of little importance. Go back to your homes!" The gentiles were left very displeased by such an answer. They thus also appealed to the mandarin governor [i.e., the county magistrate] of the town, but he gave the same answer. Finally, furious and ashamed, they recovered their idol, cleaned it, and held their festival. (Varo 1678: 361v)

The officials criticized the ritual masters for their decision to abandon the god in the hands of people who did not recognize its supremacy ("you did something truly bad in bringing [the idol] to their house"). This seems to indicate that local headmen and officials did not subscribe to the same conception of ritual community and cycle. It is well known that officials were often critical of the organizations behind the celebration of religious festivals, since such events sometimes offered opportunities for local riffraff to earn money and bully others. In this case, however, the source underlines that the official was "very devout toward the idols."

For townspeople it was inconceivable to escape the obligations entailed by the festival, since everybody in Luoyuan was territorially subject to the god, and prominent individuals were socially bound to fulfill their ritual role. The exogenous officials, instead, even if devout, could conceive of a parallel and distinct ritual world. They indeed recognized the separateness and difference of the Christians: "Christians do not venerate our idols but . . . on the contrary they disapprove of them and defame them."[55] Indeed, at the time Christianity was benignly tolerated by the Kangxi emperor, and officials knew this well. Thus, the Teachings of the Lord of Heaven had a legal right to exist side by side with other orthodox popular cults, and converts could actually choose legitimately to withdraw from the local religious cycle, without fear of official reproach. Of course, this explanation should not obscure the fact that social pressure on converts from fellow villagers to conform to local traditions remained strong.[56]

Ancestor Reverence

Other cases of iconoclasm against local gods and Buddhist shrines are to be found in Dominican chronicles and reports from Fuan.[57] While most episodes were against "idols," a few were directed against the symbols of ancestor reverence. This was a direct consequence of the Dominicans' position on the practice, which they considered to be a complex of rituals belonging to a false and idolatric religion. Unlike the Jesuits, who well into the eighteenth century permitted offerings to the ancestors on domestic altars as long as the tablets did not bear characters indicating the seat of the soul (*shen* or *ling*), Dominicans forbade any kind of tablet or offering.[58] Studies by Ebrey (1991) and Chow (1994) have contributed to our understanding of elite debates on family rituals in the Ming-Qing period. However, it appears that the issues discussed by Confucian ritualists were not those that concerned contemporary Catholic missionaries and their converts. Rather, the latter debates centered on the compatibility of ancestral rituals with the worship of the Lord of Heaven and on whether their essence was religious or "civil."[59]

In any case, it is clear that for those believers who accepted the Dominican prohibitions, the domestic rituals for the ancestors as enshrined in the traditional liturgical cycle should be discontinued. In practice, though, the situation was more complex: while most converts were compliant and sometimes even took the initiative in destroying idols, attacks on family rituals were hardly tolerated by officials or local gentry and were resisted by some of the converts.

In the earliest anti-Christian incident in Fuan, in 1637, five years after the arrival of the first Dominican, the contentious issue of ancestral rituals and respect for the calendar had clearly emerged and crystallized around the traditional obligation to make offerings at domestic shrines and graves. Following complaints from local gentry and in the wake of a provincewide campaign to eradicate heterodox groups, local officials arrested some of the Western missionaries and their converts (on this episode, see Menegon 1997). On that occasion, the Fujian maritime circuit intendant (*xunhai dao*) wrote: "I have carefully read their books. Their main idea is that by following the Lord of Heaven they will attain knowledge of the Way, and that paradise and hell are the places where we all will finally go. [To them], the human world is totally despicable; only the Lord of Heaven is worthy of utmost respect. At the deaths of their parents, they do not express any feeling of grief by crying; after their parents' burials, they do not respect the festivals in which the prescribed sacrifices must be performed" (Xu Changzhi 1855: 2.33a).

By eliminating from the ritual calendar the prescribed family sacrifices to the ancestors, Christian beliefs undermined the foundations on which the state established its control of local society. The concerns of the intendant were further revealed later in his report, where he berated some arrested Christian *shengyuan* for proclaiming themselves "followers of Confucius' teachings" (*Zhongni jiao ren*):

> Followers of Confucius' teachings should "be circumspect in
> funerary services and continue sacrifices to the distant ancestors."[60]
> ... [Confucius says]: "When [your parents] are living, serve them
> according to the observances of ritual propriety; when they are dead,
> bury them and sacrifice to them according to the observances of
> ritual propriety."[61] How can you be called disciples of Confucius if at
> [your parents'] deaths you do not grieve, and at their burials you do
> not offer libations?! You [Christians] deeply dislike the Chinese
> [ritual for] the burial of parents and consider it wrong to conduct
> sacrifices [to the departed], since [you believe that] those who
> are followers of the Lord of Heaven will live again in paradise.
> Therefore, [for you] the sacrifices performed in spring and autumn
> all belong to the category of false rites (*shu feili*). Alas, this is to
> borrow the barbarian teachings to bring disorder to the sagely Way!
> (Xu Changzhi 1855: 2.32b)

What the intendant had read and heard about Christianity, as well as his personal experience in confronting a group of rather daring literati converts from Fuan, convinced him that their discontinuance of the spring and autumn sacrifices was just a first bold step toward a complete undermining of the Confucian Way. The spurious claim by the converts that they were intent on recovering the true meaning of Confucius' teachings—as a matter of fact, a Jesuit idea—sounded preposterous to the official.[62]

Thus, the Dominican policy represented a radical challenge to the ritual fabric of local society, and it is no wonder that it elicited strong reactions. In fact, some converts at times circumvented the prohibitions against ancestor reverence, as testified by the Franciscan Augustin de San Pascual (1637–1697). San Pascual, who ministered in the Mindong mission during the period from 1672 to 1677, reported that "in Loyuen-hien [Luoyuan County], the administration of the said [Dominican] fathers, the Christians have [ancestral tablets] in their houses, adorned with flowers and *pepetes* [i.e., incense holders]. So this was what I saw once when administering there. And in Liuyang [near Muyang] I burnt some fourteen [ancestral tablets]. They belonged to an old Christian of the Dominican fathers."[63]

In spite of such cases, however, the words of the Fujian coastal intendants and of the converted *shengyuan* showed that ancestor reverence and funerary rituals—and, as a consequence, the ritual cycle of each month—were considerably affected by Dominican policy. Many Fuan Christians did reject ancestral rituals, together with the cult of gods, and had to endure the hostility of non-Christians, who, according to Fr. Varo, in 1678 still incorrectly believed that "Christians bury their dead like dogs, without any ceremony" (Varo 1678: 352v). That neophytes were well aware of the consequences of their conversion for ancestor reverence and other "superstitions" is evident in a 1671 memorial by Varo: "We [missionaries] touch upon these points [of the superstitions] only after they have been well instructed in the fundaments of our Holy Law and the articles of faith, and when they show a clear desire to be Christians. Then according to the condition of each person, before baptizing them, we distinguish what is allowed and what is forbidden among such ceremonies ... and up to now, I have seen no catechumen renounce baptism for this reason."[64]

Nevertheless, even the Dominicans had to make some concessions, as Varo admitted when he said that certain ceremonies were allowed.

We know, for example, that at least up to the middle 1680s Christians in the Fuan region were permitted to kowtow in front of the painted images of their deceased parents and ancestors during wedding ceremonies and on the occasion of the Chinese New Year festivities, although they could put only candles and incense sticks in front of the portraits, not any form of offering or ancestral tablet (see Varo 1685: 25r–v). This kind of practice indicates that Chinese Christians actively engaged the missionaries in negotiations over ritual and devotion.

Christian Time and Chinese Time: Negotiations

The difficulties experienced by Dominican missionaries in enforcing the prohibition of ancestor reverence in Fujian underline that the exacting standards of superstition-free purity set by Varo and his companions could not always be met. The introduction of Christian time, while it succeeded in eliminating some old customs—important ones at that—also obliged the missionaries to accept an array of negotiations, pressed on them by circumstances and by the appeals of their converts. Here I concentrate on two areas of negotiation linked to the liturgical calendar: first, the precept to celebrate the Days of the Lord and the other feastdays by abstaining from work and attending mass; and second, the practice of fasting and abstaining from meat on certain days.

The Day of the Lord and Feastdays

The feasibility of respecting feastdays depended on different factors, nicely summarized in 1656 by the Jesuit Martino Martini. The first hindrance to the enforcement of this precept was the difficulty many converts found in abstaining from work.[65] Martini observed: "In the kingdom of China the majority of the Christians are workers, who must obtain food for themselves and their wives by toiling every single day. If they were obliged to observe Sundays and feastdays, they could hardly obtain sustenance for their lives. They are also obliged by their officials (*praefecti*) to work, and they cannot excuse themselves by means of any agreement, since their non-Christian officials care little whether it is a feastday or not" (Vareschi 1994: 239). In fact, he observed, even officials, under danger of losing their office, must take care of the business of their yamen every day. Early in their mission Jesuits had noted that "among the Chinese there is no feast or resting day, since all days are dedicated to work."[66] Indeed, in Ming-Qing

China there was no regular rest day; festivals were mainly seasonal and, except for some of national import, were generally local in nature (Yang 1955: 307–309).

The Dominicans also remarked that regular attendance at communal religious ceremonies on a weekly basis was an uncommon phenomenon in the religious landscape of Fuan. Diego Aduarte, the first historian of the Dominican mission, reported that Chinese Christians recently converted in Fuan would meet their obligations and listen to Mass often, in sharp contrast with non-Christians, who "go to worship very rarely to their temples and [have] almost no obligation" (Aduarte 1640: II, 486; see also Bürkler 1942: 4). Missionaries elsewhere had noted the lack of weekly communal rites since the very beginning of their enterprise: in the 1601 "Annual Letter," the Jesuit Valentim Carvalho wrote that "it is very unusual for any of the sects of China to meet very frequently."[67]

Another problem faced by Christians was the opposition that their Sunday assemblies and public celebration of feasts encountered, especially in the cities. As observed by Martini, Christian meetings were regarded with suspicion by authorities, since the laws against heterodox groups forbade any private gathering, especially wherein men and women would mix. Finally, the limited number and sparse geographic distribution of the missionaries and their churches and chapels precluded regular masses for most of the faithful. The Jesuits, in particular, resided in administrative centers and made trips to the surrounding countryside, reaching certain isolated communities only once every one or two years (see Vareschi 1994: 239). The Jesuits early on had proclaimed in their catechisms the third commandment on the respect of feastdays (e.g., Ruggieri, Ricci, and Vagnone) and had even mentioned the so-called precept of the church about the obligation to hear Mass on Sundays and compulsory feastdays and to abstain from work on those days (e.g., Da Rocha). Nevertheless, regular attendance at masses and abstension from work on Sundays and feastdays was not strictly enforced in their communities.[68] One Jesuit admitted that his order would be less exacting with new converts; they would try gradually to accustom them to confession and to attending Mass only at the major feasts (Ignacio Lobo SJ [1603–?], as quoted in Bürkler 1942: 10).

When the first Dominicans arrived in the Fuan region in the 1630s, they were surprised by the relatively casual attitude of Jesuit converts toward the feastday precept, and, together with the Franciscans, they launched accusations that the Jesuits neglected the enforcement of the church precepts. They soon made public to Christians the various rules for fasting, abstinence, and attendance at Mass, based on the liturgical calendar, and proceeded to denounce the Jesuits' laxity in Manila, Macao, and Rome. Although limitations on the work of the Dominicans were similar to those encountered by the Jesuits, the friars—forced by jurisdictional circumstances—ended up concentrating their efforts in the relatively circumscribed area of Mindong and southern Zhejiang. Thus, they were in a position to monitor their communities with greater continuity—especially the larger ones, such as those in the towns of Fuan and Muyang, in each of which the numbers of converts reached almost 2,000 in the early eighteenth century.

We know little about the direct requests of Christians regarding specific negotiations in their lives. Nevertheless, from the prolonged discussions among missionaries about the precept regarding feastdays, we can see that accommodation to local conditions was necessary.[69]

Fasting and Abstinence

The practices of fasting and abstinence from meat were strictly disciplined by the liturgical calendar. As described by Varo in his catechism, in fasting there was a distinction between "mental fasting" (*xinzhai*) and "oral fasting" (*kouzhai*). Oral fasting (also called "external fasting," *waizhai*) was a way to mortify the flesh and subdue the passions, and it was further divided into two kinds: "small fasting" (*xiaozhai*) and "great fasting" (*dazhai*). Small fasting (i.e., abstention from meat) did not mean to lessen one's food intake but to avoid "the thick taste of animals"; it was still permissible to eat "the creatures of the water, fruits, and vegetables." As for great fasting, it prescribed abstention from meat as well as reduction in the number of meals. Mental fasting was a fast of the will, undertaken to purge selfishness and overcome the "seven passions." Without mental fasting, oral fasting was meaningless.

Varo added that the formal days of obligatory fasting had been reduced by the pope from sixty-three in the original European rules (*dazhai yuangui*) to a total of nine for China, mainly during Lent, and it was a grave sin not to respect them. If people fasted on the remaining days of fasting of the universal church, they would acquire special merit (*gong*). However, respecting the days of abstention from meat was required of all and was to be calculated using the "tables of feastdays" (*zhanli dan*).[70]

The ideas of fasting and abstinence were not new to China, since

Daoists and Buddhists had been maintaining vegetarian diets for centuries.[71] Exactly because fasting and abstinence were associated in the minds of most people with Buddhism, the first generation of Jesuit missionaries appears to have been very restrained in imposing strict fasting rules on neophytes. Matteo Ricci in fact provoked a Christian-Buddhist dispute with the monks Zhu Hong (1535–1615) and Yu Chunxi (?–1621) on the subject of fasting, over the different metaphysical bases for practicing it, and over the Christian rejection of the vegetarian diet, which derived from the Buddhist command to save life.[72] One of the acts required at the moment of conversion was renunciation of "pagan" fasting practices, and the Canton missionary conference of 1668 (including Jesuits, Dominicans, and Franciscans) discussed the necessity to forbid catechumens from following the dietary prohibitions of Buddhism, which excluded, for example, fish and eggs, all foods allowed to Christians (see Fan 1633, as quoted in Zürcher 1997: 636; as well as Metzler 1980: 24).

Despite such prescriptions, missionary discussions on fasting and abstinence reveal the difficulties and negotiations of practice. Since Chinese Christians were usually poor and ate mostly rice and vegetables, they did not need to be convinced to avoid meat. However, exactly because of the poverty of their diet, to oblige them to fast could be harmful to their health. Thus exceptions were listed in the catechisms and were authorized by special papal indulgence, following petitions from the missions.[73] Moreover, particular Chinese customs had to be taken into account. In the Dominican mission of Fujian, but also elsewhere in China and in the missions of Tonkin and Cochinchina, for example, customarily on the last day of the last month of the Chinese year and on the first two days of the new year, Christians were not obliged to respect fast and abstinence regulations. This lifting of the precept was due to the fact that the Spring Festival was the most important feast period of the year in China and was usually celebrated, even among the poor, with good meals and meat dishes.[74]

Christian Time and Chinese Time: New Rhythms and Congruent Traditions

As we have seen, negotiations were unavoidable, and in fact necessary, when introducing new customs and practices. Converts positioned between two worlds and two times could not conduct their lives separate from their social context. Ritual and devotional novelties introduced by the missionaries did not flourish in a vacuum, and the harsh condemnation of idolatry and magic by missionaries should not obscure the fact that existing Chinese traditions might have facilitated the acceptance of some of the new devotional practices. Thus, Christian religious practices, while introducing new rhythms and beliefs, were to a degree internalized through existing sensibilities.

Ascetic Practices

While the days of compulsory fasting and of abstinence from meat, clearly marked in liturgical calendars, were known to Christians at large, stricter ascetic practices were the preserve of a selected few. In Fuan, for example, a limited circle of converts chose to join the Third Order of Penance of San Dominic, known in Chinese as the San hui, where such practices were held in high regard.

The Dominican Third Order originated in the spiritual climate of the penitential movements of the European High Middle Ages. It obtained its first rule in 1285 as a form of lay affiliation to the Dominican [First] Order. Members of the Third Order desired to have some form of connection to monastic life while remaining in the world. They would thus try to emulate the prayer regime of monks; engage in various penitential practices (self-flagellation, wearing a hair shirt, and so on); adopt a strict schedule of fasting and abstinence; remain virginal if unmarried, chaste if widowed, or refrain from sexual contacts on fasting days if married. Charitable activities were also among their duties. Entry to the order was subject to the approval of a Dominican priest as well as of a Third Order lay prior or prioress, and it required taking special vows (including a vote of chastity for some). During the seventeenth and eighteenth centuries the rise of a more private sense of spiritual life in Europe impelled among the members of the Third Order practices such as meditation, frequent communion and confession, spiritual retreats, and other devotional practices. Recitation of the rosary and fulfillment of the obligations necessary to obtain papal indulgences for oneself or the souls of the departed (attending masses or doing penance, for example) were among the most common of such devotions (Boaga 1973–1997).

The Dominicans immediately introduced in their Chinese missions the institution of the Third Order. One of the first Dominican converts in Fuan, the commoner Andres Huang (probably Huang Dacheng; baptized 1633, died 1648), asked to join the Third Order soon after conversion. Contemporary documents report that "after admirably completing his novitiate, he professed according to the rules of the Third Order, although his life was so reformed that he [could be considered] a member of the First Order. He lived like a priest, in perfection, without missing any fast day or the penances of religious life, even when he was ill, exercising himself daily in mental prayer" (Riccio 1667: 218v). His spiritual life was closely monitored by Fr. Juan García (1606–1665), and a relatively long hagiographic account of his Christian life written by Fr. Victorio Riccio (1621–1685) describes in some detail his charitable and catechetical activities. Huang was a married, literate man of some means. Even before conversion he enforced on his wife Teresa strict rules against anything "dishonest," keeping her female friends out of the house to prevent gossip and laziness. After conversion he convinced her to "be sexually continent, separating their nuptial bed, and observing perpetual chastity."[75]

Another prominent Christian, the *gongsheng* Joaquin Guo Bangyong, traveled to Manila in 1638 and remained in the Dominican convent of Bataan for two years, solemnly professing in the Third Order before returning to Fuan in 1641 (Riccio 1667: 234v–239v). Furthermore, a cursory look at the eulogies of the dead in the Fuan mission, as found in the *Acts* of the Dominican Chapters of Manila in the first half of the eighteenth century, reveals that a number of men from the Chen lineage of Fuan and the Miao lineage of Muyang were Dominican tertiaries. Some of them received high praise for their asceticism and lifelong chastity (*Acta* 1877).

But an even greater number of women tertiaries can be found in those lists of eulogies. Vows of chastity were especially popular among converted women, who chose to remain virgins and lead lives of prayer and self-mortification. Women who led this form of religious life, which was quite popular in Spain, were known as *beatas* (in Chinese *tongzhen;* see Christian 1981: 170). The most celebrated among these women was Petronilla Chen (b. ca. 1625), who, as a child, had been a devout Buddhist, fasting and following a vegetarian diet. Through a concubine of her maternal grandfather she learned about Christianity, and apparently she was instructed in the rudiments of the new faith by a Christian uncle. Having soon memorized the catechism, she obtained baptism at age eleven, and at eighteen she took vows of chastity as a member of the Third Order of Penance of St. Dominic, continuing her ascetic practices until her death in the 1710s.[76] Petronilla was not alone: in 1695 there were at least twenty-four other *beatas* in the territory of Fuan, between eighteen and seventy-two years of age, and they all followed the rules of the Third Order, practicing meditation, recitation of scriptures, and fasting in accord with the liturgical calendar. From a surviving Chinese-language manuscript of the Third Order rules, we learn that the aims of the Third Order were twofold: "to benefit one's soul, and to be a good example for others, so that they may better serve the Lord."[77] While in the late 1640s a group of *beatas* lived for a period in a convent in Dingtou, a coastal village not far from Fuan, sharing a communal routine of religious practices in a way similar to consecrated nuns, later on it appears that most of those women lived in special quarters assigned to them by their families in their own homes. Petronilla for a long time was the prioress in charge of monitoring her sisters in religion, and communal devotions were performed weekly in a local chapel built for the women.

In sum, the Dominican Third Order was closely connected by its vows to the First Order, and its members followed a very strict regime of penance, sexual abstinence, and prayer, disciplined by the liturgical cycle of the church. Such lay organizations were not, however, unique to Fuan: in the seventeenth century around four hundred Christian lay confraternities existed in various Jesuit communities all over China. Jesuit confraternities were different from the Dominican Third Order in that they did not entail vows and their rules were less strict. They were mostly dedicated to catechetical instruction, to assistance in the funerary rituals of departed members or poor coreligionists, and to communal devotions and charitable activities.[78] They usually met once a month and were divided into groups of youths, men, and women. They thus had a more universal appeal than the Third Order, which was an elite organization only for the most devout, aiming to set an example and to promote the spiritual growth of the members.

Many forms of organized piety existed in the Chinese religious traditions of lay Buddhist groups and charitable associations, and similarities in practices and aims of such associations with the Christian confraternities has already been noted in general terms. Besides engaging in fasts, penances, and charitable activities, many of these groups privileged the recitation of sutras. Given this preexisting tradition, it is of little surprise that recitational prayer found an enthusiastic following among Fuan Christians.[79]

Daily Devotions: Recitation of the Rosary

A daily devotional practice that characterized both communal and private religious life in Fuan was the recitation of the rosary. A 1668 pocket-size prayer book from Fuan, containing instructions for reciting the rosary, describes for Chinese converts the beginning of this tradition more than four hundred years before in Tolouse, France: The Holy Mother (*shengmu*) in person had appeared to St. Dominic, founder of the Dominican Order, and had ordered him to teach people to pray over the fifteen mysteries of the Rosary (i.e., to recite the *Hail Mary* and other prayers following meditation on evangelical episodes). Now, that devotion had reached China, and since it was not a human but a divine institution, it could not be neglected by any Christian.[80] Indeed, this was one of the most enduring practices of the Dominican mission.

According to the standard practice, a total of 150 Hail Marys were divided into three cycles of fifty, to be recited daily. The five Joyful Mysteries (meditations on the life of Christ) were to be recited on "the first and fourth day after the day of the Lord"; the five Sorrowful Mysteries (on the Passion) were to be recited on "the second and fifth day"; the five Glorious Mysteries (on the Resurrection) were to be recited on the "third and sixth day"; finally, on the Day of the Lord the entire rosary was to be recited. Thus, the faithful were required to keep a watchful count of the number of prayers they were reciting, as well as of the days during which each set had to be recited. Certainly, this was the practice that most consistently set the cadence of Christian time in Fuan.

This devotion, especially popular among women, was practiced alone, in choirs in the church, or with one's family at night. An important mnemonic device used in the recitation was the 150-bead string called in Chinese the *zhuchuan*. This was one of the most popular devotional objects imported by missionaries for their converts: in a shipment sent from Macao to Fuan in 1678, besides statues, candles, and reliquaries, we find "a large quantity of rosaries" (Varo 1678: 362v).

The popularity of the rosary among converts probably contributed to the creation of a recitational pattern uniquely Chinese in flavor. A nineteenth-century Dominican described with some surprise the way Fuan Christians mixed Western and Chinese modes of recitation, a practice that he correctly believed to have originated in the seventeenth century. A leader (*jingtou*) would loudly call out, "[Let us] intone the prayers." Prayer was opened with a double sign of the cross—tracing three small crosses on the forehead, mouth, and chest, then a large cross, and finally joining the hands in front of the chest—which was a formula employed in Spain and Portugal, and in their

colonies, and used in China until the 1950s. Then everyone would kowtow and silently recite the self-deprecatory prayers (*Confiteor* and *Miser-
eatur*). They would then remain on their knees and, following the lead
of the *jingtou*, would chant the rosary "not in a low voice, but singing
in the way a choir of monks chants in semitone, since their language
is naturally musical."[81] In fact, all the various Christian prayers were
similarly chanted in communal worship.

Once again, congruent elements existed in Chinese religious tradition. The rosary as a physical object, for example, was not a novelty in
China. First mentioned in scriptures and depicted in stone reliefs in
the fourth century AD, the rosary (called *shuzhu*, counting beads;
xiangzhu, fragrant beads; *nianzhu*, recitation beads; or *chizhu*, beads
for keeping [recitations], all terms avoided by Varo but often used by
Jesuit authors) was in fact an important devotional object in Buddhism,
mainly used to count recitations of the name of Amitābha. Initially
used by monks and nuns, it also became an object for use by the laity
(see Kieschnick 2003: 124–138).

As for the recitational patterns of Christians, a congruent tradition
in China was the recitation of sutras practiced by lay Buddhist groups.
Brunner has tentatively suggested that Christian converts probably imi-
tated the chanting of Buddhist monks, or that they used the melodies
on which poems were chanted, or that they just replicated the way pri-
mers were chanted to learn characters (1963: 157). In Fuan it is not
unlikely that they adopted the forms of recitation popular among lay
Buddhist groups, such as those in the Nonaction movement, which
began to spread in southern Zhejiang and northern Fujian in the
1630s.[82]

Although it could be used for personal prayer, the recitation of the
rosary as practiced in Fuan became the most communal of Christian
devotional practices, since it required the daily gathering of the members of each family, and even of neighbors, at fixed times. Use of the
rosary was truly a confluence of Western and Chinese practices, and it
embodied the hybrid nature of Christian devotion in China: Christian
time was no longer necessarily Western time.

Conclusion

Recently, Erik Zürcher has sketched the contours of what he calls the
two "faces" of late-Ming and early-Qing Christianity. On one hand, the

Jesuits acted in China as "literati from the West" (xiru) and tried to accommodate Christianity to the Confucian world view, producing, together with their converts, a "monotheistic and puristic version of Confucianism, strongly opposed to Buddhism, Taoism, and popular 'superstition'" (1997: 649). On the other hand, those Jesuit missionaries were and remained priests, and their converts were indeed devotees of a religious cult. Zürcher concludes that "in an elite environment, Christianity had to combine two roles that were almost incompatible" (ibid.: 650).

In this essay I have endeavored to examine the religious and devotional face of Christianity in a community evangelized by friars. The Dominicans in Fuan worked mainly among commoners and at the lowest levels of the gentry class. They spread simple devotions and tried to respond to the needs of common people who had to cope with illness and death, and who were seriously concerned about their fate after death. In this the Dominicans did not differ from the Jesuits. In fact, the general neglect of the religious activities of Jesuits among the lower echelons of the literati and among commoners in China derives from a bias of modern scholarship, which until recently has privileged elite discourse. The *Litterae Annuae* and other manuscript documents from the Jesuit missions, which are filled with stories of miracles, possessions, exorcisms, piety among commoners, and conflicts with pagans, await closer inspection.[83]

However, in spite of commonality in the work of these two religious orders among the lower classes, we cannot forget that the Dominicans were opposed to the Confucianized Christianity of the Jesuits. The Dominicans introduced new practices and a new sense of liturgical time, and their converts had to make religious choices far more radical than those of the majority of Jesuit converts. For instance, besides renouncing the old gods, they had to renounce ancestor reverence. This, as we have seen, altered the structure of the Chinese temporal cycle and entailed a radical choice that other religious minorities, like the Jews or the Muslims, never faced. The potentially disruptive effects of Christian time on the lives of converts and the backlash from surrounding society, one would think, should have doomed the Christian communities of the Fuan region to quick extinction. Such extinction should also have been accelerated in the early eighteenth century by the bitter doctrinal disputes between the two parties in the Chinese Rites Controversy—accommodationists versus purists—which resulted in the Kangxi emperor exiling those mission-aries who did not respect Ricci's position on ancestor reverence and the cult of Confucius.

However, in the end, neither social pressure at the local level nor the controversy at the imperial court succeeded in eradicating Christianity in Fuan. On the contrary, Christian communities in Fuan have survived up to this day. They have gone through more than one century of Qing religious prohibitions (1723–1844); they have been the focus of massive anti-Christian campaigns in 1724, 1729, 1733–1734, 1746–1747, 1754, 1769–1771, and 1836–1837; and since the establishment of the People's Republic they have undergone the fate of Catholics all over the country, enduring repeated waves of suppression. Today, the Fuan region is home to a strong underground church faithful to the Vatican as well as an officially recognized "open church," and imposing old and new church buildings dot the countryside, catering to the large number of local Catholics. Most of them belong to the same lineages that converted over three hundred years ago.

A number of religious devotees remained Christians in spite of the resistance encountered in their locales, and they continued to uphold a complex of religious obligations that in Fujian were considered "demanding" (*yan*).[84] Indeed, Fuan converts did away with some Chinese domestic and communal rituals (such as ancestor reverence), but their choices were not of a doctrinal nature. The Dominicans—unlike the Jesuits, who welcomed some theological reflection among their converts—saw doctrine as the exclusive preserve of the church. The friars' Christians must have been given to know that infringing upon the prohibitions of the church would cause spiritual damage, endanger their souls, and deprive them of the consoling sacraments, especially confession (which indeed were denied by Dominicans to recalcitrants after 1693).[85] Thus, certain "superstitious and diabolical" practices had to be abandoned, since converts—unlike many modern people—deeply cared for their salvation in the afterlife.

The break, however, was not as dramatic as it appears. For instance, the fear of hell and the desire for salvation after death were sentiments already widely shared among Chinese people in late imperial times in the contexts of Buddhist and other popular religious beliefs. Thus, this congruence between Catholic teachings and pre-existing religious beliefs helps explain how Christianity could find an avenue into the lives of Fuan commoners and lower gentry. The promise of protection and salvation from the Lord of Heaven seemed to them more powerful than that offered by other religious systems (on congruence, see Rambo 1993).

Moreover, as we have seen, if the missionaries were to hope for success in converting more people, accommodations had to be made. The priests had to offer their converts what they needed, and in a popular milieu devotional religiosity mattered most. It is in this area that we witness the more accommodating side of the Dominicans. Their order has always been depicted as uncompromising in matters of orthodoxy, and they have been partly blamed for the "collapse" of the old China mission. However, as J. S. Cummins has observed, it is time to abandon the image of the friars as "narrow-minded bigots sabotaging the efforts of the scholarly and accommodating [Jesuit] Fathers" (1993: 3). They faced many dilemmas in their practical ministry, and they tried as much as possible to modify the Catholic orthopraxis to suit the needs of Chinese converts without endangering what in their eyes was untouchable doctrine.

Devout Christians must have contributed greatly to shaping the cadence of a new Chinese-Christian time by pleading with the missionaries to adapt the strict observances of the church to the old rhythms of domestic and communal rituals. In this area we can detect the agency of Fuan Christians. Unfortunately, their initiatives can only be glimpsed indirectly through missionary reports, since writings by Fuan converts themselves are practically nonexistent. And yet such materials, if handled sensibly, can help to redress an imbalance in the literature, which for too long has concentrated on the deeds of foreign missionaries and consequently neglected the lives of Chinese Christians.

The composite picture of the Fuan community that I have tried to draw, using the liturgical calendar as a focal point, confirms many of the conclusions reached by scholars in recent years on the nature of the Christian community in Ming-Qing China, but it also shows that the eighteenth century did not bring the collapse of the mission.[86] For Mindong converts, ancestor reverence and communal cults as parts of daily life were indeed areas of conflict. However, such conflict in the long run could be defused—though not completely eliminated—when entire families and villages were won over to the Lord of Heaven. At that point, the pressure would decrease to conform to certain local customs that were regarded as "superstitious" by missionaries and converts, and Christian religious practices, as long as they did not provoke public confrontation, would be seen as confined to villages and families and would be tolerated by local society. Through selective rejection, negotiation, and encouragement of congruent practices, Christians in Fuan in fact were able to find a niche in the local religious landscape and to survive after the Kangxi period in spite of government repressions. Thus, a balance between doctrinal rigidity and practical flexibility was found, and Chinese and Christian "times" continued to coexist. It was a precarious balance, but I would say that it remained so because of attempts at suppression by the central and provincial governments, not because of any intrinsic irreconcilability between Christian and local ritual life and liturgical time.[87]

Abbreviations

AGOP   Archivum Generale Ordinis Praedicatorum (Archives of the Dominican Master General, Rome)

AL   Biblioteca Corsiniana, Accademia dei Lincei (Corsiniana Library, Lincei Academy, Rome)

AMEP   Archives du Séminaire des Missions Étrangères de Paris (Archives of the Foreign Missions Society, Paris)

APSR   Archivo de la Provincia de Nuestra Señora del Rosario (Archives of the Dominican Province of the Holy Rosary, Manila and Avila)

ARSI   Archivum Romanum Societatis Iesu (Jesuit Roman Archives, Rome)

BC   Biblioteca Casanatense (Casanatense Library, Rome)

BNF   Bibliothèque Nationale de France (French National Library, Paris)

FHA   Zhongguo diyi lishi dang'anguan 中國第一歷史檔案館 (First Historical Archives of China, Beijing)

MEP   Missions Étrangères de Paris (Foreign Missions Society, Paris)

OP   Ordo Praedicatorum (Order of Preachers = Dominicans)

OFM   Ordo Fratrum Minorum (Order of Friars Minor = Franciscans)

SIL   Sinologisch Instituut (Sinological Institute), Leiden University

SJ   Societas Jesu (Society of Jesus = Jesuits)

Notes

I would like to thank for their comments the participants to the Qing Formation conference, especially Professor Lynn Struve, as well as Dr. Adrian Dudink and Professor Nicolas Standaert (Katholieke Universiteit Leuven, Belgium), Mr. Richard Chu (University of Massachusetts at Amherst), Professor Zvi Aziz

Ben-Dor (New York University), and the members of the China Dissertation Group at the University of California, Berkeley. I also gratefully acknowledge support for this project from the Mabelle McLeod Memorial Fund.

1. Chaves 1993: 149. Wu Li (1632–1718) wrote this poem in Macao in the 1680s. In a note to the poem he explained: "Dusk and dawn are marked only by the sound of the 'self-sounding bells.'" We thus know that here he refers to a clock and not to the tolling of a church bell. We also know it is at the beginning of a lunation, since the new moon starts rising in the western sky two or three days after conjunction.

2. "Why is it that they [i.e., the Jesuits] divide daily classes between *mao* [5:00 to 7:00 a.m.] and *you* [5:00 to 7:00 p.m.]? / They hear the bell's gentle ringing and study only at these two times" (Chaves 1993: 152). A few years later (1705), the Kangxi emperor, also in one of his poems, showed a fascination with the Western artifice of clocks and how they monitored time with precision: "Wheels move and time turns round, / Hands show the minutes as they change" (Spence 1975: 63).

3. See Landes 1983: 25; on railways and schedules, see ibid.: 285–286. On time keeping in China, see Wilkinson 2000: chap. 6.

4. Yang 1955. An exception would be the time-keeping practices (field clepsydras, drums, and other time signals) adopted in collective farming. See the reference to a Yuan-dynasty agricultural manual in Jami 1995: 174.

5. On the conceptions of time in different cultural traditions, see Ricoeur 1976; on liturgical time, see various articles in Eliade et al. 1987. On the circularity of ritual calendars, see the entry by Giulia Piccaluga in ibid.: III, 7–10. On the encounter of Chinese and Western chronology in the seventeenth and eighteenth centuries, see Witek 1983 and Zürcher 1995.

6. For a general description of the Chinese religious calendar, see the entry by Laurence Thompson in Eliade et al. 1987: III, 323–327. On the Shang liturgical cycle and its calendar, which established important calendrical conventions in the Chinese tradition, see Keightley 2000: chaps. 3 and 4.

7. "Liturgy," a word of Greek origins referring to an act or work (*ergon*) performed by or for the people (*laitos*), became an important concept in the history of religions only in the nineteenth century, when reform movements in European Christian worship resurrected it as a way to designate a particular set of cultic actions. In a general sense, scholars have come to define liturgy as "any system or set of rituals that is prescribed for public or corporate performance." Such systems entail socialization, and often temporalization by a calendar as well, so that "a principal effect of liturgy ... is to structure time, thereby making it available for conscious experience and intellectual comprehension. This in turn makes possible the further elaboration of liturgical

action." See the entry by Theodore W. Jennings, Jr., in Eliade et al. 1987: VIII, 580–583.

8. For a recent overview in English, see Chu 1997 as well as several articles in Malek 1998.

9. In line with the dominant paradigms endorsed by the church in the six-teenth and early seventeenth centuries, Adam Schall and Martino Martini SJ (1650s–1660s) did accept some elements of Chinese astrology, while Verbiest in the 1670s had a more rationalistic and negative attitude toward it, reflecting the changing climate with regard to astrology in the latter part of the seven-teenth century in Europe. See Huang 1991b: 6–7; Martini 1998: I, 171–217; Golvers 1993: 73–74; Menegon 2000.

10. For a bibliographical note on Verbiest's *Wangzhan bian* (Critique of the falsities of divination), *Wangtui jixiong zhi bian* (Critique of the falsity of aus-picious and inauspicious matters), and *Wangze bian* (Critique of hemerology), all published in 1670, see Huang 1991a: 15–16. According to classical Thomis-tic theology, there are four species of superstitions: "improper worship of the true God ('indebitus veri Dei cultus'); idolatry; divination; vain observances, which include magic and occult arts" (Herbermann et al. 1913–1914: XIV, 339). See also the *Summa Theologiae* II-II: secs. 92–96. While Chinese geomancy (*fengshui*) is probably more a form of magic than of divination, numerology and astrology are certainly divinatory arts in the Western sense. In spite of this, in early-seventeenth-century Europe only "judiciary astrology" (prediction of future events) was not accepted by the church, while "meteorological astrol-ogy" (prediction of weather and medical conditions) could be practiced.

11. On some manuscript works preserved in the Archivum Romanum So-cietatis Iesu (ARSI) that criticize geomancy and astrology, see Chan 2002, and Menegon 1995; see also Xu Zongze 1949: 110–111.

12. The Taipings proclaimed: "All the corrupt doctrines and perverted views of preceding almanacs are the results of the demons' cunning devices to deceive and delude mankind. We, your ministers, have eliminated them en-tirely; the years, months, days, and hours are all determined by our Heavenly Father.... How can any of them be good or bad? What is the use of choosing [among them]?" (quotation, Michael 1966–1971: II, 234; see also Smith 1991: 89).

13. As a matter of fact, Mei Wending and many other mid-Qing scientists ended up rejecting, as well, the Christian theologico-cosmological arguments that the Jesuits had connected to their astronomical and calendrical knowl-edge (Martzloff 1993–1994: 72). On Mei Wending and geomancy, see ibid.: 70; Smith 1991: 88.

14. On the spread of popular almanacs, see Smith 1991: 89; and 1992; as well as Huang 1996.

15. Leslie 1998 does not mention any Sino-Judaic religious calendar.

16. On Jewish rituals, see Pollack 1980: 293–294, 412. On the Kaifeng stelae and the sabbath, see Plaks 1999: esp. 44–45. Erik Zürcher calls this phenomenon "reductionism" as far as the Jewish rituals and lifestyle are concerned—that is, adoption of Chinese customs and reduction of Jewish ones. He also introduces the concept of a Chinese "cultural imperative," that is, the necessity that imported religions adapt to the Confucian order (Zürcher 1994).

17. An example is a late-imperial Sunnite calendar from the mosque of Tongzhou, near Beijing, titled "Schedule of fasting and worship of the Islamic doctrine for the year *wushen*, 34th year of the Guangxu reign of the Great Qing [1908]—taboo days of the 1,314th year after the death of the Noble Saint of the Western countries [Muhammad]." It consists of a simple sheet of yellow paper, with indications of the correspondences between the traditional dates of the Chinese year and the important celebrations and fasts of the Islamic tradition, listed under the Arabic name of the month. A good third of the space is dedicated to an exposition of the twelve Muslim commandments, a list of the important prayers to be recited daily, some of them identified by the Chinese hour, and a list of the twenty-eight bodily movements to be employed in prayer at certain precise times (Farjenel and Bouvat 1908).

18. *Shilu* of the Qing Yongzheng reign, j. 94: 4b–5b, as quoted in Leslie 1986: 124, with modifications.

19. The only present-day vestige of Muslim religious taboos in the practices of the Ding lineage of Chendai, near Quanzhou, studied by Gladney, is the omission of pork in the offerings to the ancestors, as stipulated in the genealogy. Gladney observes that the Ding celebrate ancestral worship four times a year, at the same times as their Han neighbors. Apparently only one special Muslim festival, the "cake-offering day" (1st day of the 6th month) has survived in Fujian (Gladney 1991: 270–271). On late-imperial Muslims, see Leslie 1981; 1983: 113–116; and 1986: 105–129; as well as Aziz Ben-Dor 2000.

20. On the study of popular Christianity in late-imperial China, see Standaert 1997: 593–595; Menegon 1998: 99–119; and Standaert 2001: 386–393.

21. On Aleni see Menegon 1994; *"Scholar from the West"* 1997.

22. A case in point is the Yan family in Zhangzhou, which converted in the 1630s and whose members are mentioned in eighteenth-century documents as being Christians.

23. For an overview of the Manila-Fuan connection, see Wills 1994.

24. On the relocation of the Franciscan mission from Mindong to Shandong, see Mungello 2001: 55–56.

25. Contemporary official statistics notoriously underestimate religious phenomena. The *Fuan shizhi* (1999: 1036–1037) reports 45,386 Catholics as of 1990 (8.56 percent of the total township population of 530,069).

26. *Fuan xianzhi* 1884: 9.7b, text of the "Inscription for the Reconstruction of the Ciyang Academy" by County Magistrate Du Zhong: "In the spring of the 11th year of the Qianlong era [1746], I was ordered to come and administer this city. [At the time] 20 to 30 percent of the local population was mired in the heretic teachings of the Western Ocean." In a vermilion-endorsed memorial by Fujian Provincial Surveillance Commissioner Gioro Yarhašan, we find mention of 3,000 families of converts (Gioro 1746). A comparison of the population data of Fuan county for the period between the 1391 census and the censuses of the Republican period (1941–1946) yields an average of about five people per household. This figure squares with what we know of family size in Fujian over time. Three thousand families would thus amount to a total of approximately 15,000 people; however, missionaries' sources give a number closer to 10,000, which may be more realistic. Taking the 1783 census of 123,007 as a basis (late-eighteenth-century censuses of Fujian are considered fairly reliable; see Ho 1959: 54), the percentage of Christians for the whole county would be roughly 8 percent. The number reported by officials (20 to 30 percent) is higher because they probably were considering the population of the major settlements only, where Christians were concentrated. For historical statistics on Fuan, see Chen 1991: 195.

27. Two crises touched the community in the Kangxi reign: the Calendar Controversy in the period 1664–1671 and the expulsion after 1707 of missionaries opposed to the Chinese rites and faithful to the Papal legate Mgr. De Tournon. In both cases, the absence of the Dominicans from Fuan was only temporary.

28. Report of Fr. Joaquin Royo (1741) in J. M. González 1952–1958: 372.

29. In the Ming, the *jinshi* and *juren* from Funing represented only 0.6 percent and 0.7 percent, respectively, of the Fujian provincial totals; in the Qing (1650–1820), the average was 0.6 percent and 0.4 percent respectively. Liu and Zhuang 1996: 152, 160, 212, 220.

30. Navarrete's *Controversias* (1677) as quoted in J. M. González 1955–1967: I, 297.

31. For details and further references on the vicissitudes of Funing Prefecture during the conquest, see Menegon 2002 and 2003.

32. Zhu 1985–1986: 395–397; Zheng 1992: 177; Riccio 1667.

33. Archives du Seminaire des Missions Étrangères de Paris (AMEP),

Chine, vol. 404: 81; Gioro 1746. In 1761, according to the "Relación" of Fr. Terradillos, there were eighty *beatas* in Muyang alone, and two hundred in the whole region of Fuan; see J. M. González 1955–1967: 503.

34. *Yongzheng chao* 1998: I, 257–258; *Lettres édifiantes* 1875–1877: III, 347; J. M. González 1955–1967: III, 159–171.

35. I base this statement on a number of Qianlong-period memorials on the 1746 anti-Christian campaign in Fuan, today preserved in Beijing, Taibei, and Paris.

36. The list, contained in the provincial-level interrogations of some arrested Christians, is preserved in AMEP, *Chine,* vol. 436: 151r. The books were authored by Dominican, Franciscan, and Jesuit priests. In Fuan, although many converts were illiterate, a number of them—male and female—could read the catechisms and the prayerbooks, and a few had undergone formal preparation for bureaucratic careers. Nevertheless, they were little involved in any sustained doctrinal discussion.

37. For a general evaluation of Christianity in late-Ming Fujian, see Zürcher 1990.

38. In the Portuguese dominions it was customary to follow the ancient ecclesiastical practice of numbering the days after Sunday, called *feriae,* from two to seven, starting on Monday (*feria secunda,* in Chinese *zhuer* or *zhanli er,* and ending on Saturday (*feria septima, zhuqi* or *zhanli qi*). Elsewhere, including Spain, the days after Sunday were numbered from one through six. Thus, although most Chinese Christians used the Portuguese method introduced by the Jesuits, the Spanish Dominicans numbered these days from *feria prima* to *feria sexta.* See Herbermann et al. 1913–1914: VI, 43; Varo 2000: 165.

39. Letter to Fr. Fabio de Fabj in Rome, written in Beijing, May 9, 1605, in Ricci 1911–1913: 264; see also Ricci 1942–1949: I, 271, n. 6.

40. Letter to Fr. Claudio Acquaviva, General of the Society of Jesus in Rome, written in Beijing, August 22, 1608: "The Christians come [to church] very frequently on Sundays and even more frequently on important feasts and on the major saints' days. Every year we give them a printed paper sheet [containing those dates] so that they can come [at the appointed time]." See Ricci 1911–1913: 359; also *Littera Annua,* 1589, quoted in Ricci 1942–1949: I, 270–271, n. 6.

41. Pfister 1932–1934: 116; Bernard 1945: 339. Pfister observes that no one knows why it was also translated into Syriac. Modern bibliographies are silent on the location of extant copies.

42. The text, whose printing was sponsored by Christians, is in Standaert and Dudink 2002: V, 301–333; compare a manuscript version copied by a convert in Hangzhou, Chinois 7344, Bibliothèque Nationale de France, copy at

Sinologisch Instituut, Leiden University. Elsewhere in Asia Christian converts engaged in the practice of copying or printing liturgical calendars based on the Chinese calendar. Christian calendars from China, for example, were sent to Japan in the late 1630s, after the Tokugawa shogunate forbade Christianity. Such calendars were copied by hand over and over by local underground Christians for the following two hundred years, without changes. A Japanese church calendar kept in the Nagasaki Prefectural Government Archives, copied on March 3, 1787, by the crypto-Christian Domingo Ikusuke from Urakami, is in fact based on a 1634 original. The Sundays and the saints' days written in Japanese kana are coupled with days in the regular Japanese calendar. Movable feasts continued to fall on the same dates regardless of astronomical changes for more than a century! See Murakami 1942; see also López Gay 1970: 270–271, 299; and Turnbull 1998: 138–141. On Christian concordances with the Chinese lunar calendar in the Catholic mission of Tonkin (Vietnam), see Forest 1998: III, 151–152.

43. Standaert and Dudink 2002: V, 303. *Fang, xu, mao,* and *xing* are four constellations among the twenty-eight in Chinese calendars. The days represented by these constellations are always Sundays in the Western calendar.

44. In reality, the date of Easter cannot be simply calculated based on the astronomical full moon, since it is based on an artificial "ecclesiastical full moon." Thus, special tables were prepared in Rome that were needed to set the date of Easter as the pivot for movable feasts. The authors of the *Method,* in fact, observed that "once the number of years [included in our calendrical tables] runs out, you will have to just wait for a master [i.e., a Jesuit] in the future to give you a [new] text to clarify [the matter]." Thus, the date of Easter had to be communicated from the West; see Standaert and Dudink 2002: V, 308.

45. Royo n.d. Although published in the 1740s, this calendar was closely modeled on earlier ones, rare examples of which survive in European libraries and archives. Unfortunately, on my visit to the Dominican Archives in Rome (Archivum Generale Ordinis Praedicatorum or AGOP) in November of 1998, I had to use the Latin translation of the Chinese original. The latter apparently had disappeared since it was last seen and partly photographed by José Maria González OP in the 1950s (see J. M. González 1952–1958: II, 435; a photograph of the first page of the "Lüeyan" is in I, 335). The passage I quote comes from "Ratio Calendarii perpetui a Sancta Dei Religione instituti explanatur," 9r; similar wording in Chinese can be found in Couplet n.d.

46. Male names such as Joaquin (father of Mary), Domingo (founder of the Dominicans), Raymundo (of Peñafort, a Medieval Dominican), or José (husband of Mary and protector of the China mission), and female names

such as Rosa (of Lima, Dominican Tertiary), Maria (the Virgin), or Catalina (Catherine of Siena, Dominican Tertiary), rendered in Chinese characters, were the most common. They may have been chosen regardless of the birthdays of converts but rather out of devotions in the Dominican tradition. See Sierra 1719–1739, passim; Bonniwell 1945, chap. 10, "The Dominican Calendar," 98–117.

47. In addition to the common custom of presenting food offerings every two weeks in the home shrine, a liturgy for ancestral rites as a seasonal festival was established by Zhu Xi, who suggested divination as the appropriate method to select the sacrificial days. However, by late-imperial times such divination was mostly abandoned in favor of fixed dates. See Ebrey 1991: 129, 183.

48. Indeed, sometimes existing almanacs were used by Christians to calculate liturgical feasts. Ricci, before a printed Christian calendar existed (1589), simply made notations of the feastdays on a common Chinese calendar to let his Christians in Zhaoqing (Guangdong) know the time for prayer in his absence. See Bürkler 1942: 9.

49. Varo 1720: 61b–62a. Earlier Jesuit catechisms were also critical of those same beliefs.

50. González de San Pedro 1706: 10a.

51. For examples in the region of Fuan, see Varo 1678: 358v.

52. See Pita-Moreda 1992: 231–234. On the meaning of idolatry for seventeenth-century missionaries in Latin America, see Bernand and Gruzinski 1988.

53. Varo 1678: 361v. Clearly the father of the Christian was not a convert.

54. Barend ter Haar observes: "The Gathering Head was held personally responsible for financing the collective banquet. The festivals were communal enterprises, which is proven by the very fact that the less privileged ran into financial difficulties because of the equal rotation of organizational responsibilities" (1995: 22). A seventeenth-century description from Guangdong is quoted by Haar: "When the head of a gathering is poor, he will sell off property to do it. In extreme cases, they sell off children, [for] they do not dare to retreat from the area" (ibid.: 21). For examples in the region of Fuzhou, see Szony 2002: 190–191, 284.

55. A similar case occurred a few years later at the very end of the Kangxi reign in Shanxi, where a magistrate exempted Christians from contributing to a local religious festival. Responding to the appeal against his decision presented by non-Christian villagers, he is reported to have answered: "The religion of the Lord of Heaven does not allow Christians to contribute silver for operas [to be performed in temples]. Why do you want to oblige them to do so? If Christians wanted to oblige you to contribute money to buy incense to

be burned in front of their Lord of Heaven, would you give silver to them [for that purpose]? No, you would not, because you are not Christians. Thus, the same applies to you." See a letter of Mgr. Eugenio Piloti OFM to the Procurator of Propaganda Fide, Fr. Arcangelo Miralta, dated August 24, 1735, preserved in the Archives of Propaganda Fide, Rome, as quoted in Margiotti 1958: 444.

56. In 1699 forty converted lower degree holders in Fuan bribed the local magistrate to be exempted from participating in the cult to Confucius; see J. M. González 1955–1967: I, 627. In 1730, seven years after the Yongzheng emperor's strict prohibition of Christianity had been issued, a number of Christian lower degree holders were arrested in Fuan and obliged by the county magistrate to participate in the annual rituals to the local city god. However, they promised to pay a large amount of money (600 taels) to be exempted from the ritual, and, finally, after the intercession of the local military official, who feared that complications could develop, they were exempted. See the letter from Fuan by Fr. Juan Alcober, February 27, 1730, in J. M. González 1952–1958: II, 451. In the late nineteenth century conflicts between Catholics and non-Catholics over temple festivals and other rituals were countless. At that time religious tensions between converts and other villagers were fueled by the legal meddling of foreign priests and consuls, but they also had deep roots in daily disputes having nothing to do with religion. In our seventeenth-century case, the missionaries did not intervene at all. On the nineteenth-century cases, see a number of essays in Bays 1996.

57. See, for example, Riccio 1667: 67v–68r, 163v–164r; Varo 1678: 351r, 358v.

58. The Jesuits in China invented the category of "civil" rituals and applied it to ancestral rites and to the rites in honor of Confucius, thus trying to salvage their "Confucian Christianity." Jensen (1997) misses this important point in his attempt to "manufacture" the "Confucians" as a sort of religious order in the eyes of the Jesuits (see Standaert 1999). On a similar Jesuit position in India, see Zupanov 1996: 1201–1223; and 1999: 97–101. On the tablets in China, see Dehergne 1978.

59. There is an enormous seventeenth- and eighteenth-century Western-language literature on the Chinese rites. A cache of Chinese manuscripts in the ARSI (Japonica-Sinica I, 39–42; published in Standaert and Dudink 2002: IX–XI) reflects the heated debates on rituals in Fujian and Zhejiang in the 1660s to 1690s between Jesuits and their converts, on one hand, and the Dominicans with some of their converts, on the other. On these materials see Lin 1994; Standaert 1995: esp. 15–21; Huang 1995; and Li Tiangang 1998.

60. These are the words of Master Zeng, a disciple of Confucius, in the *Lunyu*, 1/9. See Ames and Rosemont 1998: 73.

61. Quotation from the *Lunyu*, 2/5; Ames and Rosemont 1998: 77, modified.

62. On this idea among converts, see, for example, Standaert 1988; 1995; and 2001: 633.

63. Letter to Artus de Lionne MEP (1655–1713), in *Sinica Franciscana*, VII, 248–249, as translated in Chan 1996: 430. In the period between the 1650s and the 1690s, the Jesuit-Dominican debate on ritual issues, involving some Fujianese Christians, was still open, and a uniform position among all missionaries had not yet been reached.

64. Varo 1671, as quoted in J. M. González, 1955–1967: I, 400.

65. In 1537 Pope Paul III's constitution "Altitudo divini consilii" granted an indult to the peoples of the West and Southern Indies, limiting compulsory abstension from work to only Sundays and twelve major feasts, for a total of around sixty days. This constitution was not initially applied in China by the Jesuits, but was officially imposed by Rome on the China mission in 1685. For the text of the constitution "Altitudo divini consilii," see *Collectanea* 1907: 30–31.

66. *Littera Annua* of 1610 by Fr. Nicolas Trigault, quoted in Bürkler 1942: 3.

67. Quoted in Bürkler 1942: 3. Here it is necessary to qualify the opinions of these early missionaries. Christian worship in fact resembled in its regularity the strict routine of certain lay Buddhist groups, such as the followers of Luo Qing, who had periodic meetings, usually twice a month, with intense devotional activity (see Overmeyer 1976: 187–188). Franciscan missionaries reported such sectarian activities in Shandong in the early eighteenth century (see Tiedemann 1996).

68. See the catechetical texts in Standaert and Dudink 2002: I, 71 and 82 (Ruggieri); 93 (Ricci); 156–159 (Vagnone); 447–448 and 459–461 (Da Rocha).

69. An instruction by Propaganda Fide solicited by the Dominican Juan Bautista de Morales, dated September 12, 1645, clearly applied to Chinese Christians the 1537 constitution "Altitudo divini consilii" on the matter of feastdays (see *Collectanea* 1907: 31). However, the objections of the Jesuits blocked its universal implementation in China. In an instruction by the Holy Office of March 23, 1656, the question was taken up again, and the response was favorable to the Jesuit position: "The positive law [of the church] regarding fasting, the observance of feastdays, and the yearly confession and communion must be communicated by the missionaries to the Chinese Christians as

obligatory, under pain of mortal sin. At the same time, however, it is possible to give explanations of reasons for which the faithful can be excused from the observation of the precepts. At the discretion of the Pontiff, it is possible to concede to missionaries the faculty of dispensation in particular cases only, following their own judgment" (ibid.: 39). After the 1685 imposition of the precept in the Vicariates Apostolic of East Asia as defined in "Altitudo divini consilii," respect for it remained problematic. As observed by the Vicar Apostolic of Sichuan in the late 1760s, "Among the Ten Commandments ... the third one [on feastdays] is the one the Chinese, still weak in the faith, are less inclined to obey." For that reason, the Holy Office in 1769 gave a special dispensation of twelve years to Sichuanese Christians, prescribing attendance of mass in the morning but allowing work on the afternoons of Sundays and precept feastdays, except for a total prohibition of labor on four major feasts. Furthermore, in 1796 the special condition of isolated and inaccessible regions of China was accepted as a reason to excuse Christians from attending Sunday and feastday masses in most cases (ibid.: 299–300 and 389; see also Bürkler 1942: 38–41).

70. Varo 1720, 5.15b–17b. The church's general obligations of fasting in the seventeenth century were the following: all the forty days of Lent; the Ember Days (the days of fasting of the four seasons, i.e., Wednesday, Friday, and Saturday after the first Sunday of Lent, after Whitsunday, after September 14, and after December 13); and the vigils of precept feastdays. Strictly speaking, one was allowed to eat only in the evening. However, the church tolerated that the main meal be taken at noon and that a "coenula" (small dinner) be eaten in the evening. Meat, eggs, and dairy products were forbidden on fasting days. Nevertheless, it was stressed that the fasting precepts could be differentiated according to local circumstances. Thus Pope Paul III, in his 1537 constitution "Altitudo divini consilii," had allowed special rules for the West and Southern Indies, where fasts were compulsory only on the seven Fridays of Lent and on the vigils of Christmas and Easter, for a total of nine days, a rule applied to China starting in 1685. Moreover, the church precept could be overruled when it would either harm health or impede the exercise of one's obligations. Thus people with heavy jobs would be exempted. Also, the poor who only had a meager diet were excused. Finally, abstinence days in the China mission, similar to those in Europe, included each Friday and Saturday outside Lent, all the days of Lent except Sundays, the Ember Days, and thirteen feastdays, for a total of 155 days. On seventeenth-century practice in Europe and China, see Bürkler 1945: 260.

71. On the meaning of the Chinese word used for "fasting" (*zhai*), see Malek 1985. For an early missionary description of an array of Chinese fasting

practices, see Intorcetta 1668a and 1668b, summarized in Margiotti 1958: 34–35.

72. Yü 1981: 87–90; Kern 1992: 71, 328. Ricci wrote in his *True Meaning of the Lord of Heaven* that there were three reasons for fasting: penance, subduing of passions, and renunciation of pleasures and lust. He also classified the types of fasts (1985: 279–284). However, in the end he seems to dismiss fasting as a practice unworthy of much attention. On the motivations for abstinence from meat among late-Ming Buddhists and reactions to the Jesuit position, see Handlin Smith 1999: 62–63.

73. Besides Martini, Varo too observed the impossibility of respecting all the fasting days prescribed in the Roman liturgical calendar: "I do not know if one out of ten Christians could comply with all the fastings of Lent and the vigils of the [liturgical] year, as experience has taught us" (1685: 25r). On dispensations for the China mission, see Furtado 1700: 11, note b; *Collectanea* 1907: 38, 338.

74. See Bürkler 1945: 267. The matter of fasting and abstinence during the Chinese New Year was repeatedly brought up by missionaries in Tonkin and in China in the seventeenth, eighteenth, and nineteenth centuries, an indication that it remained a point of contention and that missionaries and Christians ignored repeated orders from Rome strictly to respect the prescribed fasts and abstinences. In 1768, for example, the Vicar Apostolic of Fujian, Francisco Pallas OP, residing in the region of Fuan, wrote to Rome: "Since the second day of the first moon of the coming year coincides with Ash Wednesday [February 8, 1769], local missionaries advanced a doubt to me: must the Chinese fast and abstain from meat on that day? I see in a perpetual calendar in Chinese characters, printed by order of ancient missionaries, a note: 'If the first Chinese moon falls into Lent, the Chinese shall not be obliged to abstain from meat or to fast in the last day of the last moon and in the first two days of the first moon.' [This note can in fact be found in Royo n.d.: 5r.] From this I infer that this custom has been approved and published by ancient missionaries in this empire, since many Chinese have in their hands this Chinese-language calendar so as to know when the Holy Mother Church celebrates the saints. I do not dare to give a response on this custom. I pray the Sacred Congregation [of Propaganda Fide] to give me an answer for the following years, whether this custom is to be censored and eradicated or tolerated." The Holy Office responded on July 12, 1770: "We order [Propaganda Fide] to send once more the already printed decrees [decrying this custom, issued in 1663 and again in 1760] and to communicate in writing to the Vicars Apostolic of Tonkin and of Fujian that they have the duty to apply those decrees and to inform the Sacred Congregation about their diligence in

executing them. They should also first of all delete the note read in the Chinese calendar, that is, that in the first three days of the New Year [*sic*] Christians are dispensated from abstaining from meat in case those days fall into Lent." The last act in this long process of negotiation came only on June 10, 1868, when Rome granted the faculty of dispensation in matters of fasting and abstinence on the Chinese New Year to the Vicars Apostolic of China and the neighboring kingdoms. See *Collectanea* 1907: 276 and 302 (quote).

75. Riccio 1667: 221r. The chapter of the "Hechos" recounting Huang's life is titled "Vida y muerte dichosa de Andrés Hoang, de la tercera órden de Santo Domingo."

76. Modern authors such as Garcia (1947) have offered a different surname for this woman (Liu). However, according to a list of *beatas* dated 1695, her last name was Chen (see AMEP, *Chine,* vol. 404: 81). This is confirmed in some missionary sources (Gentili 1887–1888), which call her "Tein," the Fuan-dialect pronunciation of "Chen" (see Ibañez 1941–1943). In 1695 Petronilla was seventy, and thus her birth year should be around 1625. According to Riccio, she was received into the Third Order by Fr. Capillas in the 1640s at age eighteen, thus confirming that she was born in the 1620s. Her death occurred in the 1710s, since she was commemorated in the Manila Dominican chapter of 1720. See biographical data on Petronilla in Riccio 1667: 161r ff.

77. I found the number, names, and ages of *beatas* in a letter written in 1695 by the Christian Virgins of Fuan to the Visitation Sisters of the Convent of Beaune (France) (see AMEP, *Chine,* vol. 404: 81). On the Third Order's rules in Fuan, see Royo n.d.

78. See Bornet 1948; Dehergne 1956; Margiotti 1962–1963.

79. On similarities between Christian and non-Christian religious groups, see Standaert 1988: passim. On "sutra-recitational sects," see Naquin 1985: 261.

80. "Meigui shiwu duan yin" (Introduction to the fifteen mysteries of the rosary), in Varo 1668: 46a–47b.

81. Gentili 1887–1888: III, 160, referring to the 1850s. Elderly church-goers still chant the same way today during mass, as I witnessed in Beijing in the early 1990s.

82. From some anti-Christian memorials of 1637 preserved in Xu Chang-zhi's *Shengchao poxie ji,* it appears that local officials considered Christian and Nonaction groups to be very similar in their beliefs, especially in their hostility to ancestor worship. On the sectarian groups of southern Zhejiang and northern Fujian at the time, see Lian 1989: 55–61; Ma and Han 1992: 634–640; Haar 1992: 231–233.

83. On Jesuit popular Christianity in late-Ming Fujian, see Zürcher 1985:

359–375. A recently published primary source on Fujianese popular Christianity, covering the 1640s, is Gouvea 1998. On daily life in the Jesuit mission of Jiangnan (1670s), see Golvers 1999.

84. See the comments of Jesuit converts in Li Jiubiao n.d.: 8.1a: "The rules of the [Christian] teachings are very strict, and they are not easy to follow"; and Li Jiugong n.d.: 1.15a: "There are people who are attracted by the orthodoxy of the Heavenly Teachings, but then they are put off by its severity, and they balk." See also Zürcher 1997: 633.

85. In that year, the Vicar Apostolic of Fujian, Charles Maigrot MEP (1652–1730), officially forbade the "Chinese rites" (i.e., ancestor worship and the cult of Confucius). In two letters now kept in the ARSI, a prominent Christian from Zhangzhou baptized by Jesuits, Yan Mo, lamented, "This is like being in burning fire!" when Fr. Magino Ventallol OP (1647–1732) threatened denial of the sacraments unless Yan renounce the forbidden rites. For a summary of the letters, see Chan 1996: 436.

86. See, for instance, Zürcher 1997: 650: "The two faces of early Chinese Christianity constituted an internal contradiction that never was solved, and that no doubt has contributed to its final breakdown in the early eighteenth century."

87. This claim applies only to the period before the Opium War. In Menegon 2002 I have further explored the relationship between the state and local Christian communities in Mindong during the eighteenth century, using records preserved at the First Historical Archives of China and elsewhere.

References

Acta Capitulorum Provincialium Provinciae Sanctissimi Rosarii Philippinarum Ordinis Praedicatorum ab anno 1700 ad annum 1798. 1877. Manila: Typis Collegii Sancti Thomae.

Aduarte, Diego. 1640. *Historia de la Provincia del Santo Rosario de la Orden de Predicadores en Filipinas, Japon y China.* 2 vols. Rpt. Madrid: Consejo Superior de Investigaciones Cientificas, Departamento de Misionologia Española, 1962–1963.

Aimé-Martin, M. L., ed. 1875–1877. *Lettres édifiantes et curieuses concernant l'Asie, l'Afrique et l'Amérique, avec quelques relations nouvelles des missions, et des notes géographiques et historiques.* Paris: Paul Daffis Libraire-Éditeur.

Ames, Roger, and Henry Rosemont, Jr., trans. 1998. *The Analects of Confucius: A Philosophical Translation.* New York: Ballantine Books.

Aziz Ben-Dor, Zvi. 2000. "The 'Dao of Muhammad': Scholarship, Education, and Chinese Muslim Literati Identity in Late Imperial China." Ph.D. diss., University of California at Los Angeles.

Bays, Daniel, ed. 1996. *Christianity in China: From the Eighteenth Century to the Present*. Stanford: Stanford University Press.

Bernand, Carmen, and Serge Gruzinski. 1988. *De l'idolâtrie: Une archéologie des sciences religieuses*. Paris: Éditions du Seuil.

Bernard, Henri. 1945. "Les adaptations chinoises d'ouvrages européens: bibliographie chronologique. Première partie: depuis la venue des Portugais à Canton jusqu'à la Mission française de Pékin, 1514–1688." *Monumenta Serica* 10: 1–57, 309–388.

Boaga, E. 1973–1997. "Terz'Ordine Secolare." In *Dizionario degli Istituti di Perfezione*, ed. G. Pelliccia and G. Rocca, 9, columns 1097–1116. Rome: Edizioni Paoline.

Bonniwell, William. 1945. *A History of the Dominican Liturgy, 1215–1945*. New York: Joseph Wagner.

Bornet, Paul. 1948. "L'apostolat laïque en Chine aux XVIIe et XVIIIe siècles." *Bulletin catholique de Pékin* 35: 41–67.

Brunner, Paul. 1963. *L'Euchologe de la mission de Chine: Editio Princeps 1628 et développements jusqu'à nos jours (Contribution à l'histoire des livres de prières)*. Münster: Aschendorffsche Verlagsbuchhandlung.

Bürkler, Xaver. 1942. *Die Sonn- und Festtagsfeier in der katholischen Chinamission: Eine geschichtlich-pastorale Untersuchung*. Rome: Libreria Herder.

———. 1945. "Die Fasten- und Abstinenzpraxis in der chinesischen Mission." *Neue Zeitschrift für Missionswissenschaft* 1: 258–271.

Chan, Albert. 1996. "Review of J. S. Cummins, *A Question of Rites*." *Monumenta Serica* 44: 427–438.

———. 2002. *Chinese Books and Documents in the Jesuit Archives in Rome, a Descriptive Catalogue: Japonica-Sinica I–IV*. Armonk, N.Y.: M. E. Sharpe.

Chaves, Jonathan. 1993. *Singing of the Source: Nature and God in the Poetry of the Chinese Painter Wu Li*. Honolulu: University of Hawai'i Press.

Chen Jingsheng 陳景盛. 1991. *Fujian lidai renkou lunkao* 福建歷代人口論考. Fuzhou: Fujian renmin chubanshe.

Chow, Kai-wing. 1994. *The Rise of Confucian Ritualism in Late Imperial China: Ethics, Classics and Lineage Discourse*. Stanford: Stanford University Press.

Chu, Pingyi. 1997. "Scientific Dispute in the Imperial Court: The 1664 Calendar Case." *Chinese Science* 14: 7–34.

Christian, William. 1981. *Local Religion in Sixteenth Century Spain*. Princeton: Princeton University Press.

Collectanea S. Congregationis de Propaganda Fide seu Decreta Instructiones Rescripta pro Apostolicis Missionibus, vol. 1: *1622–1866.* 1907. Romae: Ex Typographia Polyglotta–Sacra Congregatio de Propaganda Fide.

Couplet, Philippe [Bo Yingli 柏應理]. N.d. *Tianzhu shengjiao yong zhanli dan* 天主聖教永瞻禮單. BNF Chinois 7276/XII, 1 page (110 × 28 cm). Cf. also manuscript copy by a convert, 1712? BNF: Chinois 7429, 1–13. Copy in SIL.

Cummins, J. S. 1993. *A Question of Rites: Friar Domingo Navarrete and the Jesuits in China.* Aldershot, U.K.: Scolar Press; Brookfield, Vt.: Ashgate.

DeBernardi, Jean. 1992. "Space and Time in Chinese Religious Culture." *History of Religions* 31.3: 247–268.

Dehergne, Joseph. 1956. "Les congrégations dans l'empire de Chine aux XVIIe et XVIIIe siècles." In *Maria: Études sur la Sainte Vierge,* ed. H. du Manoir, 967–980. Paris: Beauchesne.

———. 1978. "Les tablettes dans le culte des ancêtres en Chine confucéenne." *Recherches de science religieuse* 66: 201–214.

Ebrey, Patricia Buckley. 1991. *Confucianism and Family Rituals in Imperial China: A Social History of Writing about Rites.* Princeton: Princeton University Press.

Eliade, Mircea, et al., eds. 1987. *Encyclopedia of Religion.* New York: Macmillan.

Fan Zhong 范中 [Timotheus]. 1633. *Tianzhu shengjiao xiaoyin* 天主聖教小引. Hangzhou: N.p. BNF: Chinois 7058, 7059, 7060, and 7379 II.

Farjenel, F., and L. Bouvat. 1908. "Calendrier musulman chinois." *Revue du Monde Musulman* 4: 548–560.

Forest, Alain. 1998. *Les missionaires français au Tonkin et au Siam, XVIIe–XVIIIe siècles: Analyse comparée d'un relatif succès et d'un total échec.* 3 vols. Paris: L'Harmattan.

Fuan shizhi 福安市志. 1999 [actual printing 2000]. Ed. Fuan shi difangzhi bianzuan weiyuanhui 福安市地方志編纂委員會. Fuan shi: Fangzhi chubanshe.

Fuan xianzhi 福安縣志. 1884. Comp. Zhang Jingqi 張景祁 et al. Rpt. Taibei: Chengwen, 1967.

Fujian Liancun gu wenhua qunluo 福建廉村古文化群落. 1997. Ed. Zhongguo renmin zhengzhi xieshang huiyi Fujian sheng Fuan shi weiyuanhui wenshi ziliao weiyuanhui 中國人民政治協商會議福建省福安市文史資料委員會. Fuan: locally published.

Furtado, Francisco. 1700. *Informatio antiquissima de praxi missionariorum Sinensium Societatis Jesu, circa ritus Sinenses, data in China, jam ab annis 1636 & 1640, a P. Francisco Furtado antiquo Missionario, & Vice-Provinciali Sinensi ejusdem Societatis.* Paris: Apud Nicolaum Pepié.

[Garcia, Quintin Maria] Jin Sheng 金聲 et al. 1947. *Zhenfu Fangjige Jiabilai lüezhuan* 真福方濟各嘉彼來略傳—*Sinarum Protomartyr Beatus Franciscus de Capillas O.P. Eius Vita.* Fuzhou: St. Joseph's Regional Seminary.

Gentili, Tommaso Maria. 1887–1888. *Memorie di un missionario domenicano nella Cina.* 3 vols. Rome: Tipografia Poliglotta.

Gioro Yarhašan 覺羅雅爾哈善. 1746. "Fujian anchashisi anchashi Jueluo Yaer-hashan zou wei Xiyang xiejiao huo min qing tongcha shenjin teyan zhizui zhi li yi jing yuwang yi jing haijiang shi" 福建按察使司按察使覺羅雅爾哈善奏為西洋邪教惑民請通查申禁特嚴治罪之例以儆愚妄以靖海疆事. FHA, 4/294/4.

Gladney, Dru C. 1991. *Muslim Chinese: Ethnic Nationalism in the People's Republic.* Cambridge: Council on East Asian Studies of Harvard University.

Golvers, Noël. 1993. *The "Astronomia Europaea" of Ferdinand Verbiest, S.J. (Dillingen, 1687): Text, Translation, Notes and Commentaries.* Monumenta Serica Monograph Ser. 27. Nettetal: Steyler Verlag.

———. 1999. *François de Rougemont, S.J., Missionary in Ch'ang-shu (Chiang-nan): A Study of His Account Book (1674–1676) and the Elogium.* Louvain Chinese Studies Ser. 8. Leuven: Ferdinand Verbiest Foundation and Leuven University Press.

González, José Maria. 1952–1958. *Misiones Dominicanas en China (1700–1750).* 2 vols. Madrid: Consejo Superior de Investigaciones Cientificas.

———. 1955–1967. *Historia de las misiones dominicanas de China.* 5 vols. Madrid: Imprenta Juan Bravo.

[González de San Pedro, Francisco] Luo Senduo 羅森鐸. 1706. *Shengjiao cuoyao* 聖教撮要. Luoyuan [Fujian]. BNF: Chinois 7044.

Gouvea, António de. 1998. *Cartas Ânuas da China.* Ed. Horácio Araújo. Macao and Lisbon: Instituto Português do Oriente and Biblioteca Nacional.

Haar, Barend J. ter. 1992. *The White Lotus Teachings in Chinese Religious History.* Leiden: Brill.

———. 1995. "Local Society and the Organization of Cults in Early Modern China: A Preliminary Study." *Studies in Central and East Asian Religions* 8: 1–43.

Handlin Smith, Johanna F. 1999. "Liberating Animals in Ming-Qing China: Buddhist Inspiration and Elite Imagination." *Journal of Asian Studies* 58.1: 51–84.

Herbermann, Charles G., et al. 1913–1914. *The Catholic Encyclopedia: An International Work of Reference on the Constitution, Doctrine, Discipline, and History of the Catholic Church.* New York: Encyclopedia Press.

Ho, Ping-ti. 1959. *Studies on the Population of China, 1368–1953.* Cambridge: Harvard University Press.

Huang, Chun-chieh, and Erik Zürcher, eds. 1995. *Time and Space in Chinese Culture.* Leiden: Brill.

Huang Yinong [Huang Yi-Long] 黃一農. 1991a. "Kangxi chao sheji 'liyu' de

Tianzhujiao Zhongwen zhushu kao" 康熙朝涉及'曆獄'的天主教中文著述考. *Shumu jikan* 書目季刊 25.1: 12–27.

———. 1991b. "Yesuhuishi dui chuantong Zhongguo xingzhan shushu de taidu" 耶穌會士對傳統中國星占術數的態度. *Jiuzhou xuekan* 九州學刊 4.3: 5–23.

———. 1995. "Bei hulüe de shengyin—jieshao Zhongguo Tianzhujiao tu dui 'liyi wenti' taidu de wenxian" 被忽略的聲音: 介紹中國天主教徒對'禮儀問題'態度的文獻. *Tsing Hua Journal of Chinese Studies* 清華學報, n.s. 25.2: 137–160.

———. 1996. "Tongshu—Zhongguo chuantong tianwen yu shehui de jiaorong" 通書—中國傳統天文與社會的交融. *Hanxue yanjiu* 漢學研究 14.2: 159–186.

Ibañez, Ignacio. 1941–1943. *Diccionario Español-Chino, dialecto de Fu-an (Houc-An) Ban-Hua zidian, Fuan fangyan* 班華字典福安方言. Shanghai: Imprimerie Commerciale, "Don Bosco" School.

Intorcetta, Prospero. 1668a. "Quaeritur: An ieiunantes in Sinis ante quam baptizentur, semper et ex natura sua cogi debeant a missionariis ad frangendum suum ieiunium, et quamvis detestentur in genere idola et omnia superstitiosa, et etiam ieiunia praeterita superstitiose facta, et expresse ac solide promittant se in posterum ob Dei amorem et cultum et in poenintentiam suorum peccatorum ieiunaturos; si tamen iustam dent causam non frangendi ieiunium an a missionariis non violato ieiunio baptizandi sint." Archivo Histórico Nacional, Madrid, Jes. 270, int. 15.

———. 1668b. "Quid agendum cum ieiunantibus in Sinis si ante baptismum difficulter inducantur ad violandum suum ieiunium." ARSI, FG 722, int. 3–5.

Jami, Catherine. 1995. "Western Devices for Measuring Time and Space: Clocks and Euclidean Geometry in Late Ming and Ch'ing China." In *Time and Space in Chinese Culture,* ed. Huang and Zürcher, 169–200.

Jensen, Lionel. 1997. *Manufacturing Confucianism: Chinese Traditions and Universal Civilizations.* Durham: Duke University Press.

Keightley, David N. 2000. *The Ancestral Landscape: Time, Space, and Community in Late Shang China (ca. 1200–1045 B.C.).* China Research Monograph, 53. Berkeley: Institute of East Asian Studies and Center for Chinese Studies, University of California.

Kern, Iso. 1992. *Buddhistische Kritik am Christentum im China des 17. Jahrhunderts.* Bern: Peter Lang.

Kieschnick, John. 2003. *The Impact of Buddhism on Chinese Material Culture.* Princeton: Princeton University Press.

Landes, David. 1983. *Revolution in Time: Clocks and the Making of the Modern World.* Cambridge: Belknap Press.

Le Goff, Jacques. 1980. "Merchant's Time and Church's Time in the Middle Ages." In *Time, Work and Culture in the Middle Ages,* ed. Le Goff, 29–42. Chicago: University of Chicago Press. Trans. of *Pour un autre Moyen Age: Temps, travail et culture en Occident.* Paris: Gallimard, 1977.

Leslie, Donald D. 1981. *Islamic Literature in Chinese, Late Ming and Early Ch'ing: Books, Authors, and Associates.* Belconnen: Canberra College of Advanced Education.

———. 1983. "Assimilation and Survival of Muslims in China." In *Actes du IIIe Colloque International de Sinologie: Appréciation par l'Europe de la tradition chinoise à partir du XVIIe siècle,* ed. Joseph Dehergne, 107–129. Paris: Les Belles Lettres, Cathasia.

———. 1986. *Islam in Traditional China: A Short History to 1800.* Canberra: Australian National University.

———. 1998. *Jews and Judaism in Traditional China: A Comprehensive Bibliography.* Monumenta Serica Monograph Ser. 44. Nettetal: Steyler Verlag.

Li Jiubiao 李九標. N.d. *Kouduo richao* 口鐸日抄. BNF: Chinois 7114; copy in SIL.

Li Jiugong 李九功. N.d. [ca. 1670]. *Shensi lu* 慎思錄. Fuqing? BNF: Chinois 7227; copy in SIL.

Li Tiangang 李天綱. 1998. *Zhongguo liyi zhi zheng: Lishi, wenxian he yiyi* 中國禮儀之爭: 歷史, 文獻. Shanghai: Shanghai guji chubanshe.

Lian Lichang 連立昌. 1989. *Fujian mimi shehui* 福建秘密社會. Fuzhou: Fujian renmin chubanshe.

Lin Jinshui. 1994. "Chinese Literati and the Rites Controversy." In *Chinese Rites Controversy,* ed. Mungello, 65–82.

Lippiello, Tiziana, and Roman Malek, eds. 1997. *"Scholar from the West": Giulio Aleni S.J. (1582–1649) and the Dialogue between Christianity and China.* Monumenta Serica Monograph Ser. 42. Nettetal: Steyler Verlag.

Liu Haifeng 劉海峰 and Zhuang Mingshui 莊明水. 1996. *Fujian jiaoyu shi* 福建教育史. Fuzhou: Fujian jiaoyu chubanshe.

López Gay, Jesús. 1970. *La liturgia en la misión del Japón del siglo XVI.* Rome: Libreria dell'Università Gregoriana.

Luoyuan xianzhi 羅源縣志. 1831. Comp. and ed. Lin Chunpu 林春溥 and Lu Fengchen 盧鳳棽. N.p.

Ma Xisha 馬西沙 and Han Bingfang 翰秉方. 1992. *Zhongguo minjian zongjiao shi* 中國民間宗教史. Shanghai: Shanghai renmin chubanshe.

Maiello, Francesco. 1994. *Storia del calendario: La misurazione del tempo, 1450–1800.* Turin: Einaudi.

Malek, Roman. 1985. *Das "Chai-chieh lu": Materialen zur Liturgie im Taoismus.* Frankfurt: Peter Lang.

————, ed. 1998. *Western Learning and Christianity in China: The Contribution and Impact of Johann Adam Schall von Bell SJ.* 2 vols. Monumenta Serica Monograph Ser. 35.1–2. Nettetal: Steyler Verlag.

Margiotti, Fortunato. 1958. *Il cattolicismo nello Shansi dalle origini al 1738.* Rome: Edizioni Sinica Franciscana.

————. 1962–1963. "Congregazioni laiche gesuitiche della antica missione cinese." *Neue Zeitschrift für Missionswissenschaft* 18: 255–274 (pt. 1); 19: 50–65 (pt. 2).

Martini, Martino. 1998. *Opera Omnia,* vol. 1: *Lettere e documenti;* vol. 2: *Opere Minori.* Ed. Giuliano Bertuccioli. Trent: Università degli Studi di Trento.

Martzloff, Jean-Claude. 1993–1994. "Space and Time in Chinese Texts of Astronomy and of Mathematical Astronomy in the Seventeenth and Eighteenth Centuries." *Chinese Science* 11: 66–92.

Menegon, Eugenio. 1994. *Un solo Cielo, Giulio Aleni S.J. (1582–1649): Geografia, arte, scienza, religione dall'Europa alla Cina.* Brescia: Grafo.

————. 1995. "Le fonti per la storia della cultura popolare nella Cina tardo-imperiale: alcuni documenti nell'Archivio Romano della Compagnia di Gesù." In *Lo studio delle fonti per la storia cinese,* ed. M. Scarpari, 63–88. Venice: Cafoscarina.

————. 1997. "Jesuits, Franciscans and Dominicans in Fujian: The Anti-Christian Incidents of 1637–1638." In *"Scholar from the West,"* ed. Lippiello and Malek, 219–262.

————. 1998. "De 'l'histoire des missions' à 'l'histoire des chrétiens chinois.'" In *Le Christ chinois: Héritages et espérance,* ed. B. Vermander, 99–119. Paris: Desclée de Brouwer, Bellarmin.

————. 2000. "Review of Martino Martini, *Opera Omnia.*" *Journal of Asian Studies* 59.2 (May): 400–401.

————. 2002. "Ancestors, Virgins, and Friars: The Localization of Christianity in Late Imperial Mindong (Fujian, China), 1632–1863." Ph.D. diss., University of California, Berkeley.

————. 2003. "Spanish Friars, Christian Loyalists and Holy Virgins in Fujian during the Ming-Qing Transition." *Monumenta Serica* 51: 335–365.

Metzler, Josef. 1980. *Die Synoden in China, Japan, und Korea, 1570–1931.* Paderborn: F. Schöningh.

Miao Zaizuo 繆載祚. 1996? "Mushui cangmang hua Muyang" 穆水蒼茫話穆陽. Mimeograph.

Michael, Franz H., ed. 1966–1971. *The Taiping Rebellion: History and Documents.* 3 vols. Seattle: University of Washington Press.

Mungello, David E., ed. 1994. *The Chinese Rites Controversy: Its History and Meaning.* Nettetal: Steyler Verlag.

————. 2001. *The Spirit and the Flesh in Shandong, 1650–1785.* Lanham: Rowman and Littlefield.

Murakami, Naojirō [村上直次郎]. 1942. "An Old Church Calendar in Japanese." *Monumenta Nipponica* 5.1: 219–224.

Naquin, Susan. 1985. "The Transmission of White Lotus Sectarianism in Late Imperial China." In *Popular Culture in Late Imperial China,* ed. D. Johnson, A. Nathan, and E. Rawski, 255–291. Berkeley: University of California Press.

Overmeyer, Daniel. 1976. *Folk Buddhist Religion: Dissenting Sects in Late Traditional China.* Cambridge: Harvard University Press.

Pfister, Louis. 1932–1934. *Notices Biographiques et Bibliographiques sur les Jesuites de l'ancienne mission de Chine.* 2 vols. Shanghai: Imprimerie de la Mission Catholique.

Pita-Moreda, Maria Teresa. 1992. *Los Predicadores novohispanos del siglo XVI.* Salamanca: Editorial S. Esteban.

Plaks, Andrew. 1999. "The Confucianization of the Kaifeng Jews: Interpretations of the Kaifeng Stelae Inscriptions." In *The Jews of China,* vol. 1: *Historical and Comparative Perspectives,* ed. Jonathan Goldstein, 36–49. Armonk, N.Y.: M. E. Sharpe.

Pollak, Michael. 1980. *Mandarins, Jews, and Missionaries: The Jewish Experience in the Chinese Empire.* Philadelphia: Jewish Publication Society of America.

Rambo, Lewis R. 1993. *Understanding Religious Conversion.* New Haven: Yale University Press.

Rawski, Evelyn Sakakida. 1979. *Education and Popular Literacy in Ch'ing China.* Ann Arbor: University of Michigan Press.

Ricci, Matteo. 1911–1913. *Opere storiche del P. Matteo Ricci,* vol. 2: *Le lettere della Cina (1580–1610) con appendice di documenti inediti.* Ed. Pietro Tacchi Venturi. Macerata: Giorgetti.

————. 1985. *The True Meaning of the Lord of Heaven* (*T'ien-chu Shih-i* 天主實義). Trans. D. Lancashire and P. Hu Kuochen, ed. E. Malatesta. St. Louis: Institute of Jesuit Sources, Ricci Institute.

————. 1942–1949. *Fonti Ricciane: Documenti originali concernenti Matteo Ricci e la storia delle prime relazioni tra l'Europa e la Cina (1579–1615).* Ed. Pasquale D'Elia. 3 vols. Rome: La Libreria dello Stato.

Riccio, Victorio. 1667. "Hechos de la Orden de Predicadores en el Imperio de la China." APSR, *China,* v. 2 (nineteenth-century manuscript copy).

Ricoeur, Paul, ed. 1976. *Cultures and Time.* Paris: UNESCO Press.

Royo, Joaquin [Hua Ruoyajing 華若亞敬]. N.d. [1740s]. Trans. J. Kuo, rev. J. Cian. "Festorum et Abstinentiae a carnibus et Temporum Jejunii Sanctae Dei Religionis Brevis Explanatio." A translation of Royo's *Shengjiao zhanli zhaiqi lüeyan* 聖教瞻禮齋期略言. AGOP: X 2571.

————. 1741. "San hui sizhang lüexiang" 三會四章略詳. AGOP: X 2571.

[Schall von Bell, Adam] Tang Ruowang 湯若望. 1683 [preface 1662]. *Minli puzhu jiehuo* 民曆鋪注解惑. Ed. Nan Huairen 南懷仁 [Ferdinand Verbiest]. N.p. In *Yesuhui Luoma dang'anguan Ming-Qing Tianzhujiao wenxian,* ed. Standaert and Dudink, VI: 465–544.

Sierra, Blas de. 1719–1739. "Memoria que por orden de N[ues]tro P[adr]e Provincial Fr. Diego Sáenz, hago de los que tengo baptizados en esta Misión desde que vine a ella." APSR: *China,* vol. 3, 41r–53v.

Smith, Richard J. 1991. *Fortune-Tellers and Philosophers: Divination in Traditional Chinese Society.* Boulder: Westview Press.

————. 1992. *Chinese Almanacs.* Hong Kong: Oxford University Press.

Spence, Jonathan. 1975. *Emperor of China: Self-Portrait of K'ang-hsi.* New York: Vintage Books.

Standaert, Nicolas. 1988. *Yang Tingyun, Confucian and Christian in Late Ming China.* Leiden: Brill.

————. 1995. *The Fascinating God: A Challenge to Modern Chinese Theology Presented by a Text on the Name of God Written by a 17th Century Chinese Student of Theology.* Rome: Editrice Pontificia Università Gregoriana.

————. 1997. "New Trends in the Historiography of Christianity in China." *Catholic Historical Review* 83.4: 573–613.

————. 1999. "The Jesuits Did NOT Manufacture 'Confucianism.'" EASTM (*East Asian Science, Technology, and Medicine*), 16: 115–132.

————, ed. 2001. *Handbook of Christianity in China, Volume One: 635–1800.* Leiden: Brill.

Standaert, Nicolas, and Adrian Dudink, eds. 2002. *Yesuhui Luoma dang'anguan Ming-Qing Tianzhujiao wenxian* 耶穌會羅馬檔案館明清天主教文獻 *Chinese Christian Texts from the Roman Archives of the Society of Jesus.* 12 vols. Taibei: Taipei Ricci Institute.

Szony, Michael. 2002. *Practicing Kinship: Lineage and Descent in Late Imperial China.* Stanford: Stanford University Press.

Tiedemann, R. G. 1996. "Christianity and Chinese 'Heterodox Sects': Mass Conversion and Syncretism in Shandong Province in the Early Eighteenth Century." *Monumenta Serica* 44: 339–382.

Turnbull, Stephen. 1998. *The Kakure Kirishitan of Japan: A Study of Their Development, Beliefs and Rituals to the Present Day.* Richmond (U.K.): Japan Library and Curzon Press.

Vareschi, Severino. 1994. "Martino Martini S.I. e il decreto del Sant'Ufficio nella Questione dei Riti Cinesi (1655–56)." *Archivum Historicum Societatis Iesu* 63.126: 209–260.

[Varo, Francisco] Wan Jiguo 萬濟國. 1668. "Zongdu cuoyao" 總牘撮要. [Fuan?] AL: 44.A.1.

————. 1671. "Manifiesto y declaración de la verdad de algunas cosas que se dicen en dos Tratados muy copiosos que hicieron los RR. PP. Diego Fabro y Francisco Brancato, religiosos de la Compañia de Jesús y ministros de este Reyno de China, acerca de la praxi que dichos PP. permiten a sus [Chris]tianos en la veneración del M. Confucio y sus difuntos." APSR: *Ritos Chinos*, vol. 5.

————. 1678. "Relacion de lo sucedido en este Imperio de China perteneciente a los Religiosos Predicadores en los tres años de 1672–73–74; dirigida a el M[uy] R[everendo] P[adre] P[rovinci]al de la Prov[inci]a del S[an]to Ross[ari]o de [P]hilip[in]as. Por Fr[ay] Fran[cis]co Varo Religioso de la mesma orden y Ministro en dicho Imperio—Yten mas añadida despues hasta el año de 78. Por Diciembre." BC: MS 1074, 323r–363r.

————. 1685. "Puntos cuya decisión me parece ser muy necesaria para la quietud de las conciencias de los religiosos misioneros en este reino de China." APSR: *Ritos Chinos*, vol. 15, doc. 2.

————. 1720 [preface 1677]. *Shengjiao mingzheng* 聖教明徵. [Fuan?] Rpt. Hong Kong: Nazareth Press, 1903.

————. 2000. *Francisco Varo's Grammar of the Mandarin Language (1703): An English Translation of "Arte de la lengua mandarina."* Ed. W. South Coblin and Joseph A. Levi, introd. Sandra Breitenbach. Amsterdam and Philadelphia: John Benjamins Publishing Company.

[Verbiest, Ferdinand] Nan Huairen 南懷仁. 1670a. *Wangtui jixiong zhi bian* 妄推吉凶之辯. BNF: Chinois 4995.

————. 1670b. *Wangze bian* 妄擇辯. ARSI: Jap. Sin. II 45D.

————. 1670c. *Wangzhan bian* 妄占辯. BNF: Chinois 4998.

Wilkinson, Endymion. 2000. *Chinese History: A Manual.* Rev. and enl. Harvard-Yenching Institute Monograph Ser. 520. Cambridge: Harvard University Asia Center.

Wills, John E. 1994. "From Manila to Fuan: Asian Contexts of Dominican Mission Policy." In *The Chinese Rites Controversy*, ed. Mungello, 111–127.

Witek, John. 1983. "Chinese Chronology: A Source of Sino-European Widening Horizons in the Eighteenth Century." In *Actes du IIIe Colloque International de Sinologie: Appréciation par l'Europe de la tradition chinoise a partir du XVIIe siècle*, ed. Joseph Dehergne, 223–252. Paris: Les Belles Lettres.

Xu Changzhi 徐昌治. 1855. *Shengchao poxie ji* 聖朝破邪集. In *Dazang jing bubian* 大藏經補編, ed. Lan Jifu 藍吉富. Rpt. of Japanese ed. Taibei: Huaning chubanshe, 1986. [Original ed.: Hangzhou, 1640.]

Xu Zongze 徐宗澤. 1949. *Ming-Qing jian Yesuhuishi yizhu tiyao* 明清間耶穌會士譯著提要. Rpt. Beijing: Zhonghua shuju, 1989.

Yang, Lien-sheng. 1955. "Schedules of Work and Rest in Traditional China." *Harvard Journal of Asiatic Studies* 18: 301–325.

Yongzheng chao Manwen zhupi zouzhe quanyi 雍正朝滿文硃批奏摺全譯. 1998. Ed. FHA. 2 vols. Hefei: Huangshan shushe.

Yü, Chün-fang. 1981. *The Renewal of Buddhism in China: Chu-hung and the Late Ming Synthesis*. New York: Columbia University Press.

Zerubavel, Eviatar. 1981. *Hidden Rhythms: Schedules and Calendars in Social Life*. Chicago: University of Chicago Press.

———. 1982. "Easter and Passover: On Calendars and Group Identity." *American Sociological Review* 47.2 (April): 284–289.

———. 1985. *The Seven Day Circle: The History and Meaning of the Week*. New York and London: Free Press.

Zheng Zhenman 鄭振滿. 1992. Ming-Qing Fujian jiazu zuzhi yu shehui bianqian 明清福建家族組織與社會變遷. Changsha: Hunan jiaoyu chubanshe.

Zhu Weigan 朱維幹. 1985–1986. *Fujian shigao* 福建史稿. 2 vols. Fuzhou: Fujian jiaoyu chubanshe.

Zupanov, Ines G. 1996. "Le repli du religieux: Les missionnaires jésuites du 17e siècle entre la théologie chrétienne et une éthique païenne." *Annales: Histoire, sciences sociales* 51: 1201–1223.

———. 1999. *Disputed Mission: Jesuit Experiments and Brahmanical Knowledge in Seventeenth-Century India*. New Delhi: Oxford University Press.

Zürcher, Erik. 1985. "The Lord of Heaven and the Demons: Strange Stories from a Late Ming Christian Manuscript." In *Religion und Philosophie in Ostasien*, ed. G. Naundorf et al., 359–375. Würzburg, Germany: Königshausen-Neumann.

———. 1990. "The Jesuit Mission in Fujian in Late Ming Times: Levels of Response." In *Development and Decline of Fukien Province in the 17th and 18th Centuries*, ed. E. B. Vermeer, 417–457. Leiden: Brill.

———. 1994. "Jesuit Accommodation and the Chinese Cultural Imperative." In *Chinese Rites Controversy*, ed. Mungello, 31–64.

———. 1995. "'In the Beginning': 17th-Century Chinese Reactions to Christian Creationism." In *Time and Space in Chinese Culture*, ed. Huang and Zürcher, 132–166.

———. 1997. "Confucian and Christian Religiosity in Late Ming China." *Catholic Historical Review* 83.4: 614–653.

CHAPTER SIX

"Birthday of the Sun"

Historical Memory in Southeastern Coastal China of the Chongzhen Emperor's Death

Zhao Shiyu and Du Zhengzhen

TRANS. LYNN A. STRUVE

ON THE 19TH DAY OF the 3rd lunar month in the 17th year of the Chongzhen reign (1644), Li Zicheng's peasant army seized Beijing. Zhu Youjian, the Ming emperor, finding no route of escape, fled to Coal Hill north of his palace and hanged himself, thus bringing to an end the Ming dynasty's years as unifier of China. Many have expressed opinions on the demise of the Ming and the death of the Chongzhen emperor, including latter-day historians, who regard the dynastic change of 1644 as a very important event in Chinese history. But few have realized that, not long after the Chongzhen suicide, this political incident became the subject of a special sort of local discourse, which was transformed into a popular tradition filled with unusual and significant cultural symbolism.

Sayings and Practices Related to the Birthday of the Sun

In a letter to friends written on March 15, 1925, Lu Xun states: "To the present day the Chinese people have not shed primitive thinking; in fact, new myths still arise. For instance, the [ancient] *Shanhai jing* [Classic of mountains and seas] has myths about the sun, but [even today] in my home area [Shaoxing], everyone says that the 19th day of the 3rd month is the Birthday of the Sun. This is not a bit of fiction or a children's tale; it really is a myth, since everyone believes it" (Lu Xun 1976: 66–67). In folk-literature circles there have been focused debates on whether this saying qualifies as a "new myth" (Liu 1987: 227; see also Han n.d.: 1), but none of the debaters has discovered the historical memories of the Ming-Qing transition hidden behind this story.

Folklorists, however, have paid a good deal of attention to popular practices relating to 3/19 as the Birthday of the Sun, since such practices are widespread in China's southeastern coastal region (see Map 2). One scholar has found that the Birthday of the Sun is not the same in the north and the south. Many places in the north take 2/1 as the sun's birthday, but in the region that extends from the east of Tai Lake to the south of Hangzhou Bay it is 3/19 (because on that day in that region the sunrise occurs at exactly 5:00 a.m.). Each household mounts year-end candles at the front door,[1] and women form groups of three to five to recite the Buddha's name and stay overnight in hilltop temples. These folkways are most prevalent in the Shaoxing area on the southwestern side of Hangzhou Bay (Jiang 1996: 508).

In the Huzhou area just south of Tai Lake, also, people have designated 3/19 as the Birthday of the Sun Bodhisattva and have passed down this "Sun Sutra":

The sun, this bright-shining, red, gem-glowing Buddha,
Shines on the four wondrous quarters of the world.
When the sun comes out, the whole sky turns red;
Breaking through the night, I come forth without cease.
When I come too fast, I hasten people's aging;
When I come too slow, nothing at all can survive.
I pass in front of each family's door,
And call all youngsters by their childhood names.
Should the sun and moon be angered and go behind the hills,
People would starve to death and all living things suffer harm.
Without me in the heavens there would be neither day nor night.
And if I did not [shine] down on the earth, there would be no
    harvest.
If the sun did not move [as it does] throughout the world,
Great hardships would result from lack of division between day and
    night.
The sun is born on the 19th day of the 3rd month.
Every family recites the Buddha's name and lights red lanterns.
People pay respects to [ancestral] spirits on their altars,
But no one honors me, the Sun Star.
When someone passes on my Sun Sutra,
The whole family, old and young, avoids affliction stars;
If no one [in the family] recites my Sun Sutra,
Then before their eyes is only the gate to Hell.

That the sun is a bright-shining, red, gem-glowing Buddha
Is told among good men and faithful women.
If [this sutra] is intoned seven times each early morn,
Then one will never enter the gate of Hell.
At death one will be reborn in the Pure Land,
And seven generations of ancestors in the netherworld will be
    returned to life.
Try your best to practice this sincerely to old age,
And your offspring will enjoy good fortune, prosperity, longevity, and
    peace.[2]

Different versions of this text have circulated in many places. For instance, in the Ningbo-Cixi area on the southeastern side of Hang-zhou Bay it goes like this:

Recite, recite the Sun Sutra;
The sun is born on 3/19 at 5:00.
When the sun comes out it brightens the four quarters,
Pervasively shining on all living things in the great world.
With the first ray, the sun ascends in the east,
Second, it illumines Guanyin of the Southern Sea,
Third, it brightens the Thousand Buddhas of the west,
And fourth, it lights up Hell's Gate in the north.
When north, south, east, and west all are bright,
The winds and rains are smooth and rhythmic and the country is at
    peace.
When people recite the Sun Sutra,
No one in their families, old or young, has an affliction star.
In the whole world the sun is most fair,
Neither cheating the poor nor flattering the rich.
We hear that it shines the same among all people on earth.
If the sun did not shine on the world,
All things would hollowly change to dust.
Good men and faithful women, come and be devout,
Be devout by first reciting the Sun Sutra.[3]

The "Sun Sutra" in its various versions appears to be a precious-scroll type of morality book (*shanshu baojuan*). Besides propagating karmic–retributive thinking, it also conveys egalitarianism and is thickly colored by popular religion. Each version refers to the date 3/19 and uses words such as "bright-shining" (*mingming*) and "red, gem-glowing" (*zhuguang*), which carry hidden meanings: *ming* is the character used for the name of the Ming dynasty, and *zhu* contains the character for, is homonymous with, and in one meaning is synonymous with Zhu, the surname of the Ming imperial lineage. However, the texts show no other direct connection to the fall of the Ming dynasty. Moreover, no writings in other regions of the country make reference to 3/19 as the Birthday of the Sun or use phrases such as "the sun is a bright-shining, red, gem-glowing Buddha," so we may conclude that these are unusual, region-specific texts.[4]

Nevertheless, connections between the Birthday of the Sun and the Ming dynasty or the Chongzhen emperor have been found in other folkways. For instance, in Wenzhou on the far southern coast of Zhejiang, "it is passed down among the people that 3/19 is the sun's birthday. Upon investigation, this turns out to be the date when Ming Sizong (Chongzhen) died for his country. On this day in the Pingyang area women read sutras and fast."[5] Also, a story collected from a sixty-five-year-old teacher by a cultural worker in Dongpuzhen, Shaoxing, goes like this:

> In times past, when Shaoxing folks came to the 19th day of the 3rd month, they would all invite the Sun Bodhisattva, saying that it was the sun's birthday. Actually, the origin of this was at the end of the Ming. When the Chongzhen emperor was on the throne, Li Zicheng raised a rebellion and brought troops dangerously close to the capital. The emperor fled to Coal Hill and, in desperation, hanged himself. There was a Ming general named Wu Sangui who allowed the Qing army to come inside the pass. So, while Li Zicheng was delivered a blow, Beijing became occupied by Qing forces, and the whole imperial family inside the palace was slaughtered. Only one member escaped, the Chongzhen emperor's third daughter, who hid in a convent and became a nun. Because 3/19 is the day when the Chongzhen emperor ascended to Heaven, it also is considered the day when the Ming dynasty was terminated. The Third Princess, lamenting her father's death and the loss of her state, personally composed a "Sun Sutra," which was disseminated among the common people. The saying that 3/19 is the sun's birthday was generated so that people could come and make reverent offerings, cleverly deceiving the Qing emperor. ("Taiyang pusa de gushi" 1989)

A Red-Heaven (*zhutian*) Temple Association that was located in the Huzhou area has direct relevance to the regional meaning of the sun-birthday rite. The deity worshiped in the Red-Heaven Temple was Red-Heaven the Great, who, according to the lore, was the Ming Chongzhen emperor. This temple was established in the Qing period, when one could not openly express remembrance of that past ruler. So the residents fashioned a martial-type idol standing with bare feet on a small ridge of hills, one hand holding a universe circle (*qiankun quan*) and the other hand wielding a sandalwood club. The ridge symbolized Coal Hill, where the Chongzhen emperor committed suicide, the universe circle the noose, and the sandalwood club the acacia tree that he used to hang himself. In the Republican period in Wuqingzhen (a market town in Huzhou), it was popularly said that on the 24th of the 4th month "Red-Heaven the Great was born, and down to today worship ceremonies are grandly practiced here" (*Wuqing zhenzhi* 1936: 19.12b).

Zhou Zuoren, who witnessed such a ceremony, said in a reminiscence: "In the first years of the Republic when I was in Shaoxing, I saw everyone worshiping a certain Red-Heaven the Great and was told that the object of the worship was the Chongzhen emperor. The idol had a red face, loose hair, and bare feet; in one hand it held a circle, which they said symbolized a noose, and maybe the other hand grasped a snake. I've seen this idol, but because it was thirty years ago, I don't recall it clearly" (1944: 150). And Ma Xulun recounted in the 1940s:

> [My friend] Yingyu wanted to go to Songbaili on Maybike Road [in Shanghai] to offer incense at the Red-Heaven Temple, and she asked me to locate it. Arriving there, we found the candle flames and incense smoke dizzying.... Red-Heaven the Great actually is the Ming Chongzhen emperor, so the idol held a loop in his right hand and a club in his left. [Someone] told us that the club symbolized a tree and the loop a knotted rope precisely to represent Sizong's suicide by hanging. Peculiar to this temple was a whole string of heads suspended above the neck of the idol, which was not the case in Hangzhou.... The Hangzhou custom was to offer sacrifices to Red Heaven very assiduously, maintaining a vegetarian diet for a whole month. [Someone else] said that in Shanghai vegetarian fasting for Red Heaven had been observed for many generations, and that if it were neglected there would be some disaster. I responded that the meaning simply was to observe mourning by not consuming meat or

wine, and thus to impress on younger generations that they must not forget. (1984: 77)

Another account says:

> In Hangzhou everyone—male and female, old and young—
> venerates the Red-Heaven Bodhisattva. Every year on his birthday,
> the 23rd and 24th of the 4th month, in the whole city incense is
> offered communally on a very grand scale. The temples also are
> ubiquitous in the city, though all are attached to other temples,
> that is, none is independent. Believers especially are women and
> children, who in the 4th month insist on maintaining a "Red-
> Heaven vegetarian fast." Perusal of neither the various sutras nor the
> [novel] *Fengshen [yanyi]* turns up any mention of this bodhisattva;
> rather, it's unique to Hangzhou. How strange! Some say that "Red
> Heaven" (*zhutian*) just means "all heavenly Buddhas" (*zhutian*), but
> this is not so. Rather, in the early Qing some [Ming] loyalists, in
> commemorating their defeated dynasty, nominally called it a
> sacrificial worship. Wouldn't that be a pretty close explanation? In
> fact, a "Sun Sutra," widely intoned among the common people,
> commemorates a former Ming emperor. (Hu 1986: II, 222)

These examples make it clear that the Shanghai, Hangzhou, Huzhou, and Shaoxing areas all had similar practices and that in the Jiangnan-Zhejiang region, at least in recent times, a special feeling has persisted about the end of the Ming.

But let us return to the matter of the sun being born on 3/19. Apart from the example of Shaoxing mentioned by Lu Xun, do we find this point of popular belief elsewhere? Below is a list of the evidence from Zhejiang:

> Yin County: "Yin custom takes 3/19 as the Birthday of the Sun.
> The various monasteries and temples hold services and intone
> sutras. Supplement: According to the *Yuzhitang tanhui* and the
> *Shixian shu*, the Sunlight Son of Heaven is born on 11/19.
> Only in our locale is the date 3/19" (*Yinxian zhi* 1877: 2.11a–
> 12a).
> Dinghai Department: "On 3/19 the various monasteries and tem-
> ples hold services and intone sutras. It has been passed on
> [among the people] that this is the day of national tragedy for

the former Ming, which, being a taboo subject, is called the Birthday of the Sun. The *Yuzhitang tanhui* and the *Shixian shu* both say that the Sunlight Son of Heaven is born on 11/19, but the custom was changed to 3/19 by [Ming] loyalists, and this has continued to the present" (*Dinghai tingzhi* 1902: 15.6a).

Dinghai County: "On 3/19 the various monasteries and temples hold services and intone sutras. It has been passed on that this is the day of national tragedy for the Ming dynasty, which, being a taboo subject, is called the Birthday of the Sun. A popularly transmitted 'Sun Sutra' says things such as this: The sun is a bright-shining Zhu Buddha, born at noon on 3/19, when every single household lights red lanterns. Zhu is the name of the Ming dynastic line" (*Dinghai xianzhi* 1924: 54a).

Wuqing Township: "It has been passed on that the 19th [of the 3rd month] is the Birthday of the Sun. Every family offers incense and lights candles. Ming Chongzhen died for his country on this day. Whether the people, in sorrowful remembrance of a former ruler, have given [the observance] this name remains to be investigated" (*Wuqing zhenzhi* 1936: 19.12a).

Hangzhou Prefecture: "The 19th [of the 3rd month] is the birth of the Sun-Star Ruler, when households compete in burning incense and candles (according to Daoist books)" (*Hangzhou fuzhi* 1912: 76.19b).

Xiaoshan County: "The 19th of the 3rd month is popularly called the sun's birthday. There are gatherings, and offerings are made in halls. The whole night long women declare the Buddha's name and call that 'staying the night on the mountain for the sun.' In fact, Ming Sizong died for his country on 3/19, and because former Ming subjects were pained by this, they set up offerings on this day and used the words 'Birthday of the Sun' to disguise a taboo. Later generations continued the practice but obscured the meaning" (*Xiaoshan xianzhi gao* 1935: 1.27a).

Entries similar to these late-Qing records from Zhejiang appear in recently compiled local histories from Taiwan. For instance, in the *Taiwan sheng tongzhi gao* (1950–1965) an entry reads: "The 19th day … of the 3rd month is customarily the sun's birthday, but it actually is the day when Ming Sizong died for his country. People use flour to make nine pigs and sixteen sheep to simulate the imperial ancestral rite and sacrifice them facing east. Each household lights candles, wanting to make things bright (*ming*). It probably is the case that former [Ming] subjects harbored feelings for their fallen state and borrowed this [rite] to embody their thoughts. Then, after a long time it became a custom." Entries in the *Jilong xianzhi* (1954–1959), *Yunlin xianzhi gao* (1958–1968), *Tainan shizhi* (1958–1983), and *Gaoxiong xianzhi gao* (1958–1968) are all basically like this.[6] The record in the *Tainan xianzhi* (1957–1960) is especially detailed regarding popular consciousness:

> The Sun's Birthday [3/19]: This is the natal day of the sun god. In
> the morning people in every single household place an incense
> table facing east in front of the main hall, set it with worship
> paraphernalia, and line up in front of it, as sacrificial goods, nine
> cakes shaped like miniature pigs and sixteen shaped like miniature
> sheep. Then the womenfolk light candles, burn incense, and
> conduct a sacrificial rite facing the sun. As for the origins [of this
> practice], according to oral accounts, former subjects of the Ming,
> living under Qing control, borrowed the fine name of the sun's
> birthday to, from a distance, pay respects to the Ming Chongzhen
> emperor, who, on this day, died for his country by hanging himself
> from an acacia tree at Coal Hill. This is an old custom that has been
> perpetuated for over two hundred years. (Ding and Zhao 1995:
> 1827–1828)

As we know, when the Qing replaced the Ming, Zhejiang and Taiwan were important bases of Southern Ming resistance to the Qing. In Zhejiang there was the regime of the Prince of Lu, and the affiliated anti-Qing forces of Zhang Mingzhen and Zhang Huangyan were active mainly in the coastal area of southeastern Zhejiang. Taiwan became the home base of the Zheng regime and thus the site of many tragedies of resistance and suppression. But we have found very few records of birthday-of-the-sun folkways in Zhejiang local histories, and in the case of Taiwan, expositions appear only in new local histories compiled in the modern period. In other regions such as Jiangnan, where anti-Qing resistance also was ardent, except for evidence of beliefs centered on the Red-Heaven temples, discussed above, it is very difficult to find this sort of record. Is this because of taboos enforced during the period of Qing control? Or is it because the custom is actually of recent origin? Might it be a result of weakening state controls in the late Qing or a product of revolutionaries' anti-Qing propaganda?

While the late Ming and early Qing was referred to as a period when "Heaven collapsed and the earth split" by people of the time, contemporaries had mixed reactions to the dynastic disruption. In 1645, before the Shunzhi court repeatedly promulgated orders that all men shave their heads (in the Manchu style), many people were without deep remorse over the fall of the Ming. Zhang Lixiang (1611–1674) wrote: "In the incident of 1644 [when Beijing fell], aside from one or two dozen men who honorably died for their principles, the great majority sullied themselves by accepting illegitimate appointments [under the Qing]. Those who abandoned their posts and fled into obscurity, by comparison, were the clean and conscientious ones."[7] A short note prefacing a poem by Lu Shiyi reads: "On the 4th day of the 5th month, tragic news of our former ruler was confirmed. All within the four seas felt the same vengefulness as though they were burying a [common] ancestor. But there were local degree holders of the Ming dynasty who casually watched the dragon-boat races as they banqueted sumptuously on multistoried pleasure barges. I indignantly ridiculed [them]" (Feng Menglong 1940: 13.9b–10a). Gui Zhuang (1613–1673) also wrote a poem criticizing such behavior: "When students heard of the upheaval, tears splashed their gowns; / but the perversity of some minds could not be fathomed. / Officials and noblemen, resplendent in their sashes and insignia, [on] this day / grew intoxicated over translucent wine vessels amidst the songs of Wu and dances of Chu." He appended this note: "On the new moon of the 4th month there was a theatrical performance in the granary inspector's office, and from the 1st of the 5th month until the Double Five Festival [on the 5th], every day the Jiading magistrate, seductive boys and courtesans in arm, watched the dragon boats" (Gui 1984: I, 31). People had different opinions on the issue of honor, and they did not necessarily have common feelings about the demise of the corrupt Ming dynasty or the Chongzhen emperor's death. How then should we interpret the underlying meaning of the Birthday of the Sun?

Local Discourses in the Southeastern Coastal Region during the Ming-Qing Transition

Some scholars are of the view that the sun's-birthday folk practice bears a special relation with Taiwan history. The following is an example: "On 3/19 are the Sun Offerings. According to studies, on this day at the end of the Ming, Li Zicheng attacked and entered Beijing, and Ming Sizong [the Chongzhen emperor] hanged himself at Coal Hill [now in Jingshan Park]. In the period when the Ming [loyalist] Zheng [family ruled Taiwan], this date was designated for offerings to be made at a distance to the lost spirit of Chongzhen. After the Qing brought Taiwan under their control, the common people of the island feigned sacrificial worship of the sun (*taiyang* ["great brightness"] being an allusion to Da-Ming ["great brightness"]) and enabled perpetuation of this practice" (Xu and Zhang 1996: 71). Another scholar is even more explicit, saying that "the sacrifice originated with Zheng Chenggong. After Qing [rule] commenced, sacrifices for the lost Ming (the sun and moon radical forming the character 'Ming') regrettably were regarded as punishable offenses by Qing officials, so people alternatively said that [the ceremonies were for] the birthday of the 'Sun-Star Ruler'" (Feiyun Jushi 1993: 156–157).[8] Although such statements overlook the fact that this sort of practice also existed in certain regions of the mainland, they do point to the folkway's origin in the Zheng period.

Another Taiwan scholar, Weng Tongwen, has published the only study known to us on the Birthday of the Sun—an article that, however, mainly concerns the anti-Qing Tiandi hui (Heaven and Earth Society). In that article he says, using information from secondary sources, that the people of southern Fujian and eastern Guangdong celebrated 3/15 or 3/19 of the lunar calendar as the Birthday of the Sun and that this practice was actually a commemoration of Ming Sizong's death for his country.[9] Weng concludes that the celebration began with the Tiandi hui, the origins of which he traces to two incidents in early Yongzheng-period Taiwan: in 1678 Cai Yin borrowed the title "Zhu, the Third Crown Prince" (Zhu San Taizi—the only surviving son of the Chongzhen emperor) to raise an armed rebellion; and in 1726 and 1728 two cases regarding the Fumu hui (Father and Mother Society) were settled in Taiwan, the records of which indicate 3/19 as the date when those anti-Qing societies were formed. Closely associating four things—this identification with the Zhu line, anti-Qing sentiment, the date 3/19, and the origin of the Tiandi hui—Weng states that the conversion of Chongzhen's death day to the Birthday of the Sun for commemorative purposes "probably began with the Tiandi hui and only later was transmitted among the people of Minnan." Moreover, because he knows of no celebration of the sun's birthday before 1728, he concludes that the Tiandi hui must have begun around that time (Weng 1977). If it could be shown that the sun's birthday celebration appeared earlier than the 1720s, then doubt would be cast on its relation to the origins of that society. Apart from this, Weng's assertion that the sun's birthday was not celebrated in provinces other than Fujian, Guangdong, and Taiwan clearly is mistaken. Certainly it also existed in Zhejiang, but we lack evidence of how it was transmitted from one southeastern coastal region to another.

Fortunately, during the Daoguang reign Xu Shidong (1814–1873) of Yin County recorded an explanation of the sun-birthday folk practice in his *Yanyulou wenji*. This passage eliminates the possibility that the practice originated in revolutionary, anti-Manchu thought at the end of the Qing. Xu's text is worth quoting at length:

> On the 19th day of the late spring [3rd month], Dong Juexuan
> [Dong Pei] came from his old home in Gaotang to the thatch hall
> west of town, where I hosted him with some wine. After a while we
> went out to look around; hand in hand we strolled, entering the gate
> under the city-wall tower and proceeding southward from there.
> Reaching the westside curve of Moon Lake, we passed the new Sun-
> Moon Temple at the lake's taper point—the one popularly called
> the Hall of the Sun. Since this structure is not recorded in the
> edition of the Yin County gazetteer published in the Qianlong reign,
> [one might surmise] that it had not yet been built at that time. But it
> is not recorded in the current gazetteer either.
>
> All one could see was a gaping red door with many people
> crowding their way in and out. There was a din of mixed male and
> female voices from the worshipers inside. Thinking this strange, we
> inquired and were told that it was the Birthday of the Sun, on which
> people recite Buddhist and Daoist sacred texts and energetically beat
> drums and gongs to congratulate the sun and attain everlasting good
> fortune. We just laughed and departed.
>
> After a while, Mr. Dong asked me, "Isn't such a rite heterodox?"
> I replied: "[Sacrifices] to the sun in the morning and the moon at
> night indeed are the duty of the emperor. [What we saw was]
> Buddhist monks and Daoist priests making money—hardly a
> [legitimate] rite." Dong continued: "Yes, but I have seen in the
> almanacs issued in the provincial capital a list of many deities'
> birthdays, among which is that of the sun on the 19th day of the 11th
> month. One might argue that this is groundless, but long ago in a
> work titled *Yuzhitang tanhui*, in the first *juan*, I read that the Emperor
> of Sunlight was born on the 19th of the 11th month. I reasoned that

because the *yang* cycle begins in the 11th month, that point was
called the birth of the sun. At least that would make some sense.
But there really seems no reason to fix on the 19th day. Moreover,
there are not two suns in the sky, and the books I've seen are in
agreement. Even if this belief is absurd, why is it practiced differently
in different places? Why does our local custom take this date as the
deity's first coming, not changing the day but changing the month,
from the 11th to the 3rd? Is this a variant tradition, and how do so
many versions come about?"

Thereupon my expression turned serious. I straightened my
lapel, sat upright, sighed regretfully, and said: "This matter began
during the Shunzhi and Kangxi reigns of our dynasty and has been
passed along to the present. Since [its inception] was over two
hundred years ago, aspects that elders did not explain, that books
did not record, that were regarded as taboo, or that were lost to
sheer distance were not transmitted by later generations. But I know
and can tell about it. Today, 3/19, is none other than the day when
Emperor Zhuanglie [Chongzhen] died for his state. The day was
zimao in the *jiashen* year.[10] The sun sank out of sight in the north,
and the land was plunged into darkness; [the sunlight] dispersed
and did not return, and even Kuafu hesitated in his chase.[11] At that
time, our Yin was the most outstanding region for loyalists. There
were hereditary aristocrats, degree holders of the previous dynasty,
elders in long-established communities, and stubborn rustic people
who did not wish to change their allegiance. Though they knew that
Heaven's command had been given and that the populace had
turned toward a sage [the Qing emperor], their feelings of loss were
very sensitive. Lacking a means to express their pent-up emotions,
each year they used this day to mourn their former ruler. Letting
their hair fall naturally [that is, unbraiding their Qing-style queues],
they made sacrifices in out-of-the-way places and wailed at the
seashores. They gathered Buddhist and Daoist priests to perform
ceremonies and thereby expressed their grief and wishes of good
fortune [for Sizong's spirit].

"At first they just prayed quietly with heads bowed, but as time
went on people in rural areas openly recited [prayers]. If they had
stolidly used the undisguised name of the defeated dynasty to refer
to the spirit in this rite, would it not have raised alarm? So they
explained it in terms of a deity in order to fool others; they changed
the name [of the subject] and concealed the true [nature of the

rite]. Shrewdly, they vaunted it among the people, saying that this day is the Birthday of the Sun. The sun represented the ruler. The deceased ruler could not be referred to openly, so they changed a person's ghost into a heavenly spirit; heavenly spirits could not have death days, so they changed a day of national consolation to a birthday. This truly is [the legacy] of our local forebears feeling constrained in their bitterness and concealed rage. Their actions could move the wind and thunder; their cause could make gods and ghosts weep. Back then, they could understand one another by exchanging gazes, but if they tried to explain the meaning they would become choked with emotion and be unable to do so. As years went by, there came to be no one who understood the reason for [this rite]. Only now am I able to tell you about it in detail.

"Now, the local people model their actions on those of their honored elders, and the Buddhists and Daoists accept what is said by the gentry. They believe in common sayings as sacrosanct and take our words as canonical. Not understanding the ways of superior men, they just adopt external forms and lose the essence, leave the old in pursuit of the new. Thus, the ready change away from 11/19. This date probably came from Daoist books and quite possibly had been observed in our locale in earlier times. Various [loyalist] gentlemen felt they needed some explanation to fool the monks and priests into changing their ways and following the gentry practice. So they covertly dressed up the object of veneration and established it as a god in a temple, and the idea eventually extended from the sun to the moon. [The religionists] made the idols very lifelike to move the common people and to make money. Accepting this idea [of birthdays for] the sun and moon, people yearly convened in droves, but none mourned the fallen dynasty. Gentlemen of later times, unaware of the origins, have just seen the vestiges. They sigh over the perversion of ritual and laugh at the different dates. They apprehend only the clever ways of ignorant Buddhists and deceitful Daoists and do not recognize [behind this rite] the precious blood of loyal officials and righteous men."

Hearing this, Mr. Dong was abashed and anxiously bowed [to me], saying: "Really?! I never perceived this before. It must have silently been made known to you by the spirits of our locale's forebears so that you could tell me about it. Some stories are old but not true; this one has recent evidence to go on. Listening to you speak of it so confidently is exciting; I'm both pleasantly surprised and fully convinced." (Xu n.d.)

According to Xu's exposition, observance of the Birthday of the Sun was initiated by Ming loyalists sometime during the Shunzhi or Kangxi reign. His claim that in the intervening two hundred years other people did not understand this clearly, that only he himself knew, is not credible. But if what he says can be substantiated, then the practice must have predated the inception of the Tiandi hui—possibly to become, later, a resource that was used by that secret society.

Looking generally at our historical records, it seems that the Birthday of the Sun was celebrated widely in Zhejiang, Fujian, and Taiwan, and if we add the belief in Red-Heaven the Great, then the distribution expands to Jiangsu. But most of the references seem to be from the Yin and Shaoxing areas of Zhejiang. When one considers that this was the center of Regent Lu's regime during the Southern Ming and that the people of this region suffered sorely during the Qing conquest and early Qing occupation, it may be appropriate to regard the birthday-of-the-sun lore as a kind of local discourse.

Quan Zuwang (1705–1755) writes: "When the Shunzhi emperor's [forces] came down to Jiangnan, East Zhejiang resisted [Heaven's] command. Though [the region] was secured in the course of one year, alarms continued to sound from the hills and seashores for many years thereafter. The main leaders in my area of Ningbo [Yin][12] were Qian [Suyue] and Shen [Chenquan], between whose groups over forty men died righteously, the last being Grand Secretary Zhang [Huangyan]" (Quan 1982). Resistance to the Qing in this region, besides lasting a long time, also was especially fierce. Again, Quan Zuwang writes, in commemoration of a leading loyalist general: "When the Great [Qing] Army came down to Jiangnan, [most resisters] sniffed the wind and scattered; wherever the [Qing soldiers] went, they scarcely had to bloody their swords. The places most difficult to conquer were Ganzhou in Jiangxi, Yinjing County [sic] in Jiangnan, and Wengzhou [among the Zhou Islands] of our area, [which mounted resistance] quite beyond the expectations of the Great Army" (Quan 1902).[13]

The number of righteous deaths among loyalists in the Qing penetration of Dinghai city left an especially deep imprint on later generations: "The royal [i.e., Qing] troops besieged the walls for ten days before the city fell. Famous [Ming] officials who had been temporarily staying there all went to righteous deaths with great dignity, and when the residents learned of that, they did the same without a second thought. Within the time it takes to eat a meal, corpses lay in scattered hillocks. The prefect's aide, a Mr. Qiao, had them put in funerary jars, cremated, and buried near the sentry station north of the city wall in an area that thereupon was called Together Returned. That was on the 2nd day of the 9th month of Shunzhi 8 [1651]."[14] Regarding this "Great Area of the Together Returned," there are several poems written in late Shunzhi or Kangxi times that tell of ardent sacrifices to the souls of those buried there, fear of referring directly to the previous dynasty, and the frustration people felt at having no appropriate site at which to express their common grief.[15]

Similarly, many shrines were established in the Yin-Dinghai area to commemorate martyrs who died in the Ming-Qing transition, and after the Qianlong emperor publicly extolled such loyal and principled men and denigrated the "two-timers" (*erchen*) who had changed allegiance from Ming to Qing, that sort of activity became even more widespread. For instance, a Yin County gazetteer records that in 1820 a Temple to Cite Loyalty was established primarily in dedication to Qian Suyue and Zhang Huangyan (*Yinxian zhi* 1877: 11.13b). Also, in 1703 a Shrine for [Martyrs] of Complete Humanity was established, using charitable contributions, by the magistrate of Dinghai outside the north gate of the city to receive prayers for those who had died righteously at the end of the Ming. In the Qianlong period a later magistrate refurbished this shrine, creating three altars for the consorts, ministers, and gentry followers of the Southern Ming imperial scion Regent Lu, and it was expanded again in the Xianfeng reign (*Dinghai tingzhi* 1902: 21.8b–11b). This degree of enthusiasm for perpetuating memories of past enemies of the Qing dynasty is not nearly so common in other parts of the country.

Especially pertinent here is that in Yin County in the 6th year of Chongzhen [1633] a Redoubled Benevolence Shrine had been substantially renovated to receive prayers honoring a Song-period magistrate, Wang Anshi (1021–1086), and a Ming-period magistrate, Wang Zhang. The latter's administration had been very beneficial, and because he, in the post of censor, subsequently died at the capital during the tragedy of 1644, the people made yearly sacrifices to him on that day, 3/19 (*Yinxian zhi* 1686: 11.5a–b). Though Wang Zhang was not a native of Yin, nor had he died in that area's anti-Qing resistance, he still was honored by the people for Ming-period service in Yin and for having lost his life with the loss of the capital. The same Kangxi-period gazetteer that cites the Wang Zhang commemoration also records that a Shrine to a Benefactor of the People was established twenty *li* to the west of the Yin County seat to commemorate a native son, Wen Yuan. It explains that this man, while serving as minister of personnel in the Zhengde reign (1506–1522), had interceded in a tax collection case on behalf of the people who cultivated lakeside lands and that the local people also sacrificed to Wen each year on 3/19 (13.26b). This is particularly interesting in that a middle-Ming official was remembered for his service to local people on the date of the last Ming emperor's death. Was this really a commemoration of Wen Yuan, or was it a borrowing of his good name to commemorate the Chongzhen emperor as a symbol of the Ming state?

In this area we can find examples, as well, of ceremonial respect for figures from the past who were controversial or disapproved elsewhere. Above we mentioned that there was a shrine in Yin County for Wang Anshi (Wang Jinggong). This is because when he was county magistrate there he did some good things. But since Song times, rulers have all disliked Wang, and those of the Qing dynasty were no exception. Xu Shidong records in his *Yinyulou biji:*

> During the Yongzheng period when Li Wei was governor of
> Zhejiang, he sternly ordered Yin County to destroy the Wang
> Jinggong Shrine. I don't know how it can be that down to the
> present [ca. Daoguang] the shrine has not been harmed. Moreover,
> this is not the only one [to Wang Anshi] in Yin. In my humble view,
> when Wang was at court his disservices to the country were too great
> for words, but when he was magistrate of Yin his beneficial works
> were very numerous—in my home area, for instance, he greatly
> improved the irrigation. So temples [honoring him] in other places
> might be done away with, but not in Yin. This is what is meant by
> "transferring sacrifices to the countryside." (Xu 1908: 1.4b)

Thus, even a ruler's strict order could be ignored in the interest of protecting a local tradition.

Dinghai also had its peculiar ways. For instance, "at New Year's time the various households set out incense and candles ... and on Shangyuan eve [the 15th of the 1st lunar month] all the shrines and temples lit lanterns, whereupon the local people gathered to enact stories from previous dynasties, performing in troops and playing gongs and drums" (*Dinghai xianzhi* 1715: 5.77a). Whether those "stories from previous dynasties" were from the Ming or not, they probably were stories from periods of Han-Chinese rule and may have been challenges to the current order. As for the Mid-Autumn Festival, in most places this is celebrated on 8/15, but in some parts of south-eastern Zhejiang the date is 8/16. Though one source links this discrepancy to the pirate suppressions by Ming general Yu Dayou (1503–1579), another says that, at least in Ningbo, the lore is that the date was changed to 8/16 by members of the Southern Song imperial lineage and has been adhered to since then.[16] The reference to members of the Southern Song imperial lineage is intimately related to the historical memories of Southern Song loyalists in the Yuan period. Besides this,

> on 9/2 everyone in [Dinghai] city beats gongs and drums to drive away bad spirits and invites monks to set out offerings of food to hungry ghosts. It is said that since [9/2] was the date of the city's tragedy [at the end of] the former [dynasty], the Ming, unofficial sacrifices were made to the wandering spirits [of those who died violently at that time]. According to the Kangxi edition [of this gazetteer], on 9/2 of the 8th year of Shunzhi, Dinghai was penetrated and the whole city was ravaged, so it is commonly called the "day of tragedy." This occurrence, recorded in the old edition, is never brought up now. But families that were affected by that tragedy make sacrifices on this day of what they call city-massacre gruel. (*Dinghai tingzhi* 1902: 15.7a)

While the previous several examples can be said to pertain to earlier periods and thus to bear at most indirect relevance here, this last one certainly is a commemoration of a mass of people who were killed in a bloody incident during the Ming-Qing transition. This sort of transformation of a challenge to political taboos into a popular celebration is similar to the offering of sacrifices to effect universal release from malevolent spirits in the Ghost Festival (celebrated on 7/15). And this sort of local cultural tradition, that is, a tradition of historical memory, is entirely consistent with observance of the Birthday of the Sun. The internal logic of both kinds of rite ingeniously achieves the same result in different ways.

In Taiwan, where the Birthday of the Sun has been observed, we can see similar evidence of the transformation of historical memory into local folk tradition. The compilers of the *Taiwan sheng tongzhi gao* are of the view that, of the "princes" (*wangye*), figures that are ubiquitous in Taiwan popular belief, over 130 are "either loyal and true followers of the Ming Zhengs or persons of outstanding merit in the region. The Taiwanese have revered their virtue, cherished their righteousness, and sacrificed to them." The princes bear various surnames, but "Zhu, Li, and Chi are the most numerous."[17] Because the Ming imperial surname had been bestowed on Zheng Chenggong, the Zhus here are both numerically and symbolically significant. Once such figures had been absorbed into the folk belief in *wangye,* their identities could be preserved indefinitely. The example of the plot, mentioned above, on the part of a Fumu hui group in Taiwan to stage an uprising on 3/19, though it cannot be related with certainty to the Birthday of the Sun, does show that the date carried some sort of mobilization value among the masses that was deeply rooted in their historical memory.

Historical Memories Concentrated in the Birthday of the Sun

To people of the early Qing, particularly to former Ming subjects, the Chongzhen emperor's suicide and the demise of the Ming were not at first historical matters held in memory but very painful current experiences. When news of the emperor's suicide reached Jiangnan around the end of the 4th and the beginning of the 5th lunar month, the initial response was widespread unrest, which did not subside until the Hongguang emperor ascended the throne in Nanjing on 5/15. The following year around the time of the Qingming Festival (3/8 in 1645), flyers were posted inside and outside the Nanjing city walls that read: "On 5/5 we have boat races to console Qu Yuan, and hearth fires are prohibited during the Cold Food Festival to mourn Jie Zitui. On 3/19 the former emperor and empress bore their outrage up to Heaven, so on that day those of us who regret having been too tardy to accompany them [in death] will gather in the suburbs to imbibe wine as an expression of our grief and anger." And the vice minister of the Court of Imperial Sacrifices submitted this memorial:

> Your Augustness has approved a censor's ... proposal to perform sacrifices-at-a-distance to the former emperor outside Great Peace Gate. Humbly, I further propose that a separate altar be established adjacently for joint offerings to the crown prince and the two other princes [believed to have been killed], and that rites be conducted regularly each year on the [emperor's] death day. Moreover, what sort of day was that but one on which the heavenly bodies darkened in the sky and the imperial temples toppled to the ground?—truly

different from ordinary death days. I recommend that an edict be issued to the whole realm that on every 3/19 everyone shall cease all music, slaughtering of animals, and marriages, and that the yamen shall forgo all punishments, light or heavy. First, this would make a matter of record the tragic desolation of the former palace; second, it would arouse a spirit of vengeance in both the capital and outlying regions. [These prohibitions] should continue [in effect] until the [severed] head of the rebel Chuang [Li Zicheng] is presented to the spirit of the former emperor, only then being somewhat relaxed. (Li Qing 1985: 234)

Both the Nanjing government and the people regarded very seriously the important incident that had just taken place and constructed for it an especially significant day of memorial. This might be attributed to a simple feeling of sadness toward a ruler-father among the people and to the need to firmly establish a legitimate succession at court. At that time, when the Jiangnan region was still held by the Ming dynasty, people did not associate 3/19 with pain over the loss of their entire country.

But after the Qing troops came southward and the Hongguang regime was destroyed, and as other Southern Ming regimes were rising and falling here and there, even contending with one another over which could promulgate the legitimate calendar, the date 3/19 and the fate of the Chongzhen emperor gradually became less salient. And even for people who continued to commemorate, that day and that death took on new meaning. A passage in the 1877 *Yinxian zhi*, drawing on a compilation of writings by anti-Qing resistance figures from East Zhejiang, the *Yongdong zhengqi ji*, reads as follows:

In 1646 on 3/19, the day when Sizong joined the blessed, discussions at [Regent Lu's] court fell silent. So [a secretary in the Ministry of Revenue] Dong Shouyu submitted this memorial:

"Your servant has heard that loyalty and righteousness are aroused by the court, and that indifference and fecklessness result when such conviction is obscured. . . . I painfully recall how the former emperor exhausted himself in work for seventeen years, letting pass not one day without thinking about ordering the state and seeking worthy officials, not one day without making military preparations and managing rebel problems. Alas, incompetent ministers disserved their country and, in a turn of events, met with a

millennial calamity. All who have blood in their veins, can they bear
to forget the shining example of our former emperor in dying for
the altars of state? Last year when I was living in straightened
circumstances, on this day I looked northward and nearly expired
[from grief], bitterly angry [too] at how officials of the southern
[i.e., Nanjing] court either neglected or forgot [to commemorate].
No wonder their loyalty and righteousness dragged the ground and
became almost nil. . . .

"Song Gaozong [r. 1127–1162] each New Year's Day would lead
his hundred ministers in paying respects at a distance to the previous
two emperors [who had been taken captive when the Jurchens seized
North China] and would receive no [holiday] congratulations at
court. Now, the fully humane and filial nature of my ruler above is
one hundred times greater than that of Gaozong. For not one
instant does he forget to avenge; for not one instant does he forget
the former emperor; for not one instant does he forget the 19th day
of the 3rd month. In the present year, the advent of the Lu regency,
this day is the primary one for remembrance with tears of blood.

"I, your servant, request that you personally lead the officials
and the people, and roundly enjoin the various princes and military
leaders to wear mourning, wail, and make offerings, and that this be
made a regular yearly observance that will cause everyone to gnash
his teeth and cry out in anger. Surely the great ethic of [respect for]
one's ruler-father will thus be revived. Thereafter, in fathomless
regret at this disaster, gods and men will assist one another in taking
revenge on an enemy with whom the world cannot be shared, and
the restoration of central rule and ancient ways will naturally blaze
forth." The Prince [of Lu] instructed the Ministry of Rites to
expeditiously undertake this. (38.36a–38a)

Worth noting here is that, on one hand, although the death of the
Chongzhen emperor and the fall of the Ming capital both were directly
related to the armies of Li Zicheng, within two years the suicide incident was being used to oppose a substitute entity, the Qing dynasty,
and the matter of peasant rebellion had been expunged from memory.
Positioned in correspondence with it was "the shame of Jingkang" (the
reign-year 1126–1127, when the Northern Song capital, Kaifeng, was
seized by the Jurchens). On the other hand, the residents of southeastern coastal China had not experienced the scourge of the peasant
rebellions and had not developed any direct emotional association

between those and the fall of the Ming. What had affected them were the southward invasions of the Qing armies, the resistance struggles against shaving the head in the Manchu style, and the rise and fall of various Southern Ming courts. Consequently, on the surface this molding of 3/19 into a symbol was in remembrance of the death in adversity of the Chongzhen emperor and the demise of the Ming court. But on a deeper level it concentrated in one memory all the calamities that people had suffered, personally and immediately, in the southward drive of the Qing.

Historical Vicissitudes of Ming-Loyalist Collective Memory during the Qing

Traditionally, psychological research has tended to regard memory as an internal activity of the individual mind unrelated to its context. But contemporary social psychologists have seen the formation and maintenance of memories of past events as a dynamic sociopsychological process (Pennebaker and Banasik 1997: 4). That is to say, historical memory is foremost a sort of collective memory: an individual's memory of any historical event invariably will be of a social nature. Of course, memory takes place only within individual minds, and a certain number of those individual minds are bound to have similar memories of certain historical events, "but the *distributed* process of remembering has social functions and effects on a societal level. The collective memory of political catastrophes is a socially distributed memory. These events may not be publicly commemorated or preserved. In fact, they may even be institutionally repressed. But they are maintained as habits, oral traditions, monuments, and historical archives" (Paez 1997: 150, italics added).

Precisely because the nature of memory is so intimately linked to transmission and continuation, we regard the term "historical memory" first as denoting memory of historical events but also as expressive of the historicity of memory itself—the processes by which people of different periods remember, forget, reconstruct, and reappropriate those events. "The ways people talk and think about recent and distant events are determined by current needs and desires" (Pennebaker and Banasik 1997: 3). Consequently, memories of a given historical occurrence may diverge in different historical periods among different groups of people. Moreover, some occurrences have negative effects and thus, whether because of governmental prohibitions or because people find them too painful to contemplate, become "silent" and are not openly commemorated. But the intent to force someone— or oneself—to forget or cease thinking about something is always futile. Often when people are told to avoid discussing or thinking about an important matter, that matter sends down roots in their memories (ibid.: 10). After experiencing a period of deep injury and repression, people tend to seek means to express (or expiate) their feelings. So, bitterly painful memories of the Ming-Qing dynastic changeover among people of the southeastern coastal region could not be extinguished by Qing governmental pressures, but with the passage of time they took the form of stories about the bygone dynasty told in confidence, stories that retained to some degree expressions of grief and regret. This perhaps is the common fate of all historical memories.

The process of molding 3/19 into a symbol laden with historical meaning was related to people's changing estimations of the Ming dynasty and the Chongzhen emperor over time. Erstwhile Ming subjects who had personally experienced the change of dynasties could not rationally or objectively contemplate the reasons for or lessons of the Ming fall, and the 19th day of the 3rd month could always elicit feelings of grief among them. For instance, Ji Wulun of Yin County was a *jinshi* of 1631. His son Ji Lizuo "when the Ming fell renounced his status as a government student and dressed as a Daoist. Every year on 3/19 he made an offering of cooked grain and wept for Sizong. Someone asked him whether it accorded with ritual propriety for a rustic subject to make sacrifices to an emperor. He replied, 'This is what is called wailing in the countryside'" (*Yinxian zhi* 1877: 39.9a). Later, celebration of the Birthday of the Sun on 3/19 was a formalized and symbolized form of this sacrifice.

Among poets, Xu Kairen, for instance, wrote several verses, including two on "The Third Month, Nineteenth Day of 1653" and one "Eulogy for the Emperor [Zhuang]lie," in which "not one character failed to embody reflection on the former state" (Deng 1984: I, 12). A poem by Yang Zhao, "Third Month, Nineteenth Day, 1671," reads in part: "I am a subject of Chongzhen, / born in the Wanli years. / My cap and gown reflected a sagely era, / and my hair grew long in that perfect time"; and his poem "Third Month, Nineteenth Day, 1673" is tearful with regret that he did not better serve the Chongzhen emperor when he was alive ("Huaigutang shixuan," in Deng 1984: I, 76).

Compared to poets, historians might be expected to show more rationality, but in the early Qing, Gu Yingtai (d. post-1689), in writing about the end of the Ming and the Chongzhen emperor, was filled with sympathy: "[The emperor] came upon a time of disorder and had many hardships; he was unfortunate to have been born in the imperial family." Further, Gu thought that the Chongzhen emperor "had some justification," in a purported last testament, to blame his ministers for letting the country down (1977: 1382). And Zhang Dai (1597–1684?), though he criticized Chongzhen for being "too exhaustive in seeking order, too sharp in managing finances, too demanding in employing men, and too driven in enforcing the laws," did not regard him as a country-losing ruler: "Among our gentry and common people, when they think about the 3rd month of 1644, there are none who do not feel pain in their hearts and spit up blood, who, thinking about our former emperor, do not wish to have died for him on the same day" (1959: 40–42). Even that severe critic of autocracy the early-Qing thinker Tang Zhen (1630–1704), though completely unforgiving of Chongzhen's wrongdoings toward personnel, still considered him a "resolute, accomplished ruler" who "labored anxiously for seventeen years, with no foolishness about wine or women, no enjoyment of banquets or excursions—yet in the end he died for the altars of state, which even now brings tears to the eyes of old folks when they speak of it" (1985: 122).

At the time of sharpest pain, when feelings were still raw, when the people of Jiang-Zhe were still fighting against the Qing regime under the banner of the Southern Ming, they didn't need an obscure symbolic idea like the Birthday of the Sun, since they could overtly use Zhu-Ming slogans or rally around various scions of the Ming imperial line, such as "Zhu, the Third Crown Prince." It was only when such grand heroics had ended in silent submersion that the still mournful losers would seek to construct a symbol and invest it with their historical memories.

If such deductive reasoning accords with actual patterns of human feeling, then the story of the Birthday of the Sun probably was invented toward the end of the Shunzhi reign in the southeastern coastal region after large-scale resistance to the Qing had met with failure, and perhaps it was transmitted to Taiwan after the Qing assertion of control over that island in 1683. But establishing the exact inception and early transmission of this lore is not as important as recognizing a process by which a body of live experiences eventually was transformed into history—and into something that could be either remembered or forgotten. Indeed, when the continuation of such a historical memory among the populace might constitute a threat to the current order, those in power were sanguine about forcing forgetfulness. So those who would preserve that body of memory had to create a veiled analogy in order to insure its uninterrupted survival. Above we have seen that in Shaoxing it was believed that the story of a Sun Bodhisattva originated with a Ming princess, the third daughter of the Chongzhen emperor, who was thought to have taken the tonsure, become a nun, and composed a sun sutra as a repository of her remembrance. Certainly this is not credible, but the meaning it expresses is not inconsistent with the following explanation by Xu Shidong:

> When our state was being founded, our locale [Yin County] was most
> noted for its many old survivors [from the Ming] who maintained
> feelings for their former dynasty and who, every year on the date
> when Emperor Zhuanglie died for the altars of state, privately held
> sacrifices in the countryside, gathering together to bow and make
> offerings. In fear of prohibition, they did not clearly announce [their
> purpose]; rather, they resorted to the fiction that it was the Birthday
> of the Sun. The sun stood for their [former] ruler, and his death day
> was made a birthday. (1908: 1.11a–b)

Both cases exhibit latter-day belief in processes by which survivors from the Ming created a story and a popular observance in order to perpetuate a historical memory. In our view, it is probable that a southeastern elite creation was forced to take the form of a commoners' custom, and thereby an item of elite consciousness was all the more easily disseminated among the masses. But the masses, for their part, in receiving it also would have transformed its content. The elite accomplished their aim of ensuring covert transmission of the commemoration, but they could not ensure that among the masses the true object of the commemoration would be preserved in memory.

In any case, the rich, immediate historical content of the Birthday-of-the-Sun story and observance seems to have been held in the hearts and minds of its originators and early participants and not openly or widely articulated. Could it then be expected that after several generations people really would still be able to intuit the twists and turns of its past? Xu Shidong was of the following view:

> When the old survivors were almost gone and the rustic sacrifices
> lacked people [to carry them on], the Buddhist monks and Daoist

[priests] ironically rescued them and made them part of their yearly services. Ignorant womenfolk went along and made this their custom. This is the reason why the Birthday of the Sun is on 3/19, not 11/19. That the tragic feelings of loss and abandonment of the [mostly Confucian] survivors [from the Ming] could turn into something that assists Buddhists and Daoists in deluding the masses and raising money is a terribly regrettable outcome, but its inception is much worth remembering. (ibid.)

The rite for the Birthday of the Sun had changed into a general invocation of good fortune and exorcism of bad, as later generations of believers apparently forgot, through indifference, the painful memories that the rite had embodied. The conscientious efforts of those who initiated the rite were not sufficient in the long run to withstand the erosion of time. Indeed, "memory depends on the social environment. . . . It is in this sense that there exists a collective memory and social frameworks for memory; it is to the degree that our individual thought places itself in these frameworks and participates in this memory that it is capable of the act of recollection."[18] If a given memory loses its sustaining social atmosphere, then it cannot possibly persist as the memory of a large collectivity; in early Qing China it could only be passed on tenuously among literati who were familiar with its past referent.

Such literati activity exemplifies Maurice Halbwachs's point that "while a society may be broken down into a number of groups of people serving a variety of functions, we can also find in it a narrower society whose role, it may be said, is to preserve and maintain the living force of tradition. Whether that society is directed toward the past or toward what is a continuation of the past in the present, it participates in present-day functions only to the extent that it is important to adapt those functions to traditions and to ensure the continuity of social life through their transformations."[19] In a certain sense, any tradition among survivors from a previous dynasty or any particular cultural tradition within the literati stratum could be seen as serving this sort of preservative function of a "narrower society." Practitioners sought, through certain symbols, to perpetuate in highly concentrated form memory of the previous dynasty in people's minds, regarding this as a sacred duty. But they were not the official historians of the current dynasty, and their duty was not to continue the historical tradition that was required by the ruling group. Just the opposite: they saw themselves as serving not a narrower society but all of Han society in keeping alive what we might now call a collective countermemory.

In the southeastern coastal region during the Qing there always existed pockets in which this sort of memory persisted, where the true meaning of the Birthday of the Sun continued to be understood not just by a small number of the highly educated but by others as well. In this region the mood of resistance against the political center was stronger than in the north because Jiangnan, Zhejiang, and Fujian had witnessed the most important anti-Qing struggles and the rise and fall of successive Southern Ming regimes. This region had undergone, as well, a series of conflicts and cases in which hundreds of residents paid with their lives for such activities as abetting pro-Ming forces at sea, publicly protesting the harsh collection of taxes, or publishing a history of the Ming that was offensive to the Manchus. Later this region would give rise to the Heaven and Earth Society, the slogan of which was "Overthrow the Qing and restore the Ming," and in the Qianlong period it exhibited a widespread form of sorcery that attacked men's queues and outerwear—the most ubiquitous symbols of Manchu rule. Inflated by the emperor's interpretation into a seditious plot, this practice elicited intense scrutiny from regional officials (Kuhn 1990). In the early Qing such locales as Shaoxing, Ningbo/Yin, and Dinghai had been through near genocides related to their support of the Southern Ming resistance. It stands to reason that the covert meaning of the Birthday of the Sun was passed along at least by a certain sector of the populace of that region. Otherwise, the observance could never have been recorded in those locales' Tongzhi- and Guangxu-period gazetteers. It is quite unlikely that stories and sayings among the common people about the Birthday of the Sun and the Red-Heaven Temple are new fabrications since the advent of the Republic.[20]

Certainly historical memories have been passed down regarding all manner of human affairs in the Ming-Qing transition, but recorded in the official histories was just one kind, one "text," that, having been vetted and distributed by the government, became the most available and familiar. In this sphere of official opinion, it seems that from an early point the Chongzhen emperor was regarded as a ruler worthy of sympathy. In the *Duoergun shezheng riji* (Dorgon's diary of [his] regental rule), for instance, is the passage "Chongzhen after all was a good emperor. It was just that his military officials took credit and rewards for empty accomplishments, and his civil officials, in their corrupt venality, undermined the law. So he lost the realm" (Dorgon 1935: 3a). This view is similar to that reported in Gu Yingtai's semiofficial *Mingshi jishi benmo* about the content of a last Chongzhen testament. Indeed the view that a diligent ruler had been undone by poor officials soon became a virtually canonical tenet about Chongzhen among rulers of the Qing. In 1659, upon the emplacement of a stele for Chongzhen, the Shunzhi emperor declared: "The Ming Chongzhen emperor, in spite of all else, was a ruler who tirelessly sought order. It's just that he employed the wrong men who led things to disaster, and [in the end] he died for the altars of state. I have said repeatedly that if we do not quickly make [his conscientiousness and self-sacrifice] widely known, I fear that after a thousand years have passed, those who vie in lacking virtue and in undoing the state will be just like those [who disserved Chongzhen]. Alas!" (Qing *shilu* 1986–1987: Shizu, 124.4b–5a). The Kangxi emperor, also, distinguishing between the Chongzhen emperor and most rulers in periods of decline, saw to it that he was honored in the imperial temple for emperors of the past. This generous Kangxi gesture, despite some criticism of the Chongzhen emperor in the official *Ming History,* completed in 1739 (j. 74; *Mingshi* 1974: II, 335), later was pronounced by the Qianlong emperor to have been "an actualization of the firm, broadminded opinion of the whole world" (Qing *shilu* 1986–1987: Gaozong, 1210.6a–b), as he too, in his own interest as ruler, vigorously extolled loyal officials and righteous subjects from the end of the Ming and correspondingly denigrated "two-time officials" who had surrendered to the Qing.

Nevertheless, the Qing government never accorded—and never could have accorded—special respect to the Zhu-Ming dynasty, which the Chongzhen emperor represented, because that would have relinquished Qing-dynasty legitimacy. The Qing court's praise for Chongzhen was issued to him as no more than an individual who occupied a certain position; there was no wish to link him with the legitimacy of the Ming. Regardless of the permutations that the official-level historiography of the Ming-Qing transition underwent, this was basic. But the historical memory that was concentrated in such folkways as the Birthday of the Sun was a different text. It represents a longing to assert a native historical tradition, symbolized by the Ming dynasty, in opposition to the alien-ruled Qing and its self-serving historiography. In this respect, though the popular text also was favorable toward the Chongzhen emperor, it differed fundamentally from the official text of the history of the Ming-Qing dynastic change.

The effort, by circuitous means, to invest a newly made, at-large story and custom with a special historical memory was vulnerable to failure if the story and custom were not passed on, but it also held out the hope that, through an ambiguous folk practice, the memory could escape the fate of eventual extinction. Indeed, when the Qing empire reached the end of its road, this special form of memory, which had been deeply embedded in the hearts of members of local elites and had been transmitted through the stories and chants of common men and women, came to the surface again under new circumstances.

Feng Ziyou (1881–1958) wrote of a meeting of anti-Manchu student activists in Japan: "In the first part of the 3rd month of 1902, [Zhang] Taiyan argued that if we wished to promote a racial revolution, we would first need to raise people's historical consciousness, and that 3/19, the taboo day of the Chongzhen emperor's death for the [Han-governed] state being not far off, we should organize a large-scale commemoration to affect the outlook and feelings of the students studying abroad" (1957: 497). And the veteran Yu Youren (1879–1964), on the 3/19 just preceding the Republican Revolution, exclaimed emotively: "How can one limit the pain of bringing up bygone matters again? Countrymen, countrymen! Do you still remember the tragic commemoration of 3/19? Today, the vicissitudes of our ancestral country are more dire than ever. You good men, can you bear to watch our godly land again be submerged?!" (1986: 157). The date 3/19 again became openly symbolic—of the "national humiliation" in loss of one's country and extermination of one's race. The historical memory attached to it gained new content, particularly in the context of challenges from the Western powers, and the popular version of its meaning was granted legality. At this point, the Birthday of the Sun can be said to have fulfilled its mission.

Notes

A somewhat different version of this essay has been published in Chinese. See Zhao and Du 1999.

1. Year-end candles are usually used at the end of the lunar year to thank the myriad spirits that benefit humankind.

2. Recited by Huang Jingqiu; recorded in Zhong 1998: 447.

3. Jiang 1996: 507. Also in the *Baojuan liuzhong* (n.d.) is a "Wang daniang baojuan" recorded in the Republican period. It contains lines such as "On the 19th of the 3rd month [when the] sun is born, good people recite the Bud-

dha's name and light heaven-lamps. The living Buddha before our eyes must be honored; people of virtue and the Way set bright lights shining."

4. For instance, in Gongan County, Hubei, a text titled "Respect the Sun God" reads: "Sun God, Sun God. The sun is born on the 19th of the 11th month and on 6/1 mounts to the entrance of the hall." And another reads: "The sun is born on the 19th of the 11th month; every family recites the Buddha's name and lights red lamps." See Han n.d.: 5. Also, in the Qianlong period the following "Sun Sutra" was copied from the home of a follower of the White Light religion (Baiyang jiao): "Sun Sutra, Sun Sutra. When the sun comes out the whole sky turns red. It reaches the door of every home and knows the childhood name of everyone.... The sun is born on the 19th of the 11th month. Every family recites the Buddha's name and lights heaven-lanterns." See a Grand Council reference copy of a memorial dated Qianlong 38 (1773)/3/5, as cited in Ma and Han 1992: 100.

5. *Zhejiang sheng fengsu jianzhi* 1986: 215. See also Ye Dabing 1998: 393.

6. Relevant materials from these local histories can be found in Ding and Zhao 1995: 1367, 1588, 1743, 1801, and 1857, respectively.

7. "Zhang Yangyuan xiansheng Lixiang yanxing jianwen lu," in Chen 1979: II, 41.

8. In this work is quoted a passage about the sun being a "bright-shining, red, gem-glowing Buddha" from a *Taiyangxing jun zhenjing* (Genuine sutra of the Sun-Star Ruler), the content of which is basically the same as that quoted at the beginning of this essay. It is difficult to judge whether this was transmitted from the mainland to Taiwan or vice versa.

9. Weng's sources here include an appendix to Chen Da's *Nanyang Huaqiao yu Min-Yue shehui* on beliefs in certain overseas Chinese communities of Chaozhou, as well as j. 23, on folkways, in Lian Heng's *Taiwan tongshi*.

10. Actually, the 19th of that month was a *dingwei* day.

11. Kuafu was a legendary beast that, not knowing its own limitations, chased the twilight.

12. Yin was a county of Ningbo Prefecture. The city that served as the Yin county seat also was the seat of the prefecture.

13. "Yinjing County" may refer to Jiangyin.

14. *Dinghai tingzhi* 1902, "Zazhi zhi, zhongmu," 26.26b–30b.

15. See, for instance, *Dinghai xianzhi* 1715, "Yiwen," 8.22a–b and 8.28a–29b.

16. On the former, see *Zhejiang minsu daguan* 1998: 59; on the latter, see *Dinghai tingzhi* 1902: 15.7a.

17. As cited in Ding and Zhao 1995: 1377.

18. Ginsburg 1997: 259, quoting from Lewis A. Coser's translation of selec-

tions from Maurice Halbwachs' *Les cadres sociaux de la mémoire* (1925) in *On Collective Memory* (Chicago, 1992), pp. 37–38.

19. Ibid.: 353–354, from *On Collective Memory*, p. 129.

20. The late gazetteer specialist Fu Zhenlun wrote in the 1920s (of a locale in Hebei): "Miscellaneous religions in Xinhe are tremendously numerous. Because their content usually is kept confidential and not revealed openly, and their leadership and transmission also often are deceptively concealed, I refer to them by the general term 'secret religions.' Though their names are many and their precepts different, they very commonly take restoration of the Ming and extinguishment of the Qing as a major tenet." Referring specifically to one sect that had several names, including Gateway to Principle (Limen), he wrote: "It is similar to the southern Three Dots Sect (the three dots being those in the character *hong* in the reign title of the [Ming founding] emperor, Hongwu).... Its adherents strictly prohibit tobacco and liquor, and they revere a white-robed bodhisattva that is commonly called the White-Robed Great Immortal or Five Path Bodhisattva—probably covert references to Ming Emperor Zhuanglie, Chongzhen. Formerly, in the Qing period, followers trimmed their lapels and sleeves with white, and in their coiffures and queues they inconspicuously used white cords. Throughout the country, followers did things like these, apparently wearing mourning for the Ming state.... Every year they observed 3/19 ... as the Birthday of the Sun (one saying—incorrect—is that it was the Ming founder's birthday) and respectfully read a 'Sun Sutra.' Such sectarians were ubiquitous in south-central Hebei" (1929: 34b–35a). This is one of the extremely small number of references the authors have seen regarding 3/19 and the Birthday of the Sun in North China. Because we still lack evidence of such cults' earliest existence in the north, we cannot yet determine whether or not this belief was transmitted northward from anti-Qing, Ming-restorationist organizations in the south.

References

Baojuan liuzong 寶卷六種. N.d. Imprint held at Beijing Normal University Library.

Chen Que 陳確. 1979. *Chen Que ji* 陳確集. 2 vols. Beijing: Zhonghua shuju.

Deng Zhicheng 鄧之誠. 1984. *Qingshi jishi chubian* 清詩紀事初編. 2 vols. Shanghai: Shanghai guji chubanshe.

Ding Shiliang 丁世良 and Zhao Fang 趙放, comps. 1995. *Zhongguo difangzhi minsu ziliao huibian* 中國地方志民俗資料匯編, vol. 3, *Huadong* 華東. Beijing: Shumu wenxian chubanshe.

Dinghai tingzhi 定海廳志. 1902. Supplemented edition (compiled 1877). Comp.

and ed. Shi Zhixun 史致馴, Chen Zhongwei 陳重威, et al. N.p.: Zhe-Ning chujingzhai.

Dinghai xianzhi 定海縣志. 1715. Comp. Miao Sui 繆燧, Chen Guan 陳琯, et al. N.p.: N.p.

———. 1924. Comp. Chen Xunzheng 陳訓正 et al. Fasc. 5, "Fangsu zhi" 方俗志, no. 16, "Fengsu suishi" 風俗歲時 sec. N.p.: N.p.

Dorgon. 1935. *Duoergun shezheng riji* 多爾袞攝政日記. 2nd ed. Beijing: Guoli Beiping gugong bowuyuan.

Feiyun Jushi 飛雲居士 [pseud.]. 1993. *Xishuo Taiwan minjian xinyang* 細說台灣民間信仰. Taibei: Yiqun shudian.

Feng Menglong 馮夢龍, comp. 1940. *Jiashen jishi* 甲申紀事. In *Xuanlantang congshu* 玄覽堂叢書, ed. Zheng Zhenduo 鄭振鐸, fasc. 107–118. Nanjing: Zhongyang tushuguan.

Feng Ziyou 馮自由. 1957. "Zhang Taiyan yu Zhina wangguo jinian hui" 章太炎與支那亡國紀念會. In *Zhongguo jindai shi ziliao congkan* 中國近代史資料叢刊, pt. 7, *Xinhai geming* 辛亥革命, vol. 1, 497–500. Shanghai: Shanghai renmin chubanshe.

Fu Zhenlun 傅振倫. 1929. "Shehui xianzhuang zhi zongjiao ji renmin xinyang" 社會現狀之宗教及人民信仰. In *Sanhe xianzhi* 三河縣志, comp. Fu Zhenlun, fasc. 4, "Fengtu kao" 風土考, chap. 4. Beijing: Yongfengde nanzhidian.

Ginsburg, Carlo. 1997. "Shared Memories, Private Recollections." In *Passing into History: Nazism and the Holocaust Beyond Memory,* ed. Gulie Ne'eman Arad. Issue of *History & Memory: Studies in Representation of the Past* 9.1–2 (Fall): 353–363. Bloomington: Indiana University Press.

Gu Yingtai 谷應泰. 1977. "Jiashen zhi bian" 甲申之變. In *Mingshi jishi benmo* 明史紀事本末, 4 (j. 79). Beijing: Zhonghua shuju.

Gui Zhuang 歸莊. 1984. *Gui Zhuang ji* 歸莊集. 2 vols. Shanghai: Shanghai guji chubanshe.

Han Zhizhong 韓致中. N.d. "Taiyang chongbai he taiyang shenhua" 太陽崇拜和太陽神話. Unpublished paper.

Hangzhou fuzhi 杭州府志. 1912 (compiled 1898). Comp. and ed. Chen Qiong 陳瓊 and Wang Fen 王棻. "Fengsu" 風俗, sec. 3. N.p.: N.p.

Hu Puan 胡朴安. 1986. *Zhongguo quanguo fengsu zhi* 中國全國風俗志. 2 vols. Shijiazhuang: Hebei renmin chubanshe.

Jiang Bin 姜彬, ed. 1996. *Daozuo wenhua yu Jiangnan minsu* 稻作文化與江南民俗. Shanghai: Shanghai wenhua chubanshe.

Kishimoto Mio 岸本美緒. 1999. "Chongzhen shiqinian de Jiangnan shehui yu guanyu Beijing de xinxi" 崇禎十七年的江南社會與關於北京的信息. *Qingshi yanjiu* 清史研究 1999, no. 2: 25–32.

Kuhn, Philip. 1990. *Soulstealers: The Chinese Sorcery Scare of 1768.* Cambridge:

Harvard University Press. Chinese edition: *Jiaohun: 1768 nian Zhongguo yaoshu da konghuang* 叫魂: 1768 年中國妖術大恐慌. Trans. Chen Jian 陳兼 and Liu Chang 劉昶. Shanghai: Sanlian shudian, 1999.

Li Qing 李清. 1985. *Nandu lu* 南渡錄. Hangzhou: Zhejiang guji chubanshe.

Liu Shouhua 劉守華. 1987. "Jinri zhi 'yuanshi sixiang' buneng chansheng xin shenhua" 今日之'原始思想'不能產生新神話. In *Shenhua xinlun* 神話新論, ed. Liu Kuili 劉魁立 et al., 227–236. Shanghai: Shanghai wenhua chubanshe.

Lu Xun 魯迅. 1976. *Lu Xun shuxin ji* 魯迅書信集. Beijing: Renmin wenxue chubanshe.

Ma Xisha 馬西沙 and Han Bingfang 韓秉方. 1992. *Zhongguo minjian zongjiao shi* 中國民間宗教史. Shanghai: Shanghai renmin chubanshe.

Ma Xulun 馬敍倫. 1984. "Zhutian miao" 朱天廟. In *Shiwu yushen* 石屋餘瀋. Shanghai: Shanghai shudian.

Mingshi 明史. 1974. Comp. Zhang Tingyu 張廷玉 et al. 17 vols. Beijing: Zhonghua shuju.

Paez, Dario, et al. 1997. "Social Processes and Collective Memory: A Cross-Cultural Approach to Remembering Political Events." In *Collective Memory of Political Events*, ed. Pennebaker et al., 147–174.

Pennebaker, James W., and Becky L. Banasik. 1997. "On the Creation and Maintenance of Collective Memories: History as Social Psychology." In *Collective Memory of Political Events*, ed. Pennebaker et al., 3–19.

Pennebaker, James W., Dario Paez, and Bernard Rime, eds. 1997. *Collective Memory of Political Events: Social Psychological Perspectives*. Mahwah, N.J.: Lawrence Erlbaum Associates.

Qing *shilu*. 1984–1987. *Da-Qing lichao shilu* 大清歷朝實錄. 60 vols. Beijing: Zhonghua shuju.

Quan Zuwang 全祖望. 1902. Beiji 碑記 for General Liu Shixun 劉世勛. As quoted in *Dinghai tingzhi*, "Cimiao zhi" 祠廟志 sec., 27.8b–9b.

———. 1982. "Ming guquan bingbu shangshu jian hanlinyuan shijiang xueshi Yin Zhang gong shendao beiming" 明故權兵部尚書兼翰林院侍講學士鄞張公神道碑銘. In *Jieqiting wenji xuanzhu* 鮚埼亭文集選注, ed. Huang Yunmei 黃雲眉, 21. Ji'nan: Qi-Lu shushe.

"Taiyang pusa de gushi" 太陽菩薩的故事. 1989. In *Zhejiang sheng mingjian wenxue jicheng* 浙江省民間文學集成, "Shaoxing shi gushi" 紹興市故事 chap. I, 568. Beijing: Zhongguo minjian wenyi chubanshe.

Tang Zhen 唐甄. 1985. *Qianshu* 潛書, pt. 3, "Renxiang" 任相. Beijing: Zhonghua shuju.

Weng Tongwen 翁同文. 1977. "Taiyang danchenjie de qiyuan yu Tiandi hui" 太陽誕辰節的起源與天地會. *Shixue huikan* 史學匯刊 7 (July): 190–196.

Wuqing zhenzhi 烏青鎮志. 1936. Comp. Dong Shining 董世寧, exp. Lu Xuepu 盧學溥. "Fengsu" 風俗 sec. N.p.: N.p.

Xiaoshan xianzhi gao 蕭山縣志稿. 1935. Comp. and ed. Peng Yanqing 彭延慶 and Yao Yingjun 姚塋俊. "Jiangyu men, fengsu" 疆域門, 風俗 sec. N.p.: N.p.

Xu Bodong 徐博東 and Zhang Minghua 張明華. 1996. *Taiwan chuantong wenhua tanyuan* 台灣傳統文化探源. Taibei: Shangwu yinshuguan.

Xu Shidong 徐時棟. N.d. (Tongzhi-Guangxu). "Taiyang shengri fu" 太陽生日賦. In *Yanyulou wenji* 煙嶼樓文集, 38.10a–12b. Ningbo: Junhe juzhenban.

———. 1908. *Yanyulou biji* 筆記. Yin County: Xu shi juxuezhai.

Ye Dabing 葉大兵. 1998. *Wenzhou minsu daquan* 溫州民俗大全. Urumchi: Xinjiang renmin chubanshe.

Yinxian zhi 鄞縣志. 1686. Comp. and ed. Wang Yuanze 王源澤 and Wen Xingdao 聞性道. N.p.: N.p.

———. 1877 (compiled 1874). Comp. and ed. Dai Mei 戴枚, Zhang Shu 張恕, et al. "Fengsu" 風俗 sec. N.p.: N.d.

Yu Youren 于右任. 1986. *Yu Youren xinhai wenji* 于右任辛亥文集. Shanghai: Fudan daxue chubanshe.

Zhang Dai 張岱. 1959. *Shikuishu houji* 石匱書後集, j. 1: "Liehuangdi benji" 烈皇帝本紀. Shanghai: Zhonghua shuju.

Zhao Shiyu 趙世瑜 and Du Zhengzhen 杜正貞. 1999. "Taiyang shengri: Dongnan yanhai diqu dui Chengzhen sinan de lishi jiyi" 太陽生日: 東南沿海地區對崇禎死難的歷史記憶. *Beijing shifan daxue xuebao* 北京師範大學學報, 1999, no. 6: 10–19.

Zhejiang minsu daguan 浙江民俗大觀. 1998. Comp. Zhejiang minjian wenyijia xiehui 浙江民間文藝家協會. Beijing: Dangdai Zhongguo chubanshe.

Zhejiang sheng fengsu jianzhi 浙江省風俗簡志. 1986. Ed. Zhejiang minsu xuehui 浙江民俗學會. Hangzhou: Zhejiang renmin chubanshe.

Zhong Weijin 鐘偉今. 1998. "Huzhou de riyue chongbai" 湖州的日月崇拜. In *Zhejiang minsu daguan*, 446–447.

Zhou Zuoren 周作人. 1944. "Yangjiu shulüe" 陽九述略. In Zhou's *Kukou gankou* 苦口甘口, 150–155. Shanghai: Taiping shuju.

HAN-SCRIPT GLOSSARY

Aizong　哀宗
An Lushan　安祿山
Anhui　安徽
anshen　安神
Baigou　白溝
Baima　白馬
Baiquan　百泉
Baiyang jiao　白陽教
"Baoxun"　寶訓
Beijing　北京
Beizhili　北直隸
benji　本紀
Bi Gan　比干
Bianjing　汴京
Bianzhou　汴州
bing　丙
Bo Yi　伯夷
Bohai　渤海
Cai Yin　蔡寅
caipeng　彩棚
Cao Cao　曹操
chahui　茶會
Chan　禪
Chang'an　長安
Changshu　常熟

Chaozhou　潮州
Chen　陳
Chen Da　陳達
Chen Ping　陳平
Chendai　陳埭
Cheng, King　成王
Cheng Yi　程頤
Chenghua　成化
Chengzong　成宗
Chi　池
Chindŏk　真德
Chinhŭng　真興
Chinp'yŏng　真平
chizhu　持珠
cho/jo　祖
ch'ŏk　尺
Ch'ŏlchong　哲宗
chong/jong　宗
Chŏng Yagyong　鄭若鏞
Chongde　崇德
Chŏngjo　正祖
Ch'ŏngju　清州
Chongmyo　宗廟
Chongzhen　崇禎
Ch'ŏnsu　天授

Chosŏn　朝鮮
chou　丑
Chu　楚
Chuang　闖
Chun, Prince of Wei　魏國王淳
chunfen　春分
Ch'ungnyŏl-wang　忠烈王
chungsa　中祀
Chunp'ung　峻豐
Chunqiu　春秋
Cixi　慈溪
Da-Ming　大明
Dading　大定
Dadu　大都
Daiyuan　大元
Dalinghe　大凌河
Daming　大明
dao/Dao　道
Daoguang　道光
Daozong　道宗
Dashun　大順
Datong　大同
Daxue　大學
daying　大迎
dazhai　大齋
dazhai yuangui　大齋原規
de　德
ding/Ding　丁
Dinghai　定海
Dingtou　頂頭
dingwei　丁未
dizhi　地支
Dong Juexuan (Dong Pei)　董覺
軒 [董沛]
Dong Shouyu　董守諭
Donglin　東林
Dongpuzhen　東浦鎮
dongzhi　冬至
Du Fu　杜甫
Du Jingquan　杜景佺

Du Mu　杜牧
Du Zhong　杜忠
dui　隊
Eastern Jin　東晉
Elai　惡來
engongsheng　恩貢生
erchen　貳臣
Fan Zhongyan　范仲淹
fang　房
fanli　凡例
Fei Lian　飛廉
Feng Quan　馮銓
Fengshen yanyi　封神演義
fengshui　風水
Fu, Prince of　福王
Fu Tingxian　傅廷獻
Fuan　福安
Fujian　福建
Fumu hui　父母會
Funing　福寧
Fushe　復社
Fuzhou　福州
gaiyuan　改元
Gangjian huizuan　綱鑑會纂
Ganzhou　贛州
Gao Jie　高傑
Gao Shi　高適
Gaotang　高唐
Gaoxiong xianzhi gao　高雄縣志稿
Gaozong　高宗
Gaozu　高祖
Geng Jingzhong　耿精忠
Geng Yinggeng　耿應庚
gengchen　庚辰
gengshen　庚申
Gong Dingzi　龔鼎孳
Gongan　公安
gongsheng　貢生
Gu Yanwu　顧炎武
Gu Yingtai　谷應泰

Guangdong　廣東

Guangning　廣寧

Guangpingdian　廣平淀

Guangwu　光武

Guangxu　光緒

Guangzhou　廣州

Guanyin　觀音

Gui Zhuang　歸莊

Guide　歸德

Guo Bangyong　郭邦雍

guohao　國號

Guomindang　國民黨

guwen　古文

Haibin　海濱

Hailing Wang　海陵王

han　函

Han　漢

Han Xin　韓信

Hangzhou　杭州

He Yinguang　何印光

Hebei　河北

Heilong River/Heilong jiang　黑龍江

Heisei　平成

Henan　河南

Heshui　河水

Hŏ Mok　許穆

hong　洪

Hong Chengchou　洪承疇

Hong Fuji　紅拂妓

Hong Niangzi　紅娘子

Hongguang　弘光

Hongje　鴻濟

Hongwenguan　弘文館

Hongwu　洪武

Hou Fangxia　侯方夏

Hou Fangyu　侯方域

Hou Fangyue　侯方岳

Hou Jin(guo)　後金(國)

Hou Xun　侯恂

Houyuan　後元

Hu (Weichi) Jingde　胡(尉遲)敬德

Huai, Emperor　懷帝

Huai River　淮河

Huaidong　淮東

"Huaigutang shixuan"　懷古堂詩選

Huaiqing　懷慶

Huaizhou　懷州

Huang Dacheng　黃大成

Huang Jingqiu　黃景秋

Huang Zongxi　黃宗羲

Huanghe　黃河

Huangjue　皇覺

Huangzhou　黃州

Hubei　湖北

hui　會

Hui (county)　輝

Hui (people)　回

huishou　會首

Huizong　徽宗

huodao shi　火刀石

Huzhou　湖州

Hwayang Academy. See Hwayang sŏwŏn

Hwayang chi　華陽誌

"Hwayang chi pal"　華陽誌跋

Hwayang sŏwŏn　華陽書院

Hwayangdong　華陽洞

hyanggyo　鄉校

Ikusuke　幾助

imsin　壬申

Injo　仁祖

Inp'yŏng　仁平

Iryŏn　一然

ji　己

Ji　汲

Ji Kang　嵇康

Ji Liuqi　計六奇

Ji Lizuo   紀歷祚
Ji Wulun   紀五倫
jia 甲
Jia She   賈涉
Jia Sidao   賈似道
Jiading   嘉定
Jiang Yun   江雲
Jiangdong   江東
Jiangnan   江南
Jiangsu   江蘇
Jiangxi   江西
Jiangyin   江陰
jiansheng   監生
Jianzhou   建州
Jiaobodong Mengweng   椒柏洞
   夢翁
jiashen   甲申
jiaxu   甲戌
jiazi   甲子
Jie 桀
Jie Zitui   介子推
Jilong xianzhi   基隆縣志
Jin 金
Jin Shenghuan   金聲桓
Jingkang   靖康
Jingshan Park   景山公園
Jingtai   景泰
jingtou   經頭
Jinguo   金國
Jingzhou   荊州
Jingzong   景宗
Jinhua   金華
Jinling   金陵
jinren   金人
Jinshi   金史
jinshi   進士
Jinzhou   錦州
Jizi   箕子
Jo Wichong   趙位寵
juan 捐

junzhu   軍主
juren   舉人
Kaeguk   開國
Kaifeng   開封
Kangxi   康熙
kapcha   甲子
Kapcha sahwa   甲子史禍
kapsin   甲申
kapsul   甲戌
Kija   箕子
Kim Sohaeng   金紹行
Kim Tŏngnyŏng   金德齡
kimi   己未
Koguryŏ   高句麗
Kŏnbok   建福
Kongzi   孔子
Kŏnwŏn   建元
Koryŏ   高麗
kou zhai   口齋
Kuafu   夸父
Kwangdŏk   光德
Kwanggaet'o   廣開土
Kwangjong   光宗
kwŏn   卷
Kwŏn Sangha   權尚夏
kyehae   癸亥
kyŏngin   庚寅
kyŏngjin   庚辰
Laiyang   萊陽
Lanxi   蘭溪
Latter Han   後漢
Latter Jin. See Hou Jin
li (distance unit)   里
li/Li (structural order,
   Supertime)   理
Li 李
Li Bo   李白
Li Huajing   李化鯨
Li Keyong   李克用
Li Mi   李宓

Li Senxian   李森先

Li Shimin   李世民

Li Shiqi   酈食其

Li Wei   李衛

Li Wen   李雯

Li Yan (the storied advisor to Li Zicheng)   李巖

Li Yan* (homophonous name)   李焉

Li Yuan   李淵

Li Zhenyuan   李貞元

Li Zicheng   李自成

Lian Heng   連橫

Lian Zhenji   縺貞吉

Liancun   廉村

Liang   梁

Liang Huafeng   梁化鳳

Liang Xi   梁熙

Liangxiang   良鄉

Liao   遼

Liao River   遼河

Liaodong   遼東

Liaoshi   遼史

Liaoxi   遼西

Liaoyang   遼陽

Lieguozhuan   列國傳

liezhuan   列傳

Limen   理門

ling   靈

Liu   劉

Liu Bang   劉邦

Liu Bei   劉備

Liu Chang   劉昌

Liu Song   劉宋

Liu Wuzhou   劉武周

Liu Yuan   劉源

Liu Zheng   劉整

Liu Zhongzao   劉中藻

Liutao   六韜

Liuyang   留洋

Lixue zongchuan   理學宗傳

Lu, Prince of/Regent   魯王/監國

Lu Qi   盧杞

Lu Shiyi   陸世儀

Lu Zhonglian   魯仲連

luan   亂

Lunyu   論語

Luo Qing   羅清

Luo Rucai   羅汝才

Luoyang   洛陽

Luoyuan   羅源

Luqu   臚朐

Lüshi chunqiu   呂氏春秋

Lüshun   旅順

Mandongmyo   萬東廟

mao (constellation)   昴

mao (one of "twelve branches")   卯

Mao Wenlong   毛文龍

Mao Zedong   毛澤東

map'ae   馬牌

Mei Wending   梅文鼎

"Meigui shiwu duan yin"   玫瑰十五端引

Mengzi   孟子

Miao   繆

Miao Shixiang   繆士珦

Min, Emperor   愍帝

Mindong   閩東

ming/Ming   明

mingming   明明

Mingru xuean   明儒學案

Mingshi   明史

Mingyi daifang lu   明夷待訪錄

Mingzong   明宗

Minnan   閩南

Munmyo   文廟

muo   戊午

Mushui　穆水
Musin nan　戊申亂
Muyang　穆洋
Muzong　穆宗
Nagasaki　長崎
Namin　南人
Nanbeichao　南北朝
Nanjing　南京
Nanyang Huaqiao yu Min-Yue
　　shehui　南洋華僑與閩粵社會
nei　內
Nei guoshiyuan　內國史院
Nei hongwenyuan　內弘文院
Nei mishuyuan　內秘書院
Nei sanyuan　內三院
nianhao　年號
nianzhu　念珠
Ningbo　寧波
Ningde　寧德
Ningzong　寧宗
Niu Jinxing　牛金星
Paekche　百濟
pal　跋
Pan Gu　盤古
Peng Zhican　彭之燦
Pingyang　平陽
pumo chi kuk　父母之國
pyŏngjin　丙辰
Qi　杞
Qian Suyue　錢肅樂
qiankun quan　乾坤圈
Qianlong　乾隆
Qiao　喬
qin　琴
Qin, First Emperor of/Qin
　　Shihuangdi　秦史皇帝
Qing　清
qing niu　青牛
Qingming　清明
Qingzhou　慶州

Qinzong　欽宗
qitalei　其他類
Qu Yuan　屈原
Quanzhou　泉州
Raozhou　饒州
renwu　人物
Renzong　仁宗
sabyŏn sadu　四籩四豆
Sajiktan　社稷壇
Samhan sŭbyu　三韓捨遺
San hui　三會
sang chi sipnyŏn　上之十年
Sanguo zhi yanyi　三國志演義
Sanlüe　三略
sau　祠宇
Shaanxi　陝西
Shandong　山東
Shang　商
Shanghai　上海
Shangqiu　商邱
Shangshu　尚書
Shangyuan　上元
Shanhai jing　山海經
Shanhai Pass　山海關
shanshu baojuan　善書寶卷
Shanxi　山西
Shao Yong　邵雍
Shaoxing　紹興
she　社
shen　神
Shen Chenquan　沈宸荃
Shengjiao zhanli zhaiqi lüeyan　聖
　　教瞻禮齋期略言
shengmu　聖母
"Shengyu"　聖諭
shengyuan　生員
Shengzong　聖宗
shi　勢
Shi Kecheng　史可程
Shi Kefa　史可法

shibazi　十八子

Shiji　史記

shijiang　十將

Shijing　詩經

shilu　實錄

Shixian shu　時憲書

Shizong　世宗

Shizu　世祖

shu feili　屬非禮

Shu-Han　蜀漢

Shu Qi　叔齊

Shun (rebel regime)　順

Shun (sage ruler)　舜

Shun, Emperor　順帝

Shunzhi　順治

shuzhu　數珠

Silla　新羅

sillok　實錄

Sima Guang　司馬光

sin　申

sinch'uk　辛丑

sinsa　辛巳

Sizong　思宗

Sŏ Kŏjŏng　徐居正

Sŏin　西人

Sŏndŏk　善德

Song　宋

Song Luo　宋犖

Song Mei　宋玫

Song Quan　宋權

Song Xiance　宋獻策

Songbaili　松柏里

Sŏnggyun'gwan　成均館

sŏngsang ch'ilnyŏn pyŏngjin　聖
　上七年丙辰

Songshi　宋史

Sŏnjo　宣祖

sosa　小祀

Southern Ming　南明

Southern Song　南宋

Su Dongpo　蘇東坡

Su Qin　蘇秦

Sui　隋

suibi　隨筆

suicha　歲差

Suizhou　睢州

Sukchong　肅宗

Sumen　蘇門

Sun Qifeng　孫奇逢

Sungjŏng ibaeksamsipsa nyŏn
　sinyu　崇禎二百三十四年辛
　酉

Sungjŏng sa sinyu　崇禎四辛酉

Sungjŏng samsipsa nyŏn sinch'uk
　崇禎三十四年辛丑

Sŭngjŏngwŏn ilgi　承政院日記

Sushu　素書

Suyang　蘇陽

Suzong　肅宗

Taebodan　大報壇

Taech'ang　大昌

T'aehwa　太和

T'aejo　太祖

taesa　大祀

Tai Lake　太湖

Taibei　臺/台北

Taiding, Emperor　泰定帝

Taigong Wang　太公望

Taihe　泰和

Taikang　太康

Tainan shizhi　台南市志

Tainan xianzhi　台南縣志

Taiping　太平

Taiwan　臺/台灣

Taiwan sheng tongzhi gao　台灣省
　通志稿

Taiwan tongshi　台灣通史

taiyang　太陽

Taiyangxing jun zhenjing　太陽星
　君真經

Taizong 太宗
Taizu 太祖
Tan Qian 談遷
Tang 唐
Tang Bin 湯斌
Tangun 檀君
tao 套
Tao Qian 陶潛
tian 天
Tian Lanfang 田蘭芳
Tiancong 天聰
Tiandi hui 天地會
Tianfu 天輔
tiangan 天干
Tianming 天命
Tianqing 天慶
tianxia 天下
"Tianzhu shengjiao zhanli zhaiqi
    biao" 天主聖教瞻禮齋期表
Tianzuo 天祚
Tong 佟
Tong Yehu Kehan 統葉護可汗
tongzhen 童貞
Tongzhi 同治
Tongzhou 通州
Tonkin 東京
tushen 土神
ŭlsa 乙巳
Urakami 浦上
ŭryu 乙酉
waizhai 外齋
Wanbao quanshu 萬寶全書
wang/Wang 王
Wang Anshi/Wang Jinggong 王
    安石/王荊公
"Wang daniang baojuan" 王大
    娘寶卷
Wang Daosheng 王道牲
Wang Daoxing 王道性

Wang Duo 王鐸
Wang Kŏn 王建
Wang Mang 王莽
wang ri 望日
Wang Shizhen 王士禎
Wang Wenkui 王文奎
Wang Yangming 王陽明
Wang Zhang 王章
Wang Zishou 王紫綬
wangye 王爺
Wanli 萬曆
"Wanli banian siyue shiwuri" 萬
    曆八年四月十五日
Wei-Jin 魏晉
Wei Yijie 魏裔介
Wei Zheng 魏徵
Wei Zhongxian 魏忠賢
Weihui 衛輝
Weishao Wang 衛紹王
Wen, Emperor 文帝
Wen, King 文王
Wen Yuan 聞淵
Wenguan 文館
Wengzhou 瀚州
wenhua 文化
Wenzhou 溫州
Wenzong 文宗
Western Jin 西晉
Wŏnjong 元宗
wu 戊
Wu 吳
Wu Cheng 吳澄
Wu huangdi shilu 武皇帝實錄
Wu Li 吳歷
Wu Qi 吳淇
Wu Sangui 吳三桂
Wu Weiye 吳偉業
Wu Yingji 吳應箕
Wu Zetian 武則天

Wuqing　烏青
wushen　戊申
Wutai Shan　五臺山
Wuzong　武宗
Xia　夏
Xi'an　西安
Xian, Emperor　獻帝
Xianfeng　咸豐
Xiang Yu　項羽
Xiangcheng　襄城
Xiangfu　祥符
xiangzhu　香珠
xianshi　現時
Xianyang　咸陽
Xiao Fengxian　蕭奉先
Xiaoshan　蕭山
Xiaoxian　孝獻
xiaozhai　小齋
Xiaozhuang　孝莊
Xiayi　夏邑
xieshuo　邪說
xing　星
Xingbu huidian　刑部會典
Xingjing　興京
Xingshan　杏山
Xingzong　興宗
Xinhe　新河
xinsi　辛巳
Xinxiang　新鄉
xinzhai　心齋
Xiongnu　匈奴
xiru　西儒
Xiyu ji　西域記
Xizong　熙宗
xu　虛
Xu Dingguo　許定國
Xu Heng　許衡
Xu Kairen　徐開任
Xu Shidong　徐時棟

Xu Yougong　徐有攻
Xu Zizhi tongjian gangmu　續資治通鑑綱目
Xu Zuomei　許作梅
Xuanzang　玄奘
Xuanzong (Liao)　宣宗
Xuanzong (Tang)　玄宗
Xue　薛
Xue Suoyun　薛所縕
Xueyuanshe　雪園社
xunhai dao　巡海道
yamen　衙門
Yan　嚴
Yan Mo　嚴謨
Yan Zhenqing　顏真卿
Yang, Emperor/Yangdi　煬帝
Yang Zhao　楊炤
Yangzhou　揚州
Yanling　鄢陵
Yao　堯
Yesu shengdan　耶穌聖誕
yi　乙
Yi　李
Yi Ik　李瀷
Yi Yin　伊尹
Yijing　易經
yimin　遺民
Yin (county)　鄞
Yin (state)　殷
Yingzong　英宗
Yinjing　陰涇
Yinxu　殷墟
yisi　乙巳
yong zhanli dan/biao　永瞻禮單/表
Yongcheng　永城
Yongdong zhengqi ji　甬東正氣集
Yŏngjo　英祖
Yongle　永樂

Yŏngnak　永樂

Yongzheng　雍正

yŏnho　年號

"Yŏnp'yo"　年表

Yŏnsan　燕山

you　酉

Yu Chunxi　虞淳熙

Yu Dayou　俞大猷

Yuan　元

Yuan, Emperor　元帝

Yuan Chonghuan　袁崇煥

Yuan Shizhong　袁時中

Yuanfeng　元封

Yue Fei　岳飛

Yun Hyu　尹鑴

Yunlin xianzhi gao　雲林縣志稿

Yuyuan jun　榆園軍

Yuzhitang tanhui　玉芝堂談薈

Zha Jizuo　查繼佐

zhai　齋

Zhang Dai　張岱

Zhang Han　張翰

Zhang Huangyan　張煌言

Zhang Jinyan　張縉彥

Zhang Juzheng　張居正

Zhang Liang　張良

Zhang Lixiang　張履祥

Zhang Mingzhen　張名振

Zhang Quan　張銓

Zhang Taiyan　章太炎

Zhang Wenguang　張文光

Zhang Xianzhong　張獻忠

"Zhang Yangyuan xiansheng
　　Lixiang yanxing jianwen lu"
　張楊園先生履祥言行見聞錄

Zhang Yi　張儀

Zhangzhou　漳州

Zhangzong　章宗

zhanli dan　瞻禮單

zhanli zhaiqi biao　瞻禮齋期表

Zhaoqing　肇慶

Zhejiang　浙江

Zheng　鄭

Zheng Chenggong　鄭成功

Zheng Lian　鄭廉

Zheng Sixiao　鄭思肖

Zhengde　正德

zhengshi　正史

Zhenguan　貞觀

zhi　治

Zhili　直隸

Zhiyuan　至元

Zhong-Xia　中夏

zhonglie　忠烈

Zhongni jiao ren　仲尼教人

Zhongtong　中統

zhongyong　中庸

zhongyuan　中原

zhongzhou　中州

Zhongzhou renwu kao　中州人物考

Zhou (dynasty)　周

Zhou (king)　紂

Zhou, Duke of　周公

Zhou Islands　舟山

Zhou Lianggong　周亮工

Zhou Yu　周瑜

Zhouli　周禮

"Zhoushu"　周書

Zhu　朱

Zhu Hong　袾宏

Zhu San Taizi　朱三太子

Zhu Xi　朱熹

Zhu Youjian　朱由檢

Zhu Yuanzhang　朱元璋

Zhuanglie　莊烈

zhuchuan　珠串

zhuer　主二

Zhuge Liang　諸葛亮

zhuguang   珠光

Zhulin qixian   竹林七賢

zhuqi   主七

zhuri   主日

zhutian (all Heavenly Buddhas)
   諸天

zhutian (Red Heaven)   朱天

zi   子

zimao   子卯

Ziyang Academy   紫陽書院

Zizhi tongjian   資治通鑑

Zizhi tongjian gangmu   資治通鑑
   綱目

zu/zong   祖/宗

Zu Chongzhi   祖沖之

Zuzhou   祖州

CONTRIBUTORS

Lynn A. Struve is Professor of History and of East Asian Languages and Cultures at Indiana University, Bloomington. She was trained in sinology principally at the University of Washington, Seattle, where she received her B.A. in Chinese Language and Literature, and at the University of Michigan, Ann Arbor, where she earned both an M.A. in Chinese Area Studies and a Ph.D. in premodern Chinese history. She teaches courses on the imperial era in China, premodern East Asian civilization, and world history in East Asian perspective. In research, she specializes in the political, intellectual, and cultural history of China in the late Ming and early Qing period, especially the Ming-Qing transition of the mid-seventeenth century. Her recent work largely concerns the dynamics of memory in journals and memoirs of that period. In addition to authoring two monographs—*The Southern Ming, 1644–1662* (Yale University Press, 1984) and *The Ming-Qing Conflict (1619–1683): A Historiography and Source Guide* (Association for Asian Studies, 1998)—and a book of translations, *Voices from the Ming-Qing Cataclysm: China in Tigers' Jaws* (Yale University Press, 1993), she has edited a collective volume, *The Qing Formation in World-Historical Time* (Harvard University Asia Center, 2004).

Mark C. Elliott is the Mark Schwartz Professor of Chinese and Inner Asian History at Harvard University. A specialist in Manchu studies, he began the study of Manchu language and history at the University of California, Berkeley, where he earned his Ph.D. in 1993. His training there, along with several years of study and research in Japan, Taiwan, and the People's Republic of China, enabled him to explore a range of issues relating to the Qing conquest experience of the seventeenth and eighteenth centuries, culminating in his book *The Manchu Way: The Eight Banners and Ethnicity in Late Imperial China* (Stanford University Press, 2001). He is also coeditor of *New Qing Imperial History: The Making of the Inner Asian Empire at Qing Chengde* (RoutledgeCurzon, 2004). Other recent publications include "The Manchu-Language Archives of the Qing and the Origins of the Palace Memorial System" (*Late Imperial China*, June 2001) and "The Limits of Tartary: Manchuria in Imperial and National Geographies" (*Journal of Asian Studies*, August 2000).

Roger Des Forges is Professor of History at the State University of New York at Buffalo, where he teaches courses on Chinese history, Asian civilization, and world civilizations. He received his A.B. degree in the Woodrow Wilson School of Public and International Affairs at Princeton University and his Ph.D. in Chinese History at Yale University. He is interested in problems of continuity and change in Chinese cultural, political, social, and economic history, which he increasingly views in a larger Asian and global perspective. His publications include *Hsi-liang and the Chinese National Revolution* (Yale University Press, 1973); *Chinese Democracy and the Crisis of 1989: Chinese and American Reflections*, coedited with Luo Ning and Wu Yenbo (State University of New York Press, 1993); and *Cultural Centrality and Political Change in Chinese History: Northeast Henan in the Fall of the Ming* (Stanford University Press, 2003).

JaHyun Kim Haboush received her Ph.D. from Columbia University, where she is currently King Sejong Professor of Korean Studies. She previously taught at the University of Illinois at Urbana-Champaign. Her major publications include *A Heritage of Kings: One Man's Monarchy in the Confucian World* (Columbia University Press, 1988), which has been reissued as *The Confucian Kingship in Korea: Yŏngjo and the Politics of Sagacity* (Columbia University Press, 2001), and *The Memoirs of Lady Hyegyŏng: The Autobiographical Writings of a Crown Princess of Eighteenth-Century Korea* (University of California Press, 1996). She also edited *The Rise of Neo-Confucianism in Korea* (Columbia University Press, 1985), *Culture and the State in Chosŏn Korea* (Cambridge: Harvard University Asia Center, 1999), and *Women and Confucian Cultures in Premodern China, Korea, and Japan* (University of California Press, 2003). She is an intellectual and cultural historian of premodern and early modern Korea. Her major areas of interest include diglossia, the concept of the public sphere and Confucian political culture, and "premodern" nationalism.

Johan Elverskog is Assistant Professor in the Department of Religious Studies at Southern Methodist University. He received his B.A. from the University of California, Berkeley, and his M.A. and Ph.D. in Central Eurasian Studies from Indiana University, Bloomington. His research focuses on the history of Buddhism in Inner Asia. He is the author of *Uygur Buddhist Literature* (Brepols, 1997) and *The Jewel Translucent Sutra: Altan Khan and the Mongols in the Sixteenth Century* (Brill, 2003). A new monograph, "Our Great Qing: The Mongols, Buddhism, and the State in Late Imperial China," is in preparation.

Eugenio Menegon is Assistant Professor in the Department of History at Boston University. He studied Chinese language and civilization at the University of Venice (Italy), received his Ph.D. in history from the University of California at Berkeley, and was a research fellow at the Katholieke Universiteit Leuven (Belgium). His research focuses on Chinese late imperial social and religious history, and Chinese-Western cultural relations. He has written several essays on the history of Christianity and Western knowledge in China. He is also the author of an Italian-language biography of the Jesuit missionary Giulio Aleni, who was active in Fujian Province in the late-Ming period: *Un solo Cielo. Giulio Aleni S.J. (1582–1649). Geografia, arte, scienza, religione dall Europa alla Cina* (One Heaven: Giulio Aleni S.J. [1582–1649]): Geography, art, science, religion from Europe to China) (Brescia: Grafo Edizioni, 1994). His current book manuscript, "Ancestors, Virgins, and Friars," explores the religious history of northeastern Fujian in late imperial times, concentrating in particular on the interactions between Chinese Catholics and local society.

Zhao Shiyu is Professor of History in the Department of History and Dean of the Center for Rural China Studies at Beijing Normal University. He received his B.A. and M.A. in Ming-Qing History and his Ph.D. in Folklore from the same university. His research concerning the political and social history of China from the fifteenth to the twentieth century is represented by such books as *Huangfu shezheng wang Duoergun quanzhuan* (Imperial regent Dorgon, a complete biography; 1986), *Li yu Zhongguo chuantong shehui* (Petty officials and traditional Chinese society; 1994), *Yanguang xiangxia de geming: Zhongguo xiandai* *minsuxue sixiang shi lun* (A revolution looking downward: historical views on modern Chinese folklore studies; 1999), and *Kuanghuan yu richang: Ming-Qing yilai de miaohui yu minjian shehui* (Carnivals and daily life: temple fairs and local society since the Ming-Qing period; 2002).

Du Zhengzhen, formerly Professor Zhao's research assistant, is now a doctoral student in the History Department of the Chinese University of Hong Kong.

INDEX

Agūda (Jin Taizu), 36–37, 38, 40–41, 43, 45, 46; historical records of, 52
Aleni, Giulio, 191
almanacs, 183, 184–186, 199
Altan Khan, 148, 150, 162
"Altitudo divini consilii," 229–230nn. 65, 69, 70
Alverson, Hoyt, 13, 14
ancestral rituals, 205–208, 218. *See also* Rites Controversy
Anderson, Benedict, 7
An Lushan rebellion: as historical referent in Ming-Qing transition, 78
anthropic principle, 12–13, 22n. 18
"arrow" of time. *See* linear time
astrology and astronomy, 183, 184, 197. *See also* Mei Wending, Schall von Bell, Adam, Verbiest, Ferdinand
Augustine, Saint, 10, 13

Ban Gu, 123
beatas, 194, 198, 213–214
Beijing, 31, 42, 49, 77–78
Benedictines, 183

Bergson, Henri, 10
Bianjing. *See* Kaifeng
Bi Gan, 96, 103n. 51
body time, 17–18, 23n. 20
Bo Yi, 87–88
Bourdin, Martial, 142, 146
Buddhism: 185, 211, 216; chanting and recitation in, 216; and Mongol identity, 149–154 passim, 156; and political legitimacy, 144–146, 151–152; and ritual, 156; social function of, 157; Tibetan, 145, 148, 155, 166
Bumbutai. *See* Xiaozhuang, Empress Dowager

Cakravartins, 144, 145, 152. *See also* Buddhism, and political legitimacy
Calendar Controversy, 224n. 27
calendars, 4, 17, 183; alternative, 7–8, 132–136, 166, 171; Chinese (luni-solar), 97, 160–161, 183–189, 197, 199; Christian liturgical, 183–184, 185–186, 196–198, 210, (in Japan) 226n. 42; Gregorian, 183, 197; Jewish liturgical, 187;